AT THE WATER'S EDGE

Essays in Faith and Morals

William L. Roth, Jr.

Foreword by Timothy Parsons-Heather

The Morning Star of Our Lord, Inc. is a nonprofit, tax-exempt, 501(c)(3), religious and charitable organization which is incorporated under the Laws of the State of Illinois. It has been established for the dissemination of various apologetic works in defense of the Truth of the Holy Gospel of Christianity. It is the intrinsic role of this Corporation to provide pastoral consolation to those lacking in faith, the infirm, homebound, incarcerated, deprived, dejected, and those who are otherwise suffering humanity for the sake of the Glory of the Kingdom of Jesus Christ. All proceeds from this book are being donated to other charitable causes to help feed, clothe, and house the poor, and for the reproduction of this spiritual manuscript for distribution on every continent of the world. If anyone would like to contribute to this worthy cause, you may do so through the following postal and website addresses.

The Morning Star of Our Lord, Inc.
Post Office Box 8584
Springfield, Illinois 62791-8584
www.ImmaculateMary.org

Published by The Morning Star of Our Lord, Inc. Used with permission.

ISBN: 0-9671587-1-0

Printed in the United States of America

AT THE WATER'S EDGE

Essays in Faith and Morals

TABLE OF CONTENTS

Part I - Let Us Not Forsake The Generations Past

Part II - At The Water's Edge

Part III - The Truth Shall Set Us Free!

Part IV - Now, It is Our Time to Respond

DEDICATION
to
Suffering Humanity

It is with heartfelt love that I address you who are Suffering Humanity for the sake of our Almighty King, the Lord Jesus Christ. With the Powers of Heaven, I proclaim to you that your Deliverance is breaching the horizon of your lives at this very moment. It is the Most Blessed Virgin of Nazareth who is miraculously transforming previously indifferent people such as myself into an advancing armada of conversion and invincible grace which bears you the reason that your hope for Redemption has never been in vain. This Grand Lady of the Highest Honor in Paradise has set Her sights and intentions upon delivering the comforts of Heaven to the doors of your souls; and nothing, and no one, has the capacity to stop Her. The war that you have waged for the dignity of humankind and the happiness for which we all pine is all but won. I ask you to spend these final moments of your generous reparation polishing every last inch of your beauty so that upon your grand entrance onto the eternal stage, the Light of God which beams from you may blind us all with the Love that even our souls long to envision. Nevermore shall you be ignored; not in a million eternities will you ever be left to fade beyond our sight or our gentle attention. Your every wish will be our command and your most subtle glance a kiss to our grateful hearts. It is you who have served by being effaced into the bedrock of the world, holding-up societies and institutions, supporting dreams and ambitions, and providing a secure cap over the abyss so that we would never fall too far to be saved. You have blessed the Earth with the vision of God in the Mystical Flesh of the Savior of the world.

Therefore, I dedicate every word that I can speak, all the prayers I can invoke, all the actions I can take, and all the books that I can write, especially this one, to the breaking-down of that final wall which separates us from the liberating dreams that are approaching to unite our hearts and set us free in the Triumph of our Immaculate Mother, the Ever-Blessed Virgin Mary.

William L. Roth, Jr.

That men may appreciate wisdom and discipline,
may understand words of intelligence;
May receive training in wise conduct,
in what is right, just and honest;
That resourcefulness may be imparted to the simple,
to the young man knowledge and discretion.
A wise man by hearing them will advance in learning,
an intelligent man will gain sound guidance,
That he may comprehend proverb and parable,
the words of the wise and their riddles.
The fear of the Lord is the beginning of knowledge,
wisdom and instruction fools despise.
Hear, my son, your father's instruction,
and reject not your mother's teaching.

Proverbs 1:2-8

Foreword

If ever a time was ripe for the world to step-back and take a good long look at itself, the hour has come for us to do it as we enter the 21st century with haste. The problem is, we are all so busy struggling to survive everyday life that we cannot find any opportunities to relax and reflect upon what we are really doing. We have a lot of pondering to do about how we would each want our lives to turn out; and none of us is immune from having to face the music of the cold, hard facts of hitting the stone wall of reality head-on when times get tough and we seem to be so alone. I used to think that people like Bob Dylan and Arlo Guthrie pretty much had the ability to sum-up life with a few lyrics in their better songs, but the tunes slowly faded-away, while the problems they vocalized have remained. I was nearly twenty-five years old before I found-out from a personal friend that it is not so much how we evaluate life which matters, but how we set-out to achieve the best of what our existence is supposed to become on an optimum plane, where God knows and sees us well. I have never been one to hail religion as the center of all universes; but the older I get, the more I realize that God is truly calling us to understand who He is and exactly what He wants us to do. I guess you could call it a "religious" experience when these feelings first entered my heart; but I choose to see it as more of an awakening. I lived my adolescent years like there was no end to the possessions I wished to own, never-minding the fact that my spirit was never really being fed by anything greater than the highest notch on the volume-knob of my bedroom stereophones.

My parents belonged to the poor middle-class of American citizens, and I was the seventh of seven sons, to go with the five daughters that my folks also had. We were sent to a small United Methodist Church on Sundays whenever my parents took the time to get us all ready. I even became a choral director for this same congregation during the years while I was commuting to college in Jacksonville, Illinois, from 1972 through 1976. I met a lot of nice people there; many of whom were several years my elder. Most all of them have died by now, but I will always remember what they told me about staying united with other religious groups in my search for eternal Salvation. However, my experience with the Methodist Church was also tainted in a way that I did not truly know until I grew to be much older. The preacher gave me a book about the Protestant faith which had a section in it that lambasted the beliefs of the Roman Catholic Church. I was unfazed by it because I never really knew what they stood for anyway. But, God has His mysterious ways! I was later led by a group of friends to attend a Christmas Eve Mass at the St. Augustine Church in Ashland, Illinois, and my conscience finally told me that my soul was very near to Heaven. I cannot explain it any better than this; I just knew that the Holy Spirit whom the Methodists told me about was alive and well in this humble Catholic Church more than any other place I had ever walked into. Although I was not able to take Communion with them that night, my sights had been set on learning more about this beautiful place and seeing what I could do to become a member.

I recall that the Pastor at the Methodist Church had told me that the Roman Catholic Mass was somehow "repugnant" in the eyes of God, as well as the rest of the Sacraments they espouse, such as Confession, the Holy Orders, the Sacrament of Extreme Unction, and the like. Now that I am another twenty-five years older, I have found-out that this Methodist minister was misleading me. He has gone to his grave now and sees the Truth; and I have often wondered what he thought when he first laid-eyes on the Face of God. He surely discovered the same thing I came to know about the Catholic Church; that She is the Original Apostolic Church which Jesus Christ, Himself, founded on the Day of Pentecost, fifty days after He was Crucified on the Hill of Mount Calvary and rose from the dead on Easter Sunday. The Holy Sacrifice of the Mass which I first attended on Christmas Eve convinced me that Paradise is reflected most perfectly on the Earth by what the Catechism of the Roman Catholic Church is teaching. I had the same feeling we often get when we hear the wheels of a 747 jet-airliner bark as they touch-down on a runway, or the sound which echoes through the air when a competitor gets a strike in a bowling alley somewhere. It is kind-of a "slam-dunk" sensation when you know that irrefutable success has been achieved and there is nothing anybody else can do about it. This is how I knew that the Catholic Church was for me. So, any remarks which are made in this book about the United Methodist Church are true and provable; and I take full responsibility for their content. The Catholic-bashing that is going-on these days in America and around the world has got to come to a screeching halt because we are offending the very Christ who has saved our souls.

When William Roth asked me to compose a "Foreword" for his manuscript, I obviously took the time to read what his *Essays* were all about. We have known each other for twenty-five years, and have authored another spiritual book together called, *Morning Star Over America*, after a miraculous experience began to unfold between us following two trips to Medjugorje, Yugoslavia, where the Blessed Virgin Mary has been appearing everyday since June of 1981. For the purpose of brevity, the only thing I can add to this "Foreword" about it is to ask you to contact the Morning Star of Our Lord Corporation at the address that William has placed elsewhere in this book. His main intention for *At the Water's Edge* is to combine a wonderful collection of apologetic works under one individual cover. If you are like me, your soul will be rocked after you have read them in much the same way my heart awoke from its spiritual sleep when I first attended that Christmas Eve Mass, way back in 1977. Yes, I assuredly followed my conscience and was confirmed into the Catholic Church in 1979 with some tremendously faith-filled people of God. The subjects which William has written about in this book are unequivocally the bedrock Truth about how Jesus Christ sees the mortal world. I asked him why he was so confident that the structured positivity of his work would be accepted by greater humanity, and he looked me in the eyes and told me outright that the Angels had assured him so. After what we have both experienced since our travels to the Yugoslavian mountains over ten years ago, I had no choice but to believe every word he was saying.

I had very little part in advising William on the composing of this book, only to tell him that I was misdirected in my younger years by the Methodist Church about Catholicism in light of what I have since learned from the Blessed Virgin Mary through my own personal exposure to Her intercession. One of my favorite entries in this book is the *Essay* which states that we are a good humanity. It lifts-up the world during a time when we seem to be doing our best to put everyone else down. There has been no lack of criticism toward our work on our first book because of the miraculous claims we have made in its text. But, we are both reminded of how Jesus sent His Disciples into the world two-by-two, and almost everyone they met thought that each pair of them was under the influence of some strange fanaticism. I have later been told that the field of psychiatry calls it a *folie a deux*, meaning that two people who are closely associated can share the same delusional ideas. Well, if this is what the world thought of the Disciples of Christ, then I guess William and I fit into the same mold. However, we are not delusional because we are telling the absolute Truth about the Salvation of souls in the Blood of Jesus Christ; and the time which will bear-out the proof that we are dispatched by the Holy Spirit is definitely on our side. No Truth will ever die, and no lie can live forever. This is why we know that the spiritual*Essays* you are about to read are a portion of the Eternal Word which God is still speaking to the physical Earth; and we had all better take note of what His Seat of Justice has to say while there is still sufficient time left for us to listen.

William rarely speaks in first-person in these *Essays* because the positions that are being explored are common knowledge to nearly everyone; at least those with a conscience to recognize the difference between good and evil. His central thesis is that we are a good and decent people, despite all of our frailties, and that we are at the brink of being perfected in our conversion to the Holy Gospel of Christianity. Indeed, we are *At the Water's Edge* in becoming the people whom Jesus Christ wants us to be; but we have allowed too many artificial things in the world to distract us from recognizing that our spiritual thirst is a prophecy of our own impending death. If we do not drink from the cool waters of repentance to which we have been led, we will perish from the dehydration that comes from not accepting God for who He really is. The arguments William puts-forth in this book are sound by all measures; and no man who knows their Savior well will ever refute what he has to say. It is true that we can become a benevolent Creation, but William minces no words in outlining the reasons why we are not yet there. I often think of the joy and pride his parents and sisters must feel in knowing that he has chosen to pursue the Love of God for his life's duties above the things so many other people are chasing; such as drugs, materialism, lust, greed, self-ingratiation, and agnosticism. He comes from a family of excellent souls; for each of them would do exactly what the Son of God has asked of us all. They live by the Creed that there is no greater Love on the Earth than to lay-down one's life for his friends.

There is a strange set of circumstances which surround his family and my own. When I was a little boy, I was walking with one of my brothers and a sister from the schoolhouse in Ashland when my sister, Patty, was struck and killed by a car in front of us. It was quite a sorrowful time for our family because we had lost one of our own so tragically. The day that she was laid to rest in Keyesport, Illinois seemed like an uncertain ending for my grieving mother and father, and for the rest of us, too. And yet, it was December 15, 1959, the exact same day that William's parents began their family with the birth of their first child and oldest daughter. I have often thought of how awkward and ironic it was that my family was so torn apart by the passing of such a little girl, when William's family was joyfully just getting started. What has happened since then has been almost too surreal to recount in any number of volumes of books. But, a greater step has been taken as he has completed this manuscript and placed it before the rest of the world for the purpose of leading his brothers and sisters back to their dignity and Salvation in the Cross of Jesus Christ. I have seen thoughtful men sitting at tables in public fora all over the globe since my adulthood has come into bloom; but I have never heard a single one of them speak the Truth about who we are better than William Roth, Jr. has in this book. I watched those same men lay their arms before them on their table-tops, touch their fingertips together, and slowly draw their hands back toward their lapels as they tried to somehow reel their listeners into a clearer understanding of their expressions. William brings us closer to his breast and takes us into his private confidence in much the same way through the pages of his book, *At the Water's Edge.*

These *Essays* are a statement about the human conscience, integrity, concern, and hopes for the arrival of the better life we have all yearned to see someday. We cannot help but gravitate to his noble aspirations for the Kingdom of Heaven to overcome the Earth with the affection which God holds in His Sacred Heart for those who truly accept Him. I know that William would not wish for me to heap any praise upon his soul for compiling this magnanimous book because he is prone to tell me that only God is the Glory and only Love is the recipient of the accolades which should spring from our hearts toward the Heavenly Throne. There is no doubt in my mind, however, that if we support one another in the same way that William Roth stands before the Cross to render honors to our Savior who was Crucified there, the world will be revived in justice and peace in the matter of an instant. I cannot apologize to William for making this a part of my "Foreword," and I know that he will include it in his book because his kindness would never allow me to be disappointed about what I really wished to say in my remarks. We search onward and upward together toward the more pious planes of human mortality; and there are certain people whose fight for Love never seems to wane or grow pale in the face of social rejection. Thanks to his loving mother and father, William has become one of those icons of true Christian faithfulness, and the world is much the better for it; while he is still suffering gladly in being despised by the very people who would just as soon spit in the Face of Jesus Christ than admit that He is the only King who can save them.

William's book is written quite simply by comparison to other works, but it has some quite definitive words in its text in an effort to touch the many intellectuals who have made such a travesty of the modern-day world. I kept a desktop dictionary at my side when I read his *Essays* and finally discovered that the terms he has used to make his case are quite appropriate in their context. I am thankful that he did not make an attempt to imitate the writing-style of the likes of Saint Thomas Aquinas because very few laymen would ever bother to pick it up and read it all the way through. William's *Essays* are directed at every soul because, as I see by his words, we are all one body of humankind in Jesus Christ, and our Almighty Father in Heaven would want it no other way. There are documented deficiencies in the means by which we conduct our lives. We are haughty, gloating, hypocritical, stingy, and obnoxious to those who live around us sometimes; but we are also capable of being quite valiant in our demeanor when we truly wish to be. It seems like the old adage is always applicable that we can judge ourselves by how we treat other people who can do nothing for us. This is the crux of why some persons are poor, while others continue to grow the cache of their riches. I have never read a book in which the wealthy population of the world was so pummeled in print as I have seen in the *Essays* you are about to read. But, living the Truth through the power of the Holy Gospel, William's soulful accounting of the status of human life today is not only accurate, it is a prophecy of what is undoubtedly going to happen to the souls of those who have lived only for themselves and cast the rest of humanity into the trash-bin along their way.

Other subjects in these *Essays* deal with the intrinsic nature of Christian piety as it has been defined in the Sacred Scriptures. In a world where there exists so many double-standards and lines to become blurred, there are no dilemmas in William's book because every single one of them is resolved inside the Truth of God. There is no gray when it comes to the matter of knowing Love in the way in which Jesus has taught it, and no contradictions to be found in the final end. William has made the case for the conversion of every living soul to the Christian faith because he is, indeed, on his way to Heaven to live among the Saints. When Saint Paul wrote his letters to the Disciples of Christ, he spoke with this same confidence and assurance that anyone can make it there, if only they will concede that the Son of God is the Ruler of all Nations, rather than the contents of their wallets or how they are dressed when they greet their friends for an early-evening dinner engagement. Surely we cannot object to the world evolving to be a better place for everyone to live; and it will become so if we adhere to the Divine Principles that are delineated in the New Covenant. But, as William has so properly stated in his *Essays*, we have not even begun the task of growing to be more united in a secular way, let alone by the commission we have been given by Jesus Christ to be servants in His Sermon on the Mount. Let us listen well to what William has to say; let us heed the Holy Spirit who is alive in his humble heart; and let anyone who has the audacity to disagree with what this book confirms climb upon a soapbox and provide the rest of humanity with undeniable evidence that the Gospel according to the Saints has nothing to do with human goodness, cohesion, healing, comfort, and everlasting peace. We own a world given to us by Almighty God, and He expects us to return it to Him in the Light of righteousness someday. Indeed, His Son will come and get it soon, whether we like it or not. That is the moment when we shall judge ourselves as to whether we accepted the Truth, employed our greatest faith, and offered our contrition to the Creator whom we have so offended by our sins and transgressions. If we heed the spiritual call to piety that William Roth has made through *At the Water's Edge*, our reunion in Paradise will be a day of high joy and celebration atop the reckoning of the mortal ages.

-Timothy Parsons-Heather
February 2001

Part I - Let Us Not Forsake The Generations Past

God Assuredly Cannot Fail Us

July 5, 2000

We await the return of the seemingly elusive Host of all Creation, He who has at last left both Tolstoy and Shakespeare speechless in His path and grateful in tears; for they can now only recount the Divinity of His peerless ingenuity. He, who has so profoundly created us to be more brilliant than the reciprocating Light, to shed upon the world our reverberating Love past all dominions and to every peoples; we who are made remarkably whole in His grace, comforted by His peace, and redeemed in His Blood. Our future is already bleeding if we decline to be remade through our Immaculate Savior, the Son of Mary, whose power and absolution grows the whisper of a solitary whippoorwill into a simultaneous concert of grand pianos. This priceless Messiah has made the echo of the breezes through the distant evergreens to become a Divine orchestration of miraculous symphonies, awaiting the ovation which our souls will tender Him at last. All of our captivating intelligence is ours for safekeeping in Christ. What we make of goodness has earlier belonged to Him; and we transfer it to one another in knowing that our wilful sincerity should wish for nowhere else to go. Now, we are no longer blind, as we can see past every intersection of Truth and morality like the overpowering vision of inner-circles from atop the mightiest skyscrapers, while the daily drama of mortal life continues to unfold beneath our most delicate paths. It is still undeniable that the debate over the destiny of humankind has long been ended because the Cross is the capstone over which no other purview can exist. In that crux, time is no longer an issue with regard to the memories of our hearts as we see in retrospect the invincible ways that other devoted people have lived. If we aspire to equate our actions with their Love, we must realize that the destiny of our brothers is one and the same as our own. We are, indeed, rightful heirs of their loyalty. This is why the sun sets like a blazing horizon afire, our reminder that a more noble day is at hand and that we can shape it by the embryonic strength of our petitions.

If nothing else comes true, we must do more than just think that we are inseparable from the Kingdom of Paradise which still shimmers at the peripheral conception of our actions. If we deign to become part of that perfection, surely the immeasurable mind of God will never be unilaterally defined by His fingertips at His temples, but that He will also require the intelligent compassion of decent men to make our immortal destiny complete. We must never assume that the Almighty Father would deny our souls as being equally glorious in excellence as His Sacrificed Son through the power and consolation of His Spirit. If we do, we have already failed the Holy Gospel of faith and retreated back into the darkness of the corruptible world. We must see and admire well! If art is more than simple imagery, then prayer is a power which lies far beyond our tangible contemplations, permeating the vastness of our inexplicable hopes for something better, superceding the imagination of man, looking up with hope and yearning for all that is blissful to fall into our faces like rays of sun through the showering rains. Let this be the day when our effervescent spirits vow to survive the struggle for mere understanding because we are all travelers and counselors in the Psalms of God, the caroleers who pronounce the new beginning of humanity, finally realizing that peace means Christ, and Christ is our only easement into Grace.

Our Perpetual State of Ecclesiastical Blessing

October 12, 2000

Can the world force the calling of the intellect and implore the proposition of the moral ages before we all fade secretly into the past without ever having challenged our enemies from within? Do we dare to nourish the process of change so that everyone who prays for their dignity can at last reach for even the lowest bar they must cross to succeed? Surely we can generate a new alternative to the repetition of our stagnant successes which only mortals aspire to perceive. What won't our fears do to deceive our most imaginative prowess! It is not easy for us to discern when and where to lurch forward to grasp the last fiber of opportunity that might ever come our way because we still refuse to search for the best from our untold fortune of humanity. True greatness is often hidden behind the veils of our bland discontent and the nondescript fables which have held our own potential at bay for too many generations gone by. We have difficulty distinguishing our dreams from what may have happened yesterday and our nightmares from the cold hard facts of reality. We must concede beyond refutation that living legends eventually die and our most romantic institutions inexorably dissolve into the forgotten passageways of history.

What seems to pain us most is our inner uncertainty and the delusion which encroaches upon our psychological security when we plant our feet under the shales that lay too far in the distant hereafter. Those who must know about these things tell us that this is not a healthful way to live. That is why we must always turn to God for the uniform resilience we need to break the dawn of the future. There are stages in life and periods of remembrance, but only one prophetic and perpetual state of ecclesiastical blessing which makes all humanity one, both the living and the dead, to unite the goodness of Creation in a supernatural way, a cohesion which cannot be divided by time, mortality, prejudice, or deceit. In Jesus Christ, we discover ourselves because His Sacred Heart is the etiology of our internal being. He does not ask that we surrender our personal advancements in greatness or self-sufficiency, or that we make our identities even remotely generic or unidentifiable. Indeed, it is in the living Spirit of God that we finally exhume the previously hidden characteristics which define what our souls actually mean to the Omnipotent One who has prepared us so well for life.

If we do not accept that we are more than simple flesh and blood, fault and sin, action and reaction, we will ultimately come to realize that we are only able to do the things that we have taught one another in order to extinguish the day. We will wield nothing more than death if we settle for anything less. Faithless human capability cannot be equated with Love's Divine power because it lacks the fundamental aspect of its creative originality. The Almighty Father gives this to us through His Son and expects us to be able to distinguish the difference between His perfection and the paltry acts that we record in our memories which serve only to close the chapters in the diaries of our foes. We must effect this ongoing issue of supernatural grace upon the dais of the public fora, or we will leave the world a much more pale legacy than our unwitting ancestors inadvertently bequeathed to us.

A Few Brave Hearts Have Conquered the Night

October 17, 2000

There is greater purpose in the morning dawn than to just give us light, knowing that no evil force in the world could stop it from rising whether it wanted to or not. It is our metaphor of ultimate simplicity which reveals to everyone alive that the night cannot prey on us long enough to ever conquer our hope. There is no real need for us to worry whether our God in Heaven is fully or faithfully aright. Indeed, He allows us to affirm Him on His own omnipotent behalf! Fighting against time that will eventually expire and a body which will crumble and die, our righteous expression is all we have to reach out, a commendation of momentum for those who are bold enough to pursue it. The Holy Spirit in our hearts is sufficiently expansive to satisfy even the most insatiable of curiosities and enfold the most surrealistic of dreams. We carry within us not only a need for change, but a somewhat false and impugning requirement that the way we alter our personal traits must never destroy the essence of who we truly are, what we perceive ourselves to be, or the way we are presented to our friends and peers. It seems that there is no greater tragedy than to betray our inner-self or inhibit our desire to jump higher than we ever thought we could leap. We must never hold-back in meekness when we know that the world is starving for our decisive wisdom, bold leadership, and indispensable good will. In the age of the twenty-first century, timidity is an admission of weakness and our irrevocable guarantee that we will ultimately fail. If there is unrelenting grief in human life, it is because too many of us continue to persist in reticence while waiting for someone else to become the ballast of hope for the multitudes and scores who have yet no voice that is loud enough to be heard.

There is sadness among us because only a few brave hearts have ever dared to conquer the hands which continue to hold us down. If God, Himself, came to us in the night and told us that He was going to remake our souls into a diminutive reed of straw, most of us would assuredly implore Him that it would be alright as long as we are not called upon to be the last one to fall onto a camel's back for fear of effecting a change. "Not me!", we say. "I have no desire to become the force which might amend the present for the good of rectifying the past or forever redefining the future." That is the cowardice which is still running rampant all over the surface of the world. It is defined by outright selfishness and is projected when we see wealthy profiteers stumbling over hungry paupers on their way to the stock market door. It would be nice if we could just judge ourselves as being filled with more ignorance than greed, but we do not deserve a singular sliver toward that beneficial doubt. No, we are finally going to have to confess that we are miserable losers in the indictment with which we are faced in refusing to feed God's sheep. But, let us not allow our lack of good judgement to wiggle off the hook! It is time for us to awaken and see ourselves as residing in the very Hands of courage that have absolved our wretched souls. Because of the Crucifixion of Jesus, we are now standing upright in the perpetuity of immortal Passion, where none of us will fail if we only set out to try.

If we ever decide to search for a better reason for life, then we must mark that day in our history books because we have already allowed too many thousands to slip from the distance of our grasp. We have somehow lost the distinction for defining Christ's Love over the darkness hovering around us, if we were ever once so enlightened at all. Someone has got to stand up and proclaim that we are a more benevolent creation than the pungent cellars where we have allowed ourselves to remain. Let us vow to become the people whom God unabashedly loves so that He can proclaim once and for all, *"At last, I have found a lot of souls who can do what it takes to transcend the helplessness which they have synthesized on their own! Perhaps now I can recline alongside the gulf streams of Paradise, pulling my rainbow overtures across my brow, and rest in the satisfaction that my children on Earth are finally coming home."* In this we must believe that our Divine Creator is not relaxing yet. As long as volcanoes erupt and rivers overflow, as long as twisters rip the heartlands from the American fruited plains, and so long as the equator-skies continue to crack the soil like the back of a hundred-year-old palm, we can be confident that the Deity who made us has plenty more to say. Indeed, as long as He sees a breach in the integrity of our spiritual crest, there is no doubt that His purposes are long from abandoning their mission on the foothills of the Earth.

If states constitute republics, and nations compose the continents, then why can we not all join within the perimeter of our Triune God, apparent on all three sides of a Divine polygon from which we have no authority to escape? Why can we not promise that we will never again reject the beauty which has so lifted us to grace? We owe our very mortal being to Him who rules and overrules toward the purpose of delineating His Will and exercising the power that perfects us in His Son. It is the most foolish of prospects for us to unilaterally claim victory over a deathbed which will unyieldingly conquer us all while we rise every day from our sleep in a wholly obstinate way, naively believing in intellect that we will never encounter a reason to muster the compassion which will reshape the future of the downtrodden whom we've prayed to never become. If we are trying to shed any benefit from the Life and Death of Jesus, we would do better to accept our condemnation now. But, His is the Resurrection that makes us wilfully concede! If we look into space and find nothing at all, it is our own unwillingness to see. The fate of the stars is no poorer just because we might choose to be blind. God's design lays silently before us at every passing moment, waiting for us to open our eyes to His Truth and begin the task of taking up our arms and fighting to our last dying day. The good soul knows the clouds to be the frosting over the confectionery world that Christ is still savoring to devour. Let us not spoil in indifference and starve His appetite, but acknowledge His purposeful presence on our road to everlasting life!

Not For Me, But for the All-Inclusive Us

October 18, 2000

We will always be able to find consolation in Christian obedience because it assigns meaning to our noble wars and the coalescence of our, otherwise, mutually inconsistent reactions. When it comes to the struggle for goodness for those who inhabit the Earth, we own no greater parlance of encouragement than our sovereign intentions to make this a better world. Holy is the sacrifice we must make to diminish our own personal gain in order to grant concession to the paltry lot of the living Christ who conceals Himself so conspicuously in the terror of our brethren's plight. They are the unheralded ones who can only dream of something less-callous or a future that will contain no more darkness because of the expiative and reasoned excellence which has made charitable men whole in the sacrament of everlasting life. We are blessed to be born into an awareness where our Savior has already once tread because we now know where best to walk and what is the most useful to say. By all means, the character of our temperament is enamored by His grace at the very moment we are conceived as a new creation in the epicenter of mortal refinement, the precious womb of our mother whose labors in pain have so faithfully bestowed us to the world. It is at that moment when our feet have more than physical power even before they impact the ground. It is the point where we begin to muster the questions which define our childhood while our divine curiosity bellows our conscience into realizing that there is something greater than the hardness of the tangible world to give us a permanent home.

The depravity in which we live generates a new definition for the amendment of our humanness and an invigorated sense of urgency that says we must find our own destiny in time. We create and destroy our possessions at will, and never once stop to ask why. We pay no mind to the inquiry of the heart because we cannot see it with our temporal eyes. We hold a penchant for diversity and affection only after we are liberated from the discrimination that keeps individuals reduced to a faceless token of incongruity in a crowd of anonymous men. Our reluctance to reach for the trembling hands of the suffering poor is only a diversion which we have slothfully allowed to fester through the oblivious callousness of our habitual minds. But, the moment we allow the radiance of justice to enlighten our souls with knowledge, we will finally understand that our purpose is no longer for "me," but for the all-inclusive "us." When we think about how bad it hurts to suffer the loss of a loved one, this is the mirrored sorrow which Jesus feels when we squander a single opportunity to elevate His poor ones in the name of endearing compassion. We continue to stealthily wield the proverbial sleight-of-hand to sift the best of riches from the world and protect them with the cadence of an honorary guard, but we still refuse to command the forces of Truth that are still trying to wrest our consciences away from the clutches of our arrogant and unsavory greed.

It is inside the lives of those who are most fortunate that we perceive the contemporaries who have made human inequality real. The proliferation of agony which they have imposed upon the neglected has been exacerbated by hands who have refused to wait their turn at the first chance of exhuming the gold. The impoverished souls on Earth are our indelible evidence that the sorrowful Passion of Christ is our visionary window into God's Sacred Heart. They provoke us to measure the true identity of our loyalty to Him and the degree to which we are willing to forego our own causes of action to embrace what He wishes us to do. Jesus has been looking for a much mightier army of saints since Adam and Eve first looked God in the eye while He pined for their adherent affection as they defiantly uttered instead, " *We quit!*" That was the birth of the subterranean world and the christening of the Mission of the Messiah from Paradise to somehow salvage the Earth. It was the moment when trees could be turned into lifeless wood, more than capable of being pierced by a spike, and when humanity contrived only ceiling-wax reasons to impale their Salvation there. Our Lord has been trying to teach us to overcome our unredressed insolence through His perfection ever since. He knows full well that, if we take up lodging in material wealth or set our course for the physical world, we will only arrive at the end of our sleep with a cold splash of reality on our face. The Son of God offers the Wisdom that knowing how to love and "being" Love are spacial chasms apart, just as profoundly as one might walk through a valley of death, or choose to pass-by overhead.

Our devotion to Heaven is no less than the transference of our indelible spiritual philanthropy to our anonymous peers and a means to share the gifts of Resurrection with humanity-at-large toward the purpose of a more powerful faith. It means effecting the Gospel by never again speaking a lie, not skipping a step on the journey of life, and never failing to offer our share under oath. These undying petitions of heroism signify never conceding defeat in outfacing adversity and always believing that the fight we must win will always force the Triumph at last. The time has come for us to pour ourselves headlong into the battle for decency and the restoration of our hierarchical conscience. The extinction of our moral standards has left us with societies that are poisoned and out of control, and many quarters are already exuding a stench from the smell of the dead. The sight of poverty we see abroad and at the end of our neighborhood corners is a testament to our own lack of vision and an optical obituary to our chances of ever becoming the people we are destined to be in the plentiful Redemption of Christ. From this we can also rise from the grave because God still holds-out the best of intentions for the future of mankind that He sees. He has set a table with the finest Wheat that money can buy and has dispatched His courier Son to retrieve us. But alas! Humanity has yet failed to arrive! All we need to do is claim our inheritance in Him and we can be nothing-less than Saved. There may be division and pride in the ranks of the lost, but not within the walls of His house! Let the mansions of Earth be tenable for the patrons of justice and the makers of peace, an occupancy which will be forever blessed. Let our service be our boundless profession that nothing can inhibit us now. The humble voice of the Mother of God has told us that this will come true. There is no doubting that it will take more than a tidy sum of animosity to ever destroy the hopeful hearts which the Lady of Immaculate Divinity has won.

We must move forward now with prudent care, withdrawing our curtains to be completely ajar because the sun has arrived and we, delightfully, are its prey! Together with the resonance of forgiveness from the skies, there is no force ongoing that can ever lead us back into malevolent arms. By the time our enemies have pondered whether our faith will conquer and prevail, we will have already pilfered their reasons to oppose the resilience of our goodness and the lofty means we have employed to conquer their hatred without ever dignifying the fight. Our prayers are like ulcers in their avenues of lust, rendering them unable to assimilate another soul or raise their heads and go on. So, let them scoff at our defense of the Truth! Let them align themselves against the legions to which they have already lost. When Jesus dispatched the dead to bury the dead, He was simultaneously referring to the pompous disbelievers who are already writhing in pain as they peel the scabs from each others' back while biting to disavow their own blame. There is no justification in such a life so separated from Christ. We must challenge those who scandalously inquire, "If a law is never broken, can it actually exist?" If we enforce the Gospel of righteousness before those who violate its Creed, the infraction is against their own souls and the cost of their retribution will forever be too great for their capacity to ever sustain. The followers of collusion and hatred will always be defeated because the children of Light shall never retreat from under the guidance and strength of their Paraclete on high. He is not only our Judge, but also our superlative inner-judgement as well. He has forthrightly given us assurance that, in any effort to destroy His followers in faith, the sorcerers aligned against us have already pummeled their own partisan ranks.

The Fragrance of Conciliatory Grace

October 23, 2000

We walk meanderingly in a somewhat shadowed and spontaneous acrimony of dismal irrelevance when our defiance gets the best of our good sense and we fail to unite as one body under the Cross of Divine Redemption. Without that cohesion, our lives are the essence of contradiction and the epitome of waste. Our Father in Heaven has been watching this process evolve for a longer period than any mortal man or woman has the capacity to ever comprehend. If only we could know that *forever* does not just mean the time past tomorrow, but that there is truly no need for a new day in the manor-house of the angelic courts before whom we will rest in eternity after the Return of Jesus Christ. Do we see any suspense in the prospect that some of those whose faces we see every day may not make it across the bridge of the everlasting ages? Are we living in a state of denial while opposing the fact that the end of human mortality will usher-in the day upon which the wretched will be judged alongside the blessed and the turmoil of our rejection against the Kingdom of God will finally come to an end? Those who are trying to know Salvation and who are otherwise tendered to surrendering their consciences to mortification in Christ are the lucky ones who will assuredly bear-out the Truth that the Deicide of the Son of Mary has been the absolution of the collective soul of His own Mystical Body of faith. That is why the unification of humanity is a congenital absolute that cannot be dismissed by those who refuse to perceive life any further than the edges of their desks. The world is soon to be dissolved and a new one will be put in its place! There is no way to escape this impending reality of fate.

How we rely on the territorial jurisdiction of the manifest globe is an outright repugnance to Christ. We often refuse to opt for the spiritual pathway and knowingly deny the counsel of the courageous few who do. No wonder our daydreams are no more than a crepe-paper mirage before our wailing eyes. Somehow the lines between what we know to be true goodness and what we prefer to see oftentimes become too blurred to be clear. It is a miracle before humankind that a more defining moment is now at hand in the glorious revelations of the Most Blessed Virgin Mary. If death is swallowed-up in victory, then mortality in itself is devoured through the Triumph of Her Immaculate Heart. The legacy of the Mother of God is greater than even the most indispensable annals of history that the world might ever become fortune enough to know! Every revolutionary change toward eradicating malice amongst men has come at the humble utterances of Her prayers beyond the skies. She has implored Her Son to make it so. If we deny the righteous virtue of the Queen of Heaven and Earth, we are totally missing the purpose of our Savior whom She laid at our feet amidst the burrows in the winter of Bethlehem. Hers was no search for divinity as She walked the mortal Earth because She needed no transformation to become the Matriarch of the Saints. Her life among us was a trial that required no testing by fire because She needed no absolution to counterpose the deference of Her kindness. When God placed the Crown of Twelve Stars atop Her delicate Head, He was not remaking Her into any greater being than She had been just moments before, but was celebrating the perfection that He knew She already owned.

So, we can huddle in our quaint bungalows, sprawling condominiums, and towering penthouses all we might. But, we will never refute the fact that the Mother of our Savior has the power of the Holy Spirit to blink in a moment's discontent and Her Son will wipe the world from the face of existence like a photographic flash. For all we did to crucify Her own beloved Flesh and Blood, we would be more than deserving of such extraordinary disdain. But, Mary knew that Her dying Son had asked Her to choreograph our conversion to His Gospel from the Cross on which He died. She could have withdrawn into an introspective submission with the most benign of intentions. However, She could see from the start that She had more than enough work to do. Her prayers would be greater in the eyes of God than our simple requisitions could impose. So, She has utilized the supernatural providence with which She is blessed to appear to the Earth again. Early and often, She has commended humankind to the Blood of Her Son by walking in mid-air above churches and cemeteries, amongst sinners and Saints, and between the ranks of the chosen and despised to express the message of eternal Salvation in the Cross which so severely crushed the flowers that are blooming in Her Heart. Simeon was assuredly right when he told Her that a sword of sorrow would send Her into tears, but he could not lay claim to the prophecy which would mitigate the gravity of Her pain. We have been admonished by Jesus ever since that, if His Mother did not grievously suffer on Good Friday, then neither did He weep. But, even the most distant of admirers has seen His lifeblood of tears slowly dripping off His feet.

Chaste is the awareness which recalls the reasons for our encouragement to prayer. That is why we must somehow form a guild of solidarity which cannot be broken by the immorality of the day. No citizens in private or leaders of the world can even remotely succeed in amending this Truth. Those who reject it in the heat of summer's day are only the beginning of the many who continue to deny it in the sultry darkness of the night. It seems painfully obvious that a part of what Jesus means by the Kingdom at hand is that there is wholly another world which is just waiting to be revealed if only we will do things right, a land of exquisite collaboration that is chock-full of blessings which emissaries and diplomats could only savor to achieve. Instead of bidding farewell to the gallanted forgiveness that may have just slipped through our hands, let us greet one another with the anticipation of a crop of justice which will be harvested in time, rich enough to lavish the palates of every soul who hungers for a singular chance to begin again where there now lies only the stain of remorse and the cold memories of revenge. The boiling point for pardoning the human spirit is the absolute degree to which men are willing to forgo their own prejudices for the good of Creation at large. This cannot wait for some sense of greater purpose or a boulevard-parade to celebrate the day. The repetitive percussion of ordinary time is more than adequate to provide the firmament for our new beginnings to prevail.

Interpersonal good will is all the ambrosial, medicinal, and convalescent amelioration that humanity needs to conform to the wishes of the Redeemer of the world. All of these fragrances of conciliatory grace are not just a temporary whiff of forbearance, an armistice for the day, or a respite before the next battle, but are a proclamation of everlasting peace between the parties of old and their contemporaries anew to holster the weapons they have been wielding for centuries and take-up the course of serving both Our Savior and His people alike, while marching together toward the procession of one family of man. There is no higher purpose in the spirit of mediation than that. This is the reason of the insistent ingenuity that we can gain from the Wisdom of the Mother of God. It is our way of finally knowing with the full-blown Revelation of Christ that His Father in Heaven is also our own. The Blessed Virgin Mary is ever the inseparable ambassador in whom we can take full confidence in our standing before Him. All that has ever been known of the priceless gem of confession and the refinement of man has been honed by the lances in Her Heart. We must lay ourselves wide-open to recognize the opportunity at hand, or we will never fully know the desires of Her Son.

We can rightfully assume that Jesus wants us to accept His Mother as being the same one who bore Him to save us. But, the ignorance of the mortals of Earth is almost too profound to absolve. It was not enough for us to scar His innocuous Body beyond the bludgeoning cruelty and madness of wolves, but humankind has also defiantly tattooed His Holy Spirit with the impression that we will fight against His Mother's intercession to our last dying breath. Then, we amazingly turn around in total desecration and expect to receive our exculpating indulgences without ever batting an eye. Therein lies the brawl in which we still bubble, the true reason that we can find no sound basis for the agony of men, and the unconditional repulsion which causes the Saints to turn their backs on the world in utter dismay. Swirling among us like an angel-duster overhead is the Queen of our Salvation, Herself. She shapes the constellations with the affection of Her sight, while we continue to look downward to our feet and at the palms of our hands as though God is still an infinity away. Where is His Justice and when will come His might? When we all stop brooding that we have been left alone and behind and finally enjoin the Holy Spirit at the sanctuary of our hearts.

To Personify the Blessed Progeny of His Reign

October 24, 2000

Christianity can never be severed into a belief of the modernism of today versus the retroactive devotion of our first century faith. We are still praising the same Son of God at this hour who first taught the Earth to know Redemption from its valleys and peaks in one harmony two-hundred decades ago. We can never exhaust the originality of our prayers, the traditions of the Church, or the power of the Sacraments with the passage of time. Contrary to popular belief, those who say that thinking about religion too repetitively will eventually rub a sore spot in the corner of our brain have already conceded to the migraine offenses and distractions of the secular world. We have a unique perspective through which to envision the way societies ought to be by augmenting our own faith in the Holy Gospel. When we utilize it, we are better able to determine that aesthetical art is a single concept of thought, while artistry as a phenomenon is the process of capturing beauty at large. This reduces the effect of our perceptiveness to the pondering we employ to differentiate the two. It is in this corollary likeness through which we recognize that, if our spiritual decisiveness is measurable only in increments that can be identified by quantity, the same standard of response will be meted-out to us by the God of our fathers at the end of our lives. He is not so illogical that He will not find some figurative way to tell us that, if we have to hang our religious nightshirt on the clothesline for fear that it may shrink in the dryer, then we have fully outgrown the marginal portions of our spiritual being and it is time to move-on to a more suitable maturity toward a greater understanding of Him.

The task that Our Father in Heaven has laid before humankind is for us to determine what is the constancy of the life which He has placed into our hands. Is it just to eat and sleep, or are those only the required pit-stops we must make to finish the race? Could it be "*...to thine own self be true*," or is that no more than an antiquated pawn of complacency for those who are yet too frail to step from behind their own timid reservations? The wrinkles on our faces are no barometer as to whether we have grown wiser by the day. We are too busy thinking that the moon is an "on-button" for the supernatural intervention of God and we have yet to find a way to depress it and keep it engaged. What we must realize instead is that Divine power truthfully comes from the pulling of a chain whose links are the Sacred Mysteries of the Most Holy Rosary. It is there that we learn that we were already chosen as princes of the Royal Family of God when Jesus was borne to the Earth; but short of the death of this King, we would have never inherited His Kingdom. We have ever since been entrusted with the stewardship of His compassion which He has willed us to dispense to His heirs. And, who are these survivors who remain? All those about whom Christ spoke in the Sermon on the Mount, those who personify the blessed progeny of His Reign, and the greater company of mortal saints who will soon know the Light of Paradise in fuller exultation.

We have been placed here for more palpable reasons than to find our way past the blindness that still skewers our faith. As followers of Jesus, we are also charged with the commission of widening the expanse of the extended arms of the first Apostles that have been transferred through the ages, those tenets which we must emit with the highest of devotion, and the raw spiritual power that makes benevolent men even better than before. It is in the humble service of our ecclesiastical clergy that we can always find ourselves, knowing full-well that the oath of the bishops of the world is fulfilled in the faith of the flocks beneath their mitre. Together, these obedient incumbents circumscribe the globe with a Divine halo of exemplary clerical tenure as they fine-tune their homilies in unison with the sweet melodies of the Holy Spirit of Our Lord. Their fatherly direction before their followers on Earth is unparalleled by any other affection known to humankind today. They dispense the Sacraments to the glee and scurrying anticipation of the billion-plus souls who are already confirmed into the original Catholic and Apostolic Church. Like Christ, Himself, they stoop to wash the feet of those whose faith is powerful enough to give them pause or ignite their pious reflection. Then, it is said, we all "rise and go on" as newly embodied creatures, fit for the dignity that is commensurate of knights, for tomorrow is the sweet blessing of solitude in knowing what the future may bring, the brigade of new hopes which cannot help but come true. There is not a fond memory in our thoughtfulness that we will fail to maintain once it is firmly seeded in this sonata of Love.

The profession of our Christianity is our succinct reminder that the mystery of faith is always greater than our capacity to put it into definitive words. God knows that if our trust in Him glistens from the center of our hearts, He will see it there with clarity. There is never a goodbye to Love for the many who choose to profess it, for those who have promises to keep are the tapestries of well-wishers whose kindred shades grow the updraft of rejuvenated spirits which make the lot of men on Earth a little more consoled. This is why the stately condolences of sympathetic grace shall never fade away or wither-out in time. Whether we choose to know it or not, there often seems to be an impasse as to when the world will slip beyond the spearhead of the illusionary hills, but suffice to say that the categorical summits of the material world and the momentary hours in between have already seen their latter stage. Just as soon as we jettison the discouragement which has been too-long burdening our petitions with sedentary doubt, the crescent awareness of humanity*regained* will be among the first to know. In the meantime, and in the wake of the forests' revelations that the Earth is still alive, let us sing of the meadows and be grateful for this day that we share in the new holland life which we have garnered in our oneness with the Savior of the world. While our fortitude seems to be just lumbering along and our faith is still laboring in pain, let our discernment be not unlike the towering evergreens who refuse to desist in the recessional autumn winds or in the winter that harbors a cold and bitter penchant for stinging us just a few more weeks behind.

Who else would dare to go forward to effect the dialogue about the Kingdom of Our Lord if we, ourselves, declined? Where shall humanity learn about the Gospels, the Acts, the Pauline Epistles, and the present-day unfolding of the Book of Revelation? Through the intercession of His Mother, Our Father in Heaven has just rolled-out His modulating pulpit to our most grand and noble staircases and has asked us to reach the highest landings to evangelize His Truth. Christians bear both the authority and the divine absolution to declare that our souls have been cleansed by His Blood, and that we hold no reservation in asserting our higher station over those who reject Him with pride. If we promise every whimpering hemisphere through the power of His New Covenant that Jesus Christ has broken the endless knot of mortal sin on the Cross, we have become a feather in the same Dove who once hovered in the heights above the River Jordan as he watched John the Baptist christen Our Savior before man. John was not wiping away any original stain because Jesus had none to extract. The fact He was attempting to prove is that Christ would be Baptized and go to His grave for the sake of our own purification, while He simultaneously put the question before the world as to whether we would follow or be disinclined. So far, we have gotten the baptism part down alright, but it is the mortally sacrificial remainder whose integrity has yet to be resolved.

If the life of a Christian were not almost intolerable to bear, anyone who is insurgent enough or adept in artifice could mimic it like a varmint in a hole. But, pain is an injurious insult which proves that our Divine Resurrection is the Truth over the fatal intrusion of death. All anyone has to do is go to any funeral home and he will know that there has to be something better than this seemingly final end. If God would allow the deceased to speak just one more whisper from the confines of their satin-lined chambers, they would soon tell us that they have already seen Him and that everything He has told them is true. We picture the beauty of where they might be through the onslaught of our emotions, but we really cannot capture the moment or the resounding chime of accord with the soul of the flesh we are about to lay to rest and the Creator who has taken them back home. If only we could see in faith through that semi-permeable veil, we would know at last that the doctrine of our Catechism is the root of the skyward tree where our own eternal life is just now beginning to bloom. There is no need for any new interpretations of the Gospel that we have been reciting since the first Holy Word was inscribed. It is, instead, our yielding compliance with the conversion that we seek about which the Seraphs and Cherubs still sing. Their lyrics remind us that faith is a blessing from the heavens, but cannot be found gift-wrapped under a tree. It is a bounty which grows from within us, one that we must open our hearts to receive.

Spiritual Jubilation and the Translation of Existence

October 26, 2000

There is a certain mystique in our emulation of Christ because we are exuding an aura of genuine divinity that the world has already rejected. Humanity proclaimed it loudly and clearly on the Hill of Mount Calvary on Good Friday. But, they need not have rejected Salvation for those of us who have succeeded them! Our Lord is a timeless regeneration of our inherited immortal perfection. What could we assume to be the content of a conversation which might occur in Paradise between a person whose deceased body has just been interred in a tomb and that of someone else whose death was more than a dozen decades before? The earlier decedent might be heard to say, "Ha Ha! I got to see God before you did!" But, they truly hold no such bragging rights in Heaven because there are no latent, sporadic, expired, or bygone times to recall. Every saint who arrives before the Throne of God is embraced by such a comprehensive Light that no one can possibly conceive whether time ever existed or remember any confounding senses of their previously lesser selves, their repressed thoughts of discomfort, or the repulsion of the social elite. That is why we should all dance through mortality with only broad smiles on our faces and no smirks of regret, reaching forever in confidence while pulling-out all the stops and running gleefully on the high-side of the thoroughfare of life. Why? Because, through the joy within our new being, we just can't seem to slow down or take another pause to cower from our long-lost inward shame. Our spiritual jubilation should be of an unflappable exuberance in the Holy Spirit while the deliverance of our newborn children brings us to shout-out our gladness that the Almighty Father has validated our Love for the larger family He brings.

There are those who appeal to no such happiness in God's supernatural Light. Some of us place very little value in the dignity of human life at all. Those who favor the execution of the convicted live according to this taurine standard of hatred. It is as though our public leaders are driving down an interstate highway while confronting an animal from the wild trying to cross the road in their path. Believing that they are seeing a lesser form of life, they do not bother to slow down for fear of upending themselves or being late for their next photo-opportunity to further inflate the cellulite obesity of their grandiose illusions of who other people may think they are. To them, it would be a crisis to detour their route to see the supermarket bargainers or miss the chance to say that they are saving the rest of us from the criminal carnivores of the predatory world. They have not a single clue that all which is righteous is attributable to God and that a parable about the Truth can be made from almost everything they do. Our affiliation with the Prince of Peace places us in a chosen deposit of filial allegiance with the visionary conquerors of unrest who stand in diametric opposition to the makers of war and whose sartorial charm still boasts of breastpins and brass stars to celebrate their victory in defining the Gospel over the drawing of political lines between the oceans of Earth. No display of skyrockets from our billets below has ever been able to compete with the awesomeness of the Creator of Life when He occasionally gives the command to unleash the bolts of lightning that set our forests afire. While the prayers from our souls are reaching ever more powerfully toward the celestial spires, the hands of those who deny Redemption are still digging for the concession of that elusive toy-whistle in the bottom of their crackerjack box. They had better hope they find it soon and begin to frantically pipe for God's attention because He is swiftly paddling away with the rest of our souls in the berth of His arms like the survivors inside the safe haven of Titanic's lifesaver boats.

If we expect to be joyful for the new ages to come, we have no choice but to let ourselves flow onwardly to our inevitable reunion with the Glory of Heaven. We will know our beloved family of Saints when we get there if we start now with our pronouncements of Love. Just as we do not lose the fluency and poise of our native tongue simply because we may be visiting another land, we will be able to speak quite comprehensibly with everyone else whose body has gone to its grave. There are no partitions to separate our souls from the fullest Light unless we, ourselves, choose to erect them. Time becomes a nonissue and neither can the various and sundry repercussions of our unleavened remorse cause us to fall short of joy. If a mathematician totaled the sum of the age of every person who ever lived on the Earth, he would still fall painfully shy of ever conceiving the briefest of seconds that ever passed into the hindsight of God. It is in this translation of existence that Jesus sees our world as strangely as we have already imagined Him to be. What does a room filled with applauding people look like to a little child who sees only an inordinate number of impacting palms mimicking a gathering of sea-lions on a wave-crashing shore? If we are to become the people whom Christ calls us to be, we must perceive our tangible world like that same innocent youngster looking so curiously at the things that cause him to squint his own eyes. However, our official primeness of life does not have to be perplexed by such interior confusion or lack of spiritual reference within the framework of our higher pursuits. It is said that, if we live long enough, every day will seem to be the anniversary of something that has happened before. But, we do not have to wait until we grow older to see those commemorative moments finally falling into place. By embracing the civility of Love even as we speak of the moment, we can envision ourselves in the broader sense as the other side of life and the world as we know it become united as one.

Love is many things to those who know Salvation, but nothing to someone who tries to hold-out on his own. It is like making the game-winning shot at the buzzer, hitting a grand-slam home-run to win the World Series, and taking the checkered-flag as champion of the Indianapolis 500, somehow all rolled into one. It is the gratitude we hold for our fallen countrymen whose widows we feed every night. The choice that Christ made to Redeem His Creation prevails over any vacuous excuses we might concoct to not try. If only our hearts will awaken, we can know Him as the composer who placed the grand finale on the score that is now playing across the airwaves in Heaven. We might be able to turn the world's jukebox music on and back off again in our heads, but the melody of Love wrought by our Savior can never escape the depths of our hearts once it starts echoing there. No sequestered chamber quartet or orchestras in the dark can replicate its beauty, and no one sporting a white wand can ever bring it to an end. Salvation is that permanent because the suffering of Christ has been made so severe. The eternal integrity of His Crucifixion on the Cross is proof that this will always be true. There is no doubt that humankind has breached His mortal Flesh in nearly every conceivable way, but we have never had any power within us to put the slightest glitch in the armor of the Divinity He still wields. The indelible nature of His Passion is still as pristine as the Holy Spirit, itself.

Icons and Missionaries Against the Adversary of Poverty

October 27, 2000

The Church is the ongoing breath of life for spiritually hungry children and the followers of the Christian faith. She has been led for centuries by giants among men who have gained nothing material in return; no profit, no fame, very little encouragement, and almost no respect from the secular world. The unique part about God's Faith Church on Earth is that it is composed entirely of sinners who, but for the chastity of the Holy Spirit, would fall to temptation over and again. Through every generation of its historical blessing, the Church is still the cynosure of all that humankind deserves from the hand of the Almighty Father through His Sacrificed Son on the Cross. This living fountain of holy fortitude is still going strong, awesome to the touch, and wise unlike no other; not hollow like a reed, but filled with integrity to rival the core of a sedge. Through all of the staggering stillness through which She summons the wicked from amidst the whispering crowds of nonbelievers, the Catholic and Apostolic Church has been the mainstay of tradition against the horrid insurrection of the wretched few who have attempted to destroy Her since the lofty tongues of fire first rained down from the floodgates of Heaven. If humanity is to capture the revealing preparation that is required to see their Savior again, every soul alive must come to a newfound identity through the Sacred Sacraments which God has so kindly dispensed. We must all recognize that the teachings of Christ are manifested through the Holy Father in Rome because the Chair of Saint Peter is the moral authority for the entire contingent of nations. It is herein again worthy of notation that the last pope of the twentieth century and the first of the one now at hand, His Holiness Pope John Paul II, has been the exemplary bastion of righteousness for the entire civilization of mortal men. Never once has he allowed his attention to digress from the message of human dignity under the Cross and in the Resurrection of Jesus Christ from the grave.

There have been tens of thousands of Roman Catholic clergymen since the dawn of the early Church who have held to the single Truth which has always been founded in faith; that the origination of everlasting life from the Throne of God is located where the Last Supper and the Crucifixion of Jesus Christ intersect, specifically the Holy Sacrifice of the Mass. This miraculous reality can never be altered or face the dissolution which befalls so many peripheral factions that already fail to withstand the testament of God's allowance when He asks for a show of hands to reveal those who openly accept Him. The Blessed Trinity; Father, Son, and Holy Spirit is the professorial Creator of this perpetual catechesis. Through our responsiveness to His grace, we learn that the Divine Nature of God cannot change, Jesus Christ *refuses* to change, and the Holy Spirit gives humanity the resilient interdependence and beholding desire to stand by them all, whether we suffer the pratfalls of plight, interrogation, persecution, confinement, or martyrdom itself. This is the supernatural precept which keeps the Sacraments new. Through all the centuries that have already passed and the multitudes of priests who have now come and gone, The Body and Blood of the Savior of the world, present in the Most Holy Eucharist, has always remained the same. As long as there is bread and wine within the reach of human hands and a Catholic priest is alive to consecrate them, we will be able to celebrate the Holy Sacrifice of the Mass because these devout men are the loving instruments of our Lord to the infinite degree.

The priestly vocation is much more than someone who walks the streets wearing a white collar and somber black cassock. A priest is our father, consoler, advisor, teacher, and friend. He ministers to our needs in times of joy and in our darkest occasions of sorrow. It is never a call of the wild that sends men into a religious vocation of the priesthood or brotherhood, or women to utter the cloistered solemnity of their convent prayers, but a summons from

God for them to go *into* the wilderness for the sake of rescuing His lost sheep and helping Him mend the fractures of the broken and oppressed hearts they find in seclusion there. From the sacristy door to the confessional walls, and from the lectern pulpit to the Altar of Sacrifice, our Roman Catholic priests deny their very selves for the good of every other man, day after day to the Glory of Christ, emitting His Light with courage into the world where only few mortals before them have ever dared to tread. These icons are missionaries against the adversary of poverty in hundreds of forgotten places where the consciences of more influential men are too afraid to go. Their mortification before the Table of the Lord is to the bold enhancement of human conversion at the cost of diminishing themselves. Their goodness is written by compassion for the poor, counsel for the wicked, forgiveness of the penitent, and encouragement for the blessed. These humble evangelists depend quite dearly on the sanctioning of our prayers, as they assuredly beseech God to help us in return. The Christian laity would be sorely remiss and quite guilty of a gross dereliction of spiritual duty if we refused to support them by lifting them up before the world and praying deeply that they remain strong in their advocacy of those who are entrusted into their care.

When our priests recite their morning Offices and offer their meditations of the Holy Hours, they are always reminded of their passion for God, asking Him to lay His healing hands on the very ground upon which His humble servants walk. If we do not respect them, then our attitude of disdain is one that God will certainly despise. They stand at the dawn of every morning to bring Creation to purity, expecting nary a pittance of reimbursement in return or an ovation from the world. When we look into their eyes, we must always be moved to ask, "What more can we expect from ourselves?" Are we prepared to take it on the chin in defense of our Christian beliefs? Do we admonish ourselves as well as one another to live-out the Apostles Creed we have professed? Do we honor our Father God and our Mother Mary, in whose custody we have been placed? Do we ever promise Him during our petitions on Sunday that we will return for the Manna of Life all the rest of the days of the week? If we answer these questions to the oblation of our First Communion, we will recognize that Jesus has built a dynasty of victory through which we cannot fail. We are the living cells of His Mystical Body which has yet to be transferred into God's Triumphant Church that surrounds Him in Heaven. Our souls are the maturing nuclei of everything that will soon come to be, each of us united as one flesh and prepared for the statesmanship of everlasting life; impregnable by any pain, unknowable to the gritty pangs of suffering, too happy to stoop for sorrow, and unable to remember the hollow taunting of our misguided tortures of grief.

We shall not be shamed by any new banishment from Heaven when that time of Glory arrives because humankind will never be able to violate the Will of God again. The thousand years' reign of peace on Earth will be more than just time to be passing; it will be the magnum opus that we take to our Salvation and only a brief millennium inside an otherwise timeless eternity of complete satisfaction. No one will ever be able to deplete our conscious awareness of realizing that everything we are doing now for human condolence is a precursor to the higher consolation we will all find when we arrive at the gateway of Paradise. Through everything we are seeing in this modern-day world, we fully understand that the Holy Gospel can never be held hostage or subject to the contemporary liberalism of the "anything goes" persuasion or the so-called inclusive interpretation of unsavory conduct which we know deeply inside to be repugnant in the judgement of God. Such crass and arrogant demagoguery is unfair to those who yet feel forsaken and disenfranchised while they are still painfully trying to find the triangular root of their spiritual elevation. We can depend on this, too, to be the latter-day enemy of the Catholic Church that Her priests and Her flock will eventually have to conquer. The outright stir-headed debauchery of the physical world is destined to fall at the feet of the Saints. The only question yet to be answered in our lifetime by Jesus Christ is, "When?"

The Encyclopedias of Our Most Memorable Hours

October 30, 2000

The Blessed Mother continues to call for prayer of reparation from humanity, but the world keeps asking "...reparation for what?" God is seeking signs in us that we are willing to own-up to our individual and collective faults and misgivings and to recognize that we can amend them only in Him. We are implored to focus our testimony on the Holiest Fruit in the vernacular of His Living Word, Jesus the Christ who died on the Cross to bring us to justice. We must never compromise our struggle to convey the standard of righteousness to those who still lack the fundamental understanding of human absolution. Is it because we live in a world which fights-off the spiritual aspects of Christianity with such a vengeance that we cannot seem to locate His higher grace? We are told that 80% of Americans believe in God, but very few of us plan to do anything with it or reach out in faith until His Son finally returns to judge us Face-to-face. It is not inherently cynical to point-out the aspects of our society that keep us from praying for more help, any more than it is uneasy for our detractors to ask why. We are unequivocally and absolutely head-over-heels in infatuation with the material world and *nolle prosequi*, unwilling to pursue the sacred calling that our Father in Heaven deigns to be necessary for

His people. Our physical possessions have locked us inside a cycloid of supply versus demand, need competing with whim, necessity over luxury, and the focal marketplace before responsibility. There still exists in us the inevitable desire to hold fast to whatever makes our lives more palliative, doing our best to save for a retirement that may never come while staving-off any inadvertent obsolescence of our fortunes while we wait.

When Jesus told us that the wind blows where it wills, He was also speaking about the changing tangible uncertainty that can make or break us in the passing of an hour. Well-to-do Americans wake every morning from their sleep wondering how they can retrieve something even more beneficial to add to their wares. Unfortunately for them, they now find themselves in the unenviable position of pulling up to the table of plenty, trying to sell God the unlikely story that they are still hungry while talking with their mouths full. No wonder He refuses to offer accreditation to what they are clamoring about. He realizes that the compass of the human conscience cannot rest in the daunting task of satisfying our lust for wealth and power or upon the defamation of our brothers' first opportunity of finally climbing out of the social broadleaves. If we heed the call of our greater potential, we will always demand the best sacrifices from ourselves and complement the most gracious decency in others, offering whatever it takes to assist the poor to tear-down the remaining blocks that lay in their passageway to dignity. We owe them the dispensation of greater personal security, spiritual enlightenment, physical health, and peace of mind. We often brag that we are making great strides in removing the barriers which divide the rich from the poor, but we are only lying to ourselves if we believe that we have made any headway worthy of being noted by the eyes of higher Paradise.

There seems to be a differentia between our perception of what actually exists before us and what we have chosen to believe. When a late-night comedian throws an index card through a windowless frame to the sound-effects of breaking glass, we try our best to associate his fallacy with what he wants us to assume. That is the same spoof that we are trying to impose on God when we tell Him that we are comforting His sheep and feeding His lambs. What would happen if Jesus Christ appeared before us just prior to our condign eternal judgement and rendered everyone on the Earth unable to hear? Would that same comedian be able to improvise his skit anymore? We might see the index card flying alright, but he would never be able to convince us that there was ever a pane of glass in the hole. Such is the type of divulgence that Heaven is about to make of our deliberate falsehoods and devious assumptions when we proclaim to have done enough to alleviate the suffering from the world at our hands. Then, we will finally see that there is a completely unexplored frontier of agony which we have yet to conquer standing right before our eyes. Our awakening will come, but will it be too late to matter? We know inside whether we are resisting the Holy Spirit or are responding with obedience to His already stern admonishment. When we begin to cry in shameful defeat in the face of our losses to the forces that are tempting us to turn our backs on the poor, then we are finally at the crossroad of conversion and have entered into the foyer of repentance, newly prepared to give our souls over to God. It is a decision which we eventually have to muster on our own. Surgeons certainly may be able to open our chest cavity and implant the heart of another man, but they cannot install a spiritual awakening there.

One of the causes of our error is that there is such inequity in what people profess to do and what they are actually accomplishing. We need to follow the example which has been set before us in the Sacred teachings of Christ. Through the Holy Gospel according to the Saints, we see that God does not hand us a blank page and ask us to write down what we want out of life. He asks us, instead, to read and comply with what His Son has already inscribed. It was recorded into Creation quite poignantly by Our Savior on the Cross. Whatever inequity that exists today is of our own making. We have seen many poor people sitting in their quaint quarters reading worn-out bibles with practically every sentence and paragraph underlined in pencil or ink, while the bibles of deacons and reverends do not even sport a bent page or a random bookmarker. Yet, they still stand on their tribunes and scream into the faces of their congregations about how much Jesus needs their greater sacrifice if He is ever going to succeed in converting the lost. If you approach these same leaders and tell them that there is a loose thread in their robe, they would be afraid to pull it out for fear that their entire hollow evangelism might fall into shreds. That is also one of the problems with the freedom of the American democracy in action. Too many publicists are speaking about politics and not enough about the Truth. We do not have the separation of Church and state in America just so our fellow citizens are at liberty to celebrate their faith. We also maintain our autonomy from God so that masses of people can be more free to reject Him!

If we were to take a survey of what Americans most like about the United States, they would say "Freedom!" If we posed a follow-up question of "Freedom to do what?", they would say "Anything we want in the privacy of our own lives!" Therein lies the problem. We give them just enough rope of indifference to hang themselves out to dry before the God who has created us all! When we take our capitalist march onward into the other parts of the world and claim that our state sponsors no belief in Jesus Christ, we are describing an atheist's dream and forcing an utter nightmare upon anyone else who has a sliver of spiritual conscience. It is true that we are all conceived by God and are given an individual identity, specific nature, subjective form, and personal consciousness. That is our blessing; but it is also our calling to pursue Him in return. We are demonstrably able to manipulate the rest of the world, but we are almost helpless in the challenge of remaking our lost image before the heavens and restoring the reputation that we had before the first man and woman fell from their place in the sky. If we love one another within the framework of the mortal time in which we are cast, our Father in Heaven will do the rest to reinvent what is lacking inside us. The past is the time that we have lived to prove it, the days we have survived which have long since become an inanimate object in the encyclopedias of our most memorable hours. The words we have spoken and speeches we once delivered are now only faceless epitaphs of moments gone by. What we do to give them new life through our expressions in Jesus is entirely of a more noble accord. We must embrace His perfection as though it is the last time we will ever have the opportunity to touch it again. Parlous powers, principles, and potions cannot bring death to the divinity of unconditional human Love.

If we only knew what command we have been given through the Holy Spirit, we would set-out to convince every nonbeliever that he has to accept Salvation in Christ Jesus, or die fighting in the process. It is true that a pelican may never become a swan in this life, but for all of our tepid attempts to succeed at humanism, we are still animals in the woods, taking our last gasps of desperation before we expire in denial of our inexcusable faults. There is a transformation of the inner-being which can be brought to light; and we must deliver one another on the rafts of our affection to that once distant shore. If we can harness our conflicting emotions at the outset, we will be brought swiftly to our feet and on our way there. Such uneasy shyness is our call for the stability of a higher reasoning. Taking a look at what criteria we employ to lay-out our lives is a good way to see this more clearly. There are very few people who would not go back again to the age of thirty-something and change a major decision that was made which might have completely amended their life as they know it. Now, we are further down the road and realize that it is only the calling to the more charitable self that brings us lasting prosperity toward peace and harmonic justice for all. We have to choose wisely because God allows us only so many days to succeed. There are a million places to land on the surface of the ground when we are falling from the sky wearing a parachute, but only a single opportunity to do it without dying. That should give us pause in considering how we continue to mark the days without eventually choosing the next one to say, "I am going to give my soul to Jesus today, or I will never live onward in the Kingdom of Heaven to tell it."

In case we have not yet recognized it from when we were little children, wherever we fall asleep at night is also where we wake up. If we quit the fight for spiritual supremacy over the forces of the world, our sleeping disinterest will cause us to rub our eyes at the end of time with no higher station in the universe than we had just moments before. We boast of the choices we have made to devote ourselves to the Son of God in America, but we do quite little in our cold vanquished crudeness to make it come true. We hold to matters of the flesh as though they are a lifeline to the unseeable beyond. It is time that we recognized that corporeal impurity is like a contagion to those who do not have the will-power to fend it away. Indeed, if they do not break free soon, their future will ascend to no greater purpose, no more grand allegiance, and with no higher motivation than corpses could have probably achieved. God may have blessed our American nation, but He has yet to force the change of hearts which will end the tragedies that come far too often to face. Where is the effectiveness of the good will to which we claim to bear witness if we do not share our spoils with those we falsely deny that we hate? There is a litany of evidentiary facts which show that we are not yet there. The daily news is replete with the infringements and disasters that are making the Saints from above still cringe regretfully and shake their heads in disbelief. What would they make of that celebrated sports-star who was robbed of a $55,000 wristwatch while waiting on the street for a stoplight to turn green? Which is more the crime, to take it from him illegally, or to selfishly wear it in the first place?

In another part of the country, a family's boa constrictor forced himself loose from an empty fish tank and squeezed their young son to death. A father was convicted of deliberately injecting his little boy with the HIV virus; and so-called "artists" have created a depiction of Jesus Christ submerged in a glass container of urine and the Blessed Virgin Mary situated in a frame with dung smeared all over Her face. Elsewhere, a pair of defendants were convicted of blowing the face clean off of a federal building, effecting the homicide of 168 innocent men, women, and children. A hermit in Montana with a grudge against society is now in prison for mailing homemade bombs to people he just doesn't like. Public officials are hauled into court on a regular basis for embezzling millions of dollars of taxpayers money while other candidates spend more than a billion more in one election cycle to seek terms of office for positions that pay barely five-figures a year. The president of the free world has been impeached for allegedly lying under oath about an extra-marital affair that he later confessed to committing; children are inducing drugs by the truck-loads, then shooting, robbing, and raping their peers as though it is the commonplace curriculum of their academic day. A young mother is imprisoned for drowning her two biological children in the back of a car that she was said to have deliberately allowed to slip into the bottom of a lake. In another nearby display of our unrestrained gaunt incivility, a professional boxer decided to chew-off a piece of his opponent's ear. The federal government allows nearly-newborn children to be killed by having their brains grotesquely extracted by a person wielding a vacuum machine in the name of a woman's right to choose; an African American is dragged to death behind a pick-up truck by a group of white people who think that he does not deserve to live; and a homosexual is beaten and left to die while strapped to a fencepost in the stark seclusion of a country hillside. Is this the American culture which God has shed His grace upon? Who do we think we are kidding? We are on the brink of seeing that the table of justice is about to be turned on us. We are the culprits who have allowed this monstrosity of evil to go unchecked within our borders; and we will be the ones whose errors of omission will be counted in the final analysis. It is as though we are down to the final game in the series of time and are facing certain elimination.

A Cortege Upon the Death of Our Personal Aspirations?

October 31, 2000

What awesomeness we behold in the potential that the Sacrifice of God has given us to grow forward in faith! Gone is the plausibility through which we might have otherwise tried to hoodwink Him into believing that the appearance of our acceptance of the Truth is not actually our backs turned the other way. It would be a crisis of no higher degree if we allowed this final burst of spiritual energy to slip beyond our grasp. However, our curiosity for what we have yet to discover keeps sending us back into isolated caves and their brother cape caverns which are flooded to the brim in the belly of the seas. We leave the speed of sound in our tracks to get to the other side of the world, venting our effluent frustrations into the trembling hemispheres we leave far behind. How does this really differ from the covered wagons who fled to the west in search of gold in the face of drought and genus enemies who wanted nothing more than to huddle alone? We were not running for the lesser of abandonments back then; we were only fleeing from the one that was worse, the same as we do today aboard our airships of unleavened metal, creaking hinges, and cracking seams. We have become so completely absorbed in the vast wasteland of human discovery that it has afforded us no greater supple advantages than we have ever captured before. And yet, to this day, we carry-on in courageous daring and dynamic strength to continue striving, ignorant of the calamities which still await us somewhere, while God has forced the storage of our most elegant flywheels and frigates into morbid places where they can make war no more.

The soothing acreage we seek is not in the tingling analgesia of pride that bellows up our back, but in the centrifugal compassion and well-spring of tears which will soon flow once we realize that we encounter our Salvation only in the goodness we bring. If we could just give this vision a better chance to survive, we will finally understand that we are glaring into a blinding flash of God's Light while simultaneously looking toward the face of a clock which stands as only a darkened silhouette before our eyes. The Messiah who has so profoundly enshrined us as princes of His Kingdom already knows that we are infant relics in the boulevard of time who will soon be escorted to the fulfillment of our most unsuspecting premonitions. How can we be sure that this masterpiece of good fortune is ours for the keeping? Because we can see the Divine countenance beyond our hopes and hear the clicking of our futures in the darkness. Our frail human nature is to follow these essences toward something recognizable and tangent with the super-real, to find a substance that truly matters to us, through which we can rest assured that the origin of all life is only a millisecond away. God knows that we cannot fail in Him even though, in His pious eyes, we are a wholly motivated collection of otherwise ill-bred, insolent, and turbulent people of extraordinary potential to succeed. We own a spherical conscience which we have somehow allowed to lay flat in the basement of Creation as though it was never a star in the heavens with oscillating rings, but a delinquent mat on the floor on which the worst of Our Savior's enemies have uncontestedly trespassed without care. Jesus Christ knows that we are quite capable of crafting an artful stratagem when we truly want to prosper on our own or when our lives are suddenly on the line. But, we still claim to be immune from engaging His wrath while dodging His warranted retribution when it is so obvious that it would be exactly what we deserve. We are the inventors of medicine, life-saving machines, and supersonic modes of inter-communication, and are oracles in assessing the Earth in the most ingenious of ways. Our appetite for victory has left the beasts of the universe laying prostrate in our paths, jaundiced with confusion as they watch over us with awestruck optimism while they witness humankind accomplish the revamping of the modern day world, still suitors to God in our quest for more liberty and incessantly hungry to engorge our almost insatiable desire for more of the same.

The winds of our minds are not unlike the swirling vortexes of the intellectual dreams which we have allowed to flourish above the white caps of our still inalienable privilege to seek, find, assemble, and destroy. What we call constants and stabilities are only erratic and erotic attempts to capture the capsule of Truth that is buried not below our arrogance where we have been digging for centuries, but light-years above and beyond the paltry achievements which we still refer to as the indomitable human experience. God owns the total collection of hues that He calls endless life in the supernatural hierarchy of Paradise where the angels fly freely to adore Him. Ours, however, is but a monochromatic backfield which keeps us from knowing ourselves the way we will eventually come to be. We would have to place three-dimensional glasses over our eyes to see what rests beyond our present comprehension of this impending omnipotent degree. That is why there was the epiphany of Jesus on the sixth day of what we have determined to be the first month of every new year. It was His own revelation which commands us to not only climb to the summit of Love, but to fly freely in His Mercy away from our failures as proudly and with more artistic grace and aerodynamics than the collective space shuttles Atlantis, Discovery, and Endeavour in synchronized side-by-side launches could ever deploy. Living in us now is the expiatory manifestation of the Divine Being of Christ, something more amenable than our spirits will ever fashion on their own. This sudden flash of recognition is ours to grasp for the taking, warehouses more than a continent of verbosity or quantitative moods, and a wholesome revolution past the idle charm of palaver with which we will never once be able to deceive God into believing that our error is really the truth. He understands that we are yet an imperfect species, even as we pray for His intervention to be transformed into the best people we could ever possibly conceive. He will never bow to the intimidation of the flamboyant jesters who earn a living out of cracking wise about our mortal condition or by making a satirical parody of His eternal grace.

Despite all of the sadness which has followed humankind for seemingly centuries without end, we must not perceive our passage into immortality as being a cortege upon the death of our personal aspirations, but rather a march of certitude that we will be triumphant in fetching every good blessing which is now being dispensed from the balconies of the Saints. They silently call us to take heed once and for all to the endearing voice of the Spirit of God, casting-away the deception that He is not really there, patching our way back as peninsulas to the solemn forgiveness we can find only in Him, never again sitting alone and forlorn as islands in the stagnant bays of disgrace. We do not need to calculate our responses as though we are cleaning out our closets at home, deciding what to throw away and what we wish to keep. The Sons of the Most High are telling us to run completely out of the house and reach into the sky with our fists pumped in the air while attesting to our Creator, "I am now ready to go!" That would finally make Anton Chekhov's *Proposal* only a corner kitchenette in the mansion of holy matrimony and the oil in the lamps of the fair maidens who are still awaiting the Bridegroom from Paradise to bubble over with joy. If it is acceptance which we are seeking from God, it will come in the form of our confidence that the Cross has already eclipsed our Great Seal, the family Crest and Coat of Arms, the signatures of our companies in battle, and the emblems that have underscored the casualties we have borne, all united as one. If we train our dispositions on the goal of the mystical endowment that we gain in the Savior of the world, the frequence of our interludes with the storied galaxies above will increase to beyond what we could ever imagine in the remaining days of the Earth. Then, we will finally be able to place our lips on the Grace Cup of everlasting life, vowing an "I do" farewell to the Last Supper of human mortality, while making its crystal-clear echo a first toast to our inauguration into the hallways of infinite peace.

Feeling Inept Before the Majesty of God

November 1, 2000

Let us not shudder in fear of an existence which is so entrenched in misery that we fail to take up the fight of rooting it out. It is time to live-up to the spiritual indictment that Christ has issued against those whose defiance toward Him leads them to the promotion of rancor and division solely for the sake of being combative. Jesus said that He has come to divide us through the power of the Holy Spirit alright, but He means the sheep from the goats and the wheat from the chaff. If our families are going to be broken, let us ensure that it is because we are still trying to help one another find a better understanding of who Jesus is and how we can respond to His calling as one people under the Cross. As His loving Christian faithful, we follow a humble lineage of fractured patriots who have known no other life than to pour-out their beings before humankind at large. While people today are busy walking the catacombs of their lost memories and singing dirges to the death of their squandered opportunities, let us take them to the face of the keystone of life's meaning, the Crucifixion on the Hill of Mount Calvary. Too many souls are running amok in any direction they can find away from holiness while believing that their own better judgment has somehow been crushed to death by a collection of chips which they have allowed to fall where they may. The behemoth task before us is much more than just wiping the tears from the eyes of the weeping; we must give them reason to stop crying altogether. We may not all be soothsayers with the mantic capacity to divine the future or declare the prophesy for the next generation, but we can sure enough make a difference in strengthening and dignifying the one in which we live.

Faith in Jesus Christ is not a dietary supplement for those who are barely struggling to stay alive in the world. It is our main course in the banquet of Love for the people He has come to save. Our own pathologies and small peccadilloes are sometimes enough to make a seasoned sailor blush, but we must somehow work around them while reaching out in prayer to help ourselves and others to be pure. It is difficult to keep Americans focused on the age-old message of the Holy Gospel because we are all too prone to opt for change solely for the sake of change, willing to gamble away our best station of philanthropy for the cause of being able to say, "Look at me! I am different from you!" It all springs from how we detest being pooled into a crock of sheepish groupies whose fancy is no greater than the culture of the talent on the stage. We often camouflage our personal distinctions that make us one accord in Christ because we try to celebrate our freedom to be hailed as counterproductive citizens before an establishment which just doesn't seem to understand the aspects of who we really are. We do this to the disdain of the angels and at the expense of our moral courage and the likeness of decency that we should have been espousing all along. Although Christians do not always walk around wearing a sunny disposition on our sleeves, we are also no slouches when it comes to carrying our share of eternal hope. The world calls us eccentrics because we see humankind through the parapet of Jesus Christ and not their flashy symbol of unity under a red, white, and blue flag blowing in the breeze on the peak of a coppertop dome. Some people may get their jollies tying themselves to telephone poles in protest of contemporary civilization, but those who know their destiny in Paradise gather under stately paper birches to recite the Sacred Mysteries of the Most Holy Rosary in thanksgiving for the Truth.

The pleasance we have come to know in the Holy Spirit is divinely inspired from the Throne of God. This is the direct diffusion of grace from Heaven that the Blessed Mother has been telling us about for dozens of years. If gentlemen will tip their hats to a beautiful lady walking down the street, they will fall to their knees in awesome wonder when they see the Roman Catholic Church just as Christ comes to claim Her as His Bride upon His second arrival to end the world. There is nothing wrong with feeling a little inept before such majesty of God. But, the kind of helplessness we desire is to be walking along a beach somewhere when the most prophetic rhyme comes to our mind and we have nothing within miles with which to write it down; so we are forced to etch it in the sand. It is a mathematical certainty that, if our poem is from the Paraclete of God, there will never be another wave splash against that shoreline until we can trace-down a pen and pad and come back to copy it again. What Jesus is searching for in us is whether we are willing to take up our arms in imitation of Him. It all comes down to a matter of effort, both spiritually and physically. He knows that very few of us would ever fight the cross-town traffic to take a meal to the poor people living alongside the tracks, but we would declare it to be a national tragedy if we ever let a blocked pore on our face fester into a pimple. What we dare to do is most often less than what we really should be accomplishing. If we bring this fact up to our neighbor next door, he will almost certainly say, "Hey, I have kids to raise and a family to feed! Besides, how will they ever succeed if I don't keep them in competition with the rest of the world?" Then, we can tell him that he has just hit the nail on the head. What are we really competing for that is not putting someone else's avenues to prosperity into the trash?

There is a popular saying nowadays which essentially asserts that whatever we build, our followers will come. This is a great tragedy for America because most of us are fulfilling the prophesies of the Gospel that are putting us to shame. We build anything we can possibly conjure from our resources to distract our children from their Salvation in Christ. Their plans and expectations are founded upon the shifting sands of materialism and capitalistic greed. Once the chairman of the Federal Reserve Board opens his mouth, it is like the entire economy of America being brought to a line-screeching halt. Millions of U.S. citizens mark his every move with an almost revered trepidation, but they will not even stop for a moment to ask who Jesus Christ really is. We can thank our Almighty Father in Heaven that these priorities are about to change. You can almost sense it in the air as this new millennium begins to unfold. The Earth is a container of gasoline and the hungry poor are the spark with which God is going to blow it into pieces. If we view Creation as a fair day in the morning, we can all but lay-out our best wagers that there will be thunderstorms before night. Those of us who know Him are already aware that the Cross was not placed before us just so the Hallmark Company could put solemn faces on their greeting cards. As truthfully as Our Savior was bludgeoned beyond recognition and hung there to die, we are also responsible for fulfilling our part of the deal. "Take up your crosses and follow me" does not mean to just carry a crucifix in our pocket. It is our promise that we will also face the same rejection and indignity in the darkness of the world if we expect to share His everlasting Glory in Paradise. The Truth will always come out in time because God knows everything we do. It has often been said that we don't know when our lives will come to an end, so we should never leave anything in our attic that we would not want our survivors to see. This is the same concern we should have as we live everyday when it comes to the matters we are trying to conceal from the heavens. When the Holy Gospel is finally fulfilled, nothing which has ever been committed will be unknown by the rest of the world, save the substance of the penitential confessions we have sacramentally made.

It seems as though humanity holds an utter repugnance against withstanding physical pain and enduring mental distress. We regard them as a two-headed prehistoric monster that tries to squeeze the life from us as though our feelings are some type of exoskeletal accordion. The diminishment we sense in our body is the tugging and pulling of our resistance against permitting God to perform the miraculous works of converting the world through our interior agony. That, however mysteriously, is also what fasting is all about and is the self-denial which allows us the grace in the Holy Eucharist to crave Salvation on the Earth and taste its purifying sweetness at the same spectacular moment. All of this is contrary to the discriminatory druthers that our minds keep trying to force us to believe. However, Christ Jesus knows it to be our victory over the transitory world, and much to our benefit in conceding to the greater purpose of absolution in His Blood. Perhaps He is calling us to perceive mortal life as our "Anticipated Mass" in observation of the Feast of The Resurrection that we shall soon celebrate in the full sunlight of Heaven.

Come All You Saints to the Aid of Souls Gone By!

November 2, 2000 - Feast of All Souls

We have exhumed the earth beneath our feet, drilling completely to the core in search of the layers of shale, flint, coal, crust, paydirt, topsoil, and seed. We have found lavenders and greys, oils and flagstones, all in an effort to take a profile view of this strange dark world which keeps us afloat in the atmospheric void of the cosmic unknown. But, while we are busy combing the grassy knolls where our progenies choose to play, let us not forget the layer that we have interred just below our feet, the tungsten graveyards of those we once held in our arms. We call them "cemeteries" for short, but they actually hold the remains of the geniuses who have kept our hopes alive; our lovers, poets, and dreamers who would never surrender to the cold stiff winds or the ravishments of mortal dismay. They were our practical romantics and educators, power wielders and homemakers, an electorate of unparalleled obedience in the orders of the day. Resting in those unheralded domains are our grandfathers and children, blacksmiths and lawyers, doctors and healers of our spiritual faith. Each one is now blessed to have seen their Creator, and hopefully have remembered our names to Him, too. They have been actors and lecturers, playwrights and pontiffs, clerics and sisters, and courageous dogmatic soldiers. Lest we forget, they have met their passing before us in tune with the praises that are so appropriately engraved on their crypts. Together, they conjoin to compose the limb of the Mystical Body of Christ which would be sorely remiss without them. We will never forget their tragedies and legacies by which we still profit and learn how to live. The plumbers and beggars, tailors and players will all be remembered for what they knew best how to do. They were bankers and teachers, farmers and pilots, mechanics and artists, judges and stenographers. All of them, professionals and amateurs, vagrants and kings alike, will be recalled most because of the way they clung to their allegiance to God. They were once so worried about what goodness they could effect in the still moistness of the sweet morning dew, but now they are made happy by what we are accomplishing in their place. They brushed their hair and stitched their flannels the best they knew how, not knowing all along that their true beauty resided within.

Gone are our caroleers and stationers, interns and salesmen; equestrians, nobles, and trustees; executors, interpreters, binders, painters, and people who conquered the seas! We have bid farewell to dealers and directors, pavers and builders, dentists, distillers, firemen, fishermen, cabinetmakers, morticians, inventors, janitors, jewelers, wanderers, princes, landlords, acrobats and musicians. We shall long remember how they worked the fields with their calloused hands, turning the wrenches, and penning the ballads we offer today. They built the bridges we ramble across and sculptured the skyscrapers where towheaded pigeons retire to warble in throngs. The world will always know of their comedy and morality, those who were willing to take the risk of uttering the words that have forced the remembrance of our more humble days. What a miracle would resume if we could all be known for the goodness we do now in the name of the preservation of the human family in the same way we recall the best of those who have long passed away. For they to whom words came easy and others who did not know what to say, their mortality has ended and they rest now from their labors under which they never once demanded to quit. It is us who still live the parenthetic lives between our birthdays and our last, never fully knowing what revelations are recoiled beyond the golden horizon that will soon greet us head-on. This should give us strength and desire to seek-out the God of all Dominion in the name of justifying our faith through the consolation He brings. We must not only be lovely in His sight, but loving as well; willing to mediate the disputes which broil beneath our collars as to whether we will ever relent or eventually catch-on to the full Light of day. Our Almighty Father in Heaven has given us a self-guided will, but He denies us permission to employ it to the advancement of our own personal whims. He has commanded that we follow in the extraordinary perfection of His Son, leaving behind our playpens and bayonets, and to forego our carnal desires in the interest of glorifying Him. We have the right to say "No," but we risk being condemned for ever allowing our refusal to pass through the cracks in our lips. Just like that delicate layer of remains which resides barely a meter below our feet, we are helpless on our own to create a more scrupulous way. We face temptation at the break of every hour, but are never once allowed to entertain them for fear of taking a fall. We hold fast to countless personal aspirations, but we are perpetually admonished that it would be best not to pursue them for now.

Instead, we are told to build up our treasuries in Heaven, but we are not allowed to expend them quite yet. God has set-out to make the nations prove their loyalty to Him, to the windy souls and deep forest greens His divinity will search to unearth anyone who is still unbeknownst to His grace, realizing well in advance that He already knows where they are. He does not seem to care if we are kneeling over our bed while reading the daily news or flying a Lear jet high in the sky, nowhere does He call for our allegiance to a scripted ongoing fantasia that has nothing to do with Him. He celebrates no partisanship other than to His Kingdom at hand, and requires no dues more capital than the fullest of our faith. Jesus Christ is somewhat of an ideologue when it comes to setting our goals because He knows that the bar for our achievement is set awfully high. If we try to steal away or run into the wheat fields of the farmer next door, we are truly only eluding ourselves. Why must we be so crucified when Our Savior has endured it already? Because the entire Trinity was excruciated when we killed the Messiah on the Cross. God was offended because His Love was violated on the Earth. Jesus willfully gave-over His entire being so that ours could be spared from the grave. And, yes, the Holy Spirit is tortured to this very day when we lay our lives on the line to defend His Truth to the rest of the world. When we are so despised, rejected, banished, punished, and martyred for the Gospel of His Son, we feel the stinging Passion of the Heavenly Paraclete to the depths of the netherlands, calling-out for us to never give up, never give in, and to always trust in ourselves.

Our hearts are often the casualties of war in the prosecution against untamed evil and horror; wounded warriors in the campaign for no more than a chance to say at last, "I have fought the good fight; I have won the race." That is what the legend of those expired souls is all about. It is victory, honor, salutation, and reward. It is also a renaissance, a thanksgiving, a Resurrection, and a joy. No mortal who has ever passed the triumph beyond the grave will wish to come back again unless we ask them to turn their faces our way. It is not that they do not love us anymore, but merely because they require our yearning for Salvation from the God before them who has finally chosen to reveal His Face. So, let the jets defy the gravity above us and the clandestine torpedoes enforce their full-speed ahead; but we shall go gallantly about the business of assuring the suffering souls in Purgatory that we will never forget them in the solemnity of our prayers. We prove it in the echoing of their past and the promises we make at their wakes, uttered again so profoundly as their requiem Masses are celebrated with such stately grace. Believe it now or dissent, all is not yet right within the confines of the incredulous world. But, we will make it so by remaining bonded in the chain of immortality with those whom we call the deceased. If we ignore their inclusion, we will be trying to bargain with Heaven at the expense of our own spiritual plight. But, when we pray on our knees for their Salvation, the prospect that we might precede them home is a highly improbable case. Our thermostatic degree of compliance is not nearly the absoluteness we will find in our Almighty God. *Come all you Saints to the aid of souls gone by! Hear our petitions! Grant them a swift reply!*Although our impish faces and squinty eyes cannot quite show it yet, we are all much more in love with God by the world they left behind! We have learned through their lives that we should never allow anyone to deceive us into believing that the Truth can be divided into one parlor over the next, or that it really does not matter at all. All Love is Divine and excelling! We shall grip that sacred portion with the clasp of their undying flame until we satisfy our hungry eyes through the feast of their smiling faces again.

Never Lose Hope, Our Day in the Sun Will Come

November 6, 2000

We should always be grateful to those who have held both custody and control over their conscience to have aided so many others through the centuries to become aware of our longevity and atonement in our living Christian faith. Without their love and unceasing dedication, the prospect of the world's population having been even as much as one-fifth converted to Salvation in Christ Jesus would have never become possible. There have been both wars and rumors of wars for all of those generations; but thanks to the living saints before us, humankind stands poised to saunter ever so gracefully into the arms of God like a long-lost sheep on a cold winter's night. Contemporary humanity owes its ancestors yet another monumental debt of gratitude, especially to those who have been responsible for the custodianship of our nuclear arsenals and conventional weapons of war. It is only their good judgement and prayerfulness that brought them to leave the Earth beneath our feet as circular in scope and green to the touch as when they originally found it. We all have a great deal to learn from the spooled tempers of the ageless chosen ones who have avoided what might have become some of the greatest tragedies in the history of Creation. The Third World nations, Eastern Europe, and the tiny island of Cuba are much the better for their discernment. What types of thoughts must have entered the minds of those upon whose decisions rested the fate of so many other lives? It could not have been terribly unlike a pianist sitting down at a fine Wurlitzer keyboard one morning and discovering that all the high notes were suddenly on the left side of the scale. They may have thought they were prepared to tickle the ivory as on any ordinary day, but the grievous consequences before them seemed almost too foreign to be true. If not for their lofty contemplations and negotiations of peaceful accords, these dire moments could have led to a certain annihilation of human life as it hung in the balance. They have since surrendered their tenures to the new ages which have come, but we shall never forget the battles for peace they have won.

That is why it is important for everyone alive to embrace the cultured civility of the Holy Spirit in our hearts. Whether we are seen as someone who has the street manners of a barbarian or the table etiquette of a bear, we can all become more urbanized through our union with the pardon and patience of the Savior of the world. Even those who are addicted to drugs and alcohol can be transformed into some of the most holy people who have charged the gate of injustice. There is no doubt that such illicit substances turn once-strong men into tepid has-beens whose legacies now rest on a catafalque in the middle of the downtown square. Many others still spend their lives winnowing-away the hours in lechery and deceit instead of trying to bring themselves into the same community as those who are wearing a revitalized conscience on the lapel of their Baptismal gowns. The Truth of God can conquer any such defeatism and help all who seek Him to ascend to a more befitting poise in the Blood which Jesus has shed on the Cross. Such enlightenment is the resurgence in strength that everyone needs; and we do not ever have to darken the door of a rehabilitation center or enter a state of suspended animation to do it. All we need is to open our hearts to the Messiah! There is no mandate for dabbling in the culture of metaphysics or the hypnotism of transcendental meditation. We can also refrain from turning ourselves into contortionists while bracing our minds for the steely obedience of those who practice yoga. As long as we say, "Lord Jesus, help me," God will deliver us to the precipice of who He wants us to be.

Indeed, our acceptance of the Holy Spirit is like gaining strength through the experience of in-flight refueling as we soar high above the clouds in divinity, not once having to descend from our happiness and never again impacting the hard reality of the tarmac of Earth or depleting our moral resolve over the rolling ocean with a thousand miles to go before we reach the mainland shore. The key to this station of the psyche is our newfound peace which lives within the decision we have made to be holy. It springs forth from the gird of justice that flows from the tongues of those who profess the Gospel of Jesus Christ. His Love is the acceptance of our new hope in Redemption and the harmonic rhapsodies which flow from within. It is not vain to demand our dignity from the rest of the world. From this day forward, when someone else asks how we bear the losses of life, we will not be forced to say that we have simply learned to live with them; we can proclaim from the depths of our hearts that we have chosen to survive without conceding at all, despite the darkness they bring! The reflection of this resiliency is in our meditation upon what it really means to be reborn in the Sacred Heart of the Son of God. If we taut the focus of our eyes concisely enough, blurring our vision of the present day strains, we can see faces in the distant background and profiles from our past. These are the ancestors of the people whom we have really chosen to become. It is no accident when this finally occurs. God does not ask us to stand at the peak of a hilltop and command the lightning to strike at our feet. Indeed, it already lunges at those who are randomly unawares, prodding them with a mammoth jolt of the supernatural when they least expect it to happen. This is the sudden awakening our souls feel once we have given ourselves to Heaven. It is as though we are suddenly springing from our sleep, looking at the past we have led, and saying, "Oh my God, what have I done?" His response will always be that we should defend our solemn promise to return to Him through the intercession of His Mother at the hour of our death.

It is certain that nobody is immune from facing temptation. That is why we ask our Father not to be led into them. But, to not accept His guidance defies our own appointments of charm and grace to our, otherwise, benign spiritual demeanor. The preferable legitimacy we must employ is to pray *before* we are tempted so that we will recognize anything which tries to get in our way. Satan boasts that dead eagles cannot fly and prisoners have no means to travel; so he tries to make everyone else believe that they are just as firmly entrenched in the bondage of the Earth. We are not confined to the flesh just because we presently live within its dimensions. We are free to engage our spirits with the Firmament of Paradise, knowing full-well that our liberation from anything that tempts us is only a Hail Mary away. So, if life is showing us only its bitter side, we can gain strength in calling upon the piousness through which our predecessors once survived. There is a remarkable story to be told about how our greatest heroes conducted themselves in moments of seismic horror and catastrophic loss. We can only imagine the crowds who huddled around the likes of the most beloved popes and the charismatic leaders of benevolent democracies, and how they said with admiration, "This giant may fall someday, but he will never really be gone." That is why we choose to remember them and is the reason we must continue to imitate their grace. The hyacinth grandeur of their moral leadership should be hailed among us as the standard to which we are all eventually held. It was their imitation of Jesus Christ which made them that way.

We should never lose hope, because our day in the sun will come. We owe a great deal more than a soft alliance to our inner-selves by being forthright against those tenacious doubts which keep trying to haunt us and hold our inclinations down. We must remember that not all illnesses are contracted from the physical world around us; but some are borne from within. However, we have the wherewithal to succeed in becoming giants of purity if we will only allow ourselves to be. Any turpitude to which we might bow is a malfeasance of our own conscience, a malady of our spirit, and a sickness which can be cured. Jesus told us the Truth about this when He said that nothing impure can come from outside, but only from the insipience of our unchallenged core. By the same token, our strength through the Holy Ghost must also be raised like a ladder at the origin of our moral constitution. If we resign ourselves in any way toward moderation in our love for God, the ongoing hedonistic forces of the everyday world will never allow our conversion to survive the fall. The materialistic and lustful influences which we still battle against will devour us with the skill of delicatessen connoisseurs and spate us into their bubbling soup like a fine brandy into the bottomless sheen of a lead-crystal champagne glass. The key is that we must never allow Satan to secure an opportunity to coerce us into becoming victims of his lies. He attempts to delude us into believing that his vultures flying over our heads and his schools of sharks preparing to engulf our souls under the swirling waters at our feet are really God's obedient worker bees trying to protect their Queen or gentle gypsy moths fluttering about the filament warmth of an outdoor street lamp in the darkness of the night. Our struggle for purification in the flames of Christ's Love is always more revealing than that. He gives us the Wisdom to recognize His Presence through the distinctive means in which He truly offers it, not the way which our predatory enemies demand that *they* want Him to be.

The entire direction that we lead our lives depends upon how we really comprehend all of this. There is no question that we shall never be the beneficiaries of an ill-gotten fortune if we will only adhere to the principles of the Truth which we have been fostering all along. We will be rich in kindness only if we are strong in faith. No surly indictment can force us to do anything else if we really do not desire it to take us down. Our guilt would otherwise always precede us; and what ascension toward goodness would there be in that? It is somewhat rhetorical to ask why a person would donate their illicit profits to charity only after having been found to have taken them in bribes. What portion of sacrifice could that ever possibly define? Why could they not have seen fit to address the needs of the suffering poor long before they had ever been accused of procuring such a cache in an unethical way? That is not how Jesus wants us to approach Him. We must wholly accept His grace because we love Him outright, not because we stand to suffer the loss of our public discretion by appearing errant and greedy before the rest of the world.

Compassion is the Product of Sympathetic Eyes

November 7, 2000

To conclude that we have loved and fought, and have even feigned affection and offense does not even come near to captioning the kaleidoscope behavior of the human family today. We should concentrate not so much upon who we once were and who we are now, but the people we all hope to become. Sometimes our thoughts rush into our minds like a sweeping campaign of persuasion, at other times we really do not know what to believe at all. The true purpose of life is not whether we have taken every fortress or secured every hill; but that we know how to defeat and overcome the adversity which is still lapping against our inner-shores. Our rise to spiritual maturity is not to have suffered every heartache known to man, but to understand and console those who have endured them before the rest of us. The essence of genius is not to be able to bring closure to every problem we encounter, but to evaluate which ones are truly worthy of solving at all. Life is only a fairytale to those who do not really care how it ends. For the rest of us, however, we know that we will be tested for the remainder of our days in seeking the best we can derive from the world as it is. The power of the intellect is not to predict and decipher the balance of every equation, but to know that some things can never be equaled, while others must not be inhibited from being united as one. This is why the common denominator of justice and peace is Love; while hatred must never be allowed fractioned entry in the final quotient when God calls the world to answer. Compassion is the product of sympathetic eyes and perceiving reality well, knowing what effects our generosity evokes from others, and making the most of what we have to sacrifice in serving as our brothers' keeper. That is the charity of the spirit which is defined in the revelation carried through the centuries from the first noblemen to ever wear the golden rings of Paradise. Every soul on the Earth must take their place in the marching ranks of mortals who have passed beyond the horizon, just shy of the foresight of the millions who remain at our sides. Reckless renegades are only remnants of a society which has gone awry. But, they must not be written-off as unretrievable or ever cast aside. They are the ominous ones whose premises are yet to be determined, those who will soon complement humanity at large by becoming an integral part of everything that is fully righteous and blessed.

There is still a great deal to be said about how we envision life, nature, and God because the lines between them sometimes become blurry and obscured. It need not be this way. If our perception maintains the clarity that our Creator wants us to behold, we will envision a spray of sunbeams fanning through the clouds onto the ground below as being the divinity of the Kingdom of Heaven seeping from around God's finger in the dyke of our Salvation, just before He allows His Son to burst through the floodgates of our exile to end mortal time. We cannot recognize the beauty of the natural world without bringing His presence into focus at our own consent. But, our minds are somehow impregnated with the determination to seek out only the grief that He seems to allow. It is difficult to be optimistic when the rest of the world rewards greed with honors-cum-laude and glamorizes pain and suffering, war and death, and lust and perversion as the goals we must struggle to achieve to be famous in the journals of other men. It is equally as difficult to perceive God with loyal deportment when He seems to take the people we love the most from within our midst and places them into their graves, while leaving us surrounded only by the strangest and more ignoble ones. This only appears to be true because we choose to view our daily lives with such a tart and compartmentalized concession. We believe that all news is bad because we watch it in one-hour increments every day; and all they ever talk about is the latest scandals and who made the highest profits before the gavel fell at the New York Stock Exchange. We do not realize that there are twenty-three hours' worth of better news to hear if the networks would only see fit to report it. The facts become more apparent once we have lent ourselves to the opportunity of surveying what we actually see through the lenses of the Truth. Yes, times are difficult because eight of ten people who walk the Earth have already turned their backs against the Love of Jesus Christ.

You do not have to be a carouser to wake up with a headache in the morning. Pain springs from our point-blank collision with existence as it is, not just as we comprehend it to be through the purview of the Holy Gospel. That is why hope is forever ours for the taking. It is true that not every welfare recipient drives a Cadillac Coupe de Ville or spends the weekend on holiday at the Waldorf Astoria Hotel. There are people who are truly in need now being aided by those who care enough to help them. Others who will listen to almost anyone else with a story to peddle are called liberals; and those who cannot tolerate people who are different from themselves are seen as too harsh and conservative. They are the ones who will never allow a stutter-step in the enforcement of public laws; and when anyone gives them an answer of "More than likely...," they respond with the inquisition, "How much more?" The truth is that there is a little of both of these eccentricities at work in all of us; and life goes on from there. Every picture *has* to be worth a thousand words because some of their images are far too poignant to ignore. They do not all need to have a date on the back to remind us of the tragedy of the moment. It is still raining on the corpse-strewn battlefields of Normandy, St. Petersburg, Korea, and Southeast Asia because our tears continue to soak the photographs with the shame which was brought upon humanity there. Indeed, it may also be true that the best speeches in the world have yet to be written, and the most venerable eulogies have not yet been uttered by those who will survive. Jesus Christ is teaching His children who have long been thinkers and revolutionaries to believe that thoughts cannot replicate confident action, and our responses need not be the direct result of blunt-forced traumatic wars. It is alright to celebrate our diversity as long as it does not loosen our moral integrity or the right of God to mortify our souls for the good of His Kingdom to come. For whatever the reason which is still unknown to us, there seems to be a prevailing and unconscionable assumption these days that we are permitted to do whatever we wish with our own personal lives as long as we do right by everyone else. Helping each other to seek a better way is just fine, but it must not be at the expense of diminishing our own spiritual reflectance before the eyes of the Lord. There is no doubt that God still considers benevolence and charity without self-control as an aberration of the highest domain, the abominable beast which will breach the fine line between our inner-selves and the spotless posterity we must all eventually embrace.

Jesus has not placed our raiment of perfection high atop the shelf of Creation where we cannot reach it. By all means, He wishes to elevate us to new levels of goodness, never compromising God's standards or stooping to ratify where we choose to remain. Flags of victory belong at full-staff on a pole with the wind breaking at their seams, not crumpled inside the gutter in shambles with raw sewage rolling by. We will never fool God into believing that we are a better people than He can see for Himself. It is not as though we can provide Him a self-portrait of the fairness of our faces, sporting a gleaming smile and a twinkle in our eyes, hoping that He will take to His knees in infatuation at His first glancing sight. The Omnipotent Father who has made us knows that we are really trying to conceal the 400 pounds of obesity and wastefulness just below the bottom of our snapshot, disguised under the name of our falsely fashioned identity. The King of Creation will never fall for such pitiful deceit as that. We must surrender and expose our entire being to Jesus Christ in order to be saved; body, soul, mind, strength, and heart. He knows that people who walk around in a slump are not really cowards, but are just tired from being beaten down by the burdens of the world on their shoulders. It is the love of many of these special ones whose faithfulness the devil is trying to steal which has kept the world afloat. They have already been hit by the flying lead of Satan's treacherous tribes; we just do not see them bleeding quite yet. If we give the best of ourselves to the vision that Christ wants us to see, we will be able to distinguish His Truth from the lies that abound; and we will always anticipate in advance what is important enough to pursue. Then, we will understand what it means to effect the summoning of His Kingdom on

Earth. It is exemplified in knowing that every one of the world's billion Catholics should camp-out on the doorstep of the United States Supreme Court Building to force the overturning of laws permitting the abortion of unborn children because it is so obvious that it will never be done at the polls. It is in taking the lessons of the heart *into* the heart, not to the heated rhetoric of the politics of dispute. These are the hopes which will change humanity at last; and this is the opposite of feigned affection and transparent faith. Indeed, it is the Truth that is still fighting to come out of us and the people in Christ we will become!

Sailing Upon the Keel of Thanksgiving to the Celestial Lights

November 9, 2000

The puzzling ambiguity and inexplicable enigma which has lulled humanity to sleep in complacency has nothing to consume for its survival but our own indifference toward the rest of the world. We live in a land in which braggarts rave joyfully about their lust for longevity and the hollow victories they have pilfered to inundate their huckleberry appetites. Desire has displaced the self-denial that Jesus Christ summoned so profoundly from His people in the Sermon on the Mount. If we perceive the resonance of the collective human voice as a bell ringing-out from our churches, many are their own campaniles who stand separate from the whole, unwilling to concede their own personal definitions of Salvation to the singular Cross where our absolution was forged into being. We must begin the task of blooming skyward as one flower again under the Son of God if we are to bask alongside the trellises of His grace. Short of that, there is truly no reason for us to remain hopeful in the Providence which will take us back home. We slowly fade into the darkness as the years pass by, while our flesh dissipates to the dust from which it was originally procured. But, our souls are the Cheshire brilliance which can never be expunged by any rogue flashpoint, terror, or aftershock. For many who have already rejected the Divine assertion of our blessings, the long night's drama of their human mortality will conclude with a tragic morning breast, a moment given to outrage and disbelief, and a dying pulse of shattered misgivings which arrive far too soon as they watch their future suddenly slip through their hands. When it comes to ascertaining the material world, we have learned in one lambasting crescendo that it is truly in gaining power that we are lost, for our spirits must rise above our calculable limits and the laws of physics if we are to ever engage the highest skies.

For now, let us all sail gently upon the keel of thanksgiving to the celestial Lights, for we do not know when the extraordinary judgement of God will finally tear down the walls of our starboard audacity that holds us back from His Truth still standing in our way. When the monsoons of immortal reality finally call us to stand before the record of our errors, we shall drown in our every sorrow and rise to the break of day unprepared for our defeat. However, never will we lose the dignity of everlasting life in the vinaceous Blood of the Savior of the world. Though the battles may come, and we know that we will never win them all, we shall soon be victorious in the only ones which will succeed before the count. Our insight will always bring us to a better understanding of Love, even when life seems cruel and unfair and we have yet to completely ascend the Hill of Absolution. Our deep depression wells from our woefully insufficient attempts at contrition and a wholly unjustified lack of hope. We never do well in perfection while holding any resolve against our brothers, and this too will haunt us at the end of time. The world often seems so heartless that we are tempted to summon the nearest coroner to perform an autopsy on the consciences of our enemies, seeing that their iniquitous intentions are only lifeless cadavers laying on the cold, hard slab of death. We should disavow the adage that impropriety only matters when the expectations are low and the stakes are not too high. If this is truly the case, we had better make sure that our souls are as squeaky clean as an hourglass when the Son of God arrives to tell us the time.

As the gulf winds always recede, so goes the vigor of the faint-of-heart who would be better to know their epitome of likeness in the sheering beauty of Christian confession than to ignore the fate of their wretched souls. They can carry no guilt if their hands are wrapped around the sequined beauty of the Crucifix, leading the procession of newborn saints to the love-spangled Gate of eternal rest. In Jesus Christ, we are the mariners and clinicians of a bolder age of change, pledged to conquer our destitution in His land of plenty and no longer vulnerable to the spiritual virus of inferiority which is still trying to bring us down. What we dream is the excellent accord of our liberty to validate the biblical premonitions before those who hate us to the seat of their bowels. Our executioners are compulsively engaged in editing defamatory remarks toward people they do not even know, unaware that we have already placed our petitions before the Table of the Lord while on our knees in declaration against those who refuse to follow Him. We do not worry in mind and heart about our foes because we already compose a portion of the symphony which God is playing at the onset of the reign of His Almighty Son. Our hearts not only keep pace with the fairway cadence to snare the attention of the embattled troops; we also supply the hallowed tenor of the stately kettles, sketching the backdrops for our children to follow more closely behind. The bazaar experience of those who continue to fight against the ranks of the just is to the depths of their own confusion about who they are really supposed to be. They have forgotten that the universe is governed by principles which are promulgated by a Divine and superior authority, one who can know no error or lapses in judgement; perhaps only misfortune as is proved by the Crucifixion of the only perfect Son ever to be born.

When the Truth of Justice strikes high noon on the face of the globe, every heart will know that Love is the origin of human decency, and has most certainly become its permanent restoration. While no one has to wear a pageantry of partisan colors to be steeped in the throes of competition, they who have already conquered the ages and their detractors, alike, are running happily around the arena of Creation with the red Bloodstains of Resurrection on their robes and a three-fold inscription of affinity to underscore their victory lap. Their spiritual preparedness had never been a just-in-case scenario, but an undeniable certainty that prevailed over any defiant disbelief which tried to keep their hopes at bay. The polygons we see in life are not just begotten by the geometric angles which induce their shape; but their surfaces help us to determine how mortal space affects our lives. There are no such crusty shales in Paradise where people once tread the jagged edges that made their days so hard. We, too, must place ourselves on a course which is not contradictory to God's higher brigades, but always intersecting His Holy Will with the communal portion of our human nature. His predetermined instinct is to prevail as the signature conclusion of the mortal ages about to pass before our unwary eyes. Jesus Christ understands our frustration with our time-tested condition and patiently awaits our coming-of-age in the knowledge of His Love. When Simon Peter denied knowing Him three times on Good Friday, Our Lord did not turn to him and say, "Wrong answer! Thank you for playing!" He waited, instead, until the completion of His Passion and Crucifixion before making the call. Thereon, Peter had no choice than to believe; for what he had seen fully proved the reason why he was chosen to hold the Keys to the Gateway of Paradise and become the first Supreme Pontiff of the Roman Catholic Church. Not only is Saint Peter the custodian of our eternal Salvation, he is also our premier example that Jesus will forgive our indiscretions again and again. The fear of dying brought Peter to deny the Blessed Trinity altogether by claiming to lack any knowledge of ever recognizing the Father in the Son, the Messiah Himself, or the Holy Spirit who hovered so quietly above. How better could the Savior of humankind implicate the Divine nature of the Triune Deity and its inseparable components as one God in Three? Peter said "no" to them all by denying that he knew the Son whom he could see standing in judgement just inches before him. His thrice-rejection of the Fruit of Mary's Womb would prophesy the same absolution and acceptance which we shall all receive from the Father in Heaven as our

Creator, Jesus at His right hand as our Savior, the Paraclete as our source of endless Wisdom, and the Immaculate Mother of God as the Mediatrix of every living grace.

We should never allow the fear of death to bring us to such fright that we forego our acceptance of the source of our redemption. Indeed, how many more martyrs must die before the rest of Creation finally concludes that these brave people were standing-fast for a Kingdom which is real? How much more ridicule and persecution must they sustain before the whole world thrusts its head above the rolling waters of indignation, no longer fighting against the very Sacrificial Lamb who is trying to pardon our souls? Hundreds of thousands of witnesses for Jesus have given their lives and the years they left behind to prove to us that they were right. They have moved corals and boulders, treading through minefields and everglades in an effort to prove to dying humanity that the miracle of our deliverance which they have already seen in good faith is true. We are sinners with blood on our hands, committing genocide against the chosen lot of God's disciples who live so humbly in blocs of nations that are still trying to exterminate their races. That same blood cannot be erased by the elements of time or the turncoat denial through which Saint Peter, himself, could never stand. Arrogant men still try to walk tall, not knowing that they are crawling in ditches with nonbelievers who keep them groveling with the rest of the moles who cannot see the Light of day. This is our time for a rude awakening because Jesus has authorized our unconditional atonement toward our full awareness of the unequaled beauty that He has already prepared across the Bar. The key is, indeed, His Blood from the Cross which stands on the Hill of Mounty Calvary, the means of unlocking the supernatural mysteries we could never have seen before. It is not too late for us to make a difference in spreading His Gospel far and wide, taking His Good News to the ends of the Earth. As long as we are not laying in a coffin somewhere, we still have time before Jesus returns to tell the world about the long-awaited retirement of the resentments that still taunt us and the installation of His prominence which responds in-kind to our beckoning call.

A Persistence of Belief, A Lifetime of Christian Conviction

November 10, 2000

When it comes to facing our many sullen propositions, we should always be more concerned that we do not ever succumb to any feelings of hatred than worrying about the certainty of our passage into death. There are millions of people who cannot quite decide why their lives are so miserable; but they are basing their assessments upon how their material possessions stack-up against everyone else. The only fate which is worse than capital punishment is to die and not know why, waking up in the hands of the Savior of the world whom we do not know, watching in terror as He crimps our patented wrinkles into something more useful, larger than the state-of-the-art kenosis, and beyond any of our most extreme imaginings. That is the windfall and watershed which we should all welcome with open arms. We may go our separate ways on the trails of the Earth, but there is no escaping His grasp once we fall asleep in death, breaking free from the coma of our indifference only after it is seemingly too late. What a blessing it would be if we could somehow realize that Jesus does not ask for an immediate conversion of our souls like igniting the Olympic torch. The Holy Spirit shapes us gradually over a period of time into the saints He wants us to be. After all, that is what mortal life is all about. Just a brief moment of spiritual awareness will transform us into recognizing Heaven's time of day. Through our prayers and inner-contrition, we are brought to the understanding of this new reckoning of the years; a persistence of prevalent belief and a lifetime of Christian conviction. A simple recitation from the heart can spark this fresh beginning of our summons of faith. It is a solicited gift of Love from Paradise that cultivates, sows, springs-forth, and harvests.

If we view our Salvation in Christianity through such a progression, we must know to begin with our reversion to the childlike innocence of believing-at-will, while continuing to wear our baccalaureate clothes. We face the daunting task of pulling the sweet hours of our youth from the annals of our rearing, remembering the passage from the Gospel when Jesus proclaimed, "You must all become like little children, or you shall not see the sunlight of Heaven." This is the same Teacher who has also commanded us to put away the giddy evolutions of our youth and the pithy frankness which still echoes from our stubborn adolescence. We are to be childlike in our acceptance, but not juvenile in our conduct. This is another example of the seeming contradiction of how we should temper ourselves because Christ has asked us to redefine the living heart pursuant to His definition of holy responsibility, not how we generally view human growth and development between ourselves and our peers. The world upside down means that the last shall be first; and many who are first will be last. Doors of opportunity for the wealthy will soon become windows of vulnerability from which they will want to shut Satan out of their lives altogether, not wishing him to see them being redressed from the pride and shame that he has heaped upon them. Conversely, the shackles of poverty which have bound the poor will be the chains they will wrap around their new pulleys of dignity, elevating themselves with the leverage of the revised meaning they have found in the bountiful richness of the Sacred Heart of Christ.

Therein rests the reason all men are called to receive the Most Blessed Sacrament at the Holy Sacrifice of the Mass. No man alive has the vision to see past his own inequity without peering through the perfection which is gained in the thanksgiving Eucharist. God knows that the distinctions which divide men are always temporal and physical in nature, save the underdeveloped regions of the world where religion is the only motivation at their disposal to disagree upon. Sir Walter Scott once concluded, "O' what a tangled web we weave...," when he should have been more concerned with, "O' that our puny hearts are too frail to ultimately succeed at deception!" He understands now what the rest of us will come to know; that we shall never wield a balance of power over God because no man will ever outlive Him. Our hearts are weak, our minds grow stale, our bodies become broken, and our souls keep trying to break free from them all. Why? What does the human spirit actually realize that the rest of our being still ignores? Is it a fear of distraction, disrepute, or agony? Is it a prefigured anxiety about standing before the Throne of the Most High in the nakedness of our sins? We could call upon the wise counsel of the apostolic experts about life on the Earth, but most of them have already died. In this context resides the purpose of the Sacraments, the Mysteries of the Most Holy Rosary, and the ever-contemporary transcription of the Sacred Gospel as dictated to the Church after its birthday at Pentecost; to say nothing about the hundreds of miraculous private revelations which have been ongoing for the past 2000 years.

We remember from the Divine Praises, "Blessed Be God in His Angels and His Saints!" Does this mean that the divinity of our Almighty Father is incomplete without them? Probably not. But, His visitation to the mortal world would be sorely remiss if they were to be excluded. By all means, the very first words ever uttered to effect the coming New Covenant were brought by an angel, Gabriel, who asked Mary to be the Mother of Jesus Christ. The Archangel Saint Michael continues to wield the sword of protection for God's children against Satan to this very day on behalf of those who implore his aid. Michael holds the commission to cast every evil spirit into the fires of Hell, but very few of us ever bother to ask Him to do it. It is true that our Salvation is completed by the Blood of Jesus on the Cross, but God persists in sending His winged messengers to augment the wisdom of the Holy Spirit in our hearts. They are His tiny satellites which have been given to the people of the world, six billion strong, that relay to the Father what He already knows and sees with His eyes. Mary is the Queen of Heaven; and wherever She goes, there is no doubt that She is being escorted with a beaming smile on Her Face by an entourage of the highest order; the angels, archangels, principalities, powers, virtues, dominations, thrones, cherubim, and seraphim. This is the Divine

Court of Counselors whose collective will is also one with the Almighty Father. They are the advocates upon whom we should call for protection, even as we summon the intercession of the Communion of Saints. We cannot take our case for absolution to any Knesset, Parliament, or Congress, be they chambered, bicameral, totalitarian, democratic, dictatorial, or monarchial in nature. No mortal authority that is not led by the Holy Spirit of God can dictate the Truth about Love in the heart; for such is the residential domain of the Savior of the world, solely unique and proprietary.

It is with similar dispatch that we disseminate the Covenant of Jesus Christ to the rest of the world. There are four Gospels; Matthew, Mark, Luke, and John; and four directions on the face of the globe; north, south, east, and west. That is a compound sixteen ways to spread the Good News of human Salvation through the Cross of Mount Calvary. We cannot subvert the Will of the Almighty Father by trying to disguise ourselves as the new Messiahs of the Earth or speaking about our deliverance beyond death as anything of our own making. Humankind at large is inconsistent in telling the truth and impotent in ushering-in the daily dawn which continues to unwrap the future of the world a morning at a time. The domicile of omnipotence is the Throne of God and the Wisdom of His Seat, all encompassed by His unconditional Love; which is reason, action, Creation, reciprocity, reparation, blessing, plentiful Redemption, and grace for the people in exile below Him. When He makes us so rich in these gifts, there is no way that we can appear before Him and claim to require additional representation due to our own indigence because we are supposed to show-up penniless anyway, having tossed our last two copper coins in the Sanctuary coffers before our souls departed our flesh. It would be hypocritical for us to call for a unilateral moratorium on punishing such ignorance because we are intelligent enough to know what Jesus has been saying all along. He expects us to sincerely offer credible confessions and be true in nature before His Throne. He can always see through our belying diversions like peering through cellophane wrapping because there is no such thing as a facsimile of Love. We cannot reproduce it by machine, via cosmic Telstar, or over a modem and telephone wire. If we sometimes get the sinking feeling that the lifeblood of everything we ever owned is slowly seeping into the ground, it is the same horror we will realize if we stand before the Face of Jesus Christ and tell Him that we have loved Him in the exact same measurement as His own. Such a brash prevarication would not even evoke a chuckle in Paradise because Jesus already bears the physical evidence against us in His Hands where the beveled-end of two spikes were hammered through His Flesh. This is why the Truth will always prevail and is the reason we should hasten to be raised with Christ when our time comes to hand-over our spirits from the valleys of the mortal world.

Our Rendezvous with Destiny

November 13, 2000

It is our most redeemable course of propriety to remember to pray not only for ourselves, but for the greater world of souls whom we will all come to know in the full Light of day. There must be a more stately absolution for the people we have long despised than the frail pardoning which we offer them in passing. If we do not love them to the core of our hearts, our outward actions will always convict us; and such is a lie that cannot live for long. We should also remember to lift our supplications even for those whom we positively know could have never died unfaithfully to Christ because it is a kindred way to commemorate their lives. They will hear and answer us when we utter their names with the espousing of their intercessory and filial alliance. Humankind must leave no stone unturned in our effort to comprehend the awesome power of an individual prayer from the heart. Many of us are still trying to sculpt the future of the universe by what we know to be real, but we are only chipping away at the darkest edges of a shadowed half-moon if we do not pray to discern the humble spirit which makes our modest intentions come true. Even though our efforts may seem archaic to us, God knows that we are quite effectual in creating an image before Him which is sufficient to be recognizable in Heaven. Oftentimes we travel in and out of nations while pitting mortal life against everlasting Eternity and beyond, not knowing that they are already one and the same perpetuity. Those who delve deeply into life on the Earth while head-over-heels in traction with a succeed-or-bust motivation eventually discover that there is not really much else worth pursuing than the affection of those they love and a place to lay their heads. We cannot mutate ourselves into something wholly different from the divine beings whom Jesus wants us to be; and this should be greater than enough to suffice for our pathetic curiosity about our banal pragmatism. All-in-all, the splendor of Creation resides within our hearts; and that is all we need to remember for now.

Therein lives the reason we should stop trying to compete with everyone else for the passive goods of the material world. We try to imprecate a nasty spell upon those we perceive as our enemies who try to get to the finish line ahead of us, hoping they will stumble and fall so we can turn them over for punishment before the God whom we believe supports our achievements over theirs. Just for the record, none of us has won anything in life other than the Blood of the Cross that is worth the effort to hail before the masses and throngs. The Holy Gospel repeatedly tells us to train our eyes on how much better we can become prior to resorting to casting our dispiritedness against our neighbors and friends. The great Rembrandt did not even know of his own true genius until he painted a portraiture of himself. It was only then that he could replicate what his mirror was already trying to reveal "Is this the true man that I want my descendants to perceive?" After the passing of over three hundred years and the 3000 works he compiled, we can now answer his question with a definitive "yes." There is no replacement for how we envision remembering ourselves or where we wish to go. This process involves the transconfirmation of our physical being into a chronological place. The twentieth-century presidents Franklin Roosevelt and Ronald Reagan both spoke of our "...rendezvous with destiny" as though it was something we could achieve on our own. Neither of them knew that it was a presence which already exists in the miracle of the human spirit that they were seeking all along. The destiny has come to greet us at the intersection of our time and immortal space. Our age is the fortunate vestige of bygone legends whom we continue to mourn and versify at our malls and coffee shop counters with the folks who live down the block. They already understand the vertical Truth that is raining down upon us in droves. If we ever embarked upon rendering a novel about the resurrection of the world which is ten-thousand chapters long, we can rest assured that we could turn at random to any page of the text and our identity would be recounted to the tee on the reverse side of that leaflet in Blood. This is how close we really are to greeting the certitude of Heaven and the mandatory statutes of God.

The transgressions we have committed in life often keep us from reconciling ourselves with both the past and our future ages. If we hold remorse for them to the depths of our confessions, Jesus will place them into remission. However, if we tend to ignore them with the belief that there are a lot worse people in the world than ourselves, God will assume that we have chosen to wear our stained garments despite Him and will blanche our unredressed barbarism in the face of our own indifference and hang us before the rest of Creation to dry. We can attempt to intellectually rise above the guilt which is grilling us from the inside, but no set of stilts could ever elevate us from the gristle and error that we have wrought of our own accord. The world in the twenty-first century is definitely one for the books because we have created a spiritual quagmire against ourselves which is unrivaled by any generation before. Our backs are slammed against the macroscope of an illegitimate technology at its finest hour, while we hold no greater domination over the flight of the human condition than the first Native American to ever greet Christopher Columbus on our eastern seaboard in 1492. It seems as though the more Jesus tries to cultivate our hearts, the more we engage the fight against Him with the belief that only evil would ever attempt to make us deny ourselves before tending to strangers we do not even know. We often stand firm against the Will of God while the Holy Spirit tries to agitate our potential into a more charitable state of being. He places our arrogance into a churn of revelation until our lives are finally rendered like butter in His Hands. He then generously spreads us out onto one deathbed apiece before we ever acknowledge what is truly going on. Our indignation does not stand a chance against the searing Sword in the Sacred Heart of Christ. He has already paired us down to those who will finally accept Him and the rest who will go to Hell.

The fact remains that the fall of man ended when Jesus Christ died for our sins on the Cross. But, those who refuse their portion of that Salvation are still going down the slide. If the lips of the defiant souls who have died in complete denial of His Blood were to somehow be transformed into graphite, they would scrawl-out their horror to the rest of the world to beware against saying "no" to Redemption as they lay flat in eternal perdition, face-down on the floor of the abyss. They have come to know what the rest of us should learn before it is too late; that God is the *genius loci*, the Guardian Deity over all Creation; and He reserves the right to continue shaping it as He pleases. He evicted Adam and Eve from the Garden of Eden, and He will cast the followers of Satan into the inferno of hatred as well. We will never end the reign of the Almighty Father or be able to circumvent His power. We are helpless to stage a coup against His sovereignty that would ever succeed. The moment is at hand during which we must choose Heaven over the throes of condemnation because time is very short. Those who believe that the passing of the world is only half-way spent are undoubtedly the same ones who are paralyzed by the chimes of noon while ignoring the stroke of midnight to begin another day. Let's face it, good will is not standing in puddles around the globe these days; and our own stubbornness is the only reason why. Our morals are suffering from both rickets and arthritis because we refuse to nourish them with the Wisdom of Love and exercise them toward the dignity of our fellow humankind. We can only imagine what our grandfathers might think of the civilization we have allowed to fester which lays waste to the pure uniformity they left us to guard with our lives. These saints whose bodies are lying dormant in their stately undercrofts below are already celebrating the Truth that they will never again have to sweat over hotbeds of manual labor or shiver in the cold. But, there is no doubt that they are sitting on the edge of their seats in wonderment of the outright evil which we who have succeeded them have allowed to flourish beyond our control. While the invocation of their extreme unction was a welcome balm to their burns of mortal strife, they look back today on a world which has grown so frozen in mutual hatred that it will, indeed, take the fires of God's wrath to ever thaw it out.

We realize all of these things by our faith in the Church, but we fail to do anything about it. The Blessed Trinity hovers above us like a reliquary crown to honor the living Christ inside us; but we still somehow manage to look another way. The Triune greatness of the God who created us is more than a treble of a fractioned integer. He is the Father, the Son, and the Holy Ghost who has come in Love to save our souls, and the ex-officio presider over every baptism, confession, confirmation, Communion, marriage, ordination, requiem Mass, and Marian cenacle. Our Divine absolution could never be more propellant than that. Our virtuous health and everlasting life hinges on whether we desire to avoid spending the rest of eternity with the fires of Gehenna lapping at our feet. Focusing on this irreducible conclusion about our immortal destination, we are still searching in the darkness like a planchette passing over an Ouija board or trying to divine the purpose of life with a wishbone whittled from a stick. Only the Paraclete of God can tell us the exact location of the future we are fervently seeking. He gestures to the center of the heart as being the primal indicator of our essential prophecy and fate. Newborn life springs from within, and so it is with our eternal Salvation. If we continue to be deceived by counting the days on the calendar and marking them out with a permanent pen, we will persist in expending our lives falsely believing that each one in itself can bear the full likeness of the encapsulated Truth. The principle reason why Heaven seems so far away is because it takes most of us decades of life to ever see its Golden Gates. Christ wants us to realize that our distance from the Throne of His Father is not a spacial fact of corporeal nature, but only a matter of time. It is what we do now with the present and passing moments which will make all the difference in the end. We can be self-deprecating in our humor, but we must always maintain the integrity of our souls by every means we can possibly conceive. The only time that Our Savior ever wants to hear us uttering, "Me, me, me..." is when we are toning our voices before singing an operetta to glorify His Cross. Very little of what we do in life should be focused upon ourselves. Making an extravaganza out of everything we do is not helping matters at all.

It is obvious that we must consume food in order to stay alive, but most people in America seem to believe that eating should be some sort of an epicurean excursion or a culinary delight. Would it not be better to save our richer appetites for the Eucharistic Table at the Holy Sacrifice of the Mass? This is where all Creation becomes one whole and we are not likely to get as hungry while doing the best of God's work. The Most Blessed Sacrament is transcendental of time and place, always reminding us that, in Jesus, we will forever be properly fed. The maturity of our faith is the beholder of our fledgling trust which guides us to Salvation in Christ until our dying days are over. Getting our minds adjusted to accepting this fact in submission is somewhat the more difficult thing to do. Just when we begin to hear cyclical echoes of decades gone-by that remind us of the innocence of our youth, and we finally have the opportunity to assess the greater values of life, it suddenly comes to a close as our dreams are shattered by death. This is when we recall that God holds a greater purpose for our having lived at all and will take us toward a fuller enlightenment which we could not have known before. We will see the stratosphere as it was always meant to be and can compare it with the world we just departed. We will see all those crack meteorologists who are still scurrying to predict the global weather patterns that God put into place when He first created the universe. We will realize that we should never have gone for the jugular against our enemies because only the Holy Spirit can grant them the good offices to change their own minds. Indeed, we will be able to discern the Earth from a purview high above the clouds, having traveled to a land where the ages, themselves, have become old enough to retire. It is these same time passages that are chastising us now, for they know full-well where they are going to sleep; taking us with them in their ticking sidecars on a journey which will eventually come to a close. Is the work we are doing now for the endorsement of history truly worthy of the years that are passing? Do we actually believe that God forces us all to undergo tragedy, pain, loss, and agony to discover what Love is all about? We will soon conjugate our union with Christ with much greater emphasis than that same Rembrandt van Ryn ever thought to imply. Did we listen, did we teach, did we share, did we guide, and did we believe? These are the questions whose responses only our prayers can reveal.

"My Dear Sir, There are Three of Us Way Up There!"

November 14, 2000

In the end, do we believe that God has protracted a campaign of human misery against the elements of the world? It seems as though we are capable of feeling only what we suffer; and anything less is always proportionately too good to be true. What hollowness accompanies our lives when our memories are so vivid that they pale the affections of an ordinary day. We cannot jettison what our minds will not forget; so we try to make the best of our diminishment and carry-on doing the business at hand. We often try to compensate for this by making our environment as comfortable as we can. But, do we really need a private residence in the outskirts of Malibu and another mansion on Montego Bay as well? Does our conveyance have to be the luxury of a Brougham instead of a more modest Custom sedan? We will sooner see an international airlines allowing its passengers to carry-on their own lawn chairs for lounging during midflight before we will ever prove that God is foreign to the disadvantages which we seem to encounter as the travails of these modern times continue to unfold. The life of Jesus Christ on the Earth was no less painful or perilous than that of our own day. And, there is no one alive who is presently hidden from the perfect vision of His Love or beyond the reach of His healing grasp. If He would have returned in Glory on July 20, 1969 to end the mortality of humankind, no one would have had to tap Him on the shoulder while pointing to the moon and say, "My dear sir, there are three of us way up there!" By all means, Collins, Armstrong, and Aldrin would have been among the first ones to know. There isn't any doubt that Our Lord would have turned in-kind to this same humble soul on that last predestined day to profess with the elegance of the Trinity in His eyes, "By the way, there are Three of *us* up there, too." It marked the first time that the lunar surface had ever been stained by the corruption of human flesh; and it has long been dying ever since. The Sea of Tranquility had been previously reserved for inhabitation only by the pristine spirits having flown there alone with their own desires to succeed.

Our much revered lives are never justified by the grip of our hands on the potency of a financial account or the expanse of the distances we can travel. We are far better to acquaint ourselves with the salutation of the Hail Mary than to search for merchant heads who are lost in unknown and uncharted waters. The Most Blessed Mother of all humankind is the convener of every grace that will usher in the final age of man. She sees Her prayer groups like thousands of little newspaper carriers bearing the countless interpretations of the ongoing stories of the day. We are telling the entire world about our Salvation in Jesus in our own splendid ways, but it is all about the same Blood pouring down from the one Divine and unprecedented Cross. Can there be a sliver of righteousness left for every soul on the Earth after what we have done to pervert it? Is the Sacred Heart of Jesus large enough to provide everyone an equal share of eternal consolation? These rhetorical questions are answered to the affirmative by the Sacred Mysteries of the Most Holy Rosary. No one would have us believe that the long contemplation upon the history of our eternal Salvation is an easy one to grasp. This is why they have been called Sacred Mysteries since Annunciation Day. We must never allow our boredom to stop us from recalling the enlightenment and redemption which humanity has gained through the lives of Jesus and Mary, and the Crucifixion and Resurrection of Our Savior from the Hill of Mount Calvary and the Sepulcher where He was laid. Many of us are willing to allow the western winds to blow into our faces until the cold stings of raindrops start pecking on our flesh, not knowing in advance that, if we stand there long enough, the truth of nature will immerse us in the reality that God loves us more than any mortal man has the capacity to conceive, save the Pontiff who is seated in the Chair of Saint Peter in the Basilica of Rome. The holy children of Immaculate Mary already know to continue praying through the storm, waiting it-out in patience until Our Lady of the Snows transforms the raindrops into gentle frozen flakes which bless the Earth in the company of Rose Petals falling harmlessly at their feet.

We must never allow anyone to coerce us into believing that our Salvation does not matter for the higher meaning of life. There would be a pixel left unlighted on the ScreenGems of Paradise if one of us is somehow left behind. This is why everyone's conscience must be resurrected from the distractions of the world; a prospect that is not any easy task to overtake. God has oftentimes reminded us of the retribution which is His alone to dispense in order to procure our inward discipline because He adores us far beyond any other contextual fete. The chastening that the Blessed Mother brings is often like a course of antibiotics which has certain adverse side effects. They are meant to amend our behavior and enlighten our hearts, not to make us sick of trying to achieve true holiness or to stop striving for genuine purity of the soul. If we would only cease fighting against these overtures from God, and one another for that matter, we would be better positioned to listen to Him. We could start by turning toward our enemies in peace and making our munitions obsolete. What good is a warplane if its ordnance has been heisted by the Love in our hearts? Why bear a bayonet when there is no one left to charge the gate? In a world of perfect peace, there are no cannons to fire, no radar vectors to detect, no casualty cerements to wear, and not a whimper of a reveille or a call to muster the forces to their ranks. If we wish to be pleasing in the sight of God, we must watch for His signals, pray for His blessings, and tread lightly upon the mooring laces where His angels have docked their buoy bells to play their violins in the midst of our quite grandiloquent state of goings-on. When the Almighty Father asks for our final commitment, He is only stirring the tasty pudding that will make our own lives sweeter to the touch of His Sacred Lips. No morsel of our sacrifices in the Name of His Son will ever escape His hearty appetite for delivering our souls back safely to His side.

Heaven knows that we hold this much control over our eternal destiny because its Courts have seen the dominion which we have wielded over the Earth. The trees have become our houses and the shelves that hold our library books. The rocks are now the mantles above our fireplaces and the stony tombs of our foregone ancient kings. Animals in the wild are our sustenance and their pelts our outer warmth. We must never believe that the hosts of the universe cannot tell the Saints in Paradise what is going on around them. Sometimes we cannot know whether they are twinkling at us in assurance or turning their backs in shame on what we are doing to God. They hold-out in wonderment as their friendliest comet sails by . "Where does he think he's going?" the curiosity of Castor probably wants to know. "We'll ask him when he comes back around," replies Pollux standing right beside. And, by the time these celestial twins meet their acquaintance once again, mankind on the Earth has exhausted his three-score and ten years; and Halley's namesake has circled around for yet another pass before the Gemini hosts who are absorbed in watching him continue to play the field. They know that the same Holy Spirit who swirls among them in the heights of the heavens lives also in our hearts far below. The Paraclete is not a "creature," per se, because He has always been one with God in Heaven from the very beginning which, in itself, is too Divine to reproach. It is the voice we hear through the Eucharistic Prayers of our priests, the sonnets from the phonics of our children, and the inspirations which bloom from within the condoling solaces of our delicate broken hearts. Jesus shouts through the ominous revelry of a stampeding avalanche and the whispered muffle of a fluttering Papilio swallowtail. Indeed, the Holy Spirit of God is the only forte we lacked the very moment we were born that we had better profess before it comes our time to die. All of this is a portion of the awakening to which humankind must concede if we are to ever fully understand what our transition into eternity is precisely about. It is also the means through which we can bring humanity to an everlasting peace as we await our deliverance into Jesus' Holy Arms. The onus is in our court to make this transformation because it was our haughty human pride which first fell us from the skies. If we allow the time to expire that will end the mortal Earth and leave the world as it stands, the force of Armageddon will be the least of our worries by the time the Judgement of the Son of God is through.

Bowing in obedient Love is not so difficult to do if we will simply understand the reasons why it must be done. Razor wire is not put on the fences around prison camps to lacerate the flesh of everyone confined. It is only there to impede the ones who attempt to scale the walls. If we stop running from Love with the intention of greeting the Truth head-on, the justice of God will eventually set us all free without our ever facing harm. It is Jesus Christ who bears the scars which should have rightfully been ours to receive. By standing still and watching in silent meditation, we will plainly see that the Blood which Our Savior shed on the Cross is the condensation of God's Love for His people after it reached its boiling point, brought-on by the heat of the Passion of His Son to the expiation of our sins. This should be an experience in solemnity and peace as we watch our Salvation unfold. Instead, we are still trying to dissect the Mysteries that have absolved us as though there must be some sort of credit for us to receive. Why should we try to crawl through a window to enter a vacant house where we used to reside when Jesus is inviting us to walk upright in line with the procession of Saints through the front door with our souls dressed in grosgrain lapels and wingtip shoes? There is a new reason to hope for this joy! The Earth is not being vacated by death to make way for a another order of inhabitants. It is merely making room for the new blessed souls alongside the ones we can no longer see. We often try painfully to conjure thoughts of life the way it used to be, like when we hear a tune from the rungs of our infant days, knowing all along how painful the nostalgia will be and what a waste the years since then have seemingly become. That discomfort is not unlike trying to stifle a sneeze while we are hiding behind the door to the past for fear of getting caught being too emotional before those who see us as being stoic pillars of an obsolete world.

We have been duped by the hardest of hearts to believe that no one should ever kiss a photograph of their most dearly beloved ones or make the sign of the Cross past the outside threshold of the Church vestibule. Holding back our affection for the Love of our families is an abomination before the Throne of God. He cannot wait until we get another chance to stoop and pamper a child or clear the passageway for someone arriving in the confines of a manual wheelchair. If we can remember the times when we have waited for a pot to come to a boil or for the thermostat to finally activate the furnace, that is the same anticipation that our Father in Heaven endures as He watches over the world seeking signs of His grace. He wants us to project the best of ourselves from under the outer shell of our ordinary lives. We must remember tenderly what our founders have taught while pledging to bring new comfort to our age. If our father played the guitar and our mother an upright piano, what were they really singing about? Are we antsy enough to discover what made our predecessors go onward in blind faith and Love? Do we grieve in sorrow for having lost them to the sting of death to the point that we, ourselves, can barely face the many tomorrows which still have yet to arrive? There is no doubt that we have a great deal of praying and pondering to do. This is our age of good fortune and opportunity for positive change; for there is no prosecution of human misery which we cannot overcome in Christ.

Part II - At the Water's Edge

Human Action Does Not Stop at the Threshold of Death

November 15, 2000

There may, indeed, be an autumn chill still hovering over the world, but we are growing a new springtime of Love from the center of our hearts. The problem which remains is that we continue to refuse to let it blossom. We will usually try to do good when the demand for it stares us in the face, but almost never when we are prompted to or when we are reprimanded by someone else for being too cruel. Perhaps, this is a product of the self-sufficient autonomy of our contemporary minds. After all of the eloquence, majesty, and grandeur of the human spirit, do we ever really recognize the true greatness which we have seen come and go? Do we know that there are countless people pouring themselves out over the coals of reparation to pay for our own transgressions behind the blind facade of the everyday world? This is the greater sonata of the invigorated conscience of man to bring the future to himself and to be a part of the whole of Creation. Is it possible to become the pearl who actually discovers the oyster? Has the intuitive grace ever crossed our consciousness that the intersection between God, humankind, and His Divine Love is not so evasive or difficult to achieve? Is the Truth now standing before us too disguised by the plenary day that we cannot fully understand the definitive cohesion between Paradise and the Earth? Do we recognize the perfection in finally conquering our own error and accepting the gift of eclipsing our futile redundance? What is the true motivation that makes us write and play, or the driving force which stirs the legends to come back again for another encore or to take a second bow? It is Love, good people! It is Love! We struggle to surpass the goal-post standards and cross the finish lines, but we are never completely satisfied that they represent the finality of everything we can achieve. Our living souls squirm about in flesh, bones, and blood; but we still demand that there must be something more meaningful to living than this. There would be no need for curtains, lockboxes, or peepholes if we really took our capacity of knowing such an advantage to heart.

There are countless avenues of knowledge and action that humankind has never stopped to think about until the most recent age. We have learned after a period of time has gone by, for example, that Martin King was not so much a master of his race as he was a slayer of injustice with an invisible crown of fortitude atop his head. He did not really consider the color of his own skin when he fought for civil rights, he just knew that the Gospel of Jesus Christ was not being fulfilled. His own freedom was not necessarily the reason for his actions as he pursued the proper legislation in a democracy which was still hidden in the squalls of the dark ages. He was more concerned with the liberation of an entire nation of people from the chains of bigotry. He knew that he had to succeed in persuading over two-hundred million Americans that discrimination is a matter of the heart, while laying-down his life to prove it. How could any country which espoused mutual liberty concede to such blind tyrannical hatred? In the end, the Gospel of Jesus Christ prevailed as those who were filled with the greatest scorn were put-down by a higher power. The Reverend King knew what most of the rest of us presently understand; that it often seems like our enemies prosper more by accident than the honest people who work hard to simply survive for another day. If we will only decide to stop turning against our brothers in contempt, we will know that life is only a fallacy when we go to Church on Sunday morning and praise Our Savior's power while leaving His pilgrims out in the cold that very night. Our stance may not be an outright aberration if we have never been told that we are the ones who are responsible to help them; but spreading the error of bias and selfishness solely because that is the way we were raised does nothing to get us off the hook in Heaven. We must be in full control of the facts of the Holy Gospel in order to avoid imposing our own personal inferences on the Scriptures at large. No one really cares how we choose to interpret the reflections of the Bible if we are the ones who always come out on top. For all of the furious debate about the inequities of the world today, the only trial that matters is whether we are justified by God in Christ Jesus. Martin Luther King was exactly on target about that. He knew what everyone else should know by now. In Jesus, we are justified; for we otherwise share no good standing before God.

Amongst all of our hashing about precepts and principles, what good are we to humanity if we refuse to actuate them? Are they only barometers with which our succeeding generations can rewrite their own history while feigning an attempt to mitigate our blindness and miserable faults in the process? Where is our protective insulation against taking the fall for our children because we have not taught them well enough to live in the Spirit of Christ? We ultimately discover that responsible human action does not stop at the threshold of death, but where the shadow of our lives greets the new Light which is still being breathed into the wombs of our impregnated mothers. While the time continues to be ripe for the asking, is our ability to enamor the distinct successes of the mortal Earth only a hollow well of mirror images and shadow boxers? Do we greet those who despise our Christianity fists-first; or do we turn-tail and run to the nearest corridor in fear of defending the Truth? The courage in our hearts tells us that the reconciliation of God and man is not so much a matter of when He will come back again, but how many more hours and years we will allow to expire at the behest of immorality before we decide to dive headlong into holiness and meet Him halfway. Would Jesus have asked for our prayers if He would have meant that the world was finished on the Cross without them? Surely His Mother would not have come rushing through the global hemispheres with an alarm in Her Hands if it were not such an urgent a task. Whether we like it or not, Heaven is never in recess and the angelic courts are still in session. Surely the Queen of the Universe would not have bothered to visit us at all if Her call to our spiritual conversion was not so important.

We can wear platitudes around the brim of our hats all we want, but only by our commitment and mutual action will we ever cross the break into initiating a change. A well-trained mind does not always infer an open heart. Looking around at those who really hunger for Salvation should be enough to evoke our own reaction. What God is seeing through the eyes of the faithful is an obedience so profound that it even encourages mere mortals to be glad to sacrifice their lives to make His dreams come true. Our greatest gifts from Heaven are those that we also offer in return because God will no longer accept our burnished concessions and holocausts in the place of our unconditional Love. We must join hands as one humanity and make the struggle for unification under the Cross more intense. For most of us, winning means proudly proclaiming, "I did better than you," instead of saying, "Perhaps, you did not do well enough." If we are truly the victors we are meant to be, we will take the hands of those who are still trying to Love us and relinquish our best talents to them, wrapped in our humble generosity, while lifting them to the plateau of full understanding that redlines our gauges of goodness and spiritual strength. We often never worry as much about claiming the trophy as we do about others perceiving us as being only second best. The accolades and awards which champions receive only seal the fate of those they have beaten. Quite the opposite, God wants us to turn away from "I" after we have accomplished the most in ourselves to the triumph of others, never to hasten their demise. We should always ask ourselves, "Have I given humanity everything I own to make sure they succeed?" What good is a trophy anyway when we just hide it in our home with the rest of our arrogant hardware? Is our pride in need of so much prompting to remind us of how great we are? It all boils down to whether there is Wisdom in our hearts sufficient for revealing the prejudices that keep us from benefitting the greater world. After all, that is what conflict is all about. Oftentimes, the page becomes blurred as to whether we are reading our own diary or a fable about who we think we are.

If we watch Creation long enough, we will eventually perceive that those who rise at the crack of dawn are not necessarily the best in the heat of the hunt. The Scriptures are replete with parables about the son who fell-out, the one who refused to go to the fields, and the workers who showed-up nearer the time to quit and expected a full-day's pay for the labors they gave. They were all still celebrated by the same Father who embraces the rest of us. But, those examples are not there to excuse the ones who refuse to try. We are being reminded that they who "... know not Love" are being asked by Jesus Christ to clarify their stance, sharpen their wit, hone their consciences, and redress their own fears. The truly confident ones do not always sleep until moments before the awakening bell. Neither do they partake in making the stadiums rock to the core of their foundations just so they can be one with the whole. The wax in their ears is not enough protection from the eery canals of haughtiness that is found where masses of people ignore God in order to silence His lambs. The wax is there to provide the sheen for those who will hear only the Truth and filter out the boasting of the rest who defy His Love. The jury may still be out on what effect our interior grief is having on the physical well-being of humanity at large, but we already know that we cannot turn their faith on like a switch. It is a gift for which they must pray while seeking our petitions for them, too. If trust in Christ Jesus is like the rise of the sun or a slow-growing pellet in winter, let us begin right now to effect the process of change because we are all getting there at once. The by-product of our Christian belief is to know that everything will work out in the end because God is in control and our Salvation in His Son is real.

The Almighty Father does not want us to be surprised at the end of life to see that we have lived nowhere close to the emergence which He is seeking from our faith. Imagine the world when Jesus returns and we are caught napping in our recliners while hearing our next-door neighbor shout, "Iceberg, dead ahead!" Our futures will then make the fate of the victims of the Titanic and the Hindenburg seem like a stroll in the park. It is time for our conscious awareness to realize that eternal damnation can occur! Every facet of life can be seen in the fullness of that day; and we always do our best work in the Light of Christ. We cannot write our history while dwelling in the darkness of the past because we constantly cross-over the lines of propriety and can never remember where we left-off when we are distracted from telling our last lie. God chooses His Saints from the best of those who are about to be saved. We cannot cast lots or draw straws to determine in advance who they are. Suffice to say is that they are living in our midst already; and we should do our best to become one in their holy numbers. Our efforts should always be greater than simply determining the articles of nature and fact, but should be projected onward and upward to the spiritual succession of the galaxies as a whole, beyond the model that was first set into being from the peaks of Mount Sinai in Exodus 19. Our new call is to forgiveness, reconciliation, forbearance, and grace. The revelations which God gave to Moses were the beginning of the Word of Truth. Jesus Christ is the incarnation of the entire literary faculties of our Divine Creator spoken aloud. The Almighty Father did not change His mind when He sent Saint Gabriel to speak to Mary; He simply placed His prefigured thoughts into fuller action. That is also our own motivation for consistency in Love and our reason to stand on His Truth, no matter what the age, and notwithstanding the cost.

The entire Old Testament is the foundation for the world we cannot yet see, brought to fulfillment by the Messiah we already fully recognize. Proof is in the Most Blessed Sacrament exposed so elegantly in the Monstrance on the Altar of Sacrifice before us. If Moses has lived to enable our feet, Jesus Christ is alive to awaken our hearts. The Mosaic Law brought our consciences upright, the Gospel of the Messiah keeps us from falling back downward again; and there is a gamut of Commandments we have to obey to comply with them both. God is telling us through them that a seed will not grow unless it is planted in good soil; and a root is useless if it is left dangling in the air. This means that we must enter deeply into our Christian conviction if we are ever going to break through the crust of our own obstinance and capture the raw meaning of eternal Salvation. Sometimes we grow weary from not knowing who we will eventually become; but that is only a defeat-in-the-making which is brewing in a decanter of disbelief. The fact remains that our work is never quite finished until a nanosecond before we die. It is as though our boss approaches our desk a minute in advance of the whistle blowing to close the business for the day and hands us an eight-inch thick docket and tells us to complete it before we go home. Pouring our lives out before God takes away this type of anxiety because it gives us a perspective which we cannot find anywhere else. We know for sure that it is the source of His continuing desire to create new life; otherwise none of us would be here to confess it. He basks in the ecstasy of the endowments of His own making. He addresses an exemplary parable to those who will lend a curious ear and poses such questions as why water and the air temperature cannot peacefully coexist without one affecting the other. It is obvious that ice and humidity would cease to be, if not for their interrelation. The point which our Father is posing is that the same principle applies in making faith, Love, and prayer as equally inseparable and one. If we live every day in the same Love through which God first created our souls, we will possess, as Martin Luther King once prophesied, a freedom that will last forever.

Let Us Not Rue the Blizzard That Has Frozen His Remains

November 16, 2000

We must always be wary while guarding against violating the very trust which has already resurrected us from the grave. Contrary to popular beliefs, the well-intentioned stateliness that golden retirees exude is not an accidental intrusion of the rights of little children to play in fields wherever they may. Who will auger our fate in the making of such modesty? The answer to this question rests in the signals of the Holy Spirit who is calling on us now to be humbled before the Almighty Cross which finally pronounced Jesus as the King of the World. Heaven knows that the authority of our prayers should take us to our knees in the Wisdom that we can brandish the power of Gatling guns in a game of pixie sticks with our enemies falling away. They are the finks who hate the Truth and spread their gainful ploy to reclaim the world they lost to Christ. We will never be true heroes in His eyes if we wince at His dutiful resurgence or refuse to rage against the pungent feud which is trying to keep our hopes at bay. Gone now is the age of timidness because, in Jesus, we walk in armored rows of nobility against our despotic foes. No growling thunder from their inner-gut will ever bring us to surrender our desire to be saved; no scowl can survive our grins of pining impishness; and no grimace will ever hold us down for long. The statutory rules that powerful men often scribe into law hold no claim over the immensity of God's Word of Love because their signed and sealed idolatries are already as dead in the grave as human sin, itself. The reckoning of their better days will never pull them away from the classical Truth which is still as obvious as the nose on their faces. Our odds are on the side of victory in the center of the Cross; for It is the catapult that makes God's saints-to-be more than watchful sentinels against the wantonness of those whom Christ will ultimately leave behind.

The patrons who love Salvation will never rest until their fingerprints are brazened into the Solitary Tool upon which the Savior of the world has fully redeemed their willing souls. Jesus will soon come back again; and it will be a miracle when Capetown, Cairo, Moscow, Berlin, Paris, Rome, Madrid, New York, Los Angeles, Manila, and Tokyo all see the Son of God at once; which is quite a feat for six billion souls who could only greet a new millennium in stages on the clock. What joy will come when Hiroshima and Nagasaki see His mushroom cloud of righteousness billowing from the Eastern Garden beyond the garnet sun! We cannot be charged with making partisan wars or taking a role in embezzlement when we place our trust in the riches of Christ who dispenses His assets for free. There will be no more need for any numeration for the suffering of our pains or for us to hold fast to our self-appointed rights to complain as devoutly as we keep our wedding vows. The night's catharsis will never last until the break of day when the reality of our dreams sets in. New wonders still wait to seek-us-out while we leave our moonlit offertories twisting in the wind. No litigant would ever treat God that way once they have seen their eternal profits standing on the line. But, then again, it is difficult to recall only nothingness when it is all you ever had to hold onto. It is time for us to assign our depositories to the new empowerment we have gained beyond the loophole of ever dying in vain.

The Love of Heaven makes our hearts so rhythmically in sync that we cannot ever turn away. Neither a knight on a stallion or a fortune in a vault could ever fell us from such grace. Jesus knows that we will never deny His rapture because we are helpless to extol our prejudices while the fear of God is firmly lodged deep within our throats. The sound of our free-will dying is not like a whip cracking on a slab, but the resounding groan of the Crucifixion still echoing through the years. We often look at God most sheepishly while cringing beside our adolescent companion named Death, who is still too young to know the Truth. "We shall take our losses as they come," is our sorrow's canned response. There is no other way to lift the lien that corruption holds over us now, no means to calculate the mass, and no sandbags to lodge against the barrage of destruction we will know unless we stake our lives in Christ. The courtier of our excellence is only one Gentleman away. He strikes lightening bolts upon the ground, but knocks only gently to tell us that He has arrived to take us to the Ball. If we become anaesthetized by the scandal of never opening the door for Him, our grief will harrow us for the rest of our lives and beyond. But even still, we place a simple asterisk beside our vanity and continue to go on. The Holy Paraclete has come to tell us that peace is now at hand with many casualties aboard who are wearing their Martyr's Crowns as they sail aloft with Jesus to the City behind the sun.

So now, the prose and poetry are the living semblance of our age. The dove and the whippoorwill don the suddenness of extraordinary grace to the mourning cause that has cleansed our souls. They fly united with pity and Love, their solitary hearts given to this peculiar new discovery of conciliatory caverns which are hewn from the mountains of our stubbornness. With one in our hands and two in the bush, we lift them all past the gifted gates of humility to the letter of our confessions, never again to be concealed in caustic gales or under battered stones. We shall go no more to seek our musings before the spoiled invasions of warrior tribes versus diadems. Our patience will unfold the future with a momentary pause because the midday eagle always spreads his wings a feather at a time. In the midst of his ornate loftiness, he cranes his neck to search for dying patriots to bless, those who are bludgeoned by misfortune and deceit, victims of the Earth who lay so quietly on their backs while the remainder of its swilling societies continue to go about their work. It is not indignity which lances their flames or dilutes their strength to proceed; but the disappointment that they could not remain amidst the eagle's flight until the Son of Man returned. They grieve their loneliness and breach of trust, not seeing anymore the reflection of the Light that glimmers so clearly on the breastplates of the Chosen Ones. We will know in due time what clefts impede their symmetry, those wailing thoughts which cast away their hopes with their muted lips still wrenching. Wherever hindering vacuums continue to stall imparted hearts, that is also where the centerfold of monoxide carnivores make waste and mutual disarray in the devouring of our faith.

This is the modern age of the Son of the Most High; and no longer will our strangers' wakes fail to make us mourn them to their deaths or impede their eternal passing for which they have waited far too long. No tears can ever overflow the Biscayne potteries to quench the thirst of violets. Yet, no one knows what strife will come to smear the rouge on languished mothers' cheeks who wonder still whether their sons will ever come back home alive. An antiquated age still soars above our Bishops' caps which tries to hold our servants down from stirring the oceans to march again toward the interior plains of the Americas, still boasting of their freedom from sea to shining sea. God will eventually drown our bureaucratic blasphemy and expose the dewlap balderdash that makes our headlines scream. Life will still go on until the Creator of the Universe says, "Stop! Let's take your breath away so you will never die again!" He knows that there is a beard inside every man still begging to emerge so as to mock the timid ones who have fallen from above his brow in much disgrace, never again to darken the doors of his consciousness until he greets the Morning Star. "Advantage to the persecuted ones!", cries Jesus as He volleys another atheist into the cauldron of eternal flames. He also knows that these are the songs of encouragement which nary will ever be replaced by elegies or memorials. If the fanfare seems too sudden to bear, then we must move to where the swallows roam, where grainy fields are combed by daggered drops of leniency.

There is no higher priest or potentate who can endure the test of divinity, nor can he stand in impurity before the Christ-Child Slain who was forced into hemorrhaging because we lost our virginity to an apple and a snake. Those blue eyes dying said, "I love you!" from a Cross where passers-by still hang their heads to grieve the arrogance of another age, our own to be precise! How dare we pose a smile on our mugs with lockets hanging around our necks while beggars still walk the streets in straps of poverty! There is no market for worn-out souls who know no solace in a world that has peddled-away its sovereignty for thirty pieces of silver which they exhumed from the bottom of a mortician's bed. They engorged their audacious greed with someone else's treasury, and then kissed the mouth of death so it could not defy their hatred in advance. No court that will judge them is more Superior than the Almighty Throne of God, who will refuse to hear their case if they decline His offer to appear before Him clad with the Blood of Redemption on their dinner gowns. If we accidently missed the reporter's mantra for today, history will always repeat itself in a better tone if we can only withstand the wait. For now, we must shed the inmate's garb that is the sin which holds us back from living-out our true freedom in a civilized society on our own. There is hope in this truth because no remorse can ever make its way forward to ignite our effigy if we continue laughing in its face. Let us hope for Love with the Nativity of the Child of Bethlehem, knowing all along that the angels atop our Christmas trees will not prohibit them from growing again, for their wings will prick the needles with the tinctures of their Love. In the meantime, the Bugle Corps plays taps again because another gallant soul has finally shed his skin. For now, narrow threads and finished linens will guard his maudlin frown with promises of a better day. Let us not rue the blizzard that has frozen his remains or castigate the cartwheels he has tossed over the bitterness with which he no longer must compete. The dead have returned to God much like toddlers in caravans, no longer cads bedecked in chivalry, while their posthumous arguments of oratory have caught landlords and lads asleep at last, adrift in the waves of wonderment as the world continues on.

Our Perilous Flight Back to the Garden of Eden

November 17, 2000

Are we really required to engage the battle of proving to the world that human Salvation is not a sudden twist of fate in which we must defend our rights against illegitimate brigadiers and rogue battering rams? The simplicity with which we live ought to be sufficient to display to our potential detractors that we are residing on the side of Christ. What a predicament must befall those who glance into our faces with their own puzzled look of bewilderment as they wonder just what makes our faith so tenable. Perhaps our demeanor provides them with only a scant revival of their more innocent days when they initially approached the world with less contention. If we were to characterize their "defiance" as being a person, could we take him at his word that he would never once concede to what we Christians have to say? Maybe a reapportionment of his crass objectives would render him a little more pliable during the interim. Our trust in Jesus will always allow us to fend-off the opposition if we will only let Him try. Who could tell by the calmness on our faces that we stand guard for an invisible society of souls who live beyond our very last tomorrow, being led by a King who had to become their servant before they would honor Him? In order to retrieve the keys that would set His subjects free, He had to go to Hell and back again. Our prayers will always stop the vile expressions and banished excrements of our enemies. There is no doubt that we will all eventually suffer our share of humiliation, sometimes even more than that if we are kind enough to hoist a *Miserere* or two upon our shoulders once in awhile. We are occasionally not completely assured as to whether everything we are fighting for will eventually come to pass. When Jesus said that we should tend to the poor and fight against temptation in order for our souls to see the Light of Heaven, was He implying the inquisition that, if there were no paupers to feed or desirables to crave, would we need to become saints at all? Would we still be trying to beseech His forgiveness anyway? The appropriate response in both of these cases is a definitive "yes."

There is nothing lacking in our perilous flight back to the Garden of Eden. Jesus proved on the Cross that human suffering is the cornerstone of our travels, as though it is in the DNA of every man who will ever see the Face of God. The struggles of life invade the most secluded chasms of our dignity with the rudest of awakenings. Our pet peeves are often transformed from being our dislike for coconut, raisins, and toggeries that are closed every Saturday, into whether we will be able to exit the world without having our heads chopped off by a furious crowed of egotistic hate-mongers. Whatever the ulterior implication, our union in the Cross disposes us to the best of God's desire to see us through the fight by satisfying His temperament in choosing to make us geniuses. That is also why He has given us the Most Blessed Sacrament. The Body of Christ is the secret of our conversion which has already been revealed and our passage into courts of wiser men who have known His Truth all along. How permeating our faith becomes when we choose to exercise it; for it is our conceptual belief in an origin of Love which has yet to be seen by those of us who remain on the Earth with the knowledge that everything we pray for will come true the very moment we die. Indeed, we owe our thanksgiving-of-the-heart a Feast Day, itself, because it is our own assurance that our lives are communing with God. The Eucharistic Celebration of the Holy Sacrifice of the Mass is our eternal gratitude. We can sand, scrape, and scratch at the surface of immortality all we like, but we will never truly know what it means to get there until we have finally surrendered our souls to the Son of God, while enjoying it in the process. There is not a single scintilla of room for us to doubt His Word because our too pragmatic approach to religion defies what we believe of everyday life. We know that there are electronegative charges in chemical bonds, but we just cannot seem to accept the fact that it is the simple magnetism of Love which draws us to the Crucifixion. When we sit alone in contemplation of this truth, we often cannot quite decide whether to accept it in raw faith or not. So, we turn to our inner-selves for advice and miraculously discover that the Holy Spirit provides the answer in our place.

One of the problems with diving head-over-heals in complete abandonment to Jesus is that our quirky doubts always seem to haunt us. If we could only realize that such displaced concern is only a reverberation of our very first victory over our fears, then we would be able to cast it aside and go on. But, no one knows what an echo looks like because we have never seen one undisguised. The canyons tell us that they occasionally see them in the wild, but their memories keep fading over time. There are no Cliffs Notes or abridged synopses about human life for the present-day because the scenes are still continuing to unfold. Our recollections seem to serve us well when all the advantages are on our side; but they are rather spotty when we have to trust someone else to ponder the decisions over our fate. That is why it is often difficult to throw our entire being into the vessel of the New Covenant Christ. We never know what He will ask us to do tomorrow. The obvious benefit is that, if we place our minds and hearts in Him for any reasonable period of time, we will never again have to feel as though we are dirty or chagrined in shame. We cannot place a stopwatch on our conscience because the persistence of temptation runs all through the day and night. We have to set our morality on overdrive and never look back again. There cannot be enough said about giving our unfettered trust in Salvation its best opportunity to thrive. When we pray, "Now, I lay me down to sleep," at night, we know that no one is pushing us into our bed or crushing our soul under their heels of oppression to coerce us into getting some rest. We simply trust that we will feel better tomorrow if we allow our minds and bodies to recover from today. So it is with our decision to place our souls into the cradle of God's consolation. When we feel the Earth begin to rock beneath us, we will know that the Immaculate Heart of His Mother is not very far away.

Conversion to the Christian faith is not an arbitrary anomaly or a deviation from the social norm because we are naturally predestined by Jesus Christ to be saved from the curse of condemnation. It is a transfer of the heart back to supernatural Love and the distillation of our incongruity through the hope we need to survive during the process. There are no hazing rites to bring us to shame because Christ has descended from the Kingdom above to restore our dignity to be not unlike His own. Neither are new converts ever subordinate to cradle Christians because many of them who are already wearing the cloak of public righteousness are still walking around in the dark. Notwithstanding the Magisterium and Hierarchy of the Apostolic Church, we are all equal in the sight of God through His Son's Paschal Mysteries, delivered by virtue of His Passionate Wounds from the mortification of our graves, and accepted all the way back to eternal peace in His Divine Resurrection. Once we have been transferred into that everlasting Dawn, we will look back on the Earth and know that the Eucharist was our mother's milk which sustained our Redemption even before we were ever borne into the perpetual Light of Day. We will recognize the Son of God as being the Communion Host the moment we open our eyes. Quite sorrowfully for many of us, trite questions keep springing forth from our overactive curiosity. "How much longer is there to go; and why must I wait? What is my part of the bargain; and when do my prayers ever matter?" The answer from Heaven is always "Sooner than you think; the Kingdom is at Hand; and give everything you own to the poor to prove your faith, for you know not the hour when the Son of Man will return!" For now, God knows that our boweries and street corners are a complete waste of time if they are not occupied by someone bearing witness to His Name. Unless each one of them is lighted by the Truth of the Cross, traffickers will continue to slam into one another in their residual darkness to the plight of their own demise. This is not the end result of some innocuous unawareness, but a product of their outright unyielding refusal to see. Our vindication does not begin with the airing of our grievances, but by bearing with them patiently to the benign consolation that sufferers procure from the offering of their unselfish deference to the majesty of the Lord.

What appears to add insult to injury is when it seems like we have given all we can possibly afford and the postman suddenly stuffs our mailboxes with unexpected solicitations from various nonprofit organizations that need just ten more dollars to meet their annual goal. God has placed no limits on what He might expect in return for the richness of His blessings. We sometimes begin to wonder which came first, the chicken or the egg. Do we receive graces from God because we are willing to sacrifice ourselves, or only after we have already done so? There is no evidence that His Love declines to enlist the order of either one. Salvation in Jesus Christ is not based on a contingency of whether our bodies might refuse to die when our name is finally called to appear in the obituary column, but is the direct result of our approbation of His Divine principles which keeps Him longing for our return to His side. It is not wholly unlike the curiosity that we exhibit when we look at the planet Venus in the twilight of the morning sun; and wonder what it would be like to go there someday. What we may not know is that there are probably just as many Venetians looking back at the Earth pondering the same thing on their own. Such is the same with Paradise; and is one of the main reasons why the King of their lot came to teach us to pray. It seems such a shame in hindsight that we decided to kill Him; for who knows what exquisite power we might be wielding by now? It is true that our faith transforms life from a glance into a mirror into a long contemplation while peering through a bay window inside a house overlooking the lake. Our spectacles are transformed into telescopes when we turn our faces to the sky. There is no foretelling what new clarity might enhance our mortal vision when we put our entire beings in Jesus Christ. What a joy it would be to discover that the scratches we have noticed in the new enamel of our spiritual conversion are only a reflection of Angels' hair upon our glistening souls.

We plot an entirely new course once we have accepted the Christian faith, discovering that we no longer need extravagant accessories when building our new homes because we are quite content with only the barest of essentials. We envision forgiveness in a new light, too, because we can fully recognize how offensive we have been in previous years. Periods of history seem to become almost irrelevant as we adopt our new outlook for the future. We understand that, when Jesus first walked the Earth, He did not set-out to meet every person who lived on the globe at the time. He could have chased-down every last mortal on the Earth to dispense His message from God, but He never traveled any more than a few hundred miles away from His home. Now, however, despite the many ages which have passed since then, His Holy Spirit will barnstorm any doorway in order to reach another sinner! He pines for us to know His Father in Heaven better; even to the point of reinventing the essence of who we really are. But, He also knows that change solely for the sake of change does not imply our spiritual growth. We have to do it His Way, or we will never succeed at all. We will always be caught in the debate of confusion about who we want to be as opposed to the people our Creator is asking us to become. This is the same lukewarmness which He has promised to spew from His mouth at the end of the ages. In the process of leaving no stone unturned, Jesus asks us to grow and change simultaneously, just in case we choose to become entangled in the dichotomy of trying to define the terms. He requires no-less than our overflowing allegiance to the Cross. That is why He was crucified on the top of the Hill of Mount Calvary instead of in the bottom of a well in the ground. If our faith is going to be so bombarded, He wishes to ensure that our enemies have to deploy surface-to-air missiles to strike us instead of dropping depth charges to rupture our souls.

We, too, must be mortified like Him if we are to understand what surrendering our will is all about. He leaves every type of sign in our pathway to let us know that He is still working toward this Truth. Is being slain in the Holy Spirit a prophecy that we will fall asleep in death and wake-up in His Arms a few moments later? It is more than likely a precursor from the Book of Revelation that precedes the ecstasy which will leave all mortal flesh behind.

There is no doubt that we can grow our fuller confidence in what this noble Paraclete has come to say. Too many times, we base our assumptions on what happens in the world. When we purchase a new automobile, the odds are in our favor that we will never have a wreck. But, can we boast that we will never be knocked-off of our surfboard by a humongous wave? The pride of humanity still has us leaning toward the latter of the two. Our confidence must be more humble than that because we have quite a distance to travel before we ever arrive at the signpost which says, "Private Entrance for Saints Only." This is not to say that our hopes should ever lay low as though Satan has run them over with a giant steamroller. The breath of God will always pick us up again if he tries to do so. We are the little ones whom He will constantly help to our feet, no matter how many times we fall on our way. He keeps telling us that we must not just talk about Love; but we must truly live it in our hearts. What good is there in chewing a treat if we never bother to swallow it. We have to conquer whatever God allows our enemies to place in the middle of the road if we ever expect to arrive at our Salvation to the roar of an approving crowd.

The relationship we maintain with the Almighty Father is no balmy proposition. He knows that His domain is already the aftermath of our nearly relinquished lives; but we are presently bound in the flesh. There are no calendars hanging in the mansions of Paradise; but we who have yet to die are still trapped counting the revolutions of the Earth around the sun one at a time, *anno Domini*, A.D., in the year of our Lord. Girding ourselves in His Justice is never an easy task; nor was it ever meant to be. We keep looking up into the skies at night while sometimes remembering the ill-fated flight of Apollo 13. It is a parable that celebrates what human Redemption is all about. God wants us to envision our Salvation in Him as a narrow plane of opportunity at a precise moment in time. Without that same synchronicity, their spaceship would have never come back to the surface of the Earth for a splash down. This is what Jesus meant when He said that the Gate is small and we shall not know in advance when the Son of Man will return. He might even choose to add an epilogue to this parable which reaffirms the truth that we can practically survive the fires of Hell and still come out alive because the Cross is our protective heat shield that has survived the blasphemy and human defiance which has been trying to fracture it for 2000 years and counting. Indeed, Creation at large is still waiting in dead silence to see if we will all make it back home to Paradise in one piece. God has almost had to destroy the oxygen supply from within our midst through the explosive nature of the Earth's personality in order to direct our attention back toward Him. There is no doubt that He is not yet finished testing us; for many are the times when we will have to take our Rosaries in-hand again and say with quiet desperation, "Houston, we have a problem!"

The growth and change He wants to see can be a forced contrition if He chooses it to be the main course of His supper meal while wielding His divinity over the world. The lesson to be learned is that our faith today should not be a carbon copy of the lesser one we put to bed last night; but always more intense to the invigoration of the heart. Just like our minds are always clearer when we wake to greet the day, our Love is better prepared once we have rested in the miracle of His grace.

The fate of the Roman Catholic Church lives in perilous times. It is seemingly not enough that She is practically ignored by the faithless multitudes who live in Her midst, but She is even the victim of assailants if She dares to raise Her Head to utter the Truth about the Sacraments before humankind. The College of Cardinals is more than a collection of magistrates for the solemnity of our Salvation; for it is their Conclave and spiritual acclamation which has provided for the continuity of the infallible nature of the Papacy for hundreds of generations past. The Chair of Saint Peter is situated exactly beneath the Throne of God as though He is the sky overhead. The Altar of Sacrifice is the Communion Table to where God dispatches His Crucified Son from the Paradisial Upper Room directly into the hands of His priests. The Pontiff of Rome is a bellwether Statesman for the Christian elect who provides to his faithful children what the rest of the world must eventually accept. Never has a Pope offered any other pathway to Salvation than the original Catholic and Apostolic Church of Jesus Christ. This should provide great consolation to the millions who are only now beginning to feel the warmth of the Holy Spirit in their hearts; while raining absolute horror upon those who continue to protest against Her Dogmas by not admitting their lack of communion with the total Truth of Christianity. There is room for all souls at the Table of Sacrifice. Let us pray that everyone on the Earth comes home to feed upon Jesus there soon.

Greet the Morning While Standing at the Water's Edge

November 20, 2000

There are really no winners in contemporary secularism; only those who are crowned as champions that are lucky enough to have not lost just yet. Our horrid attempts at such a civilization has been a travesty which continues to be filled with moral injustice. God does not yearn to see human life unfolding like a suspense-filled novella that is fashioned around a revolving-door faith. Neither does He want our Salvation to be a cliff-hanger-conclusion to a reckless mortal life. This is why our conversion to His Son must come sooner, rather than be far too late for it to matter in the end. The problems we face nowadays are not merely the effects and downside remnants of our technological advancements in reproductive science and the industrial age. Quite the contrary, life itself is only a vast wasteland if we choose to expend our years toward their expiration while remaining ignorant of the Glory of Paradise. Let us now finally begin to emerge from the darkness of night and record our many blessings from God; for we may awaken tomorrow to so many at our disposal that we may be unable to write them all down. We often rise to greet the morning while standing at the water's edge, not knowing whether to advance without the surety that we may ultimately sink or be able to swim; while trying to decide if we should retreat back into the hollows of our slumbering dens. All-in-all, it would not be imprudent to look upon the world with a less anguished tenor than our embittered peers would have us to perceive. The best of humanity may be only intermittent in nature; but the light of our kind servitude never goes completely dim between our strobing flashes of extraordinary grace. After all, we are a direct Creation of the Love of our Omnipotent Father in Heaven; and therefore, are also the ripening reposit of His fruit-filled Feast cornucopia. Our periodic trepidation is always accompanied by a courage which is so darling and profound that nothing conceivable could ever confine our hopes to the netherworld below. Our souls are Love's delight and a tender night that waves anew at sleeping dawn; a provocative and competitive day which always catches the timid horizon completely off guard.

However, we wear the emeralds of sincerity on our lapels only when we turn to America and proclaim, "Once you have transformed your poplar trees into rocking chairs instead of crosses for your enemies, then shall thine alabaster cities gleam! For today, they are still drowning in the dimmed deluge of human tears!" This is the hope with which we must carry-on toward the new Light. We must approach our brothers like gladiators and pluck the tarantulas from their souls before their hearts ever wake to realize the peril they were in. Hereby stands the purpose of the poetry of Salvation and the Love who has made it come true. There is no need for us to give our Almighty Father any reason to question our intentions by approaching His grace with even a whisper of consternation or disbelief. We have moved to within the short span of a lifetime to the death which will greet us all with a sad departing! Paradise awaits our much more romantic involvement with life hereon; seemingly never to be that well acquainted for now, while we continue to be distracted by the fleeting molecular events passing by in such a galactic realm! We turn our faces away much too often while God is trying to portray His solar radiance through a montage of selective images; for they are designed to slowly draw us back to Him at the endearment of our faith. The passing fads and cultures which we celebrate through our idle ages today do very little to impact, effect, or amend the Truth in the way that He is dispensing it from His still unchanging Throne in Paradise. Defining the conciseness of our Christian conviction and living it from our internal being are wholly different avenues because the former is only a singular sigh; while breathing life into what we believe is quite another thing. It is, moreover, the continuation of our eternal destiny to practice our religious faith as a direction and a purpose, not as some simplified appearance of cameo courtesy that makes our curiosity complete. Indeed, the fulfillment of our Divine Love through our emulation of Jesus Christ is the beginning of an everlasting life which casts a pall over mortal existence and, eventually, the art of dying itself.

It is God's cordiality that greets the fleeting and salutary gloom which breaks the heart wide open; while we send our condolences back to the riddance of torture, suffering, and pain all combined; for they are the glancing arrow's crimson trilogy of martyrdom, neither exacting nor precise, but blooming in any direction it can find to survive at last. We will travel as one to the land where drakes and goslings play in hollandaise glee before the invocation and arrival of the fully redeemed; while sweet Matthew's Passion reeks the air no more with human misery! Together, the Saints wait for our return to the backdrop of a pianissimo melody, while tears of joy trickle like rivulets down their splendrous cheeks. Beneath the decks of this timelessness, we shall prevail in hovering to the floor of our smoke-filled Earth in humble submission to Jesus and finally make our escape. Wisdom in Redemption; and not man alone; is the power of the universe; for any wretchedness which dares to cross Her path will disintegrate at the very thought of the words, "I love you." It is often the fire of grief which melts the pupils in our eyes until our future sight is clear! Do we dare make the promise that war should become so scarce that we cannot make it anymore? We remember well the anguished cries of dying sergeants who gave their lives under oath so that peace will never have to surrender again. And, we recall the hatred that they exchanged for Truth in the battles and fields of dreams which have long since run parched and dry! If we believe Jesus in faith and accept the picturesque aspirations of our hearts that will take us ever closer to His Font of Merciful Love, we will stand and walk upright with our absolution in tow, never too charred to bring our failures back to His Hearth of forgiveness once again. The pulse of our American nation once beat quite strongly in cadence with His propriety not so long ago, but now it lays nearly lifeless in the street, our soiled comrades at our feet with their ruffles not flourishing so brightly anymore. Too detached are we from the majesty that once made us a kingdom worth the salt, never to be tossed aside or shaken-down by our enemies' erratic whims. But, now, we are recoiled inside a shell of shamelessness and fear; our welcome mats withdrawn as though any weary traveler might ever want to call-on us again. Our banners' stripes may not have died in vain; and though our glowing stars are almost gone; never shall they rest in peace until they have been resurrected from the grave!

There will be nothing left of time to repeat once our Lord and Savior has come! He is the inspiration who once led Oliver Wendell Holmes to proclaim, "Build thee more stately mansions, O' my soul, as the swift seasons roll! Leave thy low-vaulted past!" These are the prosaic footnotes that we enunciate during the trials of our lives; claiming to know our own mastery which has been penned by them all; they who bask so stately now in the parlors of the soul which they could never have seen before. These are the hours that are so very fleeting; and we shall never see their like again! Once we have anthologized all of the proverbial sayings of former men at the onset of their life's conclusion, we will finally know that they could not really have discovered who they were without the Love of Christ. Our fathers before us shared both singly and altogether the same incessant helplessness which brought them to place their fingertips upon the curtal of their chin and pine outwardly for God to come to their aid. Every last one of them knew that there was no supple immortality to their prayers or oratorical works until the Holy Paraclete established residence in their hearts; for without His Love or Divine Majesty, mere words are only a befuddled mass of tribal poppycock and an archival bloc of antiquity. A higher station of immortal being we shall never claim without the Three-in-One High Deity! He is the King of all the Virtues and the bastion of Truth who reminds both the Concord and Rhine, alike, that they will never flow so deeply as to drown our sorrows or take our sins away. "Only the Blood of the Lamb on the Cross will raise all ships to the Crest of Eternity!", He is quick to pronounce with His calves resting comfortably on His earthen footstool from beyond the stars.

He commands our ascension to the Hill of Mount Calvary because the deep genuflection of entire humankind that we invoke there is to the dissolution of all imprisonment and the eradication of the same stubborn malice which has placed its tenants in chains. They are held there with holy terror in their eyes; bonded by a people so lacking in faith that they will look for any justification other than their dutiful compassion to set their captives free and pray to God that He will restore their lost dignity. And, too, what of the oceanic waves who come out to play at the break of dawn everyday; with no one there to greet them but the salty dogs who rape and pillage their fathomed acreage, while never bothering to tip their bills or thank them in return. Who knows what the whitecap crescendoes might have to say if only the roaring jetliners overhead would stop to listen once in awhile? Perhaps God had come to dine with them just yesterday and took all the souls who foundered beneath their wakes back to Heaven when He said goodbye! Amen! I say to You! This is the world which we should leave behind with the proper heights of nature and all the Rios Grande! While loons and gulls may soar in schooners above the rolling seas, never will a discouraging word ever send them back to shore again! All we can promise them from our last gasp of mortality, our final bow of peace, and our starboard departure from the passageways of our legacies is that we will soon bequeath to them the utter silence from the insides of our burial tombs!

The Origin of Infinite Wisdom at the Summit of the Blessed

November 21, 2000

Jesus Christ owns the sole discretion to mold the Universe as He sees fit; but He also entertains the images of our own creativity when they reflect His benign receptiveness; not for the purpose of altering what He has already finished, but to complement His quite exquisite number of dimensions with that of our own. He gives us the thesis of life through His Love and the surrounding Nature of the world; and then sets us free to affix whatever adjectives and prepositions to life we can employ in an effort to describe the charming grace which we encounter during our passage through the linear years. The Holy Name of Christ the King is an entire essay in perfection and Sacrifice in itself. The maxim which states that art often imitates life, which reciprocally mirrors art in return, has long been an established means to perceive the relationship between the imagination of man and our Almighty Father in Heaven. It is upon this pivoting axis that our co-dependency with Creation truly revolves. The most enduring legacy in recorded history is our ability to excel in both audible and visual expression. If we are willing to take our talents just one more step further into celebrating our spiritual admonition from Jesus, we will have transformed our assessment of the human condition into a petition to the *fons et origo*, the source and origin of infinite Wisdom at the Summit of the blessed. That is a definition of faith which can be nothing less than supernatural existence in itself. It must be absent of our whimsical moods because our emotions are always changing the texture of the temporal world. Neither can desire, by definition, be a permanent facet of the pristine Hereafter because its only purpose is to satisfy its own growling appetite; unless, of course, such desire is focused entirely upon our concurrence with the Will of our Almighty Father in Heaven.

What will eventually succeed and prevail over everything which composes the intellect of man is his power to deprive his craving for the aspects of life that will never take him to a better understand of Redemption. While God rarely tells us what to drink or what to wear on our backs, the specificity of His intentions is not so difficult to ascertain. Looking around the globe provides us a splendid deposit of information that we can acquire in the process of getting to know Him better. The Holy Spirit is the center of our Christian conscience and the provocative impulse of our struggle to become saints. If we hear someone calling-out for help in the middle of a lake, we assume that he may be about to drown. Our seemingly natural instinct is to jump-in and save him, or at least throw him a lifeline so he can reel himself in. If there is a robin caught in a smokestack, we know to open the lid and set him free. What we have taken for granted is that our mortal judgement is not the catalyst for our actions in either case. Let us give credit where it is ultimately due. Only the Holy Spirit in our hearts can induce us to rescue a life that God has created, which appears to be on the brink of extinction. No matter what religion we choose to embrace, or even if we do not know that God is working in us at all, He still utilizes us in the process of preserving His creative intentions. We are, perhaps, the unwitting participants in this process of Love whether we deem it necessary to accept it or not. These are the obvious ways that He teaches us to do only good; and there are many other illustrations which are equally as obvious to detect. The Holy Bible is replete with Chapters that cite situations where certain members of the human family are only mere pawns in the hands of a more Divine Power to sustain those who are helpless and cannot fend for themselves.

Conversely, there are also those issues for which we have no clearer distinction. We thank God every morning for making our lives more prosperous; but we are still confused as to whether we are really supposed to relinquish the material gifts that He has allowed to become our good fortune by giving it all to the poor. Would we not then be left in poverty ourselves and have to beg someone else for food? Might we become as dependent on the commonwealth of our peers as those whom we had fed from the first? Many people believe that, just in case the Almighty Father has not yet noticed, our market economy could never withstand such liquidity from this rapid transfer of wealth. God's reply is to ask us to demolish our systems of currency and spread His riches before all the world, expecting no compensation in return! This is the true application of the premise which says that we can never purchase happiness from the storehouse of our Salvation. While refusing to concede to the overtures from Christ, many of us continue to believe that such a plan of redistribution would only continue to be perverted by those who cannot control their own greed. Alas! We have just discovered the flaw in the socialist shield! Never in the history of the world has Christianity and Communism ever been able to reside under the same comprehensive domain. When we are as generous as we can be, the corrupt who live among us will start stockpiling their goods and thereafter proclaim themselves to be a separate body politick from the rest who are living the Holy Gospel in earnest. This is the reason there is still inequality among men, and is also why the charitable and innocent ones remain those who are poor. Again, the Wonderful Counselor has a response for the criminals who steal the portion which is meant to sustain the whole. Their souls will spend a trillion lifetimes and more agonizing in the blue-blazes of Hell. His Judgement is as confident as that!

Trying to determine how to resolve this stalemate is the reason that many of us turn inwardly to avoid engaging the fight for what is right and just in the vision of Heaven. We seem to be caught in the paradox of accepting only, "Me, my Creator, and the Earth." However, we risk being banished from His absolution, along with those other outright thieves, if our existence is so isolationist in its approach. Here, again, is where the power of the Holy Spirit kicks-in. Through our Baptism, Confirmation, and Communion in Jesus, God has imbedded an *apotheosis,* the transplantation of His own Divinity into our hearts, which keeps our souls yearning to be free from having to choose at all. Just like liberating a bird from inside our chimney, we are naturally drawn to sacrifice what we own for the good of Creation at large. Prayer helps us to communicate both with Jesus Christ in Heaven and His Holy Spirit who is ingrained into our consciences on the Earth. His Wisdom tells us that we should reach-out further to tend to His sheep, and to Hades with whatever we need. This is the true definition of nobility, and is also the beginning of the honorable submission which inspirited God's faithful people who have heretofore gone on to reside in Heaven as the Holy Communion of Saints, getting absolutely everything they want. It is, furthermore, the reason why Jesus dispatched the Divine Paraclete to inherit the Earth on Pentecost Sunday and give birth to the Catholic Church. The Sacred Gospel which followed soon thereafter is quite clear in affirming that, by enriching the lives of our brothers, we are actually advancing ourselves. The focal point of the entire matter is that true wealth is not found in material goods or our names flashing in neon lights on the public marquee, but in the legitimate Love which defies our own death. Indeed, if not for the dying, we would probably abandon our faith on the spot, disavowing it once and for all.

It seems like humankind is never quite satisfied until all of our assumed essentials have been elevated nearly beyond recognition. Perhaps this is our physical means of trying to offset the pressure and influence of gravity. Whatever the reasoning behind it, if our incomes are raised, we spend more at the marketplace, too. Someone across the meadow starts flying a kite; so we decide to release a balloon in response. An antenna can be restrained by its limits, so scientists have put satellites in outer space. Now, some of them have even dreamed of traveling across the solar system to Mars. Imagine the boundaries we could supercede if only we could transfer all of this tangible energy into advancing the relationship between the explorative human spirit and the Supreme omnipotence of God. Nuns and priests do it all the time while they are reciting the Holy Rosary; but they rarely make the national news or catch the fancy of our families and friends. What these holy people know that the rest of humanity still rejects is that engaging the power of the Creator who has given us life is much more than conquering the constraints which wield authority over the physical world. It is true that God told humankind in the beginning to exercise dominion over the Earth. But, we have yet to learn how to breathe under water or fly through the air without wings. The strength that He really wants us to pursue is to find Him searching for comfort at the very center of our being. Therefore, He has given us yet another definition of human Salvation, an unlimited source of His omnipotence, and a new means of transcending the confining element of time. It is called prayer from the heart; and its power hinges on our full understanding of Love; knowing well in advance that there is ultimately no way to properly effect it without our consciences zeroing-in on the Cross.

We discover at last that suffering and death are key to our source of power. But, most of us try to avoid them like they will spread some sort of black plague. Do we remember the Scriptural passage that confirms that a grain of wheat must fall to the ground and die, lest it remain just a simple grain? What Jesus is telling us now is that we must die to ourselves and be raised-up in His Resurrection to ever be exhumed from our graves. It is only after we fall to the ground in Christian conversion can God lift us back into His arms for new life. In the meantime, He continues to pass one parable after another before the eyes of our hearts to try to dilute our ignorance of His grace. The crux of each one of them is the elimination of the greed of the self. This is something that no one else on the Earth can help us do; but must be completed on our own. Even on a battlefield of 10,000 men, we are all still solitary warriors in the fight because no one else on the Earth can die our own death. Neither can we place someone else's spirit back in their corpse once they have surrendered it to God. We often huddle together to conquer a common foe, but break out of the ranks when we finally get the chance to stand in victory alone. Vultures hover in flocks over a carcass to keep other predators away; but, when the time is ripe for descending upon the kill, the scene quickly turns into every man for himself. This, again, is the reflux greediness which often recurs when the time comes to deny our very selves. The Bible clearly states that the meek will conquer the world. It seems so strange that our clothiers must provide shirts and breeches for all different sorts of men; but in the Light of Eternal Day, our souls are all the same size! If only we knew how truly great are those who suffer with just the most scarce of provisions, we would dismantle our empires and pour-out their proceeds over the Earth. As long as we carry-on with the fight to capture every dollar that seems to come near the bait in our traps, we will continue to hold our neighbors to the full extension of our arms and their nose to the grindstone of whatever we might gain from them in return. Indeed, we often keep our casual acquaintances with others in a different hopper than we do our trust as to whether we would ever permit them to conduct our financial affairs. The rest of the people around us whom we have never bothered to meet end-up in the "anonymous strangers" bin on the corner of our desk.

The problem with the conductance of our lives is that we do not realize that the Savior of the world is not very far behind. We often see film footage of the top of an airplane as it is viewed while flying through the sky. What we fail to recognize is that it takes another camera from an aircraft higher above it to record the videotape. This is very similar to the way Jesus hovers over our mortal decisions. He knows full-well where we are going; He watches our every move; and He tells His Father in Heaven whether we have earned our wings during the flight. He is our interior standard of good will while perceiving the effects that our outward actions have on the rest of the world. He is our sustenance in the battle for decency and our encouragement to share the gifts which He has given us to dispense in His Name. He knows that a hard-fought peace on the Earth is never a contradiction in terms or a rival to the long-suffering health of our maturing spiritual faith. At long last, He requires our moral purity and demands our compliance with the Beatitudes which He exhorted from a Mountaintop Sermon one day. He does not want us to become the kitchen match that is laying underfoot on the floor, hoping someone else will walk by to find us there and wield the courage it will take to strike the itch of our yearning desire to be the reflection of His Light, finally setting us free. Indeed, He wants us to be the brightest ones who are already standing upright and burning in Love for Him! A small spark of our affection is all it will take to set the rest of Creation afire! We sometimes see this in God when He asks for more than a moderate faith; not really comprehending what He is seeking at first. Some people who know that their hearts are in need of a little irrigation are prime candidates for an absolute flood of awareness because there is such hesitance in them to be flushed-out from the darkest corners of life. Their spirits need to be liberated so all the world can bask in the goodness they have gained to proclaim the Truth about Christ. There is no doubt that God places a label in a conspicuous place on our hearts when we are Christened by the Love of His Son which says in bold words, "Please protect from freezing!

Will harden if left unused!" Our compliance with these simple instructions is nothing-less than the proper restitution we must make to His Kingdom for the mess we have made of the Earth.

Our Contemporary Absolution in the Blood of Jesus Christ

November 22, 2000

It seems as though God is eager to offer us nearly every conceivable means through which we can recognize His eternal existence from our station on the Earth; but most people still walk through life without ever having bothered to encounter Him at all. There are many more enlightening ways to see our journey to its end if only we will pay closer attention to the signs that surround us. The hour of our death is not just the moment when we quit the fight for trying to reach His Kingdom, but is also the place where we insert a bookmark in the anthology of the human experience upon taking a break from our spiritual studies. The continuation of Love carries-on from there. Our passage into immortality is the juncture where we stop brainstorming about our transition into Eternal Salvation and finally stand up, leave the library of the physical world, and begin to do something about righteousness from the other side of time. Some of us see death as being a feather slowly falling from the sky through the years with our destiny scattered aimlessly by the wind. Others see it as being more precipitous than that, like a plate of fine china having fallen from a cupboard which has been toppled in a terrible earthquake somewhere. However, God chooses to envision our passing into His Kingdom as an eagle taking flight with the Wisdom of Truth grasped tightly within our talons. This is the same imagery through which we should perceive His Ecclesiastical Justice while He continues to grow the ages to their culmination in the Sacred Heart of Christ. The floodwaters that cover the Earth are actually the sorrowful tears He has shed for our having rejected His absolution for so long. They pool in the lower ravines of the world like sweat in the wrinkles on His Face. The typhoon winds we often see blowing are the tempest effects of His violent sneezing at the cruel hatred of collective humankind who have so recklessly peppered the world with outright malice for centuries-on-end from one corner of the globe to the next.

If we allow the Holy Spirit to claim our souls without our reluctance, we will see life from a wholly different perspective from the ordinary picture of Creation. A hurricane slurping-up the depths of the ocean to stay on course is no more than Jesus Christ taking a drink from the palms of His Hands at the shore of a hillside stream. Volcanic cinders are only the Saints who occasionally puff on their finest cigars while watching God's most holy mortals keeping their faith below. They sometimes inadvertently miss their ash trays when rocking in their porch swings in rhythm to the heartbeat of the universe, chuckling proudly at the most amusing children who have only now begun to walk. If we could hear their audible voices, they would be telling us to keep a watchful eye on the lay of the land around Mount Rushmore because that is where Our Savior will probably postmark the impending finish of the material world, having canceled the mountainous postage stamp that depicts the faces of the four legends who are hewn so proudly there. They already know what we must eventually perceive through the power of the Holy Spirit. The planet Saturn is only a gemstone that has been set comfortably inside its rings, while the unrefined Earth is still a diamond in the rough. These are among the visions which transcend the tangible world as we know it and allow us to envision God from within His own mystical state of intrinsic grace. It is very possible to learn which metaphors are more pleasing in His sight. They are the eloquent ones that serve only to glorify His profound power and personify the bright twinkle in His eyes.

Each of the conclusions we draw about mortality should take us ever closer to examining the kind of lives we are leading now. There is quite a difference between being legally blind and wilfully choosing to spend our pastime hiding-away in the dark. We have the ability to see the interior motivations of Christ if we will only allow His Holy Spirit to inhabit our hearts. If water was not meant to be transparent, how would we know whether it is clean or polluted? It is as pure in a sprinkling brook as our holiness must eventually become. The rest of the world should be capable of peering completely through our lives and still be able to see the Cross of Mount Calvary standing on top of a Hill on the other side. It somehow seems as though there is no way that Jesus can get the world hot enough on a midsummers day to iron the creases out of our consciences without ultimately taking us down to the ground from being overcome by exhaustion amidst the sweltering heat. He is still dispensing His Word to humanity at a rate that is less than the speed of sound because He knows that we do not often listen very well. But, we have chosen instead to break-past His barrier anyway on our haughty flight to the other side of the Earth to avoid hearing what His Immaculate Mother has come to say. This peculiar attribute of humanity does not serve Heaven a single iota or enhance the future of those who flee its admonishment to the slightest degree. Our Almighty Father has given us Cathedrals and Basilicas which have stood tall in the Truth for centuries. He has provided more than enough Sacraments to last us a lifetime and offers a priceless Eternal Salvation in His Son on the Cross. And, yet, what do most of us offer Him in return? Only a feeble attempt at spiritual faith which is so paltry and impotent in nature that, if it were to ever be transformed into bread crumbs being tossed onto the ground, it would not be able to keep a pigeon alive for more than two days.

When Jesus proclaimed that the Light of His Love should never be hidden beneath a bushel basket, His words were much larger than the parable of His speech. He was saying that our faith is not meant to be just a seedling for trampling underfoot, but rather an entire forest of towering redwoods on the crest of a hill, a range of mountains as tall as Mount Everest, a field of sunflowers already in bloom, a mass of miracles having finally been seen, a Capitol Rotunda filled to the pitch with statesmen in the prime of their years, a sun shining at the brightest midday, a moon that is completely full, and a silhouette of the Old Rugged Cross at three-hours past noon on Good Friday. We will be unable to encounter these beautiful visions as long as we carry our guilt on our backs like a saddle on a horse; just standing-in-wait for another one of Satan's mavericks to try to break us again. There is no time to waste on our futures for that sort of thing anymore. It all boils down to whether we truly want to put-forth the effort to go forward to Paradise or not. Do we invent new utensils because we actually need them to survive; or are we just too lazy to do things the old-fashioned way? There will never be any absolution which is more modern and contemporary than the Blood of Jesus Christ. He has told us this identical Truth time and time again for more generations than we might care to recall. He has sent prophets and ghosts to teach us; He has parched the Earth with the sun, healed millions at His Mother's miraculous shrines, brought crash-victims back from near-death, awakened our loved-ones from decades in a coma, and continues to place His Own Flesh and Blood on our Altars of Sacrifice every day in the world. There is still a series of questions that are much too dire to be left unaddressed for much longer. Why do we hold-out in repugnance in the presence of all these gifts? Why do we not begin trying to build-up His Kingdom instead of always ripping it apart at the seams? As a great man once asked of his fellow citizens from a podium on a sunny afternoon, "How much more power do we need? What else is left to destroy?" On the other hand, however, if we ask Jesus for a reference in our application toward our reinstatement into the heights of Paradise, He will inscribe it by His Passion and humbly sign it with His Blood. No longer will we remain in the bottom of a mote with famished crocodiles chomping at our flesh; but we will be allowed back into the Castle wearing tubular bells upon our feet to the sweet fragrance of a Thanksgiving feast which is fit for a newly-crowned prince.

Engaging the World in the Truth of God's Love

November 27, 2000

Human life is changing more rapidly than we have the capacity to measure; and our disheveled hearts are still too broken to ever withstand the pain. We continuously seek a solid ground of purpose for being here, believing that there is little we can do to pull-out of the rut of our conventional slavery to material greed. If we concede that the judgement of history is an irrevocable conclusion which is unable to be amended by modern-day man, then we are also simultaneously destroying our reason to fight for change or to seek a better world. Our willing confessions to God allow us to strengthen the courage of our inner-solvency while listening intently to the Wisdom of the Holy Spirit telling us how to live. There is no doubt that Christians are led down many vast shorelines and hidden corridors; but rarely are we allowed to fall completely out into the open like a child sliding down a fire escape or a passenger descending an inflated ramp from an airplane which has been forced to make an emergency landing. It is quite obvious that we hold-in-hand the entire Doctrine of human Salvation in the New Covenant Gospel which is personified by Jesus Christ, Himself. But, the question of our faith still remains as to whether we fully understand every complete intention of the Almighty Father or the unabridged spectrum of ordinances and resolutions He will continue to require of His Mystical Body on Earth. There is no doubt that the Flesh and Blood of our Redeemer was tortured on Good Friday and then transfixed onto the Cross to die. It is equally as profound and promising that He was raised from among the Dead on the ensuing Sunday morning. Most of us have no difficulty accepting these mystical articles as being the center of our Salvation. But, what do we make of the seemingly endless and unmitigated suffering of Christ's faithful people who still live in the exile we call mortal life, many of whom will go to their deaths in defense of His Word?

Indeed, in what context do we receive the utter repugnance we often face to prove to the enemies of Love that we are loyalists to this Lamb on the Cross? Do we run and hide in fear, telling this Slain Warrior that He is in the battle all alone and our commitments have definable limits? Do we concede that our witness to His Kingship is somehow flawed by a random memory of our own making, that we remember well the blessings He has promised, but only selectively choose to decide where the line is to be drawn as to what we will ultimately sacrifice? Is it humanity who decides when we will produce definitive results toward converting our brothers and sisters who hate God outright, and what materials we will opt to surrender to accomplish it? It often seems as though our efforts in trying to understand the Mind of God is like sitting chin-deep in a pool of algebraic expressions. Once we have deciphered the equations and canceled-out everything which is effectively equal, He seems to add another unanticipated factor to one side or the other, or changes the absolute value of the constants, while allowing an entire diatribe of independent variables to invade our original premise, each of them with a previously undetermined coefficient. Now, when we are expected to find *x for every coordinate value of y* in a matrix, it is as though we are being challenged to discover how many whole integers are present in a half-gallon of water that is being poured from a flask into a container which has a bottom, but no sides. This entire postulate seems too incomprehensible and nonsensical to be real. Our memories are no longer of any use in trying to establish the future that God holds for the world because our established theorems and corollaries often have no meaning outside our physical environment; while the generally accepted mathematical principle which states that 2 + 2 = 4 is no longer a satisfactory assessment. Our power of reasoning is completely perplexed by God's ability to rearrange the universe at His own discretion and keep us off-stride by placing new curvatures in a flat plane that looked completely straight the moment we first began. What good is a proposition for the determination of relativity when reality is actually measured in a Mass of Chalices of Blood from an inexhaustible flow of Love from a Throne which sits eons above us in Paradise? How can grams and g-forces ever effect a system so dynamic in description that everything in its shadow ceases to exist, even though it is weightless and is faster than the speed of light, but somehow sits quite peacefully and still? This is the same confusion which is generated when we attempt to decide for the Creator of every living thing that our abstract conclusions can compete with His extraterrestrial genius.

If we honestly try to become one in the perfection of Heaven, we will discover that creativity and ingenuity are products of Love; and every facet of Truth is a piece of the puzzle which allows us to live in a higher state of grace. The mantle above this extraordinary structure is Wisdom and prayer because they both teach us how to assemble the priorities of our conversion in accordance with the teachings of Christ. Moreover, they are our right and left guards against any residual temptation and doubt. As troubling as it may seem, the entire fortune of humankind is dependent on our faith in this one Messiah; while the present, the future, and all perpetuity beyond them are completely contingent upon what we seek from Him in contrast to what He expects from us in return. We cannot live a better purpose on the Earth than to serve Him under the jurisdiction of our own obedience and joy. The doorway to our becoming the greatest species of any living creature is already standing wide open, while many among us are flailing around in the darkness with their eyes closed, still trying to find the knob. Jesus Christ is hovering over us at this very moment with His Holy Arms outstretched as if to be beckoning us inside His Mercy with giant rays of sunlight and the Blood of our Redemption streaming from His Vestments. If we will only accept these dispensations with the full allegiance of our best demeanor, we will know that our union in His Sacred Heart is our perpetuating process of primordial comprehension and the essential life of Creation as it continues to be dispensed from the Intellect and Hands of the Almighty Father above.

The origin of our decisiveness is always whether we choose to join the ranks of the blessed who will do whatever it takes to defend and promote the fruits of Divine Love. This is an acceptance which should be natural for all humankind to achieve, but one that only few ever master before the moment of their death. If someone approaches us and says that they just do not have the capacity to love their enemies, we should ask them if they also do not have the ability to eat their spoils in the presence of their foes. The first is just as natural as the latter, and even more life-sustaining than anything they might consume to keep their physical bodies alive. Authentic Christian Love and Communion in the Holy Eucharist are both as natural and essential to human survival as any culinary dish they might choose to devour. When push comes to shove, we must all eventually accept the fact that there are no tenable excuses for denying the Cross on which our Savior died. Anyone who states that they have prepared a case against the outright faith of those who Love Jesus as their Redeemer is a contriver whose soul is headed for the region below the Earth which is reserved for the lost and forsaken. Somewhere in their lives, they have most assuredly been confronted with the decision to follow Jesus in Truth, but have laid-down their cross instead, searching for a better way toward happiness that just does not exist. Oftentimes the way we are reared as children hangs like a tapestry in the back of our consciousness, just beyond the sight of our comprehensive judgement and potential objectivity. This is the reason why so many people are still imprisoned by the slavery of their own prejudices. The memories of our younger years can best be described as being diminishing ripples in a pond; and it is oftentimes best just to leave it that way. Today is a better time and a new opportunity to compound our own holiness and grow in affection for the Master who has Died to save our wretched souls from the recollections which still haunt so deeply.

Of course, we also hold-on to those memories that remind us of our stouthearted faith when we were yet too little to know what it really meant. The truth is very real that these moments of great heroism in Love were not just a penny in our thoughts which have grown weaker in value because of the inflationary index of our adulthood years. God sees them as being an investment from which we will reap a high reward in Heaven someday. They are worth more than a million fortunes to Him now because they were the seedlings that have allowed our faith in Him to list so strongly and proudly in the breezes of our present-day conviction in knowing that our Salvation is imminent and true. Many people wonder what it would be like to reach their senior years and be able to see a collection of "still" photographs of their actions in the past for which they were proud to be in Love with Jesus Christ. To their great surprise, they will someday see a full-length motion picture of their struggles to comply with the Holy Gospel in living color when they finally greet Him Face-to-face. Our more contemplative moments are greater than just hours of prayer. They are our direct appeal to the Almighty Father to amend the world as we know it and render it to be like the pinnacles of the Heaven we yearn to see. If we feel like that day will never come to us, we need to call upon the higher principalities who do His bidding here on the Earth. Our union with them is nothing less than our varsity march from the bleachers to the locker room to dress ourselves in perfect submission for the battle for souls to the accompanying cheers of the Hosts of Paradise. If we choose to participate in this transformation of the world into the Arms of Christ, we will have joined the most powerful elite of God's spiritual forces who wield the commission of His Divine Authority to disseminate His statutes and decrees to the lost and alone, to dispel any forces that try to get in our way, to separate, divide, admonish, and absolve those who walk in accordance with the nature of their individual spirits, and to administer the Charitable Works of Great Mercy which God has given us to command before the ignorant who need them for the survival of their own goodness.

If we do right by the Almighty Father in engaging the world with the Truth of His Love, He will enlist our souls in the diplomatic corps of righteousness and place torches in our hands that will allow us to join the Saints of Heaven in focusing His power in a unified direction of consistory flames against evil. Our union stands for the conflagration of the horrid enemies of human Salvation and the scooping of their ashes into the gaps which are left in the ground to keep the followers of Satan safely sealed in the darkness where they belong. This power is much more than just circumstantial in nature, but is also the discretionary longitude that decent men often require to succeed in setting the stage for the end of the world. The source of our strength and spiritual goodness is the Love which is congenital in nature to those who are blessed from their birth to be the followers of Christ. He clearly sees us from the inside out, while simultaneously recognizing the physical actions that drive our purpose through the labors of our hands as being His own by proxy. This is yet another reason why we shall never lose hope while waiting for Jesus to return to the Earth to redeem us. Anticipating our Salvation is somewhat like winning the greatest crown there is to achieve in the world; while knowing in the midst of the triumph that there is a better one yet to arrive. There is still another star on the peak of our jubilation which Jesus will add to our greatest mortal accomplishments. It is an elevation that is larger than life and one from which we will never again descend to the battlefield of hatred that tried to hold us down for so long. The setting of the evening sun can never take this Victory away; and a new breaking morning could never bear a challenge as sweet to the taste. When the Son of Man returns to claim His holy people, all will be "in and done" at last; and the ledger of reservations will have been finally exhausted. No soul will ever have to die again.

Now, in our modern age, we must find a way to employ various levels of reasoning that are guided by the Rule of God's Justice so we can convince even the closest of our loved ones that their "business as usual" approach to living is no longer applicable anymore. Everyone must learn that Divine purpose is always greater than self-preservation because Love always lasts longer than time, even if it appears at the onset that it almost always flourishes through the diminishment of our most distinctive personal appeal. When we reach to the wellspring of our faith without asking God why beforehand, we should remember that He never reads anything into our responses other than what He already knows we are capable of achieving in our imitation of the Love of His Son. By all means, when it comes to growing righteousness in a particular place, God does not mandate our participation in the whole, but He welcomes it quite profoundly. He is assuredly gratified by our efforts to incrementally help our brothers and sisters overcome their fears and to break-out of their shells when growing their strength in defense of His Holy Word. Heaven knows that humanity's own hesitance, fright, intimidation, and indifference must be expunged by the gifts of Love that we bear to others in the palms of our own hands. This is what Jesus has been telling us all along. "Take up your crosses and follow Me," means to allow Him to describe the conditions of our conversion as they really exist and to define in previously-untold terms whether we have truly lost our dignity or have just been "put-out" by some former pent-up frustration which has evolved to be no barrier to our becoming more holy at all.

True joy in human life is in knowing that the only authentic Christian preparedness is whether we have really conditioned our souls to stare the jubilation of our Salvation straight in the eyes and say "I accept you," before Jesus closes-out the mortal ages in Judgement. The love which God envisions for us is one so powerful that it can perceive a cross-section of the entire spectrum of Creation at once, inviting the stars to finally reside below the clouds, expecting the forces of nature to obey our every command, and never ceasing to believe in the Beatific Dawn of Resurrection Day, even when the pit of outright rejection is sitting like a cannon ball in the arch of our throats. If we continue to stand beside the Will of God in the midst of all these proceedings, we will always be humbled by the experience and He will be forever glorified. The task of overcoming our weaknesses to our carnal desires and spiritual shortcomings is never as treacherous as it previously seemed once we have crossed this bridge of hope. Indeed, the Kingdom of Jesus Christ is never quite the same. What we sometimes forget when we are baptized is that, while Jesus washes away our original sins, we still have to uphold our portion of the Sacrament. We throw the gauntlet against every form of evil that steps into our paths the moment the Holy Spirit says, "You are Mine again!" We earn our knighthood by conquering ourselves first, before we ever set-out to take-on the greater world. We do this for many reasons, not the least of which is the fact that nothing impure can come from outside our own hearts; and the plank in our eye makes it far too difficult for us to see the splinter in the sight of our brethren who are living next door.

Nothing grandiose should be read into our successes in life, except that they are always ordained by God if they are accomplished in the Name of His Son. He usually never implies that we should go about our little corner of the globe picking fights with those whose faith has not brought them to Christianity quite yet. But, the encouragement for our evangelistic efforts glows inside our hearts from nearly every side of our own good fortune. God always says exactly what He means through the Wisdom of the Holy Spirit, in the grace of the Seven Sacraments, through the nature of the universe, and within the parameters of the Divine prophecy which He has implanted into the consciences of righteous men who reside both at home and abroad. Our self-discipline must always be prepared to stampede into battle at the whisper of His Sacred Word. Since we never really know when such an occasion will arise, we should anticipate during every breathing moment that our name might be next to be pulled from the derby of anonymous heroes who must drop what they are doing and follow Him in haste. This also complements our proper preparation for the Second Coming of Christ. What will we want Him to find us doing on that unexpected moment when He comes to take our souls into the Chambers of Justice for sentencing before the entire Court of Heavenly Hosts? What we do now for Him is our answer in advance.

There are certain individuals who believe that the lives of other people are only an alibi-in-the-making and a decades-long witch hunt for a scapegoat for their own fallacious ambitions. Whereby has our civilized society come upon such rancorous cynicism? Are we really so fearful of our fellow man that we would accuse him of conducting a carefully orchestrated vendetta against others whom they have never even met? The careful orators among us continue to speak to the cadence of the "call of the conscience," while two-thirds of their listeners do not even know what it actually means. We are, indeed, a sorrowful lot of humanity if we hold-out no more hope for ourselves than that. There is hardly an American citizen alive today who has not laid down the morning newspaper after glancing through the headlines and said, "What in the world has happened to our country?" But, their question is not in proper context because they should be more concerned about what has *not* happened in our nation. We have seen the bitter taste which has been allowed to spoil our appetite for good will while our national discourse aims only at public competition and private financial gain. We have been standing idle alongside the very intervention that we have long allowed to lay in waste; and we are wholly insufficient in making the best of our opportunities to bring America together in the wake of some of our most grave tragedies. The divisive rhetoric of many extremists does very little to ameliorate the pain which still scalds the inside of the spirits of the broken-hearted who feel so terrified and alone in a country of prosperity that they just cannot quite understand. And, just when it seems like we can claim a common ground for a higher good, another season of picking and choosing evolves again, and we take to the streets once more, trying to find "our share" of the wealth which has come to us not of our own doing, but as a gift from the intercession of the Saints who love us so dearly in the Kingdom of Heaven.

It feels like only a few short years ago when personal intelligence was an asset which was employed toward the advancement of all humanity to succeed. Somehow, this benevolence passed into the night when we followed the Judiciary Branch of our tribunal government in declaring that prayer is an intrinsic intrusion of the individual rights of some segments of people in the public arena. We were once a melting pot of dignified friends whose service to one another was seen as being like a *potage*, a warm soup in the winter's cold of the everyday world. Now, however, we have become a mutually exclusive collage of strangers who just so happen to live in a communal way so as to take advantage of the public utilities which we need to stay warm and to see what we are doing in the dark. Where there was previous security in the strength of our very numbers, now we do whatever we can to imitate life on the inside of prisons by secluding ourselves behind concrete walls and barbed-wire fences. How ironic that we stand and proclaim to be "one nation under God, indivisible, with liberty and justice for all." What grief is brought to our souls when we hear the echo of the lyrics of our most majestic songs which celebrate our desire to be free just because we do not violate one another in order to maintain our diversity. There has long been the argument that the Church has played a sorely impotent role in the promulgation of most of our public laws. But, what is there to say about the masses of lay people who have been downright repugnant in their refusal to demand that their nation obey the Commandments of God, as well as those of the statutory order? Of course, there may already be enough fault-finders to go around that we do not need some sort of morality police telling us what to do in the privacy of our own homes. But, what happened to the proposition proclaiming our responsibility to keep ourselves holy and pure in the eyes of our Creator so He will never allow our sheen of goodness to be tarnished by humanity whole?

The Blessed and Immaculate Mother of Jesus Christ, Mary, Queen of the Saints, is speaking no less critically about the entire people whom God has created as we, ourselves, often do about the agnosticism of the United States. The differences of race, creed, and native tongue do absolutely nothing to diversify the mortal body of humankind who must live in the Crucifixion of Jesus in order to never die the permanent death that is coming to us all. "Nation shall rise against nation," said Our Savior as He looked forward in time to the end of the world. And, sure enough, there are now hundreds of thousands of partisans already racing across the globe wearing corselets and bearing swords against their brothers, even as we speak today. Can humanity not see that Christ is more than our Prophet and Guide; He is the only Way, Truth, and Life to our ever being raised from the dead? What is wrong with a human heart who cannot understand this? Do the tenets of their own beliefs preclude them from ever seeing their way into the full Light of Divine Revelation in the Son of God? Even many of those who embrace the Decalogue from Mount Sinai know that those Ten Commandments were delivered by the same God whose Blessed Progeny was to become the New Covenant Christ. He is the Messianic Law who has fulfilled the Words of His Father which were given to Moses hundreds of generations before Him. His purpose is toward the compassionate pardoning of sinners instead of laying them flat-out before the Wrath of God's Eternal Justice. The tendance of those who are suffering and in need comes not only from the generosity of the millions who help them to lead better lives, but from the latter's inexplicable imitation of the Root of David whom many of them still reject as being an imposter! The God of Israel has sudden news for them to hear; the Holy Spirit is not that naive! He works in and among them despite their own obstructionist views regarding the renewal of the world in the Blood of Jesus Christ.

Is this to say that we can never escape the grasp of the Almighty Father? Certainly not! But, He will appropriately place the tools of His own forthrightness in any auxiliary hands which He can find on the Earth so those who serve Him while unawares will never reject His identity on the day they die, no matter what religion they choose to practice. At the same time, He relocates those who wail in agony in the midst of these humble servants for the purpose to which Saint Paul referred as being the ullage in the suffering of Jesus on the Cross. This must assuredly be the reciprocal nature of servant and master that mirrors the way Jesus lived His Life in the mortal world. The servant eventually became the Master of all; and thereby we are every one elevated to the royal priesthood of perfect Saints by living this same orientation. Now, His Holy Mother has come to say that the perspiration from the brow of those who serve the human family in the Name of the Love of Christ moistens the saccharine which makes His Heavenly Feast complete. However, She has also added the caveat that every soul on the globe must come to the Eucharistic Table at the Holy Sacrifice of the Mass to be eligible to receive the highest gifts of grace that Her Son has to offer. In other words, good works are insufficient of their own accord to deliver us to the exact center of absolution. We must invoke nothing less than our most beneficial faith to make the connection with Heaven that God wants us to perceive. The Most Blessed Sacrament is the conjunctive Body and Blood of Jesus Christ who unites our souls with Paradise before we ever surrender our passing flesh. It is possible to reach the heavens by way of our paratactic approach to our religious faith; but God may be forced to ask us to repeat ourselves before His Almighty Throne at the end of time when we are only able to mutter the words, "I accept and I believe," while shrugging our shoulders in lack of assurance as to whether that is what we are really supposed to say.

Our faith in Jesus must be so confident that it will even take us by surprise. Many are the occasions when the Saints of old have looked back in time and said to themselves, "Did I really go through all of that?" as they take another sip from their Loving Cup. If only we can muster this same courage in what we profess to believe today, no more will anyone look cynically upon the societies of the world and ask what everyone is fighting about. They will know immediately that the end of all inequity and lack of affection is not a function of what might have happened to their country, but what was finally manifested inside their hearts to bring an end to the battles whose outcomes hold no bearing whatsoever on the completion of Creation at large. Jesus Christ finished it on the Cross with the assistance of our prayers and the same intercession of His Blessed Mother which is ongoing to this very day. What She has come to say is much more poignant than the pleasantries that we often hear from the souls who follow God in blind abandonment. Her purpose is light years more transcendent than we might be able to readily see. Let's face it, the Mother of God has come to tell us that we can make a difference in reshaping Heaven because this is the way Her Son wants it to be! We are given the Holy Rosary, all of the Blessed Litanies, and the prayers of Ordinary Time to get us through the night. Christ will keep us warm because He does not want our hearts to ever grow rancid, stale, or cold. We are the idols of His Divine Envisionment; and He will never let us stray beyond His panoramic insights of Truth. By standing beside Him to our last dying day, we will never need an exculpating portfolio or a paltry excuse to offer our Divine Master upon His final revealing of what we were doing in the dark corners of the Earth for so long.

"The Lost Steamer Who Gave No Rise to Living"

November 28, 2000

There is no question that the resolution to our sorrows is long overdue and never swift in arriving at all; while it often seems as though the few who wound our tender hearts only ignore our pain and stoop to bow only when they are panning for gold in the stream of tears we leave behind. Happiness is never a forge which finds our way too often; but the *deja vu* sadness we seem to experience is yet nothing more than the roundelay recurrence of the ordinary cycles of linear time which should have died the very moment we promised God that we would seek only His benign Sweet Heart for the rest of our mortal days. Why do we not allow the conscience of Heaven to pique our unchecked vanity so we will no longer be able to raise our heads in defense of our own regard before those who scourge us for standing upright in the Cross of Jesus Christ? More writers than could ever be numbered in a day have promised in their literary works that the "just" shall win at the last. Who is to say that they all may not succeed at the exact same time if only they will recognize the Face of Jesus in the background images of the present age and know that the battles of the Earth need not ever rage again? The spirit of their elevation defies the same crass worsted that is trying to bind us all toward grief amidst the clarion call of the greatest Good News to ever impact the earlobes of the unsuspecting world. God is offering us a spiral staircase which reaches beyond any heights that our mental constitution could possibly imagine whose newel is the Cross upon which Jesus died to save our souls and to become our Communion Bread.

If we cannot lend ourselves to accept this hope, we will not be entirely unlike the historical world which has attempted at times to obliterate whole societies simply because they thought them to be an inferior lot of men. We must vow to never again fall prey to these tyrants who promote the genocide of other races such as the Teutonic Pogrom of the mid-20th century and the so-called "ethnic cleansing" that still stains the boundaries of the simmering Earth today. We must fight against this hatred from the core of our Christian beliefs because it is the main reason why many impressionable souls are still being stricken by such idolatry and are eventually cut-off altogether from making their final peace with God. Those who violate the Fruits of Love can dress their cruel malice in pretty linens all they like; but we are called to remember that poison ivy also has flower petals and roses in the wild sprout thorns so as to hold those who might wish to pluck them by the stems from their colonial bushes at least a finger's touch away. We cannot allow the larger body of humanity to fall to the fate which has occurred inside the borders of so many single nations under siege. The eternal life of every mortal being is far too important for us to leave a single one behind on our voyage of good will and our reconciliation with the God of all the ages. The land which gives us breathing air is common to all souls; and every rolling waterway should raise us together as one.

We will always miss the mark toward gaining life eternal if we do not approach the singular Cross that has already made us pure and whole. Humanity cannot afford to settle for a lesser god because the destiny of our future always resides in the Truth. The parables which support us are sometimes too numerous to mention. We do not call upon a veterinarian for the removal of our inflamed appendix; but rather the best doctor of surgical medicine we can possibly find in practice. The same appraisal applies to gaining our Salvation at the end of time. We do not want to die and wake-up again just anywhere; we want to spend our afterlife in Heaven! And, it is quite apparent that only Jesus Christ can take us there. The same principle applies when going to the Holy Sacrifice of the Mass for the healing of our souls. We will never find the Bread of Life at an evangelistic tent-revival with clamoring cymbals and hecklers shouting aimlessly against whatever subject happens to leap into the forefront of their minds. If we pray to the Holy Spirit without truly knowing what greater blessings we might receive, the world may change the very next moment we rub our weary eyes. Of course, we often do pretty well at the petitioning part when it comes to imploring Jesus for the satisfaction of our every passing need; but we are sorely remiss in offering our prayers of thanksgiving or surrendering our more humble praises in honor of His Love. "Did I not heal all ten?" was His inquiry when only one had come back to thank Him in return.

Perhaps there is substantial truth to the accusation that we often forget the source of our indulgences once we have been absolved of our sins as though the container which has quenched our thirst is empty and we have chosen just to cast it aside for a newer source of aid. Our offerance of thanksgiving is the life hereon for the blessings we received today. It is the echo of our unity in every Eucharistic Benediction that has ever been professed around the globe.

Indeed, our gratitude to Jesus is the sweet incense of our faith which remains with Him long after we have gone back outside again to play like children in the street. If we fail to offer our subservient fondness to the Almighty Father as soon as our prayers are answered, He might reserve the right to remind us of our slippage during a time when we least expect to hear it! We must remember that there is no jury to lend their pity upon the occasion of our death. Jesus Christ is the sole determiner of whether we have kept our promises below Him. Be it fair or not, our destiny already resides in His Hands with precious few other mortals to ever advocate our cause. Thankfully for those with hearts that are still golden enough to inquire, we will always find Jesus, Mary, and Joseph standing tall for our Redemption, along with the Saints and the Angels from on High, and God-knows who else will be there nearby to beseech His forbearance on our behalf. "Let him in!" they are generally prone to say. This is why it is imperative that we call upon their intercession now, before the hours we have left remaining on the Earth finally begin to wane.

If the world was ever to be viewed in the context of being a ship sailing on the seas of the universal waters below the heavenly firmament, it would surely be one whose fate has been determined by those who have cast the Holy Gospel aside so as to ignore their Salvation altogether. Unfortunately for many, those who know Jesus very well often refuse to offer His Love to the rest of humanity. A poem to eulogize this globe that is spinning beyond control by its own audacious pride could be quite sorrowful for the reading.

The Lost Steamer Who Gave No Rise to Living

O' pitiful Earth which has such wretches in it,
With carol streaming buffets on Her deck.
Seal Her sweet magnolias beneath Her bureaus,
To save them all from dying in the Wreck.
Glad shall the midshipmen be once their fate is ended,
And rich morticians dive deeply to retrieve Her bell.
Praying as one for the borage who were tossed over,
Beseeching God to spare the dead from Hell.
Her crown princes had rejected their Wise Gondolier,
And sailed proudly toward a more uncharted dredge.
Most all the Hosts of Heaven cringing now to see Her,
Go tumbling off the side of Creation's Edge.
Their last descendent holds little hope for the departed,
Who turned their backs on their Salvation from Above.
A lost frigate that declined to engage the battle,

That would place Her aboard the feathers of a Dove.
To a Shore where its steerage would become the captains,
And Her coal porters would garner the most of all.
If ever there was a freighter with greater purpose,
She would surely have never missed this Port of Call.
The modern day Communion that they were offered,
From the Creator who hailed "The Least of These."
Still lingers near to hear their last confessions,
That will take their hearts to praying on their knees.
For now, the future of those so deeply under water,
Her course no longer sailing the ocean's crest.
Depends on the Mercy so quietly in the breezes,
Who forgives them the way that only He does best!

-William L. Roth, Jr.

Let us never forget that we cannot mortgage our future in Paradise while we are still alive on the Earth. We will never be able to return again in corruptible flesh wearing mortal clothes and expect to be able to quit the debt somehow. But, by turning to the absolution that Jesus is offering today, there will be no borrowing to plea, no bartering to beg, and certainly no need to steal away and hide. There are many souls who have asked whether their mansion in Paradise is already built or not; or if God is keeping their residence on blueprinted pages, instead, while He waits to see if they are finally washed clean in Jesus' Blood to keep them from descending into Hell. The answer is abundantly clear that we are presently in the foyer of Heaven as our days here on the Earth continue to expire because our Baptism, Confirmation, Communion, and frequent honest Confessions have been enough to take us through the door. Only our passage from death back into Life is the chasm which remains to be crossed because Jesus has already set the appointments of our stately mansions appropriately in their place. The fact remains true, however, that we will come perilously close to surrendering them if we do not keep our white garments of holiness utterly free from stain and our consciences as clear as a Cathedral bell.

We Are Growing Holier by the Hour

November 30, 2000

Trying to understand the intentions of God without inviting His Spirit into our hearts is not a divine comedy or even a slightly humorous matter. He often sits on His Throne with His Chin perched on the knuckles of His Hands and a smile on His Face while we stammer-about before Him, helplessly struggling to remove our swords that are stuck like glue in the bottom of their sheaths. The only verifiable test of the strength of our faith in His Kingdom is the passing element of time. The years will eventually tell us if we really belong to Heaven, or whether we will take the first exit ramp the moment we are called to reign-in our own error and conquer everything that still distracts us from the Salvation which Jesus offers at the end of our life. The flames of our votive candles will reflect very little light if we are not willing to offer a spiritual inferno of our own that blazes from the deep recesses of our mortal being. It seems as though we spend our entire lives trying to conquer the influences of the flesh; which is a perpetual battle because our spirits are encased inside it. However, there is no reason to believe that the envelope of our physical bodies has to become a liability toward the Love we offer to Jesus. He gives the same purity to us; and surely we can properly reciprocate of our own accord. Our sins are almost always punctuated by a certain latent feeling of guilt when we bear the Christian conscience to know that we have trespassed against the Laws of God. Some of us are simply weaker than other people; but we are all growing holier by the hour. We should never look with disdain upon those who are still fighting to gain control over their more domestic side because the prospect of their culpability does not always begin at the dateline of when they should have grown old enough to know better. It is a cruel and deceptive world; and we all have to engage our more courageous spirit to conquer it at times. God knows that there are always mitigating factors to the weakness which bring us to do something wrong.

This, indeed, is one of the reasons why we should be thankful for life here on the Earth. It is our molting season during which we can shed everything that keeps us from being recognized as totally Divine by our Almighty Father. We are sequestered, as it seems, away from the center of our origin for reasons not punitive in nature, but to await our own adjudication of ourselves as to whether we know for sure that we are worthy of being acquitted in the Blood of Jesus Christ. This is a verdict which cannot come too soon. His Crucifixion is a 2000-year-old crime that has come forward in time to bind-up our wounds and to simultaneously set us free. We must confess to having caused it, but we shall never face the eternal consequences which should properly be ours to bear. Indeed, God allows us to walk-away from the murder of His Son not only scot-free, but right back into His Loving Arms in Paradise. The irony of it all is that we must become one with this exact same Sacrifice in order to be saved as though we are assimilating it into the fiber of our souls and uniting ourselves with the sanction of its purpose. For all of our prayers and acts of good works, we find at the last that our faith is the most valuable tool in our possession because it allows us to see ourselves better than anyone else could possibly comprehend. There is no doubt that we often make the mistake of looking at our brothers and sisters in the context of what they have given back to God as compared with everything we have offered Him. We are often surprised to discover that we have actually sacrificed very little at all. How many times have we pondered the life of someone else and admitted quietly to ourselves, "Whew, am I glad I never had to go through that!"

The key to our knowledge is our trust in the Holy Spirit because He allows us to determine whether the sounds we hear in the background world are really God calling us to greater Light or perhaps the curiosity of our own imaginings trying to make us a more benevolent people than we have the capacity to be on our own. Whichever is the case, we can know only by our faith in listening to God's Living Word. We discover in time that self-determination is never the same nobility as self-denial because the former implies some sort of temporal satisfaction and does not truly peck at the core of who we really are. Knowing where Siberia is located and going there to live indefinitely are two entirely different propositions. This is just one of the characteristics of the three stages of life that we somehow seem to encounter as soon as we are able to rise from our cradles: finding God; accepting Him for Who He is; and then getting our feet wet in embracing our Salvation by jumping into the Sacred Heart of Christ headfirst. This is the only way to entirely immerse our souls in His Divine Mercy. Sometimes we cannot know where we stand before Him until the fog of our own confusion is lifted and the smoke has cleared from whence He has seared our consciences to wake us up. One thing is for certain; we will always know Him better when it comes time to recline in our battlefield bunker for the night if we spend the greater portion of the day praying for His help. Turning to His grace will also aid us in recognizing our enemies more quickly and the range of opposition we must face when we exit our front doors tomorrow.

Everything we need to know to survive is found in the Wisdom of the Almighty Father. However, we are expected to actually call upon Him to help us, not just sit back and wonder if He will make a giant splash into our consciences like an unexpected monsoon. A man once inaugurated a nation in peril by saying, "We have nothing to fear but fear, itself!" Nevertheless, this is very little consolation when the bullets of reality start flying over our heads during the times we least expect to find ourselves anywhere near the frontline of fire. What is even more worrisome is that the man who was speaking about never giving-in to fear was standing in the midst of the most developed country in the entire world. Imagine if that same 20th century democracy had to face the mean streets of the likes of Haiti everyday! Somehow this is the same way that we should perceive our stature in the conversion of our hearts to the Holy Gospel of Jesus Christ. Taking-up our crosses is never as bad as it seems when we look at how the rest of the world must beg for the slightest ounce of dignity from those who think they have it so bad. Where we stand before the prejudgement of Jesus Christ is often where we actually place ourselves. If we would only comply with His Commandments instead of trying to gerrymander around them all the time, perhaps we could face the Truth with a little more integrity and faith. Telling other people that "God will never give you more to carry than your soul can bear," rings somewhat hollow when coming from the mouth of one of our peers who has never had to suffer a pittance of anything for as long as a day in his life. It bears an eery resemblance to a soundbite from a person who has never lost a close loved-one to death or had a husband or wife walk-out on them while posing the deadpan question of, "I cannot figure out why I don't love you anymore?" Such scurrilous platitudes do very little to soothe our broken hearts. What the Gospel passage which these people are demagoging really means is that God will never ask us to carry any more than He has required from some of the greatest heroes we have ever known who have all since gone-on to become saints of the highest order.

As if life is not an irony enough in itself, we tend to add quite a surplus of our own confusion to the mix which makes our envisionment of the Mercy of God oftentimes too difficult to comprehend. Prosecutors spend their entire careers trying to convince criminal courts that the accused defendants who stand before them should all be found guilty as charged and be punished to the full extent of the law. And, yet, these same attorneys stand naked, themselves, before their God the very moment they die and try to convince Him that they are wholly innocent of their own sins and transgressions. The main purpose He holds at this point in time is trying to decide who the real criminals are in the impending process of separating the sheep from the goats. To His great credit, however, Jesus continues to see these same poor sinners through the eyes of pity with which He deals with everyone else; forever patient and always pardoning. He will wait for as long as it takes for us to evolve to His spiritual school of thought. Sometimes it is difficult to know whether we go to college to learn a trade, or to qualify later for a position in the labor force in which we will actually be taught what to do to earn a living. Our chosen vocation never begins to bloom until we have actually started it; and so it is with human spiritual conversion. We prepare to greet the real world by praying the Holy Rosary so we can best defend the statutes of God once our calling is made. Unfortunately for many of us, we suddenly realize that our gainful employment started yesterday; and our true engagement has already been commenced.

A good starting point would be for us to stop believing that getting on our knees before the Divine Power of Jesus is somehow still beneath our dignity. No powerful group of elitists wants to be told that they are not living-up to their own charter from someone else who is observing them from the outside-in. This same clique will always believe that they are justifiably punishing him by denying him permission to become one in their numbers. If we profess to be living-out the mandates which have been promulgated in the Sacred Scriptures, Jesus will never fail to admonish us to execute His Will correctly. He will always find a way to expose us as being hypocrites if we refuse to follow Him; and that is why many people protest against the Holy Paraclete and finally throw Christ out of the public debate altogether. In most contested fora, speed is not always as important as accuracy; as is the case in our battles against the everyday world. But, we must always prevail upon righteousness until we finally get it right. The concept of timing may be more important than we actually care to realize. God is fully aware of what we need from Him and is more than willing to satisfy our hunger when it is in congruence with His prophecies of the unfolding world. An airplane that is flying in a landing pattern must touch-down on the runway at a precise moment in its glide-path in order to keep from killing everyone aboard. We must likewise know the status of our faith at all times, lest we fail to completely understand the Holy Gospel we are proclaiming so proudly before the rest of humanity which we, ourselves, might tragically choose to question at the end of time.

There is no doubt that our comprehensive unity with Our Savior cannot be accomplished overnight. There are many people who immediately leap into midair while clapping their palms together toward the purpose of celebrating their Christian conversion; but they are not as eager to cheer so loudly once Satan tries to tie their hands behind their backs. Many of us have traveled a great distance in a very brief period of time. It seems not so long ago that we once produced a photograph with a man standing beneath a drop-cloth covering his head with something that appeared to be a bar of miniature stadium lights exploding in his hand. The only details he had to work with were lines of shadows and light. Now, however, we own gadgets that produce digital images which encapsulate every color of the rainbow and can even detect a flyspeck on the side of an elephant's face. God assuredly wants us to realize that we have the capacity for bringing the development of our spiritual faith into the contemporary age to the same degree. When we pray to make it so, He will do everything within His might to show us the way. It is those who do not really believe they can make it who still founder in fear. They stand in stark contrast alongside their brothers who believe that they need no refinement at all to qualify for a blessed judgement on the day they finally die. These are the ones who think that praying is somehow only the art of talking to ourselves. The next time one of them proclaims that they can find no useful purpose in praying the Holy Rosary so their soul will be better prepared to greet Jesus Face-to-face, we should ask them in retort why they feel it necessary to practice their skills on the archery range in order to be able to hit a bull in the eye. They can only dodge so many bullets in their fight against the Truth before their consciences will be hit; and the carnage which will ensue is quite a gruesome sight to behold. That is when God will turn to the rest of Creation and speak loudly about their arrogance while saying, "This program has committed a fatal error and will now shut down." And, the rest of us will know that their fondness for absolution is about to be pronounced dead.

The Son of this same Omnipotent Father knows that it is still not too late for them to amend their ways. The problem rests in the prospect that too many of us are becoming intrigued by the seemingly parallel, and yet, diametric and coexisting counterpart of human life that appears to be humming alongside God's Kingdom which He has somehow allowed to be placed into being by humankind for reasons known only to Him. The facts will eventually reveal, however, that this imagined "secondary world" is composed only of the echoes from our own mortality which keep lingering in our consciousness because we continue to refuse to acknowledge and accept the existing infinity of Paradise. There is only one eternal Salvation; and we shall not find it if we persist in pursuing everything of the Earth and nothing of the Divinity of Christ. There is a great deal to be said about the pride we take in the advancements of our industrialized world. And now, we have even invaded the laboratory for the purpose of "creating" other mortal creatures who might someday resemble ourselves. This may be well and good if the Almighty Father chooses to deposit a spirit there and call it new life. But, He also knows that we do not have the capacity to create a soul. The capstone of our responsibility resides in our assuring Him in return that there is no need for us to spend our years hacking-away at His Divine purposes because we have yet to preserve the lives, dignity, and destinies of the people whom He has already given us to love and protect, such as our little unborn children in the wombs of their mothers and the paupers laying in rags on the street. Sometimes the distinction of our own arrogant rejection of Heaven is so profound that it sounds like fingernails being dragged across a chalkboard amidst the tones of a fifth-grader's piccolo recital.

We have no power or venue that we are not afforded by the Creator of the universe; but it would probably be best for now if we would only accept His challenge to enhance the lot of those who are impoverished and to exhume the consciences of the deadbeats who will not Love His Son who died on the Cross to save us all from condemnation.

Greeting the Thunderheads with a Sweet Valor of Our Own

December 4, 2000

Sometimes it seems as though our future is sitting in the bough of a tree that has yet to be planted by anyone. Oh!, what we would give to see the meandering limbs of this towering oak in advance, sometimes! One of the main reasons why God does not place the remainder of our lives in such a vulnerable position is because He knows that we would not wait for the coming years to fall our way and we would never put-forth the effort to make the ascension required to greet them. We might, instead, search for something within our gasp and try to cut our destiny in half or, perhaps, try to rush the clock and change the calender in order to discover what the residuals of our mortality have to offer in the end. It is probably for the good of everyone concerned that the Creator of the world keeps the horizon of our lives just beyond our best reproach. He knows what scandals might be sleeping there if we ever possessed the power to prophesy the games of chance or what the racehorses may do at the milltrack everyday. This is not the type of contouring He wants us to invoke as we continue to remake our lives for the months and years ahead. We already own the authority to alter the course of human events, but only by praying for the speedy arrival of our own compliance to His Will. We must somehow believe that the torrid winds and towering twisters of lady Nature are an impressionable parable about His Love and that He wants to lay His Kingdom at our feet like giant maples being felled by the whirling tempests of the Earth. But, there is no doubt that we are still as afraid of knowing His power as we are of enduring them. Most of us grew-up as the lucky ones who once played on the floor with our tractors or dollhouses in-hand while waiting for our fathers to return from work or the grocery store so they could raise us into their arms and remind us of how thankful they were that we were their little children back then. Our Creator is no-less affectionate than any of them ever were, or anyone else for that matter, and is just as proud that we have been regained through our acceptance of Salvation in Jesus Christ.

Even though we may not yet completely understand it all, the Love of God will always effect our lives, whether our demeanor is to be confused, repulsed, rebellious, complacent, or benignly accepting in our spiritual response. He does only good, and His intentions are always manifested toward the full development of our greater incorporeal perfection. We will never be able to grow upright or bear fruit if we cannot withstand the buffets of the temporal exile in which our souls and bodies have been temporarily placed. We discover at the last that the Almighty Father actually wants *us* to become the trees and that we should wish to hold the future in our hands through the cleansing Blood of His Beatific Son. Then, we can greet the thunderheads of sorrow and self-pity with a sweet valor of our own, if only we will allow the Holy Spirit to pass gently through the archways of our branches. As time continues to unfold, we quickly learn about the beauty of God and discover the answers to most of our interior questions. We find-out what His Will truly is, when and how we must effect it in the material world, and where we should set-out to evangelize the Gospel of His Word. But, the universal design which seemingly keeps eluding us is the reason behind the incessant interrogative of "why?" Somehow, the wingtip shoes of our dignity and spirituality that the Father in Heaven has given us to wear do not seem to fit too well right now. But, if we begin to walk upright and become conditioned to the pathways of His righteousness, we can always break-them-in slowly by the transition which springs from the obedience inside our hearts. After all, that is what praying for absolution through the Cross of Mount Calvary is all about. It is our wilful interior discernment, Wisdom, strength, and resignation to the very Creator who has set our lives in motion like little wind-up toys, just before He turned us loose to wander aimlessly around the globe and to deplete our energy while struggling in earnest to discover who He really is.

Surely Our Savior does not want us to wear sandals of the everyday world to the celebration of Eternal Life at the Banquet Table in Paradise! It is supposed to be a much more stately dinner than that! We must arrive, instead, in our best apparel so as to blend-in with the rest of the Saints who are already there waiting for our souls at the door. The agony, pain, and discomfort of the spiritual conversion that we are experiencing in the modern-day world is not the paring and sewing of our original Baptismal Gown, for it befitted us once and for all on the day we were sacramentally christened. All we are required to do now is to keep it clean from stain. The struggles we are facing today are actually the tendering of our hearts to holiness so as to be able to wear it with the same purity as when God's Waters of Forgiveness first touched our souls. This is our mandate from the King of all Creation; but, somehow, we still continue to reject the piety which allows us to execute it to total perfection. For example, if we believe that we are the same person at the end of a Holy Hour who we were when we first knelt-down to pray, then we have unwittingly missed the entire point. Jesus Christ enhances the prospects of our saintliness when we implore His Divine intercession like a pit-crew chief preparing a

Winston-Cup NASCAR competitor who is about to jump back into the field for the final laps of the race. Our outlook and conduct must always reflect the better person He is so carefully shaping us to be. There is no reckless marauder or inferior despot who could ever overcome our lead, and none who would ever dare try to knock our lives off course. When Satan or any of his evil dregs attempt to trample on the goodness of our souls, Jesus will always turn to them in defiance and wield His famous proclamation, "Load well your weapons, for your pathway lies over My Dead Body, having long-since been Resurrected from the Grave!"

This is a time of new enlightenment for Christians on the Earth. Jesus has come into the world seeking bill-posters who are willing to erect monuments of faith to announce His impending Return in Glory. Unfortunately for many of us, He is looking upon a globe today which is composed mostly of illiterate delinquents who have never taken the time to learn how to read His signs. And, too, the great plague which exacerbates this awful condition is that He knows full-well that unloved adolescents grow-up to be quite angry men. This is why He wants us all to know that we already belong to the epicenter of His Love in His Agony and Crucifixion on the Cross. Although the Almighty Father may never allow us to be stricken by such pain, grief, misfortune, sacrifice, or sorrow at the juncture where human thought and physical action ultimately intersect, He will most assuredly implore us to travel courageously down nearly every conceivable avenue of preponderance before we completely understand that the Passion, Death, and Resurrection of Jesus Christ is real. While we may not be able to foresee every opportune moment for us to change into saints like goal-posts standing directly before our eyes, we can still perceive His Sacred Heart a whole lot better by comparing the lives we lead everyday with the legendary brevity of the 33 years of His own.

Sooner or later, the point of the conversion of the mortal world becomes an almost too obvious and inevitable proposition to ignore. How much more Truth can God cram into the paragraph which began with the first Word of our Salvation; known as the Annunciation, and the final exclamation point of the Resurrection of Jesus Christ from the Tomb? When will we finally understand that Jesus conquered His own mortality so our own lives would not end like a question mark left dangling in thin air over an empty cavern in the desert? Indeed, the closing of our eyes in eternal rest is only a beautiful semi-colon in the unending passage of our immortal continuation. It is but a brief pause for peaceful reflection and a breath of fresh air as we continue to speak with the voice of Divine Praises to the Perpetuity of All Eternities, the everlasting Redemption that humankind has been seeking for the last 2000 years! This is the belief we profess and the Holy Gospel by which our entire excellence is designed. A human life without faith in the Messianic Christ bears the indignation of an obsolete artifact from a second-hand thrift-store outlet. It is only refuse for the devil's dogs to scratch from the trash and devour in-full, and just valuable enough for the thieves of the netherworld to place on a shelf above a flaming cauldron somewhere. Our rise to ceaseless happiness is a function of whether we choose to hope for our own Salvation in the same way that we have always prayed for the deliverance of those who are already departed from us in death. We are able to dream about what they would do if our positions were suddenly reversed only because we have always envisioned the beautiful sight of their first encounter in seeing the Divine Splendor of God. Our dreams are their metaphysical contributions which serve to magnify our own deposits of faith from their lofty stations beyond their mortal mausoleums.

The Blessed Mother has spoken many times about the impending Triumph of Her Immaculate Heart, often referring to three concise processional periods in which we must partake for our lives to be perfected in Her Son. They are, collectively, our concession to the Wisdom of the Holy Spirit, the rapid response of the holy faithful, being those who lay their lives outright at the feet of Jesus toward their own spiritual enlightenment and the stirring of the collective conscience of the rest of the world, and the expanded period of grace and preparation of the greater body of humankind just prior to the Second Coming of Christ. The latter is an ongoing process of deeper ecclesiastical meditation and a more intense confession of the soul. Its purpose is for the conversion of the remaining lot of sinners who do not yet know their Salvation in the Blood of the Cross, but eventually will in time. They shall spend the rest of their days basking in the Light of eternal absolution because of the sacrifices of their brothers and sisters who knew the Truth all along. These crucial passages are all interconnected and woven together by the Holy Spirit in the Hands of the Blessed Virgin Mary, the Mediatrix of every grace from Heaven and the Co-Redemptress of all humankind. Through the imminent Triumph of Her Immaculate Heart, Mary is the Cauline Matriarch whom has already been enshrined beneath a Crown of Twelve Stars that is celebrated in the Book of Revelation and has been awarded irrevocable permanence at the Seat of God's Wisdom toward the conversion and repatriation of all of His children into Paradise for the everlasting ages to come, sitting now just beyond the horizon of our own expiration. Mary's intercessory Grace is the Reprise of the Son of Man and the final arrival of Jesus Christ in Glory and Truth to Judge both the living and the dead. The petals of Her Holy Rosary are, indeed, the Saints who are now in Heaven; and Her most profound Blossom is Her Sacrificed Son, the singularly-celebrated Savior of the world.

The task is now before us to locate this new meadow of beauty before the sun goes down for good. We often feel disengaged in trying because we do not always know where else to look. The pathway actually resides inside ourselves, at the core of our very being, at the pinpoint-center of our withering hearts. They are fibrillating in exhaustion from our own lack of love; but they are not yet dying in vain because most of us will eventually open them to receive the Holy Spirit just in time to be saved. We often wonder how the road to Paradise can be defined so conservatively and why the Gate seems so narrow at times; and yet, the Kingdom of God is wholly and uniquely interwoven and connected to the mortal world below. The answer is that we are still trying to find the mountain peaks while choosing to live in sin in the valleys at their feet. Our purpose on the Earth should be to prepare ourselves for the indictments of God's Justice by being better peacemakers, healers, servants, and consolers while we are waiting for Christ to return. Although this is often not an easy task to undertake, it was never really quite meant to be. If we are all to become one flock in the paradisial bliss beyond the clouds, will we not also be called to follow the Lamb of God like sheep into an equally sacrificial reparation which has already rescued the world from the fires of lasting perdition? He has put this question upon our tables in no uncertain terms! Which could be worse, being tortured in defense of the Truth for a lifetime, or being burned at the stake in the infernos of Gehenna for the rest of eternity to come? We are expected to decide the fate of our own spiritual destination before Christ ever asks for our answer.

If we choose to embrace this "Troth" of humility, self-denial, penitence, subordination, and holiness, we will be swiftly on our way to being greeted with the Mantle of Sainthood before we ever relinquish our souls to death. Christians already know that such a life seems to be a cyclical rhythm of joy, emotion, suffering, and sorrow. But, these same feelings somehow find themselves in syncopation, not synchronicity, with the forces of the Divine and miraculous which make their way to the surface of what we truly believe. When we live the example that Jesus has left before us in faith, our happiness will always be the more prominent melody to which our gleeful souls shall dance and the strain from which all other arrangements in life are derived. We are reminded of the reason we own mirrors and why we erect them in their appropriate places inside our homes. Without them, we would never be able to know how other people see us; while we often forget that they can only perceive the outer-shell of who we really are. Even as we exit the friendly confines of our personal abodes, we are the only ones who can produce a suitable image from inside our hearts for the rest of Creation to see. Is that person always the image and likeness of Christ? Do we emit the Light of Love by our words and actions when we take our souls onto the streets? By the same token, the reflection of our loyalty to Jesus is how God sees us as His Holy Spirit is perched in the parlours of our faith. We must always strive to become as pious as the Perfection who is looking back at us, and to taut our souls inside the Hands of Our Almighty Shepherd so He can shear us bare of any residual hesitation we might possess while living-out the Holy Gospel for the rest of Creation to see.

God Doth Have A Sense of Humor

December 5, 2000

If the faith which Jesus freely gives us is as strong as He intends it to be, other people will be able to feed from it to the good of their own enlightenment, counsel, consolation, and direction. There is no disguising a Christian soul amongst a crowd of nonbelievers because he is always the one with the aura around his face. The Blessed Mother once offered a parable about seeing a group of people standing in a foyer listening to one of their members speaking; but we do not have the advantage of being able to hear anyone. How do we know which one is talking? The one whose lips are shaping his words, of course. This is not unlike the ability of the world to recognize in whom the Holy Paraclete has taken residence. We know by physical signs that there is Wisdom and knowledge in the spirit of this fortunate soul. He is the one who truly cares about the condition of the lives of other people; while some in his midst could not give a finch about how the rest of the world survives. The gentleness of the children of Mary is one of their greater assets and most distinctive attributes because they understand without apprehension that the Blessed Mother is the Trestle who connects their souls to the Blood of Jesus Christ. When we convoke our Rosary groups at the center of Her Immaculate Heart, we will feel a certain sense of ease and inevitability about our own Salvation when it comes our time to die. She has told us many times that it is nonsensical for us to believe that God would ever surrender our souls to the abyss below the Earth when He has already borne the grief of the loss of His own Son to the Cross to save us. He is presently thanking Himself because He now holds Jesus back at His side again.

The Truth cannot be hidden that the awful torture which Our Lord endured to expiate our sins has filled the cup of human Salvation to overflowing; and the dew that is forming on its golden sides is comprised of the hundreds of thousands of sacrifices that His little people have made throughout the centuries which have served to convert the sinners whom He placed in their midst. Through their unification with the Cross and their own agonizing pain, the Resurrection of the Mystical Body of Christ is now a foregone conclusion.

What is yet to be discovered is whether everyone alive today will be a participant of it. People who believe that all souls have the opportunity to be redeemed already live in this beautifully amberic state of Love amidst the commotion of a quite stubborn and cynical world. Their anticipation is not to be diminished by the ranting of any faithless naysayers who seem to have nothing better to do than try to destroy someone else's hope. The impervious confidence of Christianity tells us without a hint of ambiguity that Heaven will always help us, God will generously bless us, Mary will humbly teach us, Jesus will boldly protect us, the Holy Spirit will clearly guide us, and the Cross will courageously Redeem our souls. The Truth cannot be disseminated much more generously than that. We have already been told that the signs which lay in the offing are now being described as an absolute *mirabile dictu*, a marvel to relate to humanity, because of their ascribed linkage to the Will of the Almighty Father, the Love of His Sacrificed Son, and the Divine Nature of His higher Creation.

Jesus Christ knows that the outcome of our work in His Holy Name will always bear the reflection of His Love and that we will foster the sweetness of His peace, chastity, decency, healing, and compassion because of the Life He has given us to share. His Immaculate Mother has told the world about the Compass of Light that our conversion to Her Son is already bringing to humanity. It is an Arch of new awareness and the brandishing of Eternal Justice. We are called to be like little children in our movement toward the Cross. But, do we know what this really means? Perhaps it is the impression we held of the world back when we were younger and how our lives eventually influenced us to become the elders we are today. Maybe that is why we had two pet cats, but never really knew what their function was. Could this Arch also possibly explain the reason why we kept a bunny rabbit in a cage for fear that it may have run away and we would have lost our fuzzy little friend? Somehow this Compass of Light is precisely the kind of a comprehensive review of our lives as a whole from whence we remember the more simple facets that once existed before. If it is, it certainly has a lot of explaining to do. On the more gentle side, it might be the reason why we always wanted our bedroom to be on the corner of the house where we could see the trains go by and watch the cars passing each other on the street. Sometimes we would get out of bed when we heard the humming engines of our best friends' sports cars and flip the light switch on and off just to tell them hello again. No doubt, it must also be why we painted a giant mural on our wall to remind us every day of the fashions we liked the most. Whatever the extension of this archway of trust, we also recognize it as being the reason why we envision the present moment as our true best of times; that it is finally our day of resurgence in the sun when we can finally boast of having nothing more in our grasp than the bountiful Love of Jesus Christ, while we still cling with the grip of death to the mustard-seed that has become our new partner of Love and our life of higher hope.

This fresh springtime of Christian peace is our commission to take hold of the passing opportunities to do better which once kept slipping beyond our grasp in the years gone-by; like offering our opinions to people who really care to hear them now, giving advice to strangers who have never trusted us before, and seeing little children the same way we always wanted to be perceived. Now, it is alright to scribble in the margins of our homework papers if the notion strikes our fancy; and we can push-away that bowl of hominy which almost made us as sick at the dinner table as when we took our first sip of beer, knowing full-well that nothing else we taste in this life will ever be that bitter again. Indeed, it is the Truth in knowing that, by the time Our Heavenly Father is finished cultivating our hearts here on Earth, not a single ghost from the past will ever be able to haunt us again. We can now approach our lives in Jesus with determination, self-control, and the advance knowledge that we have already begun to succeed. Who is to say? We might even begin to see the better side of circuit judges who really do care about justice, and municipal policemen who are seemingly more interested in preventing crime than they are in inflicting punishment. Yes, this new season of enlightenment is in knowing that the hopes we once held as little children are speedily on their way to coming true today and that our teachers in times-past were not really disciplinary monsters whom nobody else would even hire to carry logs from the woods to burn in their fireplaces. We can now behave like benign preschoolers in a world of dread and fear where God is our Omnipotent Father and the Blessed Virgin Mary is the Mother we always wanted to have. We can go to sleep at night beneath Her Mantle to the tune of sweet-nothings resounding in our ears and the Angels reclining at our feet.

The more gruesome side of the mortal world seems to subside somewhat when we beckon the Hosts of Heaven to take our sorrows away. This does not imply that it is not still there; it just simply means that we can face it better than we ever could before. We can pray with more confidence that every heart can feel like our own if only they will cast aside their inner-abstention and invite the Holy Spirit to reside in them as well. Their awakening from the depths of night can be like our own enkindled spirits; for we rise from our beds and know beyond any silhouette of delusion that Emanuel is with us today. We no longer live life in degrees or ever wonder again just what the parameters of a stone's throw might be or the exact measurements of a "skosh." We begin to see seemingly impossible events in the world and automatically attribute them to our Almighty Father in Heaven.

Who, after all, was the first to say that, "God doth have a sense of humor?" Everyone has heard about eight-year-old DeAndra Anrig who found herself airborne when the string of her kite was snagged by an airplane flying over Shoreline Park, California in March 1988. The little girl was lifted ten feet off the ground and carried 33 yards before she ever let go! And, what about the fisherman off the west coast of Sweden who found an engagement ring that had fallen into the sea in 1994, only to be consumed by a mussel and turn-up two years later in a shellfish which he had caught by chance? The amazing wonders of humankind never seem to desist. The newspaper headlines ran amok about the story of little Kristin Loendal, a nine-year-old girl from Oslo, Norway, who was hit by a car while riding her bicycle in May 1998, tumbled through midair, and then landed in the bed of a pickup truck that was traveling in the opposite direction. Other than a few bumps and bruises and a nearly broken heart, she was not injured at all!

Let us not forget Ali Abdel-Rahim of Egypt who was pronounced dead after having drowned in the coastal waters off Alexandria Beach and regained consciousness in a morgue refrigerator in which he had been laying for over three hours. He was awakened by a loud bang and unfamiliar voices and grabbed the hand of an attendant who was trying to close the drawer in which he was temporarily entombed. As if that is not yet enough, a 22-year-old Bosnian man was chasing a fly out of his attic window and plunged 59 feet into the Limmat River in Ennetbaden, Switzerland, surviving the fall with only slight injuries. He bounced-off the roof of his tenement building and the awning of a nearby restaurant and into the depths of the rolling waters below. We also wonder whether God was chuckling when an employee of the Coors Brewing Company in Golden, Colorado flipped the wrong switch and sent 77,000 gallons of fresh brewsky into a nearby creek bed? On and on, the list of quirks continue to emerge to stir our tufts of humor and truly have us wondering whether God has played any hand in modeling them. This same approach to life and lightness of heart is our awareness that Heaven's Compass of Light is quite far reaching, indeed.

Rediscovering Ourselves All Over Again

December 6, 2000

When Adam and Eve proudly told God that they had chosen to become His equal and fell on their faces into original sin, all of our souls were seared by the firebrand of their profound disobedience. Not even the many historical Doctors of the Church have ever held the power to remove the scars which were inflicted upon us at the beginning of time. However, through His infinite Love and Divine Wisdom, God chose to sacrificially remove the stains from our "being" by placing the Scars on the Body of Jesus Christ, instead. Our souls can never be purified by any other means. They cannot be blanched, distilled, dissembled, eradicated, or diffused in an effort to make us the pristine children we were first created to be. Only the Blood of Jesus Christ can remake us into those perfect people again. Our initial purity will never be restored by employing any form of antiseptic, ammonia, chlorine, peroxide, or a magic potion from an artesian well. Neither can our transgressions be forced into remission by applying any camphor, cortisone, pumice, or any sparkling lavaliere that we just so happened to pick-up at a local pawn shop to wear around our neck. We would never know where or how to apply them appropriately, anyway, because our souls are completely invisible to everyone alive except the Hosts of Paradise. Not even a powdered cleanser or gritted paper could ever scrape away the corruption we have inherited from the first Fall of man. Only the waters of our Baptism and the Blood of Jesus Christ can make us pure and whole once again. We should always remember that we are born into the world with a human composition which is fully knowable to Him, but not with an identity that He easily recognizes as being one with His Own. It is only by what we do in the short span of our lifetime that allows Him to finally turn His Glorious Face in our direction and call us by name. Sometimes we ponder all the ways we might remain anonymous to Him; but after we summon the Holy Spirit to take rest inside our hearts, we are as singularly extraordinary in distinction as the Saints in Heaven, themselves.

For now, are we not just a minuscule blade of grass in a meadow somewhere or a grain of sand in the desert, or a sliver of wheat in a field, or a flake of snow in a plummeting avalanche? Indeed, are we not simply a face in the crowd of some six-billion people who live on the surface of the globe? If we refuse to make our intentions known before the Holy Cross on Mount Calvary, that is all we will ever become. It is a decision which must be made through our most contemplative thoughts and implemented through the Love we already share with God. It is widely known that the process of developing the retentive power of the memory is called "mnemonics," and is a counterpart and complement to the sentimental allurements of the heart. The former is a deliberate exercise in obsessive consternation, while the latter is an involuntary response to our insatiable desires for grace, a stronger spiritual faith, and a revived moral constitution. The mind has oftentimes been regarded as being somewhat like a snob to the soul, but the heart is always its best of friends. Let us allow our thoughts to be not so much the solvency of our anguish and sorrow, but the dais upon which we place our more noble of traits which will allow us to say "yes" to God from the inside-out. Our collective composition has been Passionately ensanguined by the Blood of Christ so we can be made new again in every possible means and so we may become completely enraptured by the Absolution that no man has ever before been able to secure on his own.

So, as soon as we grow old enough to find-out who we are in the midst of the frail mortal world, God suddenly asks us to rediscover ourselves all over again. He does this through His Supreme perpetual Nature in the presence of the Holy Trinity, of which He is One of the Three real and distinct subsistencies in the singular substance of Truth. This is the same Love which He asks us to embrace with the belief of innocuous lambs; and these are the facts as we have known them to be true from the first moment that Mary offered Her Fiat to the Archangel Gabriel. It is also why our spiritual faith should never once be characterized by any transparent presumptions or some enigmatic layperson's faulty hypotheses. The Almighty Father has already told us that His Kingdom is unequivocally real and He wishes for each and every one of us to become a new person living inside it. Thereafter, we shall no longer be granules of stone or slivers of hay anymore. We are to know beyond the farthest recesses of our interior hearts that God not only appears to exist, but He is the definitive Creator of all humankind and the vertical compression between the physical world and the spiritual constructs of His higher perfection. However, He is also quite aware that there is an exponentially incalculable number of opinions and lifestyles of His people on the Earth who often harbor too many hidden chronic and deep-seated animosities toward one another with regard to their different races, religions, philosophies, and attitudes of behavior that are not likely to be reconciled overnight. What the Holy Spirit is now attempting to do through the millions of good Christians who believe in Him is to remake the larger family of man into a single composition of one voice that is comprised of the various elements of diversity which still exist simultaneously and to superimpose His own vision and power over all the world like a warm woolen blanket covering our souls in the dead of a long winter's night. God is calling us all to the mountaintop of His holiness and He fully expects that the frostbite of hatred and indifference of the knaves around us will be nipping incessantly like daggers at our feet.

How does Jesus intend to pull-off this seemingly impossible coalescence? By dispensing the Seven Sacraments of the Holy Roman Catholic and Apostolic Church onto the Earth below Him, under the leadership and guidance of the Supreme Pontiff in Saint Peter's Square in Rome. These multiple Graces are the superabundance of God's own pious faith in His people so that we, too, will come to believe in Him as we commend our souls to His Merciful Heart. Our grandfathers and their own before them never once retreated from upholding the stature and quality of the explicit spiritual excellence which has become the foundation of our contemporary faith today. They all accepted what God's humble people still seem to agree upon now; that the erelong arrival of the Savior of the World in Redemptive Glory could never come anytime too soon . Moreover, they also embraced the same benevolent Mother to lead them to Him who is speaking through the Holy Spirit in the world once again. Mary, the Queen of Heaven and Earth, is the foremost and preeminent Matriarch in every universe of Creation. No other woman could ever approach Her stationed perfection or come close to imitating Her charm. She has been sinless from the very beginning of Her Immaculate Conception, ever since God placed Her beautiful soul into the womb of Her mother, Saint Anne. This humble Lady of Perpetual Help is a Saint of Her own Divine inclination who consistently replicates, defines, reflects, and expounds the Will of our Almighty Father in Paradise. The messages which She has come to dispense to humanity are far greater than any highly developed composition of transcendent verse or poetic reams of expression; they actually reflect the essential Commandments from God on High to be heard by the same souls on the Earth whom Her Son was Crucified to redeem.

Now is the suitably proper and befitting time for us to conform our larger purpose in life to complying with God's kind, obliging, and professorial statutes and ordinances which have been handed-down by the Faith Church on Earth for hundreds of years and counting. The preciseness of our faith must ring as clear in God's sight as the heavens that are blue; never to be shaded by a hint of doubt or opalescence, and never cold or clammy to the spiritual touch. By all means, we should carry our faith in our hearts like babes in their cradles as we approach the Altar of Sacrifice for the Eucharistic Celebration of the Holy Mass. We often enter the Sanctuary with our consciences wailing aloud; and God has never once failed to answer us back again. That is why we must come forward to His Table of Love with the absolute purpose of amendment in our hearts. This is much more than just our mutual rapprochement or our forewarning to do better whenever we find the time. It is our plea to Our Father in Heaven to accept us as we truly want to been seen by Him. As soon as the opening processional begins to commence the Holy Mass, our own contrition must be the macebearer for our profession of faith as we earnestly acknowledge our offensive nature and the cause of our actions or negligence that may have led others into temptation, fear, harm, or regret. The Penitential Rite which ensues, formerly known as the *februarius*, is the secondary occasion of our expiation, purgation, and initial blessing, not to be confused with the primary Sacrament of Reconciliation into which we should have entered long before Mass ever began. No one should dare to take a position in the roll-call of communicants or approach the Sacred Host while having any knowledge of any residual or venial transgressions in their hearts, let alone any perverse or rancid mortal sins that shall certainly take us to the doorway of Hell if we do not confess them before we lay our bodies down to die. It is only through this willing acknowledgment in what we have done or failed to do that we are capable of transmitting, progressing, and proceeding together toward a deeper unity within the Passion and Crucifixion of Christ.

We must forever acknowledge that the Sacred Mysteries do not just represent an honorary remembrance of Christ's 2000-year-old Passion and Death, but rather is the same ongoing Crucifixion which is taking place on Mount Calvary right before our very eyes! This is why we believe, desire, and trust that everything we pray for will eventually come to pass as we place all of our petitions in the depths of the Redemptive Cup! There is an old archaic expression which declares that we too often, "hope against hope," sometimes. What this really means is that certain people still cling to their elusive expectations, even when the present factual circumstances do not warrant it anymore. That is not what we are doing when we participate in the Holy Sacrifice of the Mass. The type of faith which we hold in our hearts is, instead, one of a true and credible anticipation that the fulfillment of the Holy Gospel will occur yet in our lifetime. If we approach the Sacred Altar with only a spavined disbelief about our own true worthiness in Heaven, this is what God will allow us to carry away in our hands; even though our souls are all still indented with a new mark of Grace every time we receive the Body and Blood of His Sacrificed Son. Some people do not truly realize the expanse of the miracle which occurs every time we receive Holy Communion. There are principals, priors, magistrates, and abbots who would walk a thousand miles apiece to become as perfect as we are the moment the Body of Christ makes contact with our tongue. This is the faith in which we believe and the Most Blessed Sacrament whom we embrace as being the Salvation of our souls and the Conqueror over our detention to the grave.

What? This is Opportunity for the Many?

December 7, 2000

There is no doubt that modern Christianity is the all-inclusive, logical, justified, principled, sanctioned, and authorized belief in the Triune God of all humanity. Every one of us can take great solace in this preeminent Truth. Through all of the ironies, miscalculations, and seeming contradictions in what we see in the everyday world, we continue to realize that Jesus Christ is fully in charge of His Kingdom in Heaven and is still shaping Creation below on the Earth. But, when we begin to look around at the perceptible aspects of nature and the conduct of mortal men, we oftentimes wonder what impression He actually wants us to render from the attributes of life which do not seem to be congruent with His Light of Love, His lessons, and His teachings. No matter what we choose to do while we live in mortality, or with our death hereafter, our soul will always exist somewhere; and we must begin now to make plans for that inevitable engagement. As we continue to witness the unfolding of the universe, we always have the inner-urge to assess the process of its socialization when compared to our own knowledge of ethical propriety and justice. Thereafter, we decide to participate in it when and where it seems fitting that God would be better served by our efforts. But, many underlying incongruities continue to haunt our souls almost everywhere we look these days. There is no doubt that thousands of us are still praying for the end of the drought and blight which have ravaged the driest areas of the globe as a whole; while we look across the distant hemispheres in awe to see that it is already raining in sheets over the expanse of the teeming oceans. How much more backwards could this ever be? We have willingly conceded that our birth from our mother's womb is not accompanied by a table of contents for daily living or a syllabus in our hands to tell us what time the Truth may arrive; but we know full-well that we must master the art of divinity correctly if we are ever to be made acceptable again in the Mind and Heart of God.

Our efforts are hindered somewhat when we see things that just do not seem to make any degree of good sense. The greatest inequity always emerges with regard to the distribution of wealth among the peoples of the nations. Why does it seem like God allows the richest magnates on the planet to dictate the standards by which the poorest of all must comply in order to borrow their money? It is as though they collect themselves in a board room somewhere and say, "What exorbitant interest rate shall we charge them this week,?" in an effort to collect as much usury as they can before they finally get caught by the Interstate Commerce Commission. How can these same wealthy autocrats align themselves with a conservative social movement in America which pretends to be"pro-life" by nature, and yet work so hard to persuade the very government they disdain so much to execute the highest number of convicted felons within a given calendar year? In this same vein of hypocrisy, it is almost an elegiac expression of gross contradiction to celebrate the life of someone who has just given a million-dollar scholarship fund to their Alma Mater and is forced to drive past their neighboring ghettoes and county breadlines in order to get to the commencement ceremony at which they will receive their Doctoral Degree in Human Letters and their philanthropic Award of Personal Distinction. Could not the poor on the streets to whom they turned their backs have used the money better, rather than enhance the prospect of graduating more intellectuals to place in the pool of lawyers and brokers who will eventually inherit control of the ongoing new economy? On top of all that, there are those precious faithful Roman Catholics who traveled to attend the ordination of their new Bishop at their midwestern Diocesan Cathedral in December of 1999, only to discover that they were turned-away at the door because the event was being held by "invitation only," and the crowd inside consisted mainly of Protestant leaders, prominent politicians, and glory-seekers who would never attempt to attend a daily Mass if their very lives depended on it. The poor souls who fill those church pews day-in and day-out were apparently just keeping them warm until the "real" dignitaries finally found a good enough reason to show-up. What a whitewash of deceit in the making! God knows that the "first" in His Kingdom will eventually be those little prayerful servants who came to receive the Holy Eucharist like clockwork without ever requiring the need for someone near them to bang a gong, crash a cymbal, take a bow for a flashbulb photograph, or to gloat before a newspaper reporter in order to honor God the way He should be properly worshiped and praised on every other day of the year.

Indeed, as if that is still insufficient, many have been the times when loving Catholics attended the various Novenas which are celebrated throughout the Christian Year, praying for peace and charity in the world, while those who really need to pray come racing-by on the avenues outside the front door of the vestibule in BMW's, Cadillacs, Corvettes, and Lincoln Town Cars. As if to add further insult to injury, the ushers then take up a collection after the Holy Rosary is recited to help feed the poor, while those who have just driven-by them stop at the next intersection to pump $40.00 worth of gasoline into their cars to keep them purring along. Is something amiss in all of this tawdry evidence? Those who have very little money in their pockets go to their respective parishes to pray for the conversion of the rich, yet they become the ones from whom the collection is solicited. The discussion of these greater issues in our private lives with regard to how they affect our interpersonal affairs and the public at large should always be centered around the Most Holy Eucharist. Perhaps now, everyone will know the real reason why the Immaculate Mother of God is trying to lead us all to the Most Blessed Sacrament for a little dose of the Truth. She knows full-well that the maturing agenda of the Earth is a much larger prospect than the flat surface we see from our purview on the ground to the nearest horizon everyday. Her call is to a much more geodetic survey of the needs of humanity by enlisting our spiritual support for people we do not even know who live past the curvature of the globe from where we make our homes at night.

Just when it seems like we finally understand the proper order of things and the apparent list of priorities that God has laid-out before us, we are hit smack-in-the-face with those glaring inconsistencies again. The happiest day of our lives is when we take a bride or a husband during the Sacrament of Holy Matrimony. But, how almost mythically excruciating it must become for surviving spouses to ponder their departed loved-ones after spending decades on-end being one in their singular flesh. These mourning heirs can only recline in a livingroom chair where they used to enjoy talking about the topics of the day and think about the hands they once held for so long that had served them so well, now being folded neatly together by a complete stranger working in a funeral home because there is no life inside to move them anymore. Such traumas of the heart are almost too numerous to mention nowadays, but an essential fact remains true through it all. God still loves us to the death; and we must always believe that those who have died have gone-on to His Celestial City of Light where we shall all bask in the sunshine of Eternity someday. Humankind must never forget that the genial protection of Jesus' Love is always sympathetic, cordial, and favorable to life, growth, strength, comfort, and peace. He knows what we suffer because He has endured the same Agony before us. It is as though He is standing now in Paradise wearing His Vestments of Kingship amongst the Angels and Saints who honor Him there; while He has dedicated the purple Maniple near His left sleeve in remembrance of the countless sorrowful hearts who are still enchained by depression and fear on the mortal Earth below.

The subject at hand always returns to our ongoing struggle to overcome and avoid the human error which prevents us from seeing His compassionate Heart to the best of all possible worlds. His urgency is not only that we work toward the greater containment of our sins, but that we eradicate them altogether from ever taunting our souls again. We can do this by dedicating our spirits to contemplative prayer and through serving those who need our help the most. The flow of spiritual Wisdom from the Throne of God is much more than a channelizer, watercourse, river, or a brook. We can never once complain that we have ever suffered from a lack of His telling us what to do. The Holy Spirit has almost deluged us with such an advisory briefing in the person of Jesus Christ that we could all live to be a hundred years old and never be able to scarf the foam off of His cold ready-stein. We often tend to rush-to-judgement about what the subject of God's designs really mean in our emphatic demands for receiving something more, and in our brash and intemperate immoderation which keeps us all from waiting in patience for His responsive predicates to finally arrive. It seems almost too unbearable that our Creator seems to be holding all of the playing cards in His Hands; but we tend to forget that we are the ones who are concealed so cunningly in the cuff of His Chasuble now. Satan cannot win a paltry pence anymore because those who embrace the Divine Love of Jesus Christ represent the infiltration of His righteousness into an otherwise oblique mortal world. We do not have to wait for the hidden intentions of our Almighty Father to completely unfold before we can know in advance what they will eventually be. Jesus Christ *is* His Holy Will Who is already revealed to Creation.

Now, we do not have to dwell on the anxieties of the unknowable future anymore or rue the ironies which we cannot seem to rectify because Jesus has transfixed their solution in place. He is simply waiting in the wings of Paradise for the rest of the world to come-up to His spiritual speed. We see the reflection of His soul in the natural universe and in our own affection for the true greatness of His lofty dignity, imposing character, sovereign grandeur, and the overwhelming patience of His Divine Mercy. Now, we can live in harmony on the Earth and everyone else whose spirit is bound for Heaven will like it all the more. Indeed, if peace always remains the essence of itself, there can never be any war inside its midst. It must be wholly free from ever again falling victim to the halters of disrespect, the bindings of hatred, the snares of neglect, or the scorn of isolationism. Jesus Christ is the Author and Finisher of our faith; and He has sent a Divine tranquility into the world that we could never exhume from under the ground by ourselves. If peace ever took-on a detectible frame, it would surely appear like an apparition of a mighty steed with streamers on his tail, tall in stature, with a blond mane, blue eyes, and a glowing halo above his head. In truth, we must all become the horsemen of this great icon of Love and human decency if such a hallowed placidity is ever to deliver us on his back before the elegance of the King of Redemption.

At last, we must all turn to the Roman Catholic Church to make us the saints we are supposed to become. Our journey is one of total renewal, reparation, faith, service, absolution, and reward. Our heart tells us that these things unfold from inside us the very first moment we hear a priest say, " *pax vobiscum*, peace be with you!" Our struggle is always one of opening the heart to a greater degree and knowing that we cannot just "think" that we are Christian people. There is no room for the absolute rationalism which some people would like to see play a more prominent role in the Catholic Church because human reason cannot be separated from the Guiding Hand of Divine Revelation and can never, itself, exist as an adequate source for discovering the Truth or sustaining our religious faith. God has made an express demand as a condition of our acceptance of the New Covenant Christ that we must place all our hope in His Sacrifice and Resurrection as the cause of our Salvation from the very moment He first enters our hearts. Jesus has redeemed our souls with His entire Mind, Body, Soul, and Strength because He is the complete Revelation of the Love of God for humanity. Hence, we should be willing to offer Him nothing less in return. We must lift our suffrages to His awaiting ears and refrain from trying to calculate His every response in advance of our prayers. If we never do anything else regarding our relationships with other people toward the maintaining of world peace, we must never once allow ourselves or those who represent our spiritual interests to ever yield to the temptation of redressing old wounds or to breach our solemn promises of forgiveness that we have mutually exchanged in the past.

God always recognizes the legitimacy of our faith by how much we are willing to love our fellow man, by what we will give-up to prove it, and by what sacrifices we are willing to make when we first hear His Voice calling in the night. If we "...harden not our hearts," we will succeed in becoming the likeness of His Son and, therefore, be pleasing in the sight of the entire Paradisial Court. The miraculous intervention of the Holy Spirit does not depend upon us for His own survival, but we most assuredly cannot become a more benevolent people by locking Him out in the cold. Those among us who doubt this Truth are reminded of the great Saint, Thomas. He once proclaimed that he would not believe Jesus to be the New Messiah until he could place his hands into the wounds of His Sacrificed Body which had only recently been raised from the Tomb. Just for the record, the name "Thomas," means "twin," and we have yet to know whether he ever truly had one or not. Perhaps humanity-at-large can now become his identical brother and, somehow, go back in time and remind him that we could never be influenced by his lack of blameless faith. Let us be the sibling who never doubted for an instant that the Holy Son of God has been Resurrected from the Sepulcher for good! We must live this prophecy now and invite Saint Thomas to come to our aid in the ongoing struggle for Truth which the people of the modern age so desperately need to win!

The Dignified Virtues of Our Spiritual Convalescence

December 8, 2000

We sometimes wonder why our hair turns gray, our eyes begin to wince, and our souls grow weary in a world in which we seem to hold absolutely no sovereignty over what we see before us or where we are eventually going. Our consciousness is seemingly pummeled from the first moment we awaken in the morning until we cry ourselves to sleep at night by the tragedies which have befallen humanity like a hailstorm in the wilderness. We wonder why so many societies have almost made a sport out of spitting in the Face of God as though it is some sort of unstoppable global pandemic that has now spread completely beyond our control. Those who really care about solving the awful onset of mental depression and our dissatisfaction with the status quo pray from the plunkets of their inner-being for some type of gnostic nobleman to step from behind the sunset hills and finally bring all of this to an amicable end. The horrendous carnage we see before our eyes everyday almost defies the imagination of what could still become our worst nightmares of disillusionment, poignance, the mystifying, and the surreal. They are a series in a greater portion of defining anomalies which splatter the reality of the unfolding world that, when combined with the extraordinary and mundane, compose the never-ending saga of human events that pass before the curtain of mortal life as time keeps traveling by. There are other such scenes, however, which are somewhat more subtle and sensitive to the restless spirit than their counterparts seem to be. A persistent description of life presently exists that is not hailed very often because it is an unsavory connotation to the situations which we often take for granted, a subtitle to a novel that has never been written, and a caption to a photograph which is almost too painful to take. We look through the bittersweetness of our tears rolling down our cheeks in shocking amazement at what we see sometimes.

What are some of these almost "hallowed" and preemptive visions that we have seen which tell us a greater story than anyone else could ever speak or write? There is no challenging the fact that each one of them indicates a progressive world which is still in transition, a series of events that are pending and not quite concluded; and perhaps others which have come to full closure while the remnants of their passing have left an indelible echo of pain, pride, or even social chagrin in our hearts. Perhaps some of them would include such occasions as when we find certain artifacts from years gone-by, like an antiquated baby carriage that has been left stranded in someone's attic for over fifty years, or seeing an ancient upright piano sitting beside it with a tarpaulin covering its top. There are many additional visions which give us a fleeting moment to reflect upon what has once been, and what may follow when we are least expected to notice. It is a hollow feeling to look at a cape launchpad in Florida about an hour after a space-shuttle has taken-off into outer space, as if all eyes are now looking only toward the heavens, while the support that never waned remains in secluded elegance in ashes upon the ground. And, some people shrug in contemplation when they see a Major League Baseball diamond in the midwinter off-season with two feet of snow covering the pitcher's mound in swirling powdery drifts. Others have the same sentiments when they walk into a huge empty auditorium or a field gymnasium following a crucial convention or a decisive sports event that has finally revealed who the real winners and losers are.

There are countless less-celebrated sights, too, that bring just a moment of hesitation to the casual thoughts which compose our mental disposition. It is a strange feeling to see an old abandoned automobile seat sitting all by itself alongside an interstate highway a hundred miles from the nearest exit ramp, or an artificial limb laying haphazardly in a pile on the hallway floor. Just as remarkable are such things as a pair of eyeglasses that were seemingly just tossed onto a closet shelf with no lenses in their frame, an empty antique refrigerator with its doors standing ajar, a Crucifix found in the bottom of a bunker on a battlefield from a war that has long been over, or perhaps a busy intersection where the stoplights have malfunctioned and the traffic is jammed from bumper to bumper with the sound of horns blaring through the air amidst people screaming at the top of their lungs. Imagine what it would be like to enter a courtroom and find all the jurors wearing tuxedos with derbies atop their heads. What about the occasion when we have seen a hearse stopped at a gas station while waiting their turn at the pump ahead of us? We have often wondered whether there was actually a corpse inside, but were always too hesitant to let our curiosity be known to anyone. Other situations seem to stop the clock on the wall altogether as if all time has become one, while others garner only our slightly parting glance. Do we recall ever seeing a television playing in the lobby of a school commissary somewhere, but there was not a soul within a hundred yards to watch it? And, what are our thoughts when we see an empty wheelchair sitting in the middle of a sidewalk downtown, or a lightbulb glowing in a lamp that has no shade to cover its glare? Is the sight of a pair of stained curtains blowing outside a second story window without a screen to hold them back a statement about the economic conditions of the poor souls who live inside? What pause do we take in finding a spent shotgun shell in the middle of a drugstore parking lot, or hearing a crash in our house through the bedroom wall in the middle of the night when we have lived alone for years? And, every one of us has cringed at the thought of seeing someone plummeting to the ground after leaping from an airplane when their parachute has suddenly refused to open. We would much rather see a geyser of crude-oil come gushing to a hundred-feet in the air on the hidden acreage of a farmer's land who is about to lose everything he ever had because he cannot afford to make the mortgage payments anymore.

Even through all of this, humanity somehow maintains his drive to carry-on in the name of survival and the bequeathing of his heritage to the ages. Our hope may be slightly frayed right now, but it is never quite permanently deferred. It might be cracking a little at the seams, but it is not yet broken in-half. Indeed, it may be increasingly more difficult to unearth it by the hour, but it shall never become certifiably extinct. Since God first set our spirits upon the soiled Earth below our feet, we have been almost infatuated by life and the universe at large. It is in not yet knowing the reason why that we continue to fight for the Truth. Once we have consummated our charge for discovery, we will understand at last that every decent aspect of our lives resided inside us all along in the presence of essential Love. We will know at the end of time that Love has never been a matter of frequency, as today's popular culture would have us believe, but is instead a measure of our sustained and intense desire to see the unveiled revelation of the future first-hand. As we embrace our brothers and sisters more closely in this age-old creative desire, we see ever more distinctly that our Love is also our longevity, commitment, sincerity, surrender, and servitude for all we will ever become. Our Love exudes the dignified virtues of sympathy, modesty, discretion, and faith. It is our spiritual convalescence, our new renaissance, our interior purgation, and the widespread expression of our finished identity. The only thing that Love is "not" is any force which diminishes the Divine, the perfect, the pure, and the anticipation of safely delivering new life from the womb. Love can be violated by any malevolence that breaches the peace in our hearts and the community as a whole as it has been so appropriately defined by the Holy Spirit of God in the New Covent Scriptures. Love is our sustenance of life, our emollience beyond our death, and our resuscitation from the boiling waters of any self-incrimination which may try to hold us back from forgiving ourselves before Heaven at the end of time. It is the wings that have supplanted our legs and the vision which has taken-away our blindness in light of the unknowable galaxies that still reside at a distance just beyond our reach. It is the integrity of our innocence, but not with the slightest hint of naivete. Moreover and again, it means never stooping to exploit someone else's uninhibited personal affections for the advancement of our own private whims or material gain.

Indeed, Love is the spiritual energy of our hearts, our genuine trustworthiness, and our interior goodness come true. Even after the passing of a seeming infinity of centuries which have slipped into history by now, true Love is our admission that we still do not have all the answers to the question of why we cannot yet contain our faults and spiritual misgivings to the height of our best control. It is our valued confession before Almighty God that we really do not know how to love our suffering brethren on the Earth as we really ought, but we shall never quit the fight until we, ourselves, have become the noonday bell in Creation which rings so loudly that God is forced to place His ageless Hands over His temples to keep from hearing our call. If we do these things well, Jesus Christ will lift our feet from the muck of our own transgressions before they dry into permanent cement and we become stuck in the mortal world forever like a clothesline post in a prison infirmary. If we love Him both now and forever, Jesus will grant us His patented rights to celebrate life everlasting with Him in Paradise. By seeing the evasiveness of our own reality well, by never growing stale in our faith because of the trite backdrop of the everyday world, and by growing our Love for Salvation to its highest peak through the Wisdom of refusing to give-in, we will have already booked our flight on the Chartered Bliss of Eternity which is bound for the far eastern skies.

The Holy Trinity Will Always be Inseparably One

December 11, 2000

While we are trying to respond to the inquiries from those who are curious about the miracle of Christianity, we must be cautious never to place a definition of it before them that is more difficult to understand than the very faith we are professing to espouse. Our Love for their Salvation must be as simple as the little Christ Child who was laid so innocently in the Bethlehem manger. This is one of the reasons why so many people have been turned-off by the seemingly precocious writings of the great Doctor of the Church, Saint Thomas Aquinas. His witness to Jesus Christ, however, is quite a welcome aberration from the norm because, through his works, hundreds of thousands of apprehensive intellectuals who think that other writings about human redemption are somewhat schmaltzy and infantile are eventually brought to conversion through the dimensioned conclusions of his spiritual treatises. Most of us would rather hear a more prismatic accounting of what it means to be a Christian, i.e., without the effuse deployment of what many perceive as being the private lingo and professorial jargon known only to studious theologians and the practicing clergy. When we begin to initiate the use of incurrent dogmas and testamentary ecclesiastics, that is the point where the faith of most common people finally gets off the bus. What kept Saint Thomas from fully realizing this will always be a source of curiosity for many contemporary Christians. There is some good news to report, however; as the Blessed Virgin Mary has told many people in the world through interior locution that Saint Thomas is now back to playing with his toys in a sandbox outside the Mansions of Heaven once again.

Quite conversely, we are to never forget the wisdom that Thomas Aquinas brings to a material world which is seeming to become ever more complicated in its own right as the days continue to pass. Indeed, his own benign genius must have led him to employ the principle of, "...your faith is weaker than mine for no good reason at all, for I am convincingly more the greater intellect than you!" Whatever the purpose he had in mind, he was not saying that those who are little and simple in their approach to the Cross are the antithesis of the formal Truth which is explicated through the Holy Gospel as God has revealed it through Jesus Christ. The purpose of anyone else's conclusions about how to become more holy are never generic in nature because they draw upon the specifics of how the entire body of humankind must become one unified entity in the Messiah of Salvation, to whose Judgment we shall all be subjected on the day we eventually die, if not before in His Glorious Return to Redeem us. We must somehow begin to grow more rapidly toward a spiritual enlightenment that is greater than the product of our simple majority or the plurality of our distinct opinions. If the prophecy Jesus has promised is to come true that the entire world of the living will become whole and without diminution at the end of time, and it certainly will by then; we are not as likely to see it occur in our lifetime if we keep trying to relocate ourselves to be farther and farther apart. To this inevitable end, we must always prosecute the same litigation upon our own personal consciences if we ever intend to unite them with humanity at large. A good beginning would be for each of us to realize that human life was never meant to be centered around the revolving tripolar axis of physical nourishment, reactionary stimulation, and the sensations of the tangible world.

After all, we are not living in a think-tank or giant test-tube somewhere, or an environmental biosphere where our sole purpose is to define our relationship with the physical Earth or to see just how long we can survive with the gradual relinquishing of our most vital signs. Human mortality is a real thing to behold, and we are not crash-test dummies who are immune to the fetish encounters of everyday life or the sudden collision we experience with reality everyday. Obstacles really do get in our way, corporeal pain truly hurts us to the core, and broken hearts are almost always too grievous to bear. Our bodies begin to ache, our minds often throb, and our feelings sometimes grow too numb to matter anymore. However, we will all discover at the end of time that human existence is actually much like a giant metaphor for a much greater and prefigured perfection that we have, thus far, been unwilling to forge. And, the fleeting moments which seem so everlastingly fragile are not really God's incessant barrage of hammer-strokes to keep our spirits nailed to the floor of Creation for the purpose of preparing us for the shock of greeting His Love somehow in fear. There is a much higher resolution for His having placed us at random on the surface of the rotating globe than that. We must begin to perceive our reason for living as our realization of the Divine Revelation which is about to take us all to a new and unconditional freedom with Him, a proposition for which there is no singular parable that could ever prepare us too much. This is why now is the time for our mutual precognition in advance of the great absolution which we have awaited a seeming eternity to receive. Jesus has told us through the Wisdom of the Holy Spirit that His Crucifixion has taken our souls away from the world as though we are standing on a plateau which is 10,000 feet high in the air. His Virgin Mother has come to warn us to be more careful where we choose to tread because we are still blindfolded by our own mortality and wandering perilously within an inch of its edge!

God did not evict Adam and Eve from the Garden of Paradise as a function of not loving them anymore, but because they proudly tried to equate themselves with His creative power. He realized that they would never be happy thereafter, knowing that they were standing naked in front of the Truth at the time. So, as a compassionate means of teaching them to Love again and to ponder the expanse of His own disposition, He sent them into exile on the Earth in blind abeyance until Christ had the opportunity to purify them, and the rest of us too, from our own inherited sinful nature. The Almighty Father knew that Adam and Eve, unlike Himself, did not possess the power to create something out of nothing. If they could, they would surely have never relied on the temptations by which they were pelted from a snake on the ground to get what they wanted from God. When we fast-forward a seeming eternity from then, Jesus Christ descended upon the very Earth to which they were banished, clothed in sinless human flesh, and told everyone who would ever live there that God has decided to change His Mind. We are now allowed to return to Paradise through our purgation in His Blood and, low and behold, we can have anything we want. There will be no fruit trees from which we will have to be sequestered; and we will be able to place whatever we desire in our own hands without having to beg the Almighty Father every time He turns around to proffer a smile. The first man and woman ever to be created were the product of the Love of God, not an effect of His own inception, because He has no beginning or end. When we return to Heaven someday, we will take-on the attributes of Jesus Christ in every conceivable way. We will be required to do so, or we will never be allowed to enter it from the first. Beyond that factual provision, what we wish to make for ourselves in the Kingdom of Salvation is a function of our own individual rights. Satan will be permanently confined to Hell by then, and there will be no one else left to tempt us into violating God's Law of Love again. Quite precisely, the thought will not even own an avenue through which to enter our minds because of our newfound perfection as the Mystical Body of the Resurrected Christ.

That is why it is so important for us to engage the march of returning to the original essence of our spiritual perfection while we live here on the Earth today. This has been a labor of Love upon which no other chore in history has been able to encroach quite yet. Again, humanity seems to be too preoccupied with the prospect of relative numbers as opposed to finally getting righteousness down-pat once and for all. We remember the beguiling mind-set of the countercultural mid-twentieth century American youth movement as being the ideology which asserts that anything which exists in massive quantities must somehow be godlike in nature, and that a horde of randomly selected components must surely possess some sort of awesome creative power of its own. After all, this is what the Woodstock phenomenon was all about in the late 1960s. We could not bring ourselves to conclude that the true meaning of "peace" meant to embrace the Sacraments of the Church, so we gathered like a giant collection of factionists to drown our frustrations in disparaging music, chemical contraband, illicit sexual unions, and political speeches against an ongoing war in Southeast Asia with the hopes of discovering the true meaning of life somehow on our own. If the nomadic people who attended that raucous event would have accidentally discovered a humongous pile of hair or fingernail clippings that were said to have been collected from everyone who lived in the colonial days, they would have knelt-down to worship it as being a god in the flesh. The fact remains prevalent that we missed the point back then, and most of us are still grievously short of it now. God does not necessarily reside in the immensity of an inexplicable quotient or a concept of rare historical descent, but in the essential substance of perfect Love. That is how one Savior redeemed the entire human race on a singular Cross on Mount Calvary, almost 2000 years ago. It is also why our spiritual piety is not so much a function of our obsessive repetitiveness, but is the sole attraction of the genius of Heaven which we find in the Holy Paraclete who is still pounding like the dickens to locate the center-most point of our petrified hearts.

Jesus Christ is not simply a passive or provisional aspect of the personified human species located in time, but is the permanent replacement for our mortal lives beyond the Earth which we see with our eyes. By living and dying in the presence of His Grace, our souls become uniquely perfected within His Being, by His Sacrifice, and through His Paschal Resurrection, much in the same way that the Holy Trinity is now, and will always be, inexplicably and inseparably One. The flatly erroneous and "contravisional" approach to life by those who oppose human Salvation altogether is not even in the ballpark of looking in the direction of the end of mortal existence, let alone what may happen to their souls thereafter. If we plead to God for a sign that we are living within the parameters of His Divine acceptance, He will always tell us that our own faith in asking Him *is* that sign. This tells us that our every act must always originate from His Holy Will, displayed to perfection in His Crucified Son. We must remember that human life is not wholly unlike an unabridged book, or a volume of books, or even a thousand libraries; but none of them would be worth the making if we ever missed-out on living a single page. It is oftentimes too burdensome for us to bear the daily quintet of the rotating series of morning, midday, afternoon, evening, and the dead of the night. But, as long as we make sure that our every action, affection, and thought revolves around Jesus Christ, all of time will become one to the elation of our sorrowful hearts. It is as though there is a sunbeam of light shining through our bedroom window onto the floor which never seems to pale or go away. It is a signal of God's original and perpetual Love in a material world that is obviously growing more deficient by the day. If our difficulties in life are viewed as being like a vertical slash or a pendulum of interior grievances, we must somehow find a way to overcome each of them individually by transforming them into a spiritually collative "1" through the imposition of our left-flank processional flag of courage based upon the foundation of our faith in the power of God. It always takes the inception of our fixated trust in Him to keep our goal to be first in His Kingdom from fading into the past, while the rest of the hashes around us would rather ignore the Holy Cross than to look the Truth in the face.

Sometimes, however, we place so much emphasis in making the grade for the purpose of conquering the system that we fail to recognize what lessons the experience was actually supposed to be teaching us. We are not all instantly expected to become "Little Jesuses" through the passing of a single night. On the other hand, however, it is not as though we are making an unfounded presumption about a set of circumstances which do not actually exist. We are, indeed, supposed to imitate His loving perfection during every situation that comes our way. Should we go out searching for them in advance? If we are to become perfect evangelists, we should. But, it seems as though a plentiful lot of opportunities approach us in everyday life nonetheless without everyone on Earth hanging a shingle in front of their door which says, "Christianity is Spoken Here." That is also why we must read the Sacred Scriptures from cover to cover, and know what they are really talking about. We usually never recall the exact synoptic details of the four Gospel teachings, but we for sure had better retain the concept of the original theses of righteousness and faith if we ever expect to call ourselves blessed. It is only in humbling ourselves in this same manner that we will eradicate the seeming jealous envy and outright conspiracy of trying to indict our fellow man for any weakness we may find in him so we will have less competition on our way to the top of the corporate and socioeconomic ladder. There is no doubt that more people today need to refrain from the disdainful habit of placing their objectionable sentiments on the front line of demarcation where they refuse to believe in God so they can, instead, finally begin the process of elevating the desires of their souls toward expressing the higher valances of their spiritual integrity. We recall the story about a father who had to rush to a hospital emergency unit where his young son was taken after being injured in a lawn-mowing accident, severing both of his arms and legs. While he and the rest of his family sat wringing their hands in the waiting-room chairs, the doctors worked feverishly to reattached his son's separated limbs before it became too late to save them. After the passing of about twenty-four hours, a nurse finally emerged into the hall to tell them that the boy had just been taken into the recovery-room area, then to be transferred onto another floor to receive Intensive Care.

So, the little boy's father goes into the hospital courtyard about an hour after that to relax and smoke a cigarette, and greets another man sitting on a bench in the middle of the square. The crouching second man is seen wiping sweat from his brow and looking outward toward the father with his own sense of urgency on his face. The pensive father tells him what a terrible accident his son has apparently survived, and speaks of the long ordeal to reattach his severed arms and legs by the doctors to whom he owes the best of his days. He did not want to burden the other fellow too much because he seemed to have some pretty serious pondering to do of his own. But, after listening intently to what the father has to say, the second man walks back into the hospital door after getting his breath of fresh air. When the father goes back into the consultation room with the attending physicians to learn the prognosis of his child, he learns to his astonishment that the man who was sitting on the common-area bench was none other than the lead surgeon who had just restored his son's ability to live as normally as everyone else in the world. This is a parable about how Jesus listens to us sometimes. Christ does not stand proudly before humanity and beat His breast with pride that He has saved our souls from burning in Hell. He listens quite intently through the lives of those whom we once thought to be common everyday men. He is a champion of Divine healing who is concealed so eloquently in the poor and those who serve others without a public reward. Yes, He is like that humble surgeon who turned to the father of the very fortunate son as if to say to him, "the true champion is your adolescent child who endured his pain so profoundly so you could be introduced to the miracle of the Cross today."

Social Rank, Material Fortune, and Interpersonal Power

December 12, 2000

One of the sweetest Fruits of the Holy Spirit is the perfection of our ability to maintain our self-control. Of all the clement attributes which Jesus places into our hearts through the magnanimity of His Love, taking special care in what we do and say is probably the most difficult one to pursue. It is not because we somehow become over-confident in the way we continue to live in our brilliant Christian faith, but more a matter of when and where to wield the virtues of humility and placidness in a world that usually wants nothing to do with either one. The prospect of our pondering always sends us back to the list of the Spiritual and Corporeal Acts of Mercy which the Almighty Father has promulgated for us to execute on His behalf. Did Jesus not tell us that our dutiful labors of "admonishing the sinner" would get us tossed through the swinging-doors of the mortal Earth to be found in contempt by the rest of society? There is certainly no smugness in our hearts when we have to pick ourselves up from the gutter after having been thrown there by an anti-Christian society whom we have just told would eventually reject us. We are oftentimes cast-out as being public enemies for correctly prophesying the behavior of the very people who are castigating us from the first. For some unexplained reason, many of those among us share the unfortunate distinction of being unwilling to comply with the wishes of Jesus solely because they do not like the person who is speaking in His stead. Humanity as a whole shares an intrinsic tendency to resist moral order, external commands, pious suggestions, and at least a bare minimum set of standards for their modest spiritual expectations.

We do not, however, have much difficulty in taking stock in our own internal persuasions which often take us to greater influence in social rank, material fortune, and interpersonal power. Most people who excel in the public theater usually own a quick wit, the ability to capitalize upon a passing opportunity in a moment's notice, shrewdness in the field of business management, the art of effective communication, and an impressive personal appearance. Indeed, an entire group of such talented people can take control over the governing economy of a given nation in a flash. The characteristic structure of their interwoven qualities is often a marvel to behold. But, what-say their attention might be turned in the direction of the Son of God? What, in His Holy Name, do we suppose this group of highly-trained individuals might accomplish in bringing justice to the Earth if every one of them suddenly awoke from a good night's sleep and simultaneously decided that it was finally time to convert the entire world to the Gospel of Jesus Christ? The Holy Spirit would now have a field day and a place to lay His weary Head in quarters where He had previously never been allowed to even enter the door. All of a sudden, we would all possess the true definition of a "new world order" at our hands! Imagine the possibilities of a globe of nations who hold a keen heart and ready conscience for what God really wants them to do! The spiritual enlightenment and hemispheric healing which would follow close behind would be almost too great to bear without the rest of us falling in ecstasy to our knees.

Finally, those who maintain the material lock on the fortune of the world which truly belongs to everyone would make prosperity available to the poorer souls who need to benefit from it the most. Humanity would finally apprehend the meaning of Love through the inevitable signs from God that would follow. The traditional characteristics and significant nature of the end of the world would begin to roll upon us like a wind-swept bank of cumulus clouds. The media would report at last that the dimensions through which our Creator has chosen to reveal Himself as the Triune Deity is the end of the line for anyone who is ignorant enough to dare to oppose Him. We would see the Holy Spirit running amok in every city, county, parish, and state. Jesus Christ would become the greatest opportunist we have ever seen in the history of the universe! How the collective voices of a converted ruling-class of newborn citizens in Christianity would unfold the Salvation of the entire body of humankind would rival the celebration of every New Year's Eve in the past 2000 years, all rolled into one. Then, should any mad-dog followers of Satan come frothing at the mouth in an attempt to devour the most innocent of God's children on the Earth, they would quickly be scorched into ashes by the Love of Jesus' faithful flock like a flamethrower being blasted toward their face. This is the infinite influence which the Cross wields over the good and the bad, alike. Decent men will become even greater heroes, and the souls of deadbeat thugs who will never belong to eternal Salvation will be forced to retreat into their farthest point inside the pit of Hell since the Son of God first walked-out of His grave.

When victory finally arrives in the form of the conversion of humankind, we will see the Truth like it has never before been revealed in our contemporary lives. In the blink of an eye, people will stand in shock to see what God will do with His Creation. The ancient pyramids will be the stately pedestals upon which the outer-planets will come home to roost in our midst. The Great Wall of China, the sprawling masses of continental railroads, and subterranean fault-lines all over the globe will open like gargantuan zippers, and out will climb the back-up troops that Jesus had placed beneath them just before He ascended into Heaven to help us win this last great battle of righteousness. If we Christians believe that every human event is determined by the ultimate goal of Love for the purpose of the Redemption of our souls, then we must know that these are the triumphant echoes which are still ringing from the Cross as it stands bearing the Lamb of God who takes away the sins of the world. The issues of race, mentality, location, and time will not matter anymore when this final sprint for the finish-line begins to ensue. And, Jesus will not just be standing there like a stuffed-shirt general on the top of a hill, seeing whether we will eventually succeed. He will lead us into the pack of nary-do-wells after having armed us so profoundly with the cloak of His Grace that we will take the enemy by storm and not a single one of us ever suffer so much as a scratch. It shall, indeed, be the *ne plus ultra*, the highest point of eternal Victory that humanity will ever know.

The world must eventually realize that the Blood of Christ in which our souls have been bathed is more than some rubefacient ointment that must somehow make its way through the tenacity of our skin. Our Salvation in the Crucifixion of Jesus immerses us from the inside-out, taking our very spirits back to Paradise while the flesh of our bones falls sheepishly to the ground. The precedent to this Wisdom is the Passionate process of how, under Pontius Pilate, we sinners effectively tortured the Son of God until He bled to death with the bark of a tree gouging into the gaping lashes on His Back which was shaped into the form of a "plus," signifying that God is positive that He wants us all to return to His Side. Now, as we live in the Holy Light of Jesus' Resurrection with which we see to walk upright, our transgressions against the Almighty Father in Heaven have been vanquished, dispelled, exempted, expunged, destroyed, annihilated, erased, removed, and obliterated from ever casting a shadow on the backdrop of Creation again. Only the image of the Cross remains on the horizon of our predestined future. And, while so many faithful followers of the Holy Gospel have wondered why Jesus' legs were not broken the moment He died, the answer is not that difficult to retrieve.

It was widely known that it was a custom to break the bones in the legs of those who were crucified back then as a final indication that the deceased would never set foot on the mortal earth again. But, the Holy Spirit did more than just hover above the Mountaintop that day. His prophecy was about to be fulfilled that the Son of Man would soon be raised from the Tomb and walk again like He had done just three days prior. Of course, he could have healed Himself with the touch of a Hand if His legs were to have ever been broken, but those who believed in Him had much more hope with which to pray when they saw that this Man was somehow different, that He died an innocent execution, that His Soul would not be gone for long, and His legs would soon bear the weight of our own resurrection from the grave while dancing to the sweet melodies of our own Gloria, Praises, and Honor in the process. This was His gift of anticipation for the souls who stood by His side with the faith to believe in His Word. Others have asked whether the Holy Name of the Crucified Savior ever appeared in the necrological obituary column of the local daily express, if they ever had one in His day, only to find that they would have had to print a retraction for the headlines of the Monday Morning News. Everyone who knew Him in Love realized what we all know now; that Jesus Christ represents the sustenance of human life throughout all of immortal existence. He is our preservation against the tollways of time and the supplier of our every requisition for making our way back home beyond the everlasting ages. Those who knew Him saw more than the Immanuel who had come to live in their midst. They saw the brilliant courage of a perfect Man in the flesh who was good natured, frank, kindly outspoken, and tender of heart; the kind of compassionate human being whom we all want our sons to become. He was, and still is, our sublimely indispensable Agnus Dei, Corpus Christi, and Spiritus Sanctus, all present in the Almighty Father who is now inherent in the Earth.

The sounds from the uttering lips of Jesus can still be heard in the twenty-first century world. It is curious to recall that, even though His voice had been somewhat softened by the excruciating pain and suffering which had been imposed upon Him on the day He laid-down His Life for us, every soul on the Hill that day could hear the intonation of His very last words, even those who knelt so very far away from Him in the back of the crowd of watchers. He spoke with a profound confidence in the Will of the Father even then, as He Christened humanity for their new liberation from sin and death. The Crucifixion of our Lord took place on a summit which is called Golgotha, or *gulgoleth* in Hebrew terms. This "place of the skull" could never mute-out His expressions of affection, consecration, and commendation which He made the last in His mortal Life to His Mother Mary Immaculate and our representative for the present day, His Apostle, Saint John. It was at this "place of the skull" where Jesus Christ brought human Redemption to a head.

The Honorable Piousness Knocking on Our Doors

December 13, 2000

If we men should coldly design our shallow deftness with which we expect to conquer the war-ravaged world, we might do as well by tendering our bourgeoning consciousness to the more noble of things so that, whenever we fail, no more shall the hollow briefness of weeping solemnity haunt our poor selves again. The blustery cold and wintery midwestern midnight blues always give-way to the warmth of the early evening sun of gladder spirits who, in themselves, have flown a more delightful course of love. Will God show-up someday soon and summon His ready reservists, the more righteous of His flock, and make ornate veterans of them all? Or, will He concede to the olfactory legacy that we have left behind, against which only the dead can compete? We are, after all, a long and lost trailer of too broken hearts, smitten and despised, overly burdened, and yet still overjoyed. Humankind is too much in love with life to be so forlorn, too good in faith to ever be forsaken, with not a particle of adeptness in the cunning do we possess, but properly positioned against the stars to be so supernaturally blessed. The slumbering oversight which has now become our broad awakening is hidden in the withering of the past, while every Abigail is her father's budding cup, and in them both, all humankind has found a newer hope. Let us not utter our reluctance quite yet so as to prevail in the final cast, for it is too late for us to turn back now, and far too soon to retreat into the shadows of the hovering night. We shall fall in love with solar spires and singe our souls, too timid to raise ourselves and try again, and not near as ample as those who listen so clearly to the crispy sounds of the bristlettes who cry just beyond the street lamps of their consciences, while we still shiver in the dampest corners of our fears, afraid for reality to finally set in.

Who could have known that Love is not a project of democracy in the works, or ever a compromise of the ancient Truth? The appeasement of the schizophrenic willow trees does not even inspire a dirge to wail, for all the world is surely listening intently to what they have to say, but like our hearts in quietly beating, they are not yet speaking so loudly as to be heard. While we almost never force our pleas of genuflection upon the lives of other men, we sometimes cannot keep from reaching for the bait left in their traps. What high-wire walkers we have become with no way to call ourselves down or to judge where we must go from here because we have suddenly lost our way back home! The abrupt hiddenness of our perception gives us rise to see our lives as a button not in the hole and a valor which has never once been claimed. What viral seediness grows from our lack of trust in God, for we are an armistice that has already been broken and a genesis of exemplary shame. Our minds grow weary from hearing one iambic pentameter too many and being teased by a whatchamacallit that never really had a name to call its own. We all must die from a grief which never seems to ebb and from a pleasance that never fails to surrender too soon. One disaster seems to impishly mirror the next; and our victories are always too sparse to ever be seen in swells. Now we know that the parables of Jesus are always meant to induce a reaction of compliance on our own, not just our pining to make their symbols disappear for good.

It would be nice to place every sliver of our contemptuousness in Christ, but we are too afraid that the world might try to rob us from behind or pilfer our ruffled dignity should we ever turn our backs on its brawny fascia again, so keenly erected within the steely poise of our gentler thoughts. We are often much too easily swilled into complacency, our goals set on more distant impressions, making us an easy prey to discouragement and any random temptation, and quite the slimmer pickens for the righteousness which caters the Feast of moral Truth. We once owned a sufficient lot of passing days without shattered dreams to bear, but it seems like we can scarcely hear their faint echoes calling anymore. Shall God stoop to dispense our undeserving guerdon if we are still too frail to raise our hands to reach for Him right now? No wonder the smirks of the arrogant crowds never take the time to scoff at what we do for Christ these days. Are our pale intentions even bright enough for Him to try to stretch to capture or squint to see every once in awhile? Our lamenting sentiments might be more befitted toward what His Nature truly reveals in the Most Blessed Sacrament, the Holy Eucharist, within whose Body our very future rings. Can we bring ourselves to befriend the honorable piousness that keeps knocking upon our entrance doors all through the day and night? We must approach Jesus Christ amidst the shuddering depths and thunderclaps of the Almighty Hands who yearn so profoundly to hold our souls once again; for we, too, beg to see our prodigal decency finally wandering almost unwittingly through the portico of our aching hearts like a deer longing for a stream. It would not hurt us a single smidgeon if we would try to convince ourselves that the humility which we are still lacking en masse is not really a penitentiary ground.

Indeed, our humble submission is not even a holding pen where we must check our spirits at the door to come and go as we please because thousands of centuries of mortal men before us have looked far and wide and have never found so much as a single constraint or conscripting predator there. There is no fooling the inner-man as to whether he is being loved by the rest of humanity or not. The emptiness inside his heart is as real as the world he sees, and not some paraplegia that has rocked his mind and soul into permanent sleep as though no one is really ignoring him. God wants our aversion to His holiness to be suspended for all of time and to shrivel-up and blow-away like the maple leaf which once covered Adam's loins, the one that has now taken refuge once and for all in the dark abyss below the Earth because his soul is not so naked anymore. A writer once penned the words, "Death, be not proud...," and that is what our conversion and spiritual confession is all about. Do we love God's children sufficiently and will they be able to tell Him so someday without lying before His Sacred Face? This is the fateful question which could determine whether we ever see the towering treetops on the lofty peaks of our final Absolution having finally come-to-pass. Repentance is the fruit of an inspirited heart which grows more bountifully in the everyday world than it might in the Garden of Eden. If we honor our Almighty Father by appealing to His Reverence through the Immaculate Heart of Mary, we will have stationed our eternal Triumph for good.

The Sacred Heart of Jesus is the oarlock that will keep our spirits from slipping through our hands as we row toward the falling waters in the distant beyond. What we often fail to recognize along the way is that the pit at the bottom of our deathbed bears a spike as large as the Washington Monument which will lance our souls into unending perdition if we do not take to the air at the last moment in time on the wings of the perfection we have gained through the power of the Cross. Ingesting the Holy Eucharist is overwhelmingly the same as feeding upon our Eternal Salvation, itself. There is no time like the present to tuck our napkins of Confession beneath the chin of our faith which overlays our souls and allow God to nourish us all back to Life once again. So, we come before Him rich and poor, frail and mighty, intelligent and illaudable, but always ready to be remade whole in the lofty percussions that still resound from the final chime of the hour when Jesus exchanged His Life for the full, invariable, and prime ex facto atonement for our sins. Now, any extemporaneous and prayerful soliloquies we may see fit to deliver to ourselves would not be too unwelcomed by the ears of the Holy Spirit living inside our hearts, who is lent so graciously in hearing again how great art the God of Abraham.

Inquisition

Where are you, humanity? Where do you belong, and where are you going?
Where is my sister, where is my brother, what of my father, what of my mother?
Today, I am a dying Rose. I weep for Love, I weep for those who sit in woeful thought alone. I bend in sorrow from welts of time; I grasp for things that once were mine, but in the end, I lose them.

But, where is Love? Do I have any? Where is my Death? Where is my memory?
And you, O' great merciless strength of Time, where are you going?
I feel your pull. My heart is showing the signs of age.
And, I see you Death! You cannot hide! I see you coming! I know that you won't stop whether I'm in Peace or I'm enraged.

You are a thief, O' Time. You rob the day of life and light. And, you rob me of my breath and youth. Is the coming 'morrow something new? Will there be anything left that I can keep? I know there won't. I loathe you Time, you are a thief! Why don't we sing? Why don't we dance? But, then, there'd only be the chance that it would end again and I would just sit and wonder what's the use.

What I would really like is to be a poet! He's one who sees the end of all!
Or, is there really a man that tall?

-Timothy Parsons-Heather
September 30, 1975

A Sequel to "Morning Star Over America"

December 14, 2000

I would like to pause in the ongoing text of this accounting of the intercession of the Blessed Virgin Mary to provide a quasi-summary of the important issues that She has raised to date. As I have indicated before, this book is a sequel to our first edition of, *Morning Star Over America*, in which my brother and I have provided an intensely detailed record of the unfolding of Our Lady's miraculous messages for the entire world. While the preeminent text of our Diary has already been distributed in many parts of the globe, we still have quite a distance to travel in evangelizing the Gospel of Jesus Christ through the other various means at our disposal. We call upon everyone on the Earth to join in the struggle for goodness, equality, righteousness, faith, prayer, and conversion to Jesus Christ as the Savior of our souls. For over ten years now, the Immaculate Mother of God has been speaking directly and audibly to my brother and me, continuing to offer messages about our transformation into the perfect people whom Jesus wants us to become in Him. While Her words always carry the urgency of the Book of Revelation, She still exhibits the patience of the Holy Spirit in teaching us all how to change our lives and to conform to the wishes of our Almighty Father in Heaven. She has told us many times before that, if this were not possible to achieve, She would certainly have never appeared in the first place, and would have probably given up trying to change us long ago. That is an additional reason why Our Lady has asked my brother and me to perceive the past ten years as being much more than a partial segment of the passing lineage of our lives. Our hearts have literally been taken away from the everyday world and transplanted into the timeless Hands of Her Son.

The Blessed Mother has described Her maturing relationship with us over the last ten years as being like a charismatic "decagon" of events with an actual spiritual body whose broader dimensions have been determined by the longevity, strength, and sincerity of our prayers. Each of the years has been uniquely different in its own right, but they have all been the collective growth of our trust in God to take us where He wants us to go. From February 22, 1991 forward, my brother and I have grown from the timid and confused "material boys" we once were into two people who have finally come to understand with the clarity of Love that nothing in the world can compete with the Divinity of Paradise for consoling the human spirit and raising our consciences toward the higher things of life. The basic principles of Our Lady's words have never wavered from whence they first began over a decade ago. Self-sacrifice is the key to unlocking the secrets of the inner-soul, and prayer is our only means to hold it within the grasp of our hands. We must take to our knees and ask God for the intervention of the Holy Spirit to soften our hearts and to beseech His glorious assistance throughout all our days. Our every thought should lay another stepping-stone on the pathway of our desire to go to Heaven, while we promise Jesus our deepest devotion in searching for Him more religiously when we receive the Most Blessed Sacrament as our Eucharistic Bread of Eternal Life.

The Blessed Virgin Mary has taught us that our forgiveness of one another is the beginning of our deliverance of the custody of the mortal Earth into the final Reign of Jesus Christ. There can be no interchange of mutual pardon and good will if we do not center them both in the Love which we find in His Sacred Heart. Again, looking back on *Morning Star Over America*, we can see the process through which the Blessed Mother has vowelized Her lessons from centuries-passed to help those of us who now live in modern times recognize the unchanging nature of the Love of God. Jesus is the consummate and singular Messiah for all the ages because His Birth in Bethlehem and His impending Return in Glory are both the essence of the same "Advent of the heart." While we cannot yet envision them as being simultaneous events in the history of Creation, everyone else in Heaven already sees it this way. They bear-out the same yearning conclusion of our anticipation, rebirth, and renewal for the family of man; not an anxiety or fear about how the world may end, but our confident assurance that our souls have already been saved through the Blood of the Cross and Our Lord's Resurrection from the grave. It is toward this higher state of spiritual enlightenment and stirring of the conscience that our messages from the Mother of God have forthrightly proceeded. And, there are several persistent and recurrent themes which keep running through them like a common thread of urgency. Let us make a brief summary recollection of them here.

* First, and foremost, we have the capacity through the Divine intercession of the Blessed Virgin Mary to become more holy people than we ever previously thought we had the potential to be. If there is one thing for sure, this Immaculate Lady recognizes the power of the Holy Spirit and the Blood of Her Crucified Son to remake any human being into His exemplary and perfect likeness again.

* We have no reason to believe that the world will come to an end in the horrible mess into which we have allowed it to deteriorate. Whether we choose to accept it or not, Jesus Christ is in full control of His Kingdom; and He is now in the process of empowering His flock on the Earth to prove it outright. The source of our strength and progress is always found in the virtue of our

prayers. There is nothing in the world any more potent in forcing a change for the better than when we place our intentions before the very God who has created us.

* Humankind is absolutely and irrevocably helpless to do anything of a righteous nature unless we call on the Holy Spirit to be our guide. He does this through the invincible power of the Cross, to which we all must go for the Wisdom to know the Truth and the pathway which will lead us to Redemption.

* The Holy Sacrifice of the Mass is our most transcending way to attend the Last Supper and the Crucifixion of Our Lord concurrently, as though we were present in person on the very day they took place. Whether we choose to believe that we are somehow miraculously transported backward in time over twenty centuries, or whether God brings Good Friday to the day in which we are now living, time is a nonissue with regard to the agelessness of the Eucharistic Celebration. We are standing on the Hill of Mount Calvary from the moment we walk into the church to bow on our kneelers and the priest calls the congregation to order.

* Our recitation of the Sacred Mysteries of the Most Holy Rosary is, in itself, a supernatural event. God has been dispensing healing graces through this Marian Consecration since His Mother first dispensed the Rosary to Saint Dominic and made the notable Fifteen Promises to him about the predestined good fortune that would come to those who devoutly recite it.

* The idea that Christians are somehow supposed to be a timid society who must resort to begging the rest of humanity to yearn for Salvation is a boldly errant misconception. By the Wisdom of the Holy Spirit and the legacy of the Cross, those who have accepted Christ as their Living Redeemer are the most powerful mortals on the Earth. No one should apologize for knowing the Truth of the Gospel, and should be proud to boast about it whenever such opportunities arise.

* The temporal world is only a physical distraction to the human soul and a means through which many people are prevented from entering a closer relationship with God. Those who seek the gift of inner-peace must always refrain from lowering themselves to participating in lewd conduct, idolatry, materialism, illicit matters of the flesh, and infidelity to the Holy Spirit.

* The Hosts of Heaven, inclusive of the Saints and the countless Legions of Angels, serve mortal humankind to a much greater degree than we could have possibly ever discovered on our own. The Blessed Mother has repeatedly asked us to call upon the Communion of Saints for their intercessory prayers before the Throne of God in our hours of greatest need.

* The Church Suffering, composed of the Poor Souls in Purgatory, is a truthful and agonizing spiritual mortification in a real identifiable place. We must conjoin our perpetual petitions with theirs as they serve-out their last sentences toward the goal of purifying their souls, making them presentable to stand before God without an ounce of shame in their hearts. Again, Our Lady has made it clear that *we* are responsible for praying for their release into Paradise.

* We must obey the Holy Roman Catholic and Apostolic Church to the best of our faithful service, including our allegiance to the Pope in Rome, toward the eradication of the ongoing culture of death throughout the world, i.e., the end of abortion, capital punishment, and so-called mercy-killing. We must be loyal to the profession of our Creed and reject sin in all forms. In this same Church, we must espouse the virtues of all Seven of the Sacraments and embrace the pious fruits of Love, fasting, prayer, penance, peace, and conversion.

While this abbreviated summation is in no way exhaustive, it allows us to see that we still have an immense amount of work to do in order to become the people whom Christ will eventually deliver to His Father's side in Heaven. He, too, dictates the principles which will always help us to do better along the way. We should never forget that the purpose of His Passion and Crucifixion is not only to prevent those who accept Him from going to Hell when they die, but also to destroy hatred from ever trying to pierce their human hearts again. Such disdain is the poison that always destroys fond relationships between men. Jesus sees our world with a much greater perspective than we really know. A hundred years in His sight is somewhat how we feel when we see the second-hand click past a number on our analog wristwatch. Indeed, Heaven is not even enveloped by the element of time like we are here on the Earth beneath it. While we may possibly envision Creation as being like a golf-ball resting comfortably on a tee under a palm tree somewhere, Jesus sees the globe as having already been driven all the way past the fairway of our mortality, onto the green of our new spiritual awareness, and leaning over the edge of the last hole on the course of our lives, getting ready to fall into the Cup of Everlasting Redemption. He knows that the Cross is the "flag" for which His faithful children have been aiming all along, and the Holy Rosary is the Iron which has clad us in the Grace of His Immaculate Mother and lifted our souls into the heights of our conversion amongst the celestial clouds. This is how close He stands to returning to the Earth and ending our life as we know it. If any angel should sneeze somewhere amongst the distant stars, it might be sufficient reason for Christ to decide to make our world come tumbling-down into the foundation of His Truth once and for all.

The fact remains apparent that we human beings are still having difficulty distinguishing greed and luxury from the bare necessities of life. We continue to be absorbed in pursuing the accumulation of wealth, while ignoring the fact that we cannot take a penny of it with us when we finally die. And, should we choose to horde our resources to the further suffering of the poor, we may arrive before the Face of God and hear Him say, "You have already had your mansion! Get out, and do not ever come back! I do not know who you are!" This would be the worst news that could befall the ears of any wretched soul. There is no doubt that we must enlist the further counsel of the Holy Spirit to help us discern the broad differences which will always exist between entertainment and immorality, responsibility and opportunism, ignorance and wantonness, righteousness and sin, justice and vengeance, and Love and infatuation. We do not have to bend our minds into the shape of a pretzel to understand what God really means by repentance. The simplicity of the Holy Gospel clearly states that it is through letting-go in life that we are truly able to hang-on to Salvation forever. The intrinsic nature of God's Wisdom tells us that human vanity is a "closed" system and a sub-part of a greater obstinance which mortal men hold against Heaven because it exists only to serve the self. If we cannot reach-out to the suffering souls who live among us, we have only destroyed our own good fortune before the Man-God who has saved us.

There is also no denying the fact that peace inside the heart and peace-universal almost never spring from appeasement, but from a shared compromise of mutually Divine instructions which are dispensed by the power of the Holy Spirit. While God will never compromise His Truth, He eventually takes us all closer to it by our greater understanding of what we must surrender to get there. Obstructionism and corruption will never lead the human spirit toward our higher unity with the perfection of the Kingdom of Heaven. Indeed, the maxims do not stop there. When all is said and done, we will learn that defeat in the pursuit of righteousness is never the final outcome of the synopsis which we are still living a day at a time. And, fundamental fairness is always a relative issue because its definition is contingent upon who we choose to ask. Doing what is right in accordance with the Christian Gospel is not always fair in the eyes of the vast *immoral* majority. The Love of God is not a whimsical farce or some intangible force of nature existing in a vacuum somewhere. Jesus Christ is a real human being who has been Resurrected from the Tomb in which His Body was laid soon after He was killed on Good Friday, almost 2000 years ago. You cannot get any more real than that. He knows what everyone else who lives in the Holy Spirit has come to accept. Those of us residing on the surface of the globe will all die before death, itself, ever stops killing us; should the Son of Man not yet Return in Glory to suspend that ongoing procession. In order to overcome it, we must predispose ourselves to receiving our Divine Advocate, the Paraclete, inside our hearts if we ever expect to comprehend what God holds in store for our future. Whether it is composed of Everlasting Life or eternal condemnation is entirely our decision to make.

Part III - The Truth Shall Set Us Free!

Blessed is He Whose Heart Has Not Forgotten

December 26, 2000

Somehow, it seems as though we can never truly know God until our hearts have finally been trampled underfoot by those who despise us because of our Love for Him, or until we have fallen and grieved from inside the extrememost pit of utter human despondence, certainly not before we have been forced to look at the world from our dungeon chains upward, and only after we have seen our own frail existence through the purview of the Passion and Crucifixion of Jesus Christ. Moreover, it is only subsequent to our having been effectively discarded by the rest of the world that we can really know what it means to be regained in the Most Sacred Heart of God. The frozen hatred which has been shown toward the followers of Jesus in past centuries makes the prospect of a nuclear winter look like a sunny day on a Floridian beach. It is as though life is not grievous enough in that the globe is starving for inter-reactionary Christian Love, but those who finally decide to espouse its righteousness are often commonly scoffed at, spate upon, banished, persecuted, and abandoned as being useless wretches with seemingly nothing else to do than to seek after some invisible God whom no one else cares enough about to even consider as being alive. It is a monumental miracle that Christians can maintain the genuineness of their faith in the face of such impetuous opposition, but it is even a greater marvel that Jesus does not strike-down His mortal enemies who wreak misery upon His loyal children before their nihilistic indignance ever gets a chance to leave their heathen lips. He assuredly must be waiting for them to discover that they are only standing alone in their opposition to the Truth because even Satan, himself, will swiftly abandon them after destroying any hint of goodness which may have otherwise survived their own indifference. Of course, he will take their souls to suffer perdition in Hell, but they will thereafter be on their own to endure the eternal consequences of their individual corruption without a single scintilla of consolation from the evil scoundrel who finally led them there to rot.

However, the mortal world is not yet concluded, and the Kingdom of God on the Earth is still unfolding to this day. Jesus Christ has not surrendered the soul of anyone now alive to the depths of such an agonizing fire. He knows full-well that true conversion can spring from the first whimper of a sinner's humble contrition. Great mountains can fall into the valleys below at the descent of the first stone to break free. A single God has created the entire universe in which billions of celestial bodies reside. One Savior has redeemed the entire human race from languishing in unending condemnation. One

Angel named Gabriel invited One Immaculate Conception to accept the Baby Jesus in Her Womb; One Paraclete has brought the Infinity of God's concise vision to all good men with the faith to believe; and One Love is comprised of the same beneficent Matriarch and the Blessed Trinity which has so profoundly triangulated the entire earthen globe in search of the lost people of Jerusalem, ourselves included for good measure. Our Almighty Father is calling-out for a sweeping change to the face of the Earth, for a collection of men and women who will finally stand and proclaim that He owns us outright, and that He is our only Salvation from the desolate confinement which we call human life. If we are to be fishers of men, we must courageously vow to forge every ocean and cross every stream to find our brothers; and we must fall to our knees with baited breath to hear them say "yes" to their own personal purification in the Holy Spirit of God. Then, the mystique of majestic perfection will overcome the world with a new propriety and a higher hope, sustained by people who are promised to Salvation by their internal hearts, openly and promptly willing to be the infirmarians for those who are still suffering the pangs of faithlessness and the guilt of their own transgressions.

What is it about a vehicle or common carrier that gives it the connotation of having greater eloquence, capacity, and stateliness when it is said to have multiple engines? We hear announcers and broadcasters say, "All the boosters have ignited," or pilots calmly saying, "We are going to disengage engine number four for the rest of our flight because it is running a little warm," with such calmness in their voice that the process seems almost too routine. Is it because their flying machines have the reputation of being so invincible now that they simply rely on secondary auxiliary engines to complete their journey through the skies? Is there some sort of inherent revered power in the plurality of their huge cylindrical turbines? This casual sense of security is not unlike the confidence we have gained in knowing that the entire Court of Heaven is presently holding us aloft in Love before God so we can know Him better despite our own temporary weaknesses or our occasional miscalculation about true reality which might hold our good offices at bay for a moment or send our consciences down the wrong path for a brief interlude of error. If only we could see that the Divine and omnipotent allies of supernatural intercession are already helping us through the trials of daily life, we would expend a huge sigh of relief and be not so afraid of believing in Salvation in Jesus anymore. We often take for granted that our peripheral vision is working involuntarily to perceive the rest of the world upon which our mind is not really concentrating, but it would be like pulling teeth to ever get the enemies of Love to believe that the Kingdom of Paradise is just as close to us now as the next blink of their eyes.

Indeed, our pupils move back and forth almost automatically when we read sentences on a page, and we do not even think about what is causing this tracking motion to proceed. Do we ever stop to ponder about the mysterious relationship that exists between our ability to see Creation with our eyes and everything before us that is constantly begging for our undivided attention to be seen, as though there is some invisible force-field of subliminal contact between the two at the exact position where our vision is brought into full focus? Whether we encounter the world by form of habit, ritual, accident, or direction; the fact remains true that the environment which exists just beyond our focal point does not disappear simply because we are not presently looking its way; and the Kingdom of God is likewise no-less apparent. All we need to do is entrain the desires of our hearts, our faith, our consciences, and our actions toward the direction of the Son of God on a collective and universal scale, just like those rolling mountains or flying machines somehow unwittingly do, and He will miraculously turn our heads away from the ordinary world and reorient them toward the pristine signature of His Preeminent Divineness. Then, we will not feel so hated anymore; and that is when we shall realize that the Holy Spirit is within us as Christ's Mystical Body on the Earth begins to assume a shape which is fully complementary to the citizenry of Heaven.

There is no denying that we will be voluntary captives under the protection of the filial affection of God if we ever finally comprehend who He is because we will then begin to sense together the early autumn reminiscence of prim assurance that the new springtime of His comfort is with us at last. We will have fallen deeply in Love with Christ for good as we are divined by His Spirit to recall those foregone memories of the good times of life and the way it used to be, those passages of endearment which we vowed to never forget from whence they first occurred, but somehow they quietly slipped beyond the forfeiture of the luring weeks and the adept cunningness of the months that wiled away. In Jesus Christ, these momentous remembrances can be retrieved forever, for they can be seized once more, and nothing will ever be able to steal them from the origin of our hearts again. Then will we be able to stand upon those conquered mountain peaks and proclaim with ferocity, "*Blessed is he whose heart has not forgotten, and they who shall retrieve those bygone charismatic hopes, another instant of Love to never slip away, to grasp that brilliant age of new enlightenment with ease at last, forever theirs to hold and keep.*" It is true that all time is one in the Holy Cross upon which our Savior laid-down His Life for the cause of our newborn resiliency. So, what do we make of these ever-passing ages? Do we only set them aside for as long as we can bear it or horde them somewhere for our future posterity? Should we toss them into the winds of the inexorable centuries, or somehow build upon them and never once look back, or perhaps ignore their presence altogether? Surely they must be profit or fare for something better to come, more than a linear means through which to remember when our fathers died or to recount them as a passing lot of finite moments in a parable about human multiplicity to be savored only by the generations which will follow close behind.

If we simply wish for God to bring human life to a close while we stand beside the road criticizing His every move, we would do better to watch that proverbial pot come to a boil or stare at the telephone in the hope that it will ring at any next second and announce the fateful news which we have been anticipating from not so very long ago. Never to destroy anyone else's hope, but life is more daily than that accord, and we have a great deal of work to do before we can "will" Our Savior into returning in Glory again. There are yet fields of towering youth who still need planting in the foundations of Christian Love, and elder statesmen who are almost ready for the harvest of death to whom we must begin to listen in earnest. Every soul who has ever uttered the Truth of the Holy Gospel has left a pastoral divot on the mortal ground where they once walked before; and that is how humanity is still being cultivated to this day to receive the seed of spiritual conversion. For those who believe that life is only a piece of hornbook paper, a makeshift satin canvas, an empty treadle hopper, or an abandoned minnow well, we are all expected to fill our jigger of mortal time with our impressions of the solemnity of the Crucifixion and Resurrection of Christ through our most useful works. By the time our individual lives come to an end, we should have left no pockmarks of impurity on the face of the Earth, but should otherwise ingrain the evidence of our own compliance with the Will of the Father on every facet of life as we know it to be, in every society whose artful wares are tendered to such humble resignation, inside the burrows and alongside the broadways of every city street and darkened alley, and written with sweat, blood, and tears across the carcases of every dying rural skyway with the intensity of the prayerful Litanies of the Holy Family springing from our hearts.

There is still too much tragedy for our consciousness to ever absorb in a single lifetime, but there is also too much hope in Jesus Christ for us to ever be destroyed in regaining our joy in His Holy Spirit. We are born into the world with a slap on our buttocks and screaming tears rolling from our squinting eyes, while our proud families boast of their new progeny with smiles abroad their adoring faces. But, we depart the Earth in lonely death, laying on our backs in sleeping silence, while the tears now roll like deluges down the cheeks of our sole survivors who mourn the loss of one of their own. What happens in between these two diametric events is all that matters to the greater world we leave behind. What do we eventually do with our hands to reshape

Creation into the likeness of Paradise before we are forced to drop them at our sides in death? And, what will our children's children, our nieces and nephews, and their contemporary friends read about our solitary attempts at evangelizing the Holy Gospel as handed-down to us from the first-century Saints? Will they proudly eulogize us as being the great Christian philanthropists who surrendered our last material possession to the poor while giving everything else to the propagation of faith across the more distant continents to forward the advancement and healing of those whom God had commended to our care? We must turn in preparation for this noble goodness to the Papal voice of the Holy Father in Rome for the nurturing of our strength and conviction in Christ and to aid us in our struggle to know the difference between self-preservation and sacrificial Love. Every grace-filled Sacrament, indulging observation, prayerful solemnity, cause of celebration, and responsibility to effect our faith is delineated in the Roman Catechism; and we shall all be called to justice by the Messiah of the New Covenant according to how we each comply with the Sacred Gospel which we have professed and the Holy Spirit who penned it from the start.

There is a specific message to the Western Hemisphere, particularly the post-modern States of North America, with regard to our compliance with the wishes of the Holy Father, who sits upon the Chair of Saint Peter across the Atlantic Ocean from our most Eastern shore. The Capitol of our nation is not located in New England "proper" solely because it was the first frontier to be colonized; but so that the ears of our governors can be better lent to the Truth which keeps pouring-out from Vatican City about what true freedom really is. It is not found in some unprincipled collection of material wealth or in an organized promulgation of public laws, but in recognizing that a capitalist democracy will ultimately fail unless it chooses to follow the Truth of Christ. Even the longitudinal time zones bear-out this inevitability, for every Feast and liturgical occasion is observed at Saint Peter's Square in Rome well before it ever makes landfall on the continent of America. Is God sublimely telling us by the aspects of the tangible world that we should also follow His chosen Pontiff in every other aspect of human conduct and benign spiritual demeanor? "Turn to Jesus Christ and you will truly be the land of the free and the home of the brave," is what the Holy Father is proclaiming to those who fill the chambers on Capitol Hill. He knows what the rest of God's children have understood for 225 years and counting, that the United States is too absorbed in its own blind patriotism than to truly know what it means to seek freedom from sin. We launch our fireworks a week too late, it seems, for God to give a care about glancing from His Throne in the Mansions of Paradise to our raucous carousing on the streets far below. Christmas Eve comes and goes, and not a fizzling rocket of celebration is ever fired into the nighttime skies to thank Him in return. But, just wait a week longer for a new year to roll around and humanity erupts into uncontrollable songs and exotic dances as though, somehow, the Creator of the Universe has given them 365 new reasons to celebrate their own audacity in rejecting the Passion and Crucifixion of His Son. The fact remains persistently true for those who have not yet accepted Salvation in the Blood of Jesus Christ that time is not their friend at all! And, should they continue to twist and jive in their cordoned avenues just because the calendar has expired again, they might discover quite the sorrowful way that they have only been drowning-out the sound of another series of spikes being driven into their coffin lids, for which there is no other escape than the power of the Crucifixion of the Son of God.

We are not predisposed to suffering the indignity of burning forever in hellish fires if we will just awake from the hypnotism of the everyday world. We are all royal priests in our own God-given way who will soon exchange our palliums of faith for a new Vestment of Living Redemption forever to come. God does not only want our love, purity, and holiness to shine from our souls like a flame in the darkness, but He also requires us to spread our Divine likeness of His Son throughout Creation as though our pious character is a giant candelabra radiating from our souls like the extension of our fingertips reaching for the Manna of Life from the Altar of Sacrifice. After all, we are every one His little children who yearn quite pitifully for the comforting embrace of our Heavenly Father above, beyond the throes of the Earth. Our Love for humankind must reach into the involute galaxies and beyond, sharing the fruits of the Holy Spirit with our brethren like a multi-headed field planter being pulled across the flats of the circular globe by the gargantuan power of the Paraclete at the depth of our inner-souls. We are His spiritual contractors, ambassadors, emissaries, laborers, servants, and messengers, all rolled into one body of human flesh inside the radiant beams of the Holy Cross. Indeed, the Mother Church of Roman Catholicism is the Seven-Sacrament source of our ecclesiastical profundity in the material world, making us ready for the Final Season of Love while the element of time continues to prepare us all for the rich harvest of Salvation at last.

The Seven Sorrows of Mary - Jesus Is Love

December 27, 2000

If simple human "moxie" is a vigorous courage which takes its definition from a trademark soft drink by the same name, then surely "kellogg" can best describe the intense diplomacy with which we must approach the more delicate issues that often seem to stand so stubbornly between our peers and their almost unconventional conversion to Salvation in Jesus Christ. Of course, we offer our deepest apologies to the 20 th century Nobel Prize winner, Frank Billings Kellogg, if his spirit should be so inclined to take offense by our invocation of his great service in making our point about imitating the fruits of peace which God has given us to pursue with intense resoluteness. However, even he finally admitted that peace is much more than a simple mutual coexistence of particular races of people on the globe, absent of any physical conflict between the several nations. World peace is not only defined by a lack of ongoing war, but the elimination of the conditions that ultimately lead to war, such as quartered poverty, political aggression, bigotry, greed, and discrimination. There has never once been an international dispute which was not initiated by a group of opportunists who wished to violate another society's principles of government or personal and religious beliefs. There has been untold human suffering which always accompanies these storied conflicts, but it is often disregarded as being a suitable means to a much more amicable end. That, in itself, is an extreme example of rife contradiction for the record books! What about the countless border skirmishes which no one else bothers to notice that claim thousands of lives every year while the rest of humanity goes about conducting its daily business? Surely we can collectively redefine our shared vision of global peace if we are ever going to end interpersonal confrontation as we know it.

There is a purpose, however, for human suffering which is allowed by God to ensue for the manifestation of His unfolding Kingdom. It does not include an all-out persecution against mortal dignity for the purpose of gaining material wealth, but is more spiritually directed toward the purification of the enemies of righteousness. The Almighty Father will always carefully apply any suffering that exists in the world to the backdrop of the Cross of His Son, but the agonizing pain which springs forth from crippling diseases and forsaken hearts is always of the highest firmament in the portraiture of His Love. The physical torture which was heaped upon Jesus Christ is the Passion that has saved our souls from spending eternity in exile from Heaven. But, the internal sorrow which His Mother endured is just as profluent toward making final reparation for our sinful errors. We recognize that such suffering by anyone in Creation may be quite as obnoxious to the senses, but it is never made of poison or venomous to the soul because it always paves the way for the purification of the greater world of men. The Seven Sorrows of Mary are an example for the rest of Her children to recall when asking for Her Divine intercession.

1. *The Prophesy of Simeon that a sword would pierce Her Immaculate Heart*
2. *Her Flight into Egypt*
3. *The loss of the Child Jesus in the Temple*
4. *Her meeting with Jesus on the Way of the Cross*
5. *The Crucifixion of Jesus on the Cross of Mount Calvary*
6. *The deposition of the Body of Christ from the Cross as it was laid in Mary's lap* This was quite poignantly depicted in the inspirational "Pieta" of Michelangelo
7. *The laying of Jesus' Body in the Sepulcher*

These wholly terrifying interior griefs were almost too overwhelming for such a beautifully delicate and charming Mother to bear in a single lifetime. Together, they represent more than anything which Saint Paul might have guessed to be lacking in the Cross of Jesus Christ. Her tears and dolors were as deep and agonizing as the Wounds of Her Sacrificed Son for which we offer the balms of our own mortification to this very day. And yet, the prayers we raise from our hearts for the conversion of sinners are as equally important as every lash and heartache that Jesus and His Mother ever suffered to bring the sins of mankind to an irrevocable end. Sometimes we believe that our best efforts are having only a marginal effect toward altering the mind-set of the world to do better, but our work has taken-up where our Savior and His Mother once left off. Our Lady is still quite displeased about the condition of Her children's souls today, and Jesus is yet offended by those who continue to mock His Sorrowful Crucifixion while ignoring the moral graces of His Seven Holy Sacraments. Sometimes we feel like we are only the mosquitoes at the dinner party or the termites squirming under the surface of the real world at hand. But, if we work long enough by gnawing away at the stubbornness of those who are opposed to Christianity, we will eventually topple their haughty pride into a heap of splinters laying in ruins on the ground. This does not come about without our own suffering in the mix because God also allows us to share in the same grief which once befell His Divine Son and His Immaculate Mother as they, too, tried with overwhelming success to deliver us to the post-baptismal bay of His Infinite Mercy.

There has never been a person who has gone to Heaven who did not yearn to be redeemed before the day they died. If someone asserts anything otherwise, he is only trying to fool himself. Therein rests the preposition to what kind of suffering may come to us in the present-day world. Most Christians are fortunate enough to die naturally on their own without somebody else killing them for their faith in advance. While it is quite a noble facet to become a martyr for our religious beliefs, most of us would just as soon usher that salvific cup to our neighbor's door as it passes quietly in the night.

But, the little things we do for Jesus on a daily basis are oftentimes just as magnificent in reflecting the power of the Cross. We have seen on many occasions that screen writers often base the entire synopsis of a major masterpiece on a subtle idiosyncrasy of a randomly anonymous person. God is no-less the accomplished laureate when it comes to elevating our more simple works in spiritual terms. He reserves the right, the power, and the capacity to turn our world around in circles, upside-down, inside-out, and backward again at the slightest hint of our interest in knowing Him to a greater degree. He can make our happiness in Him so extreme in joy that it will always counter any distance our hearts may be taken toward the opposite direction in total despair. We never have to snap our fingers to get Him to notice the silence of our whimpering. All we need to do is place a set of Rosary beads in our hands and we will have effectively echoed our desire out-loud for Him to turn our watering eyes into the sweetest wine of laughter again. There are silhouettes and profiles of familiar faces which remain on the Earth long after our Catechism teachers have passed-away to pose as our examples of loving kinship, and nearly every other kind of incentive to do God's work in their wakes in almost every direction we choose to turn our heads today.

The power of prayer is more palpable than humankind may ever know in time. People who beseech God to keep certain thoughts from entering their minds awaken the next morning and often cannot remember what they were actually praying for. They have somehow become mysteriously like the intellectual child adolescent named Joel Wittenberg who once proclaimed to his biological parents that a contemporary cultural argument can be made against every spiritual virtue which Jesus presented as the Beatitudes in the Sermon on the Mount. He apparently believed that they are too archaic for our technologically advanced secular societies and cited the need for them to be debated in a more public way. Therefore, in order to prove his case, he challenged his parochial high school Chaplain to debate the issues in the district gymnasium in front of the entire student body one day. However, by the time he had asked the Holy Spirit for guidance on his behalf for a higher state of Wisdom, that same Chaplain had given him a box containing a series of alphabetic letters and asked him to go to the marquee beside the boulevard and advertise the scheduled event for the rest of the world to see. But, as he arrived at the edge of the parking lot, he had forgotten what words he was supposed to spell-out. So, what did he do with his bucket of letters that were intended to announce his upcoming debate against the Beatitudes, once hailed as being the great title bout of "Joel v Issues?" He had no other choice than to carefully rearrange them on the marquee to depict his newfound simple slogan of, "Jesus Is love." We know that nothing is certain in life except for God's desire to save us from Hell and His complete means of expressing it through the aspects of the universe, supernatural facts, Divine art, the prophesies of the Saints, the physics of the material world, and through the power of His Paraclete inside our fibrillating hearts. There is no greater product of the Truth than that. And, we must listen to Him with the curiosity of little children. If He tells us to go into the backyard and grab a handful of wind from the western breezes and bring it back to Him intact, we had better know beyond any shadow of doubt that we are fully capable of doing it.

We have all muttered to ourselves and never known that we were speaking aloud until someone else asks us what we have said. That is the same comfortable nature with which we must come to know Our Savior at the core of our very being. Love should be our natural state of life, our means of communication, our reason for dressing for the day, the way we open our curtains, and the last sentiment we paraphrase before we close our eyes at night. Uniting with the perfection of Christ is just that simple. No one seems to understand why people yawn during certain times of the day because they do not know that it is our body's built-in modem of stimulating our respiratory system. We yawn and inhale when we first rise from our sleep so that our breathing pattern can be restored to its normal rhythm and our lungs can be refilled with fresh air. Shortly after we have been awake for awhile, our natural respiration is restored and we do not yawn anymore. The same thing happens when we stand and walk outdoors after being cooped-up inside the confines of our homes sometimes. Likewise, in the evening hours when our body begins to slumber for the night, we yawn because our systems are starting to shut-down and we do not draw deep enough breaths to take-in the amount of oxygen we need. Soon after we fall asleep, we hardly require any oxygen at all and the yawning stops again. This is a primal function of the involuntary responses of the human body to survive in the physical world. There is no difference in how we accept the graces from God which keep our souls aloft in purity. When we do, we suddenly begin to challenge ourselves to do many things that the early Saints once accomplished without ever having to ask themselves why. We sing melodies from our hearts that we have never even heard before. A complete stranger can approach us and we have an intrinsic feeling that we have known him all our lives. This is the natural reciprocity which Heaven bestows upon us when we finally give ourselves to Christ.

Long Live Mother Teresa of Calcutta!

December 28, 2000

No one who has an appropriate heart ever likes goodbyes or endings, especially ones that are permanent or sad. That is why we should always greet one another with a demeanor which speaks to Love, one with an all-encompassing gentleness and divine poise that brings-out the more redeeming qualities of ourselves, our friends, and our peers. One of the worst things which can happen in life is wishing that you will never encounter someone again or thinking to yourself, "Maybe we will get along better the next time we meet." This, in itself, is an admission that peace and good will among men has never really been secured. The truthful commission rests not in what we do to impress other men, but what we do *for* them, especially if they are poverty-stricken or somehow diseased. The list of great servants in the line of Jesus Christ could fill more pages than it would take to wrap the entire world in grace, even if it were to be singled-spaced and require a magnifying glass to read them. What these humble children of God have done for so long is to peel the encasement of shame from around that same globe which has been wrought by the rest of humanity who could not care less about how their brethren survive the night. Living the light of Divine grace always requires an intense degree of charitable aforethought so as to always be able to meet the needs of the poor before they are forced to stoop to begging on their knees for someone else to come to their aid. There is one worthy servant of God whose life should be remembered especially by the people of our age.

Mother Teresa of Calcutta actually combed the streets of her seaport city in an effort to reach those whose paths had not yet led them to her compassionate embrace. Her discerning spirit allowed her to grow infinitely in the Wisdom of God as she readily recognized the suffering of Christ in those who hungered for physical and spiritual nourishment, alike. The squalid living conditions in India and Albania where she served humankind so well has all but been eliminated for thousands of paupers who are still being blessed by the prayerful lives of the Sisters of Charity. Mother Teresa wanted everyone on Earth to envision the healing of all nations in the same way that she and her humble nuns have slowly nursed the natives of India back to health once again, one soul at a time. Those who are the beneficiaries of such saints as Mother Teresa are not only lifted out of the oppression of being poor, they are taught to know the Holy Spirit in themselves in a much more intimate way. Let us never forget *The Quotable Lewis, 1440; Taliessin Through Logres (1948), chapter V, paragraph 33, Page 359*, "Christians naturally think more often of what the world has inflicted on the saints; but the saints also inflict much on the world. Mixed with the cry of martyrs, the cry of nature wounded by Grace also ascends–and presumably to Heaven. That cry has, indeed, been legitimized for all believers by the words of the Virgin Mother, Herself–'Son, why has thou thus dealt with us? Behold, thy father and I have sought thee sorrowing.'"

Hence, we live at last in the likeness of this Holy Mother who also yearns to see the smiling faces of Her little servants on the Earth living-out the Will of God. This is the dressing for suffering at large, that the Mother of Our Savior would ensure Her unity with our efforts in such a worthy cause. We shall know forever to imitate Her stately Wisdom in remembering to call upon the same Son to whom She gave His Virgin Birth for security and consolation. That is Her way of invoking the power of the Holy Spirit, and it is assuredly the way in which Mother Teresa lived. This special nun did not spend her precious-few dollars advertising for certitude across the airwaves for more impressionable people to see, she got down on her knees in the filth of the slums with pity in her hands to make the world a better place for countless dying children, abandoned orphans, hungry widows, and people with crippling disease. She willingly offered her entire life as the magistral grace which is still being dispensed from the very Throne of God in our day. It is no wonder that there are already millions of laypeople, countless holy representatives, testators, advocates, witnesses, and priestly postulators who are urging the Vatican to move toward placing her sweet departed soul onto the fast-track for swift ecclesiastical canonization. Her life was much more than the pious perfection which we saw gleaming from the depth of her eyes. She was a self-disciplinarian and the exemplification of sacrificial grace. No one in the world knew how to pray better then her, and none was greater in her willingness to do it, even as much as twenty-four hours a day when she was still strong enough to endure.

Above everything else, Mother Teresa was an obedient daughter of the Immaculate Mother of God who knew the power of reciting a single Hail Mary as well as the Supreme Pontiff in Rome. She once stated that she would remember the holy shrine of Our Lady, Queen of Peace, in the Yugoslavian village of Medjugorje by offering the angelic salutation before she retired every night to ensure that the Will of God would be done across the summit of the mountains there. And, let us make no mistake about it, she could rumble with the best of them when the occasion was presented to publicly denounce abortion in defending the rights of all unborn children in the wombs of their mothers. She once told an obstinate pro-choice American president not very long before she died for him to send her those little children after they were born if no one else cared enough about them to advance their dignity from the womb to their full stature in human life. She was a warrior princess for their cause, and many expectant mothers carried their unborn children to full-term and new birth at the urging of this great Saint.

Mother Teresa also made it clear that her King was the Almighty Savior of the Cross, and her Queen was His Blessed Virgin Mother. Never once was she ever intimidated or shaken from her faith by the wealthy, powerful, or affluent, those who claimed a higher sovereignty before God, or those curiosity seekers who called on her only so they could be seen as being "chummy" with an impassioned maiden of holy honor. As for the latter, she usually sent them away with their tails between their legs in shame that they had given no more than the exiguous tip of the iceberg from their fortunes toward the advancement of those who had only little to their name. Mother Teresa could spot a hypocrite a mile away and held no reserve in telling them so. But, beneath her humble habit beat the heart of a silent champion, 87 years strong before she was finally taken to Heaven to receive her eternal reward in September 1997. Her soul to this day is still an heroic, shining, stately, royal, and splendorous gift from God to the Creation He made with such care. If the 20th century could ever be called blessed, it is because of the love and service of Mother Teresa and the Papacy of the Holy Father Pope John Paul II, who inspired her excellence so profoundly. The extraordinary character of her Christian conviction will be remembered long after Jesus Christ returns in Glory to claim His Mystical Body into Paradise for the endless ages to come. She was a venerable fountain of Love for the millions who knew her up-close in a most personal way, and those who had never laid eyes on her glowing face at all. There was no poverty of material or faith on any spot on the Earth after she laid her humble feet there and tread its path.

Although small in physical stature, she was a giant among men who taught us right from wrong, how to better understand the Holy Gospel of Our Lord, and what it truly means to pray from the heart. Her quick wit was attributed to her trust in God for all things in life. She once suffered a brief spell of faintness and responded in reply, "Oh, that was just a blessing from Jesus Christ." Not only did she nurture the victims of famine, rubeola, AIDS, and countless other diseases during their gruesome hours of suffering, she always remembered them to God in her daily supplications and implored the rest of humankind to do the same. There was never a single unkempt soul that ever asked for her help who was once turned away. Just as surely as Mercy and Pardon follow us all the days of our lives, Mother Teresa saw the Face of Jesus in Paradise when she died and must have heard him say, "Thank you! You are the one who cared for me for so long! Welcome to your new home!" And, that is why we remember Mother Teresa with the richness of princes in the wake of her life. She is now one with the entire Communion of Saints who continue to help God's helpless children in exile. We should lift our intercessory prayers to her everyday, just as she taught millions of others to do when she walked the

Earth in such noble grace. Everything she stood for was in common with Salvation. How proud our Heavenly Father must be to have welcomed her into His open arms! His absolute dominion, mastery, and abundance of Love for all of His people shines with great magnification into the world through the eternal soul of Mother Teresa of Calcutta. We should be so fortunate as to see her once again in the not-too-distance foyers of everlasting life. If we reflect the same commission which she espoused in helping God's "least of these," there is no doubt that our reward will be as rich as the bounty she has received from the Sacred Heart of Christ.

Pope John Paul II on the Value of the Family

December 29, 2000

Any time there is a conflict between human hearts where innocent people suffer from loneliness and despair, or when broken spirits overshadow our capacities to perceive new hope, or when the gravity of sin appears to be more attractive than our spiritual faith and moral perfection, then we have yet to accomplish the goal of attaining unconditional Love. The very first venue through which we are all exposed to knowing the difference between happiness and defeat is in our relationships within the circle of our immediate families. The gradual deterioration of the ties that bind us together from the crib to the front exit door has caused many of the tragedies which have stained the face of American civilization from one coast to the next. Public leaders and private citizens alike often speak about "family values," but they rarely mention the word "love" in their attempt to define what they really mean. The way some parents have ignored the spiritual needs of their young innocents is no less than an egregious abdication of their pastoral duties as guardians of their children's faith. The sequestered familial experience in which human beings are cultured makes an everlasting impression upon our conduct in the later years of life. From early childhood to our giddy adolescence, and from our becoming teenagers to statesmen, we must always be exposed to Love as it has been so uniquely defined by Jesus Christ in the Holy Gospel of the New Covenant. He has stated that His Spirit has come to divide us one from another, but His words resound the condition which exists only if we refuse to heed the rest of His wise counsel. Jesus is the great source of peace and cohesion in our families and in the world; but we are, indeed, divided by His Commandments if as few as one among us refuses to comply.

We are called to understand that every member of our immediate family is as important to the whole as any of the rest. There are so many forces which are still trying to divide us today that it seems almost impossible for us to remain under the same umbrella of our Christian pursuit. Pope John Paul

II spoke to the issue of the American family when he visited the Unites States in October 1979. He said, "When the value of the family is threatened because of social and economic pressures, we will stand up and reaffirm that the family is necessary not only for the private good of every person, but also for the common good of every society, nation, and state. When freedom is used to dominate the weak, to squander natural resources and energy, and to deny basic necessities to people, we will stand up and reaffirm the demands of justice and social love. When the sick, the aged, or the dying are abandoned in loneliness, we will stand up and proclaim that they are worthy of love, care, and respect" (Washington D.C., October 7, 1979). The Holy Pontiff was telling us a generation ago that the institution of the family must include those who are not even related to us by biological origin or the conditions of adoptive law. If we cannot love the members of our nuclear families completely, will we ever be able to reach-out in that same love to the rest of the world to commune with those who are so in need of our help and affections?

Our advancement toward a greater good will for humankind at large begins at the spiritual center of our individual hearts. We will always be a sorely diminished people if we continue to allow our biases and anxieties to deteriorate the fabric of our relationships into some type of paranoiac desperation or a discontented intolerance because it is the seed from which outright hatred is sprung. And, once that ugly head of malice has been raised, it can take countless centuries more to ever bring it back under control again. Sometimes our feelings are suspended in midair by our personal insecurities and prejudices against those who have attempted to invade the aspects of our individually-peculiar impressions of the world, as fragile as they might be, when their intentions may be quite as benignly simple as only asking us to accept their love. Many people have somehow come to believe that our collateral environment is no longer sanitary if we allow the opinions of unknown strangers to fester like a mole in the circumference of our midst. What we really need to recognize, instead, is that the superfluous speech of daily life rarely, if ever, reveals the true inner-self because most of us are more interested in how life affects us inside as opposed to how we can change humanity for the better as a whole. This type of spiritual reclusiveness does not really help anyone in the greater scheme of things, especially those who often run and hide from the very Truth which will eventually set them free. It is becoming increasingly obvious that Jesus Christ is the answer to every question as to why we are still a frail and broken society of frightened hermits instead of a bristling community of conjoining friends.

Saint Isaac of Stella bestowed a great wish upon the human spirit in A.D.1169 which is still quite applicable in our modern day, "May the Son of

God who is already formed in you, grow in you, so that for you He will become immeasurable, and that in you He will become laughter, exultation, and the fulness of joy which no one will take from you." Therein rests the reconciliation between relatives and members of the same family, between precincts and parishes, between nations and provinces, and between races and celestial worlds. Our hearts must be a living repository of inviolate hope; never disinterested or indifferent concerning what our subordinates might have to say, but always much more than capable of recalling any moral precept in a flash, spotting an offense against the Truth the moment we first see it, sustaining our higher senses of virtue and love, and protecting our inner-emotions from the aggression of any unsuspecting emotional attack. There is no doubt that God has created human life, but He has also subsequently left it to us to comply with His moral certainty and to complete the journey back to His Kingdom with propriety and response. We owe it to our loved ones and ourselves, alike, to maintain the fiber of our dignity before the rest of the world so that our descendants can learn from our intelligent legacy and the rules of moral law which we leave behind, a benison for their final inheritance. There have been a trillion tears which have fallen to the earth on the road to reclaiming our human decency. But, weeping does much more than just evacuate the sorrows from inside our hearts; it also makes amends for the transgressions of those who have so offended us in the sight of Jesus Christ.

God laid-out His Plan for our purification when His Son was placed on a stony slab in the Tabernacle Tomb where He was buried on Good Friday. There is no doubt that this same deathbed of rock was His Divine way of explaining to Creation that the hearts of humankind will open only after they have conceded to the responsibility for executing His Crucified Son. Now, He has been raised again, and God has fully done His part to absolve us of our crimes. We, however, are still the stoic and impervious pessimists who have failed thus far to soften the rigidity of our doggedness to allow Him to come back. We were once like the boulder of confinement for His Sacrificed Flesh; and we are still as stubborn as frozen mountains when He comes to knock upon the chambers of our hearts as the Holy Spirit now. We quite often treat Him like a mange-infested canine, no more than a mere pet peeve of ours, ironically too much a thorn which is somehow piercing *our* brow, demanding that He go lie down and stop clawing at our hearts in an effort to get inside for the comfort of our love. We often fail so miserably because too many of us cannot seem to decipher the mysterious "code" that will lead humanity back to trusting Him again. Fortunately, there is no such calculation or positioning required for our spiritual conversion inside the seed of Christian faith. There are most certainly many Divine Mysteries that still surround the Blessed Trinity, but the code for our conduct is found quite readily in the Sacred Scripture teachings. The Mystery of our Salvation is no more complicated than that. If we become like the little children whom Jesus asks us to be, we will be fully capable of seeing the footsteps of angels in the frosting on our birthday cakes and hearing the softest whispers of their nursery rhymes when we first lay down to sleep. These resounding graces from the Paraclete on High are both real and available to the touch. It is never a matter of an overzealous imagination that takes us closer to the Kingdom of the Blessed, rather the unfettered relinquishing of our callous chicanery and the obstacles to our faith.

Just because the Son of God may have never physically walked into the family rooms of our residences does not mean that He has not had plenty more to say by the signs He places in our midst. We can remove a piece of plain bond paper from our typewriter or a copied page from the screen of our word-processor and never have to utter a word to challenge the hearts of the millions who will read about the brilliance of our love. We can console the grieving, comfort the dying, and stir the consciences of men everywhere on the globe, just by leaving the printed traces of our Wisdom in written composition somewhere for them to see. That is also why Our Savior has so generously peppered the Earth with the Truth of His Holy Gospel in the light of the blazing sun, beneath the branches of conic pines, through the touch of more gentle hands, and abounding through the Glory of the Sacramental Graces which bloom like Chinese Chrysanthemums from the priests of His Apostolic Church. The presence of God in every living thing has been left like the leaves of a charlotte novel on the ledges of Creation, just begging for someone to come along and take them home for reading in the twilight hours of their days, perhaps awaiting the closing sunset that will deplete their mortal years. If we seek-out these holy instruments as one family of humankind with our hearts as entwined as the fibers on our sleeves, we will no longer question the motivations of our friends, and no more will our siblings rival the peace for which we pray with such sincerity in our hearts. God can readily hear us pounding our breasts in fear of loneliness quite like a base drum beating next to the melodious sound of an octave oboe. He knows that our relationships often follow the principles of physics and that the friction which swelters between us only serves to expand the nature of our differences while elevating the crassness of our too evasive tempers. Eternal peace will come full circle in our day if we solemnly choose to offer every second of it back to the Prince of Peace, the Child of Mary, the Author who has come to awaken us just in the nick of time to preserve the Redemption which He has finished with such languishing in His Blood. The Holy Spirit has already dispensed to humankind the Greatest Story Ever Told; and the bells of Norman Vincent's faith have finally pealed their last. Now, the burden of our Christian conversion is vested in the fullness of our response.

"The Powers That Be; The Powers Who Are"

January 2, 2001

It is a compliment to the 21st Century Western world that we have held fast to the restraining abstinence of moderation when we surely might have otherwise been more satisfied in annihilating the enemies of our social and economic progress which has made us the envy of the universe for contemporary advancement. Being a solitary superpower amongst a family of numerous underdeveloped nations has its perks, not the least of which is being able to boast of the best in militaristic defenses and the personal development of the human individual. The down-side to our success is that we curiously continue to place a disproportionate amount of value on tangible materials and very little credence on seeking the common thread which makes the entire globe of different races singularly one. If we do not heed the call of the Holy Spirit to share the profits of our international progress with the people who have no more than a grassy hut in which to live and a camp fire to sustain themselves, we have already failed the purpose of becoming gainfully more civilized from the start. If we look at our profusion in the context of being a parabolic control of the environmental climate, then the coldest winter of materialism we have ever known is now upon us, and our spirits are becoming somewhat ossified by the brittle nature of our isolationist approach. Our self-induced allurement to the satisfaction of our insatiable appetite for temporal goods over our spiritual identity is rendering us to be a lesser people than God has heretofore intended us to become. We are often a too calculating compost of meandering lushes who hover like insects above our next prey, wondering what undiscovered stimulus we might find there, just waiting for the right opportunity to lurch forward and grab it like a leopard in the wild.

What we often tend to forget is that Jesus Christ knows who we are, what we are thinking, the depths of our motivations, our capacities to fail and succeed, and whether we ever intend to surrender any of it for the purpose of knowing Him better. We may be taken by surprise to discover that the individual skies above us may not be as permanent as we have always believed, and that we may never sail aloft among them while incognito without the more perceptive angels realizing our presence after all. What we sometimes consider to be our darkest secrets only blind us to the Truth which God has been telling us all along. If we stay on the course that has been laid-out by the very conscience we profess before the world, we cannot help but be taken back to the inherent goodness through which Adam and Eve were created in the beginning.

The crux of this obvious eventuality is whether we are yet willing to stand and fight against the seemingly countless distractions which are still trying to force us to turn-tail and run. When it comes to defending ourselves against evil legions, the children of God are never truly afraid of engaging the battle, but we can get awfully tired of being on-guard all the time. It seems as though all we have to do is stop for a breath of fresh air and another enemy of our Salvation is standing in our path, ready to blow vile smoke into our face again. If we remake the alignment of our priorities so that we are no longer afraid of fighting and dying, Satan cannot harm us with a hint of anxiety anymore.

Let's face the facts candidly; humanity has been involved in the amateur profession of delivering our souls over to death since the beginning of time, and there is apparently no wrong way to do it since no one that we have known in our day has ever come back to try again. The billions of people who have died in the thousands of years of the history of man have somehow managed, with the help of God, to get it right the first time. There is no reason to assume that we will be any different when He calls us to return and stand in His presence in Heaven. If only we could believe in the droves of supernatural manifestations which are unfolding around us every day without hesitation, we would look at the end of life not as a means of expiration, but as a continuation of our blessed gift of liberty and peace in the Sacred Heart of Christ. If there is any kind of apportionment to be made in the quantity of miracles and apparitions throughout the historical ledger of Creation, it does not necessarily favor the earliest centuries over the contemporary nature of our own. Indeed, the 20th century has been among the most prolific of them all when pertaining to the intercessions of the Blessed Virgin Mary, the Saints, and the armies of Angels from the Throne of the Most High Deity. Moreover, never before has a generation of curious citizens been afforded a greater opportunity to live-out the persuasion of placing the highest possible value on individual human life than we have at our hands in the modern-day world; what with our previously unprecedented advancements in the practice of medicine, electronic communication, manufacturing goods and commodities, our ability to locate and treat the diseased and dying, and the technical knowledge which is required to place these cooperatively preventative systems in place.

The matter of our efforts boils down to the question as to whether we truly believe that human existence should be perceived as a priceless vase on a fireplace mantle or a broken gin bottle laying in the street. If it is the former over the latter, we should begin to try harder to make what little time we have left before Jesus returns our most valued in history toward employing our every good virtue, talent, resource, and energy for the purpose of healing His Creation in every sense of the word. The purpose of our daily lives simply comes down to that. The principle roadblock from making this occur is our lack of admission that we are often too selfish and our sacred promise to God that we will begin to do better with the compassion of the Cross in our hearts is usually left unfulfilled. The problem is that our struggle is often preceded by our reputation for seeking the most opportune globular position over our neighbors and our persistent knack for grabbing every good thing in life which we somehow think we deserve. Those of us in America want to make the transition from looking at the "powers-that-be" who are located at the far-distant horizon to becoming the invincible "powers-who-are" who perceive the rest of the world through the prism of our seclusive inhibitions. Moreover, we want to accomplish this overnight, while still not knowing what to do with our good prosperity other than to please ourselves once we have securely attained it. There is no doubt that our objectives and priorities are in need of a major spiritual overhaul. In the evolution of our post-modern secular world, a thoughtful public servant is somewhat a wizard nowadays if he can persuade someone else to even slightly adhere to the basic principles of common sense and the higher admiration which we should all maintain inside the depths of our hearts for the mystical intentions of God.

We shall never truly discover the cubic parameters of mortal genius until we finally look charitably toward the poorest among us and act upon their immediate sight to alleviate their suffering. If being divine in human flesh is to be as possible as Christ has told us it is, then this goal is the saving grace on our journey to Paradise. We are much too often predisposed to complacency in the face of the unmitigated selfishness of our peers whose favor we do not wish to lose and whose character we would never dare bring into question. That not only represents a statement about their lack of charity, but about the insolvency of our own personal integrity as well. If only we could know how the Holy Spirit is already speaking inside us, and if only our nightmares of a secluded world of segregation would go away, perhaps we might rise to the occasion of putting the extraordinary needs of the rest of the world before our own individual whims. Many have been the times when we have finally attained a great personal achievement for which we have longed like sheep all our lives, but in the shock of our sudden success, our consciousness never really allows us to believe that victory has become ours at last. We often arise from our sleep and surreally discover that the Almighty Father has delivered us from the hollowness which once accompanied our every waking moment only after we have walked alone in the dark or on the less-traveled trails of our little towns while hungering for just a sliver of a chance to finally make it big. These are the same hopes and sentiments of many other people around the world who wonder when they are going to see their next meal or how they will ever take away their father's pain from lying in a bed of catastrophic illness, fear, or cerebral emaciation.

If any one of us has ever pondered why our mind never seems to stop whirling through the possibilities about how better the world can be when we are dead asleep at night, it is because the human heart is still tweaking our faith in knowing that our love is never complete while there are still little children cooped-up inside cardboard boxes on the street while their mothers are out looking for some passerby in the night who might spare her some pocket change so she can purchase a loaf of bread to feed them when the cold reality of the morning dawns. These are not vague images from someone's novel imagination that are penned for the latest New York Time's list; this is the real world as it exists today. And, for those hatemongers who state in complete defiance that paupers are on the street because they have put *themselves* there, the Son of God will soon respond to their preposterous fabrication with the reply that the same assertion will no-doubt have to be made when someone asks why the richest of all among us have mysteriously gone to Hell. Therefore, why should we not let our midnight dreams of polar extremity be more about sharing the fortunes of the world instead of calculating why someone's satin sheets are softer to the touch than the concrete ballasts of the highway underpasses where their poorer brethren have taken refuge for the night? While we often rush to the doctor to secure a new prescription for the symptomatic hypochondrias which somehow ail us like a phantom mantra and consume the pharmacist's wares like they are almost going out of style, the vagabond souls on the street whose solvency has been squandered by our own selfish greed can only hang their heads in sorrow and pray to the God who loves them that their wailing tears will eventually wash their pain away.

Too many ordinary people continue to raise their brows in pride and arrogance while proclaiming that they will make the best holders of political office because they will never leave a soul behind. They campaign for seats on the school board, the titles of mayor, representatives in the House, and all the way up the line to the highest offices in the land. They splash the evidence of their hollow promises all over the newspaper headlines everyday and invoke the populist nobility of their inaugural proclamations like Shakespeare wearing a martyr's crown. But, when the pinnacle of Truth finally arrives at their door and the critical moment comes for them to decide to either keep their promises of prosperity for all or to kick-back their spoils to the partisans who first helped them get to the top of the heap, their answer is almost too obvious to state. That is why there is such irony in a united American nation which is so afraid of being taken hostage by some foreign faction, while we have instead long been held captive by the almighty dollar inside our own guarded borders from becoming the truthful land which espouses opportunity for the oppressed and freedom for the brave. Such blatant hypocrisy will never survive the impending Kingdom of Jesus Christ; and He will undoubtedly pulverize it under His Mother's Heel as soon as His Omnipotent Father in Heaven commands the fateful word. Although He has never mandated to mortal humankind that any construct of governance should be a communistic rite; to hold on to our wealth with our arms akimbo until we are given some sort of formal dowry in exchange for our Christian charity is a sure way to divorce our souls from any kind of eternal consolation before God ever proposes that we accompany His Sacrificed Son down the aisle of absolution. His uncompromising Commandment to share and share alike infers that those who were never given an opportunity to be the best in the class or who never inherited an empire from their ancestors are still meant to be treated like Divine royalty when we see them crouching in poverty on a park bench outside City Hall.

So, we continue to discuss the issues of human rights in our public forums and how we might ultimately sever the ugly head of social indigence so we will not appear to be quite as seedy to the rest of the world when they look so fondly toward us for international charm and romanticism. We have totally and completely missed the point if we do not take at least a moment to be enlightened by the Spirit of God who knows no comparison between sovereign nations and could not care less whether our flag flies more properly than at the capitol of the republic next door. He lives in the center of our hearts where there are no politics to please, no axes to grind, and no philosophical ideologies to embrace for the purpose of ensuring our compliance to the will of the donors who have paid us to protect their private wealth. The Kingdom of Heaven is Jesus Christ at His best; and the Truth is the Gospel mandate through which His righteous elect will eventually succeed in serving Him. As has been said many times before, never has there been a dollar taken past the grave; but many are our acts of selfish shame which have made us all a lesser people in trying to pass it on to our selective heirs. Any adjective which can best describe our material greed is more than apropos these days because anguished paupers around the globe are still asking God to force us into surrendering their share of natural resources which He so generously allotted to them when He laid the first axial cornerstone to the center of the world. Their problem will not be resolved by any number of polemics or ecumenical books, but only by our compliance with the New Covenant Christ.

The Immaculate Crown of Twelve Stars

January 3, 2001

Our love for the Son of God takes its derivation from the power of His Spirit of persuasion, the same sense of communion which He employed when He lured His first Apostles away from their trades to become fishers of men. They learned much more than the immeasurable aspect of the perfection of the soul; they encountered the immortal knowledge that the Kingdom of Heaven is larger than we could ever have perceived it to be on our own. There are too many dimensions in life for us to ever keep track of them all, but only one unbounded Love which will take us back to the Garden of Eden. Our relationship with the Holy Paraclete is filled to the brim with miracles, mysteries, oracles, and manifestations. Saint Peter and his friends wasted no time in falling in line behind the Savior of the world when He came to summon them into His favor. There is no doubt that He would have quite a difficult task these days in coaxing the men of our age to walk with Him toward self-sacrifice and eternal grace. There is no present-day sudden rush to usher the Kingdom of God to the Earth in our time because too many policemen, district attorneys, judges, jailers, and prison guards would suddenly become unemployed. What good would they be in a world where there is only forgiveness for those who have sinned, alongside their proper enlightenment so they will never fall again. Indeed, what would be the use in stealing anything at all if every child of God receives an equal share of the blessings of the Earth? This may appear to be too optimistic to be true, but there is no denying that Divine Love is the recurring motif, the *idee fixe*, of the nature of God from before the beginning of the Creation He made with His Hands.

Indeed, Love is the underlying purpose of our spiritual faith and the source of every act of human decency which springs from within it, whether it be a thought of prayerful solace or the act of feeding five-thousand men from a few fishes and loaves. There is no possible way that our trust in the Lord can be misplaced on the Earth or in Paradise. Even through many of the unwritten Traditions of the Church, Jesus affirms whatever we do in His Name as a voucher toward the dispensation of His Sacred Blessing. These same Traditions are as dear to our Almighty Father as the Crucifixion of His Son, itself. We must always remember that the administration of the Sacraments by His holy priests are fixed in time because they are executed by mortal men; and yet they are also eternal and immortal graces for the souls who receive them. For those who place no value in the supremacy of the Traditions of the Holy Roman Catholic Church, they are robbing themselves of the higher gifts from the Throne of God in Heaven. Their faith is weaker than it needs to be; and their human spirits are only the poorer for it. When someone inquires of Jesus as to whether the Traditions are from Him, it is as though He is nodding His Thorn-Scarred Head to the affirmative rather than to utter an audible "yes" so as to preserve the integrity of our faith. He has asked us from the beginning of time to know that He has ratified our good works in His Holy Name, no matter what the age in which we live.

Jesus also requires us to accept the regenerative power of His Body and Blood which has reaffirmed our Wisdom to know that He is living inside us. Hence, it is not only our goodness that is at work, but the substance of His Divinity, too. There is nothing that takes us closer to conversion and Salvation which is not commissioned by Our Father in Heaven because we can muster no immaculately imaginative power on our own. The honor, respect, and reverence we hold for the perfect Fruits of the Holy Spirit are undefiled from whence they first entered our consciousness. Our echoing affection for the resonance of Christ through the tangible world is like the serein mists which follow a sustained showering of rain, the tiny droplets of moisture which somehow continue to fall once the clouds have finally moved away. They ensure that our souls will never once suffer the parching periods of reservation and doubt which often haunt other men, those who have never considered surrendering their existence to Jesus. Even though there may be no rainbows overhead every time we walk back into the fields, we know that God is still there by the Light of the Holy Spirit in our hearts and the unseen Kingdom of Human Redemption which is now fully at hand. The evidence of our conversion to the Truth rests comfortably within the panorama of a Crown of Twelve Stars, the *etoiles*, situated so perfectly around the Immaculate Mother of God. They are anything but a symbolic gesture of good will from Heaven; they are a fully ceremonial Constellation which resounds the faithfulness of the first Apostles and the stellar Wisdom that led them to creating the Original and Apostolic Church through the sublime Divinity of the Holy Spirit.

What is so revealing about these Cardinal Virtues which oscillate so profoundly about the Head of the Blessed Virgin Mary? The secret is found in the intercession which She is affording humankind before the Cross of Her Son. They shine through a random order of proficiency in remembrance of Our Lord from His Nativity to His Ascension into Heaven. Any soul can see their conversion twinkling before their eyes in the penmanship of God written across the Sky of the Firmament above the Grace of His humble Mother. *In propria persona integer vitae*, we must always preserve our purity and innocence, *Christus Crucifixus e pluribus unum*, we are all one of many in the Sacrifice of Christ, *Agnus Dei misericordia*, we are saved through the Mercy of the Lamb of God, *terminus a quo, terminus ad quem*, He is the Alpha and the Omega, *vi et armis sanctus victorias*, we know victory with holy arms, *in hoc signo vinces*, in this sign shalt thou conquer, *divinitas mater familias*, Our Lady is the Divine Mother of families, *vae victis*, woe to the vanquished, *Mater Dei Immaculata*, She is the Immaculate Mother of Our Almighty Father, *Deo gratias*, thanks be to God*!* *Ora pro patria* , pray for your country!, and *Dominus vobiscum*, the Lord be with you always! These are the sparkling signatures, epilogues, and blessings that are already glittering over the New Jerusalem as we wait in joyful hope for the Dawn of the Second Coming of Jesus Christ in Glory.

In Matters of Faith and Morals, It Certainly Is!

January 4, 2001

We are called to be little children in the Gospel of Jesus Christ, away from the cynical entrapments that are set before us by countless ruthless men, and fond of the innocence through which we once saw every soul who first approached us as we pounded our fists on the trays of our high chairs, way back when. We never really knew what it meant to be afraid until the first person came to scare us. Pain was never a factor in life until the first time we caught our little finger in the kitchen drawer. The only abandonment that we could possibly conceive is when our mother suddenly disappeared beyond our immediate sight. But, our perception and emotions have come a long way since those days of early pines. Now, we almost expect to be hurt both inside and out by the sorrows of losing our friends or our parents to death, or the home for which we have worked for decades going up in smoke in an accidental fire. We sometimes wonder where we will get the money to send our children to school or how we will pay their outstanding medical bills. When we were yet little children peeking so impishly into the faces of the adults who so adored our carefree purity, we could not have known that life would become so difficult to bear. The problem at hand is that most of us believe that the coming of adulthood is supposed to be a battle against the years. But, this is not what Jesus teaches us at all. The world is not so much inherently cruel in nature as it is adversely affected by our endless search for a more complex meaning. Unfortunately for most of us, our misguided search has sent us down a path of bobbing for material goods in a sea of confusion, running as fast as we can from anyone who would dare to admonish us not to continue, and going to sleep at night wondering what new assets will be ours tomorrow.

There is more to the acclamation by Jesus which says we must become little children before we will ever be allowed admittance into the Kingdom of Heaven than what we choose to believe. Taking our own little children as an example is a good place for us to start learning, especially in their preschool years. They rarely ask for anything more than something to eat and plenty of toys to toss around because they have never really looked beyond the glass in the front door to know that cars are not an intrinsic property of global nature and that their manufacturers do not give them away. They sit like pets in our grocery carts while we push them around through the supermarket and somehow believe that the food we purchase for our kitchens has always been there on the merchant's shelves. It is not that they never care to know the rest of the story, it is just that a lack of such information is not detrimental to their everyday lives. Is this the kind of "children" which Jesus requires us all to become? In matters of faith and morals it certainly is! We must believe the Gospel of His Truth just like those same little kids who see the produce section in the grocery store and know not in what region they were grown. We realize that Love is only from God as well as everything which composes His Creation existing beyond the scope of our sight. We live and Trust in His Word without question because that is what the Holy Spirit has asked us to do. Hence, we have become His children once again.

But, we must be wary of the skewed perception which also comes with such a fresh beginning so we do not fear the social cinema that keeps flashing in our faces everyday. When we see fishing worms, little children see rattle snakes. A Saint Bernard to us looks like an elephant from their infant perspective. Moreover, stop signs, traffic lights, and wailing train whistles do not mean a nippy thing to them; neither could they care less about civil codes and uniforms. Our growing spiritual maturity should always make us more discerning than that. Just because an enterprise may have a fancy logo and a catchy slogan to laud its name does not contribute to its good standing or status of legitimacy. The older we grow, the more it seems like the innocuous aspects of our personal lives slowly begin to fade away; but the hunger of our hearts for tenderness remains a much-too-often unfulfilled trait of our inner consciousness. The acceptable mortal character of humankind cannot survive very long if it is not nurtured by the eternal consolation which is found in the Holy Spirit of Christ. We often tend to remain in a constant period of reflection when we love one another as we, ourselves, desire to be equally embraced by God. This is never a self-effacing wish list of long-extinguished hopes or sweet dreams that have permanently been destroyed, but a new anticipation of the better world to come and the realization of our destiny in Heaven, where the death-rattle of our darkest fears is gone.

The night is more than a parable about street lights and locked entrance doors; it is an impression of our suspended expectations of what tomorrow may bring; and we face it with the full complement of trepidation, fear, resolution, and confidence closely at our side. No matter what we do with time, something will always come to take its place. Thereafter, God has left it up to us to define what goodness that future will possess. We should never consider opening our sleepy eyes to the sunrise in the east without first consulting with the Holy Spirit as to how we can make the world a better place, to somehow learn from our brothers' wit, to mend the walkways beneath our clumsy feet, to create a broader bridge of unity between the lost and forsaken, and to co-redeem their spirits by forgiving them to the max, no matter what transgressions still exist for which they stand accused. The title of "predecessor" to our new progeny is a huge responsibility to accept, but it is forthrightly ours to assume. What will we do to take ourselves back to our earlier innocence while simultaneously maintaining our wariness before the rest of the world? How well will we hope for our brothers' health, and pray for them, listening carefully to their pleas, and proceed to mend their lives? If they beseech our residual currency, will we give them our liabilities instead? If their tenure finds them lying face-down on the ground, will we help them back to standing on their feet, or walk around them on our way to someplace else? If their infirmities and afflictions find their way into our diaries, will we wish to quarantine them into a more remote location so no one else will ever be able to compare them to our own good fortunes?

Somehow, amidst the swell of all this human growth, personal development, temporal distraction, slow matriculation, and stealthy calculation, we are still required to become some of the most profound evangelists the world has ever seen. We must behave as though we are masters of filial love while maintaining the same demeanor as our humble servants. We should always teach the Truth about sacrifice and charity without appearing to be hypocrites, ourselves. We must pray deeply for the conversion of the world on our knees while still carrying water to our more destitute brothers as quickly as we can pail it. And, we must anticipate the arrival of the Kingdom of our Salvation while simultaneously keeping our hands to the plow and our minds singularly united with the needs of the suffering poor. And yet, if we yearn to see more of the miracles of the universe, do we reckon that the Son of God will leave us in suspense? The answer reverts to our faithful desire to accept them with the honesty of those little children we so often see climbing up and down the steps of the escalators alongside their distracted mothers at the shopping mall. The essence of this trust is never a blind retraction into being naive again or surrendering our higher intelligence. It means cutting-out the fat which has grown the obesity of our obstinance and jumping headlong into the bushes to see what is causing them to shake so much. Accepting that we are the children of Our Father in Heaven once again is the retrieval of our more generous side, to laugh at our own mistakes, and to cast away the disdain which has brought our vile indiscretions to a bleeding head for far too many days. At last, it means being willing to be carried like a collar around the back of Our Savior's neck in the image of the lamb for whom He gave His Life to save.

If we can fully participate in the charismatic simplicity that has made saints of the earliest ages, our Love will quickly whisk-away their centuries of despondence by the sounds of our hands and knees slapping on the floor as we crawl like toddlers into the Holy arms of God. We can hop full-bore into His lap and cry-out "Papa," and He will proudly take us in; for we are the prodigal children He has been waiting too long to see recuse ourselves from jurists' benches and fall into the embrace of our long-forgotten mothers once again. We are quite expected to ask the Angels "why" every time they turn around; and their Wisdom will always take our souls right back to the Throne from whence they came. God does not even seem to care whether we put our mortal shoes on the wrong feet once in awhile, just as long as we remember that we are supposed to be going home sometime soon, particularly on the road which will lead us to His residential Grace. For all it is worth, we are the fortunate generation which holds dominion over the advanced contemporary world, but we too often act like we are sprawled-out on our spiritual deathbed instead of living-out the promises of our Christian faithfulness. It is alright to weep when things don't seem to go our way, as long as the properties we desire are in union with the Will of God. He already knows the value of our ulterior pouting and whether there is true sincerity to our whims. All we have to do is place our every single thought in the Sacred Heart of Christ, and the Kingdom of Holy Explicitness will be finally ours to keep. We will find everything for which we seek in Jesus as the Author of our faith.

In light of our lack of perceptive awareness, our souls are suffering the angst of a form of separation anxiety from the Kingdom of Heaven that has all the classic symptoms of a child who has been abandoned on a doorstep somewhere out in the cold. Fortunately for us, however, an Angel named Gabriel came to ring the entrance bell of the mortal world and the Blessed Mother of God answered the door, allowing the company of our Salvation to come in. She has since turned to tell Her Divine Son about the sorrowful state of affairs in which we have been left; and He has done everything in His Omnipotent power to restore our dignity again. He has fought both tooth and toenail to give us a new name, to shower our beings in Baptismal Grace, and wash us clean through the perfection of His Blood. He has reared us according to His Holy Word and is now fully prepared to present us to His Father in Paradise, expecting in advance that God will adopt us as His own little children as though we had never left the chambers of His Palace. Now, we are dressed in the saintly conversion which has been dispensed to us by His Immaculate Mother. She has taught us the proper table manners by beseeching us to kneel before the Sacred Altar of Her Sacrificed Son, knowing full-well that our presence will be more dignified when we finally take our seat at the Banquet Table of Everlasting Life. So, while we are never meant to be the epitome of immature delinquents in grown-up bodies anymore, we can surely display the yearling disposition that will make the septilateral Fruits of the lofty Paraclete more sweet to our buzzing lips for the countless ages to come, bearing with them our new consolation, absolution, and spiritual ingenuity. Our Sweet Lord wishes to hear us giggling like cherubs in the satchel around His shoulder blades, not screaming for a mandate of cultural identity like some movie-trailer over-voice. He knows that our Love for Him is yet precipitously on the lam, but He has not given up in the effort of retrieving us for final deliverance to His Father once again. Even though His Mystical Body on the Earth is of all concurrent ages, we are still a supernatural element in the Eminence of His Love. Let us vow at once to become those little children who have earned His sincere affections so His burden will become more clement as He carries our souls back to His Throne of Eternity.

The Professions of the Mortals in Conclave Just Below

January 5, 2001

Our Divine Lord has asked us to pluck the strings skillfully when we play-out the symphony of His Eternal ensemble before the throngs of other men. His Truth has long been the plectrum of our faithfulness, for without His Holy Spirit to guide us through the darkness, we would have never known what notes resonate the most delightfully to His ears. When we hope and wish, pray and implore, and provide and attest for such a long time, we often begin to wonder whether what we say even seems to matter anymore. The list is long that bears the names of those who have gone to Heaven, the countless epitaphs of clerical geniuses through whose works we now know God better than we have ever attested to perceive Him on our own. There are books of Saints, Feasts of Martyrs, Solemnities of the Blessed, and Masses for the Dead. Now, at long last, we know that there is a more epoch time of peaceful grace which has yet to break past the dawn; for all the marking of the days that those who are now asleep in Christ inscribed, we suddenly incline that they are all one part in Body with Him. But for the saving grace of pretty flowers, moralizing homilies, rhythmic sonnets, and solfeggio duets, we might tend to look another way while seeking to rock our souls to sleep amidst the wait for our Salvation to finally come. Is Jesus the prodigal Master who has been frolicking about the universe for far too long, knowing that our hearts are just as broken as the lanced bosom of His Own? Can we not reciprocate sufficiently and barter for His return in satisfaction, fatting the calves of our spiritual righteousness, slaughtering the audacity of our own human will, and redressing the arena of the Earth in the most spirited decorum which He has so properly afforded us to dispense?

The memories of our grandfathers' faith are still alive today, for now they can proclaim that He came for them before they had eyes to see Him in advance. Will we be so fortunate as to know Him better than those generations before? Do we have the strength to run into the wilderness and see if He is hiding anywhere? If we build our Love in remembrance of His Holy Sacrifice, will He not come back at last? The trust which transcends our own beliefs cannot be placed in vain! This is not the time for goodnight, farewell, or bye-bye to those gleaming hopes that we have long held in our embolic hearts. The harvest fruits are ripening now, the hour is near at hand, and the Savior of Humankind is ushering-in the twilight of the morning! The oceans' waves are careening now; He has fully parted the darkness of the night with the laser of His Love; and Cana's miracle ballads can again be heard playing from the Victory on the shore! His Mother's water is now new wine; and this wine has become His Sacred Blood; and His Blood is our final Absolution after all! Let us forget about taking time for climbing to the mountain peaks to proclaim our life's Redemption, for there are insufficient glassy sands remaining to scale them now! We should begin to celebrate our Salvation from the monument where we stand! Deliverance into Heaven*is* the summit of God's peace on Earth and blessings to all men of noble will! How ironic is it that we have already come to be the chosen Elect in the Sacred Heart of Christ, but we are only now beginning to circulate our nominating petitions to bring about a better world? Men have prophesied long ago that we would never yield to the battle against the haste of an exile which is so subdued by doubt!

Now, we can bear-out the Truth of the Sacraments because, in them, we are pious again, and we can fall in Love anew. We can fully discern the amplitude of the Paraclete while He sings from the center of our hearts and choose our words most auspiciously when we tell humanity how sweet is our absolution to the taste! The surface of our community is no longer a gritty gypsum slothfulness, but a more golden rule of righteousness, fit for the new Kings we are, sparkling in the dewdrops of our ever fresher holiness, polished by the faith of our sudden sacredness, and suitable for the hour when our souls will be finally set forever in the pitchstone of God's grace. No longer do we need the reference of the stars to know where Jesus is; never again will we desist in acknowledging His Truth; and not a single instant more will we have to kiss the lackluster lines of our bank accounts in order to survive. Through the Son of Mary Immaculate, we have found the pivot of our purity; and we are never going back to bed with corruption ever again! The bridge of our infirmity has been finally burned for good; and now we can leap with joy that the olden spoils of our ancient days can just rot into abysmal smut for all we care! This is the enlightened age of our discernment when we can talk to Moses and remind Him what a good Messiah that his prophecy had foretold! We can tell Ecclesiastes that we are chaste once again, and that our hearts need not feign a struggle which we had never wished to wage from before the moment when Jesus Christ first shook the world and woke us up! Now, we are His fancied warriors who have found the lost and transformed their spirits into flowers blooming from the darkness of His Tomb!

The "people-speak" of this new day is about ridding Creation of every form of distemperature and beginning our lives over once again. It means that insolvency can be washed away more quickly than it came about; that penitence is a transverse plank in the boardwalk toward the Light of Divine Euphrasy, that prayer from the heart is our first commission which answers the interrogatories of why we ever began to hope for peace at all. Repentance is the initiation of the full expungement of our felonious discordance and saying "yes" when it means denying the wishes of the self, a far more noble investment than giving-in to mortal carnal lust, debased perversion, and brazen exploitation. With the Truth of Love glowing so tanny in our faces, how can we turn our backs and leave our consciences out in the cold? There is not a single speck of darkness or a clouded tint of gray in the Eternal Truth, so why do we need more than one paillette adorning the surface of our soul? We are members of the largesse of invincible riches, now being dispensed in the millions by the Son of Our God for transference into the Mansions of Holy Paradise. Indeed, where else would the first Apostles have gone for such grace and power? They knew, as we all know now, that moral excellence can be found only in the Master of the Ages, who once came replete in Human Flesh in their archaic day of present tense, and now in the Holy Spirit, Sacred Word, and Sacrament, to take us to the same Garden Suites where they now confer about the proper professions of the mortals still in conclave just below. So, let us be far wiser than their mere mortal loftiness and give them reason to know that they will see us once again on a more proficient day, when wrens and orioles can sing atop the vineyard slopes as we, the branches, shuffle stately in the winds. We sometimes make a poor and tepid attempt at slowly relocating our subtle eccentricities so as to create a diversion away from our more peculiar attributes, not truly realizing that we still share the identical fallible capacities to commit the same concentric foibles which are common to us all.

Mutual Civility and the Composure of Society

January 6, 2001

Part of the community of Wisdom in understanding the Will of God is to know that we are all trying to become timeless and immortal saints inside the parenthetic subpart of eternity through which the world exists. An hourglass is nothing more than a miniature turnstile, and so is the Will of Our Almighty Father to allow only one day at a given time to compose the procession of our lives. Do we surmise this to be true because He knows we cannot bear life any faster than that? Is there too much grief and sorrow for us to greet than can be engaged in less than one twist of the Earth in the vacuum of space? What is so magical about the hours numbering twenty-four, the 1440 minutes which we are allotted to complete our work, consume our meals, get plenty of rest, pray for our Salvation, fruitfully multiply our numbers, and slowly prepare for death? There is no denying that the basis for all of it must be founded in the capacity of God to know us before we ever gain the opportunity to realize for ourselves who we are and where we are eventually going. One thing is for sure, if we do not have His Love in our hearts, we might as well get in the car, travel into the city, walk into the newspaper office, and place our own obituary in the legal section because we are already dead and looking for a grave to crawl into. Indeed, when we glance into the mirror in the morning without the Holy Spirit having possession of our soul, it is a modern-day miracle that there is even a reflection looking back. If we already know that the calendar is a function of the movement of celestial masses in the spacial universe, why can we not accept that human Redemption is brought by the same God who created it from the very first?

His prominence is dove-tailed into the world like the profile of a feather, so subtly bewildering and blessed from Heaven that we are often forced to look at our lives from the purview of the inside-out to see His presence best. Ignoring the power He wields over us is no way to become better acquainted with His saving Grace. It would be interesting to see what would happen if everyone alive decided to walk backwards one day. Do we actually think we could fool God into believing that He would then be seeing His Creation unfolding in reverse or that we had finally discovered how to go back in time without imploring His aid? There are some people who assume that He is so gullibly impressionable; but they fail to recognize that, if not for His Divine intercession, we would never even be able to stand upright at all, much-less walk in any direction we choose to embark. Perhaps we take for granted that the business of life is something which even He often views through eyes of chagrin and disdain. Just because we may have the capacity to talk in our sleep does not mean that we are capable of dreaming aloud. If it is like most of our hollow platitudes, it certainly does not infer that we are capable of creating sound moral doctrine without the soul and inspiration of the Son of God to guide our thoughts. We must try our noble best to realize the purpose of His Holy Reign better than this.

If we are to accept the dominion that we have been offered over the matters of the Earth, we should allow the Holy Spirit of preservation into our hearts so as to defy the culture of death which leads many people to abortion, suicide, and euthanasia; and to protect one another from physical harm and exposure to malevolent forces which serve only as detriments to our Christian maturation. One of the problems inside America today is that those who are fashioning the standards for our cultural fecklessness do not yet understand that there is a broad difference between "garb" and garbage; or if they do, they are certainly not conferring with the provisions of their own Thesauruses. Most of them have either wilfully or inadvertently left God out of the process; and the learned habitations of our adolescent children are already paying the price. We spend thousands of dollars apiece for a global positioning system in our automobiles to make sure we never get lost, but most of us do not give a hoot whether Jesus Christ ever knows where our souls are presently located with respect to the parameters of time and eternity. We too often pay very little attention to what has been going on right beneath our noses. Humankind has excavated craters by the multitudes from the surface of the globe so as to build skyscrapers, install subway transportation systems, and create shelters to protect us against the forces of a nuclear blast; and the Earth is somewhat now the lesser for it. But, the architects of this new "development" proudly beat their chests in their triumphs over nature. On the other hand, our 2000-year-old ancestors once dug a single hole in the ground to make a plug in which to place the Holy Cross where Our Savior was Crucified; and the soul of every mortal sinner who ever lived was spared from eternal condemnation. It was the greatest ground-breaking ceremony ever to be held in the history of all Creation, but a only few hundred-thousand people in history have ever bothered to open their hearts to acknowledge His invitation to attend, let-alone offer a simple RSVP. Most of us still snub it as being an unsolicited obstruction to a greater world of fame and turn away like timid moles, searching in earnest for someplace else to bury a time capsule that celebrates the uniqueness of our prevalence.

There are a great many other statements about the inability of humankind to truly understand the dimensions, scope, and purpose of mortal life as God wishes it to be known. Our souls often grow weary from the cold hatred which we espouse. They crack, ache, sting, and bleed; but we still refuse to acknowledge that it is our own raw doing which is keeping the more balmy climates away. We need to start not only making better promises to ourselves and to the greater world at large, but we must also do better in resolving to keep them; even if it is to the point of self-enforcement and denial; and even if it means placing our own dignity in the line of fire so we can elevate the highest prospects for the successes of other men. We must hope to choose more wisely in the greater avenues of possibility that will lead us all to a more civilized society as it is defined by personal and social Love, not by expediency or paper-lace popularity before those who can do nothing but try to procure our respect through the tenuous bribery of their material wealth. No conviction could ever be more brilliant than our desire to become the contemporary poster-children of moral perfection, shared by our societal responsiveness with faith to the depths of the most blessed of hearts and the pursuit of the only goal which will ever matter in the end; the deliverance of the entire globular mass of human people into the rolling pool of Blood at the foot of the Cross of Jesus Christ.

Thereafter, our acceptance in His sight will not only be abrupt and spectacular, but a requisite accompaniment that *He* requires for His own satisfaction; knowing that His Love has made all the difference in the cumulative ages and that His Wisdom has been the firebrand which has cauterized the hole in Creation into which we might have otherwise fallen with no way to get out. Our oaths of Love must be uttered aloud so that we, ourselves, can hear them reverberating from the outermost walls of our consciences and back again; never allowing us to wiggle off the hook of our own good faith, pulling like the spirit of St. Louis Clydesdales at our sense of decency until the fateful moment when we finally drop like potato-sacks in death at the feet of our children hanging on our every last word. If we are going to be greedy at all, let it be in never wanting the slightest portion of God's Holy grace to slip beyond our grasp. No man should ever stand in the wake of a disastrous life and proclaim that he never once failed to try to make it better. Tragedy can come in many forms, but the greatest is the spiritual hero who never came to be, the honest man who squandered his own potential to share the best of his Love, and the masses of lukewarm Christians who always professed they were doing more than enough to satisfy the appetite of Jesus Christ to make the world a more peace-filled place for everyone. Not since the giants of the early ages have we seen more than a sprinkling or two of truly larger-than-life mortal beings; those who have made a difference by never inheriting a penny; the same ones who were forced to beg for their first dollar, but always gave away the last they ever had.

We weep inside with tears which almost drown our hearts because the days still lack the fire that once came from the skyscraping faith of little people in isolated and anonymous places, marching to the beat of conquering social inequity, calling for the alleviation of abject poverty in every urban slum, and embracing little children who run away from home to somehow punish their parents, only to return and see that they have suddenly passed-away while they were gone and now the grief is theirs to bear. Somewhere inside us all is a need to hoist the world upon our shoulders and carry it back to Christ, knowing beyond any shadow of doubt that He has already provided us the strength and means to do it. We must fight against the animalistic instincts of terrified men who cannot know what Love is like because they are too afraid to surrender to their personal sentimentalism. There are dark shadows creeping everywhere from which we flinch like parakeets, frightened all the way down to our toenails that one of them is harboring a murderer or hypocrite; or worse, someone who might know a little more about how to suffer with acceptance and humility than we are willing to embrace ourselves. The goodness of our mothers and fathers cannot die when their bodies go to their graves because their actions will always remain alive to speak quite loudly in their place. If we are curators of their preserved sincerity, then we must do more than just tell other souls what they were like to know; we must instinctively emulate their own emeritus imitation of the same Anointed Jesus who is now calling us back to their original station of honor, decency, modesty, and grace. No pious man is ever a foreigner to the Love which he must eventually betroth; but some of us are not even slightly close to becoming engaged to the natural virtues which will make us the children of God. We will discover at the end of time that it was not a burdening yoke which Jesus Christ was trying to fit us for; He was only measuring our souls for His presentation of our Wedding Ring.

All of this is why it is so imperative that we somehow work to increase the level of civility in our public discourse in America and abroad. We should take the life of the Pope of the Holy Catholic Church as our modern-day example. When speaking of the tenure of the Roman Papacy, we have seen some of the most gently courageous and pious men to ever pass before our eyes than the recorded history of humankind has ever known. They have understood what it means to be persuasive and to win without destroying the internal dignity of those who opposed them. We seem to have lost our ability to comprehend the difference between stable competition and outright mean-spiritedness these days. A "time-out" is a term which is used to define a pause to readjust our external strategies, but now also alludes to the necessity of isolating someone for illicit conduct while they are trying to bring their distemper under control. Hockey games that were previously held at arms length because of their violent content are now being hailed as a cultural advancement in the likes of healthful sparring. We bestow great commendations upon those who commit unsportsmanlike conduct, while sending the well-behaved into the mean streets to learn how to become more obnoxious and aggressive everyday. All of this misplaced logic is at the cost of our mutual civility and the composure of society at large. Our domestic patrimony is missing the guidance of more upstanding fathers because our families are still falling apart at the seams. Where there is *not* Love, there can be no moral righteousness. The highly contentious and partisan nature of our ongoing public conduct is lent to the destruction of our desire to be God's children anymore. Hereafter, we must understand that the argument about the restoration of the presence of the Holy Spirit in our hearts is not, after all, an abstract debate, but a mandatory discourse about whether we are truly going to become the image of Christ in our own particular way.

Self-Actualization and Our Own Submission

January 9, 2001

There comes a time in human life, or perhaps more often than we realize, when we must step-back from the protrusion of ourselves into the breadth of society and take stock in how the rest of the world really perceives us amongst its greater peers. There is nothing defeatist about evaluating our approach to everyday life, knowing in advance that our purpose must not be self-destructive or intentioned to be too critical in the end. The often sedentary reaction of other people to our daily demeanor rarely enhances the accuracy of their innermost feelings about whether we are allowing the reflection of Jesus to flourish through our exterior moods. Sometimes it seems like the skies could open at any next moment and a mysterious airship will descend from beyond the outer-atmosphere carrying the best of the person we once were and the greatest potential we might ever achieve in two separate seats. We wonder in the interim how we will ever finally fuse these two totally distinct individuals together, both lacking in any characteristic definitiveness, but who exist to make us the total person of perfection that God wants us to be for the future. What a moment it would be to somehow stand alone on the tarmac one day and greet these two distinguishable identities whom we always hoped to become and to be automatically assimilated by them into one true greatness without ever having to do anything more than surrender with our bare hands in the air. Unfortunately, however, this seems not very practical because we are being called to be single-minded in one contemporary Spirit of Truth through the Gospel of the New Covenant Christ. We *are* who we are; and therefore, we must improve upon the nature of our character without expecting some imaginary alien to deliver a magical clone to take our place, one who has already been perfected while nobody else was watching.

We know many things to be true because we have already walked near the line of total spiritual utopia during different moments in our lives; and there is no reason why we cannot make them come true again. Our goal is to finally relinquish anything and everything that is presently precluding us from being the same youngster who became the Eagle Scout, or the kid who won the spelling bee, or the same student who easily figured-out the algebraic expression on the chalkboard when everybody else seemed so stumped. We can again become the sibling who offered the prayerful return of thanks at Christmastime when our brothers and sisters were still too shy to speak. The reason we have not yet become single-minded in Christ is because we can all envision this strange triangular personality living inside us which we have yet to blend into one; the accidental saint we once were as a little child, the canonized citizen of Heaven that Jesus will make of us someday, and the very confused soul we are right now. The vulcanization we seek must be of the more spiritual realm, manifested through our physical actions that concisely emulate the humility of Jesus as He lived and died on the Earth. The forces of holiness which bloom from His grace allow us to know our pristine identity in Him; intelligent, polished, capable of good judgement, and always properly poised and willing to accept the increased dimensions of whom we must eventually become; walking with the dignity of noblemen and the authority of princes and kings.

Are we yet capable and qualified to reprimand ourselves for not displaying the better-disciplined traits of our well-intentioned etiquette? Do we scoff at those who remind us that we must become even more like Jesus when we cannot clearly see it ourselves? After all, human self-actualization can never be separated from our own submission because the foundation of our worthiness in the eyes of the Heavenly Court rests soundly upon it; and that is the stricter forum through which we will all finally judge ourselves. How do we find such goodness of the soul in our sight? We might begin by looking toward the needs of the children of God who live both in our midst and at the farthest corners of the globe. Never has there been a Saint in the history of Salvation that was ever beatified or canonized who did not bear this quality of humble service in their spiritual resume. Indeed, this may be just miracle enough for the Son of God to make us all new saints before we stoop to die. When our hearts proceed with such genuineness, we can regain the spirit of determination that we once held in our heyday, while the still-kaleidoscope of mortal life takes on a new meaning because our priorities have become more aligned with the conscience of God. When we see our subtle personal insults that diminish the peace of other men as just another sleight, Jesus sees them as more aggressive attacks which break their spirits in half. The intonation of our conspicuous motivations are always revealed in the pleasantness of our humor and the politeness in which we approach the rest of the world. From this higher point of view, we can recognize the countless inequities that have been laying before our eyes since the day we were borne to our mothers.

It is a blatant departure from the Truth to allow tens-of-thousands of souls to remain confined in wheelchairs and lay paralyzed on their backs without the proper medical research to heal them when businesses in America spend hundreds of billions of dollars on new sports stadiums and fund the financial accounts required to pay their players' exorbitant salaries. Multi-millions more are being spent to build monuments to people who have been dead for two-hundred years and to compensate a segment of society for what someone else's ancestors might have done to offend their own predecessors, all who have been cold in the grave for generations past. A spirit of thankfulness must shine through our more enchanted temperament when we hear someone else try to tell us how a certain chore might be better accomplished to reflect a more equitable use of our time or to procure a product which will be more beneficially employed. What do we often retort, instead? "I have been doing it this way all of my life!" What kind of attitude is that? We discover at last that a moment's peace is a hundred times more valuable than the cumulative victories of all the wars in which we have fought for the past 10,000 years. We should allow our every inaugural speech to be about the espousal of true goodness toward our fellow men, and our anniversaries to be about remembering those who fought to the death to evangelize the Gospel of Jesus Christ, rather than when a particular faction was finally allowed their freedom to occupy a certain untillable parcel of land.

Too many of us are possessed by our compulsion to adhere to mere protocol, while too few are concerned about the facade of the final results. We must never be willing to deviate from the Truth of Almighty God, no matter what proceedings may ensue, regardless of how much we are despised, and notwithstanding the pique of our public reputation, as if it should matter anyway. Just like we embrace new hopes of our own, we must remember that another person's dreams are often as fragile as eggshells, unable to be restored or reconstructed if we should ever try to shatter them or place them in a sudden cynical light or ever try to interpret-away their meaning when they serve only to bring the dreamer toward a better understanding of Love. Life is too fleeting for us to embark upon destabilizing the fondness of our brothers' wishes, the desires they keep, or the unsolicited gifts they may have received from God, such as miraculous visions from His Throne to which they will cling like eagles until they finally greet Him in death. None of us is fully immune from conceding to those leech-like anticipations which seem almost too metaphysical to the touch, those impressions of the heart that comprise a more superior world, the ones which only seem to exist in the substance of fairy tales, just before the placard falls at the end of their run and fractures the poor man sweeping-up. There is plenty to be said about why we hold such thoughts; but, when adequately seen, they speak to our insatiable thirst for everlasting peace and our desire to be Christ's little children again.

Then, there are those diametrically-opposed paradoxes in which we might also wonder how to respond when we once held a romantic affection for someone, even to the point of obsession; then, after not seeing them for a decade or two, being unable to recall why we were ever infatuated with them in the first place. How about *that* for a deception of the heart? Thereafter, we are forced to place our inner-emotions on spin-control, thanking God that we never married them; or, better yet, getting down on our knees to ask Him through our frightful redress how our earlier judgement could have ever been so errantly flawed. These particular features of our ongoing discernment teach us a lot about ourselves, but they mainly just reveal how much we hold in common with other men. Never are we forced to look very far from home to hear somebody else say something that we have also always believed to be true; and seldom is the headline in the newspaper anything which takes us by surprise. So, indeed, we do place some value in how we fit into the greater vessel of life. We know from the start that the simple majority of men learn rather quickly how to survive the passages of time, never quite conquering them or making the most of their use. We are given to the Spirit of Jesus Christ so we can finally lift ourselves beyond these things and so our mutual coexistence can hold an entirely new purpose, one which is based upon reflection and destiny, not blind stagnation and fear.

The American Mass-Media as a Fictitious Enterprise

January 10, 2001

If anyone were to look-up the word "hypocrite" in their desktop dictionary and read its definition, they would probably also see a depiction of a newspaper editor beside it to augment its meaning. There has been a long standing dispute about the role of the printed and electronic media in democratic countries throughout the world, but rarely has there ever been a system of privately disseminating the news that is as profoundly secular, deficient, and wittingly fallacious as the one in the United States of America. Reporting our ongoing public affairs is often difficult enough as it is, but the process is far more complicated when those who are offering the story stand to make themselves rich by telling their patrons what they have come to know about the personal business of the rest of society. The collective media in America is a wholly-fictitious enterprise, composed of individuals who have deliberately chosen to decline the paths of life in which they might otherwise have participated in the mitigation of human suffering, having instead been self-appointed as public watchdogs over their peers when they, themselves, do very little to comply with the minimum standards they hold before the developing world as being barely acceptable conduct. For those who are still keeping score, the media maintain about seven different roles which they have acquired for themselves today; informant, inquisitor, analyst, historian, sectarian, partisan, and private profiteer. The latter, of course, is one that they strictly deny as having any formal bearing upon the behavior of their quite ignoble profession. For all it might be worth, they are nothing more than a bunch of stuffy sticklers about eradicating moral vices, rather than becoming ambassadors for the simple virtues that would make the world a better place for everyone to live. Their redundant words of vitriol about the condition of humanity do not even come close to outlining the proper solutions we require because, absent the graveness of human sin, they would have nothing else to report.

This has not always been the case, however. There was a time when someone could pick-up a newspaper and immediately read the facts about who, what, where, when, and how something transpired. Now, it seems as though the members of their editorial boards get up in the morning while thinking, "I wonder which issue we can transform into a scandal this week?" They survive in the markets only through their autocratic influence because their purpose is never mandated by the will of the general public. They claim to be just another private industry, but they make it their purpose to create dilemmas in the public sector that continue to stir the emotions of insecure people and lead their readers into a near paranoiac state about the conditions of the material world. They often celebrate social conflict and perpetuate the declaration of differences which can further divide families, individuals, and nations. They speak about the tragedy of the wars going on across the globe, but will do absolutely nothing to try to diffuse them. If anyone ever approached a reporter in a crowd to help solve a problem at a civic meeting, he would turn-tail and run, claiming that addressing such issues is not a requirement of his job description. But, if an agreement is ever reached that is unsuitable to his taste, he will be the first to criticize its implementation before the rest of the world has even seen it. He knows, as well as everyone else, that he can claim no intrinsic successes toward the development of a greater status of democracy because he is still too busy highlighting the distinctions that serve to separate common citizens from one another and lending a new limelight to social disarray at every turn. How many people have committed horrific crimes because they knew that their faces would be spread across every front page headline and television screen in the country? Indeed, the media play on the fears of the weak and the impressionable more than any daytime soap opera could ever aspire to evoke. They scandalize the mistakes of our impressionable youth, glorify their violence as a justifiable means of protest, and hail themselves as being the clarion catalysts for progressive social change.

If the general public and the media were to be depicted as being a horse and a cart, those in the media would somehow believe that the rest of the world is piled like a huge load of baggage being pulled along behind them to an unknown destination called "the future." While they try to peddle individual articles as being newsworthy, they forget that there are much greater needs to be met than just talking about today's societal problems. They often would make good sidewalk supervisors because their involvement is only to the advancement of their own professional pride. Most of their members are misguided, misinformed, profoundly disinterested, and totally unwilling to accede to the pursuits of a more civilized conscience. Not only that, they somehow believe that an act of forgiveness is a violation of their uniform code. The newspaper is prompt to print a story about someone who is accused of committing a crime; but they rarely, if ever, print a retraction when that same person is found to be not guilty. When all is said and done, it is quite clear that the media in America try to justify the reasons why people hate one another so they can keep their dialogue of digression rolling along. They often serve as a propaganda agent for interpersonal conflict, while refusing to play the slightest part in securing and preserving a lasting peace. Now and again, you might find the owners of a newspaper or televison station sponsoring a fund-raiser for the disadvantaged during the December holiday season, but they will only take a picture of the poor and refer to the poignance of their plight for the other eleven months of the year, leaving them laying in the gutter as they walk-on past for someone else to stop and feed.

The American media can boast of no participation in the procurement of social justice. If anything, they sometimes make things worse by widening the gap between certain marginal, cultural, and racial divides. They realize that they are immune from prosecution as they continue to exacerbate their own misgivings because they wrap themselves in the First Amendment of the U.S. Constitution and would brandish the arms of the Second if anyone ever tried to take it away. They always seem to be held accountable to no one, not even the courts whose judges they often endorse on election day. In order to procure new leads, they attempt to draw strange correlations between completely unrelated events; they promote the lack of absolution between individuals and sects; and they place the Holy Cross of Jesus Christ at arms length while completely ignoring their opportunity to evangelize the reason why He was Crucified in the first place, even though it was meant to save their wretched souls from spending eternity crackling like discarded kindling in the leaping fires of Hell. Their grievous indifference is lent even more credibility because their product is seen as "faddish" by nature and, therefore, is produced in such massive quantities. The mainstream printed medium is especially worse in this regard because it offers a more permanent and visible record than the issues that are brought forth across the televised airwaves. Members of the media somehow believe that their careers are a reflection of the Truth, itself, and are apt to try to assassinate the character of anyone else on the Earth who would attempt to convince them otherwise. They do not acknowledge the continental divide as being a geographic location in North America; they perceive it as being an agenda for separating its citizens by what we believe, by what we do for a living, how we spend our hard-earned money, and the color of our skin. The news media spew-forth a daily mantra of gruesome horror, discrimination, tragedy, and illusion; and then set-out to take a poll to see what effect their literary brainwashing has had on the rest of society. What they tend to ignore is that they share a greater role in shaping public opinion than most any other source of information. Then, they sheepishly behave like they are shocked to the core when they see how callous and embittered their fellow countrymen have become.

Many in the media claim to be independent in their views, but they immediately attack anyone who would dare to address their tone of arrogance while becoming as fully steeped in political partisanship as any publicly-funded entity that ever existed in history. They quite often surrender to the temptations which they have laid before themselves; mainly by refusing to engage the fight against the enticement to dabble in raw sensationalism and idolatry; but rarely, if ever, succeeding in conquering their inherent desire to place the public perception of decent men into the nearest trash receptacle. Media moguls have never quite drawn the connection between the power of their influence on the public debate and the more proper issues that would have otherwise been raised if only they would adhere to the admonishment of their more principled advisors. They will often pose an irrelevant question and thereafter offer a series of completely false solutions which, even if employed collectively, would never speak to alleviating the throes of the struggles ahead. There is not a whisper of doubt in the minds of men who own greater wisdom that, when Jesus Christ finally returns to the Earth in Glory, one of His first bold acts of Justice will be to reduce the public media's fallacious empire into a smoldering pile of rubble and ruins in a heap atop the ground.

It is often quite interesting to recall what certain recent public figures have said about the role of the media in the United States today. Jack Kennedy played the press like a Stradivarius violin and made them like it, only to see them bow at his every whim. Then, there are those who have become engaged in a more love-hate relationship than that. First Lady Barbara Bush once told her successor, Hillary Rodham Clinton, as the two were involved in a short discussion before the presidential transition of their husbands in 1993 to, "Avoid the press like the plague!" Most of us believe that the legendary baseball pitcher Steve Carlton had it about right, too. He never granted more than a press interview or two from the time he threw the first pitch of his long stellar career until the moment when he walked-off the mound to retire. There was no way that he was going to provide them the opportunity to skew what he might have had to say or to pose a moronic question whose basis was not founded in fact. The favorite of many people, however, is the former college basketball coach from the Hoosier State of Indiana, Bobby Knight. For anyone alive who enjoys a more personal relationship with the basic Truth, they could always count on Coach Knight to look a newspaper or television reporter in the eye with a grimace on his face and say in response to a rhetorical inquiry, "What kind of a &#@%! question is that to be asking me?" We all know that former President Ronald Reagan was also correct when he spoke about the U.S.S.R. as being an "evil empire," but he was ignoring the one that was just under his nose in the form of the mass-media in the free-world United States. There seems to be an unstated mutual agreement between most factions in our country that the media have a strange penchant for discovering corruption in various locales between our borders, but they offer very little progress toward developing solutions on how to prevent it from ever happening again. They almost always forget that a simple human mistake is never a universal scandal, nor is it always against the law, until somebody on the block with a big mouth skews the facts for their own private financial gain. In toto, they are the epitome of that rumor-mill.

The Sacrament of Holy Matrimony

January 11, 2001

One of the more humbling roles in the procession of mortal life is the domestic vocation given through the Sacrament of Holy Matrimony. The responsibilities which accompany getting married are, beyond any doubt, some of the most important vows that a human soul could ever be entrusted to keep; for, without a solemn promise to God and one's spouse alike, it would surely never become a bountiful sanctity. The reason for wedding another person is always founded in the multi-faceted Fruits of Divine Love. One of the attributes which makes the Sacrament of Marriage different from others is that the anointing grace of God is dispensed upon a man and a woman simultaneously; whereas the Sacrament, itself, is meant to give rise to a new creature in the physical world when the wedded couple becomes one flesh, one heart, and one licit mind, spirit, body, and oath. In keeping with the profession of the blessing of marriage, there are now two individuals who have become separable only through the element of space. In all other ways, they are indivisibly one and the same mysterious essence, not wholly unlike the way that the Omnipresence of God is also singular with His Son and the Holy Paraclete. One might think of the many contemplative vistas which become a part of the lives of those who enter the religious orders because an equally protracted prospectus should be manifested through the avocation of Holy Matrimony. The commitment is no-less consequential and the rewards are as equally fond to the Almighty Father who clothes it with His Love. He knows that it is within these Bonds of Matrimony where blessed procreation occurs and His commission for mankind to be fruitful and multiply takes its most befitting form.

For the record, there is no such thing as a marriage between two people of the same sex, nor is it ever permissible in the eyes of God for someone to be "married" to more than one person at a time. Such grave sins are aberrations from the Truth and an abomination in the sight of Jesus Christ. But, when a man and a women exchange vows in the witness of a properly ordained representative of God, the lives of the two fortunate people involved portends in-part the return of Our Savior in Glory to set the whole world aright. The Church is His Bride and He is the Groom who shall provide for every need which could ever befall His people. This is quite similar to the role of fatherhood because he is the sustainer, the head of the table, and master of the interior domain. His assignment is to have and to hold his wife, to protect her, offer her his fidelity, loyalty, friendship, sympathy, compassion, support, counsel, and sacrificial Love. And, since the two are one flesh, his wife is to reciprocate these same virtues so as to gently advise and teach each other about the difficulties of life, whether they may ultimately find themselves in poverty or wealth, or sickness and infirmity. One of the greater tragedies of the modern day, and a grievous sin in the eyes of God, is for someone to seek to become separated from their faithful spouse who has taken-ill or is otherwise permanently disabled. They must remember that their vows are not only a promise to each other, but to Christ and His Church, alike. Breaching them for any reason short of dying is an outright violation against the Truth of the Crucifixion and an act of blasphemy against the Holy Spirit who forged them into one flesh at the Sacred Altar of Sacrifice. It is appropriate to remember that the Sacrament of Marriage is a perpetual one and that it need not be renewed before death.

The imitation of the Holy Family; Jesus, Mary, and Joseph, should be the goal for every newlywed couple to hope to attain, because through such eternal beauty blossoms all other relationships which have the potential to grow; husband, wife, father, mother, son, daughter, brother, sister, and grandchild; each blooming from the marriage of the patriarch and matriarch of this extended family. The Bonds of Matrimony between a man and a woman carry much more meaning than the simple kindred spirits which exist in good standing elsewhere because they offer the world the opportunity to see how God wants His Church to equipoise its own profession of faith. Being a husband or wife provides a widened broadway of avenues through which someone can espouse the goodness of the Sacred Heart of Jesus and the Immaculate Heart of His Mother. This loving inspiration allows us to survive in happiness through nearly every conceivable distinction of mortal life; the elements of our youth, participation in the social graces, maintaining the home and financial apportionments; the laughter, the tears, the joys, the fears, and, sometimes even modesty about our more humble successes. There are so many impulses and influences which flow from the stream of Love during the many years of marriage that they are, oftentimes, too profuse to enumerate. It is somewhat like the unusually less-than-enamored wit of Abraham Lincoln when he said, "It will all become one thing." He meant that there are so many traits to being human in the mortal world and, in realizing that they all eventually end, the culmination of our days always leads us back to our singular God. So it is with the multi-dimensioned aspects of the Sacrament of Marriage.

And, then, the children come along! What a blessed new beginning for a man and his wife! If you ever took an agnostic into a maternity ward and allowed him to see the gift of new birth occur, he would exit the place singing the praises of Almighty God; for the beauty of a little child, or multiple ones at times, rivals nothing else that could ever be given to the face of the Earth. The new mother finds her soul at peace again, if it was almost lost amidst all the pains of labor; so that her helpless offspring becomes a priceless reflection of her original love for her husband and the beatific gift from Jesus in her arms which proves it. Forget about Murphy's Law; if anything can go wrong, it will; for it is now time to celebrate God's intention that life should go on! Just as she and her husband must lead their entire lives as an echo of the Love of their wedding day, they must both embrace this new little baby the way the Wise Men paid homage to the infant Child Jesus in the manger in Bethlehem. The same vows which applied at their marriage are meant, too, for the care of their children; to love and to cherish, to have and to hold, and to defend and respect. Life takes-on somewhat of a more testy turn on the domestic front when these new little ones are born. There are now cries in the middle of the night to console, new fears to subdue, bedtime stories to tell, recitals and graduations to attend, and countless grandchildren to spoil. But, this brief synopsis of a grandeur number of years does not even approach the dubious details which inevitably fall in between!

The experience of marriage is meant to be one which is blessed with holiness, tranquility, servitude, and joy. It remains all of these with great *pro forma*, according to form, and more, if only every member of the nuclear family calls his conscience toward loving again. We are created through the power of God, strengthened by His Sacramental graces, and are given every possible reason to live in confidence by remaining whole with His Church. No family will ever be blessed who refuses to be led by their father and mother into full communion with the Christian faith. There is no practice session or rehearsal for life, especially one that is filled with the bounty of marriage and rearing Christ's little children. There is no way to "resign" from the position of parent once He gives us our progeny; and we can never descend from the imperial heights which He has placed upon their souls. We are all responsible for seeing that our children are Baptized into the Faith and that they maintain their allegiance to the Creed from the instant they first recite it. When we instill this faithfulness to Jesus within their hearts, they will never once be rebellious or reject our affection, but will remain more loyal to the Ten Commandments and will be the people of goodness that we, ourselves, always hoped for them to become. We do not own the faculty to fast-forward through life to avoid the more difficult times; and we should harbor no reason to go back and transform the way we poured ourselves out in the service of the people we have known. It is God's little children whom we must all remain, no matter how many years have expired.

Jonathan King said it correctly in a song that he recorded in 1965, "*Everyone's Gone to the Moon*," when he sang, "...streets full of people, all alone; roads full of houses, never home; eyes full of sorrow, never wet; hands full of money, all in debt; mouths full of chocolate-covered cream; arms that can only lift a spoon; everyone's gone to the moon." These are the same types of extreme contradictions which often surround human life, especially for those who must tend to the monumental tasks that accompany the blessings of marriage and raising children of their own. It took this popular singer only two-and-a-half minutes to describe the waning favors which can come and go in an entire expanse of a lifetime. He speaks to the youthfulness in us all and the irony that attends our triumphs and defeats along the way. If there are moments in our married life when we wish to pause and say, "...where is my best patience when I need it?", that is when we must recall the Holy Family again. In the innocence of Baby Jesus, Saint Joseph, and the Blessed Virgin Mary rests our eternal guidance upon which we must depend as mothers, fathers, children, and siblings toward the attainment of our most purposeful existence as the loving people of God whom He has always yearned to bless.

A Humble Soul Named Ellis McPherson

January 12, 2001

I wished to produce an essay in this manuscript as a tribute to the life of a man who imitated the Love of Jesus Christ in the way I understand Him to be in the Holy Gospel as much as any other person I have ever met. He died about two-weeks before I penned this humble elegy in his memory. Ellis McPherson was born on a cold Arkansas February night in 1904 and died on December 29, 2000, back in his homeland after a remarkable journey through life which touched the hearts of thousands of simple people. While I am nearly 60 years his junior, I was fortunate to know him as my step-grandfather, good friend, and neighbor. We have all heard stories of how underdeveloped the midwestern states in America were at the turn of the 20th century; and there are plenty of heroes to speak about from that vein in our history. Perhaps my Grandpa was no more valiant than most of them, but he is about the only one I ever remember meeting so personally before any of the rest. It was much the same for everyone back then; they had large families that lived in rural areas who sustained themselves by tending to the crops in the fields. They hunted for their food in the wilderness, drank water from a well in the ground, heated it to take a bath, shivered through cold blustery winter storms, and sweat like wildfire during the dog-days of summer. They often slept outdoors beneath the trees at night to keep cool. My Grandpa was born to many siblings and wore plenty of hand-me-down clothes with lots of patches. He used to tease me about how he once had to eat crow for supper and was quite fond of black-eyed peas, hominy, possum, and fresh cantaloupe.

Grandpa McPherson married the woman who had adopted my own mother as a young child in Springfield, Illinois. His first wife passed-away in the late 1960s and is buried near Alton, the great waterway city along the Mississippi river. His body is now at rest at her side as I pen this memoire of his legacy. I had known him for about thirty years prior, since I was roughly ten years old. He was a carpenter by trade, and had built quite a few private homes, businesses, and churches that still stand in and around Madison, Macoupin, and Clinton counties in rural Illinois. He also worked in the gun-powder mills that supplied explosives to the U.S. military during WW II, and was the typical elderly gentleman who required thick-lense glasses and plenty of light when he sat down to read anything. I noticed that he was also pretty

adept at hand-crafting, too, when I saw a collection of little wooden hatchets he had whittled during his spare time
in the basement. I purchased the house next-door to him and Grandma in 1989 and was their neighbor until she was placed into a nursing home about thirty miles away. Grandpa then moved closer to his own relatives on August 15, 1996. It was not surprising to see him mow the lawn at 90 years of age, climb a ladder to patch a leaky roof, or get down on his knees to pull weeds along the fence. I remember one of his quirky habits was to whitewash the bottom of the tree trunks in the yard to a height of about four feet off the ground. It always reminded me of where someone had placed a marker when they had a massive flood in the area. He sometimes planted tomatoes in the backyard while wearing his wide-brimmed straw hat and tended to a trellis of roses that always bloomed on the south side of the front porch when the season was ripe.

Grandpa suffered from diabetes during most of his adult years, and he never allowed it to slow him down too much; but the surgeons had to remove a part of one leg just a few days before he died. In 1996, when he was 92 years old, he underwent an operation to remove a cancerous tumor from the side of his face. The doctors told us that they could not get it all out; that it had spread down into his neck and into his lymph nodes; but they had done all they could do. It seemed a mystery to me that he lived another four years without the malignancy spreading any further. During the time I lived next-door to him, I volunteered to cut his grass, but he would always make me take five-dollars for it. There was nothing I could do to reject it because he practically made me feel as though it was an affront to turn it down. He had his hands pretty full besides, since he drove his own automobile almost until the day he moved away. Grandma McPherson was rather persistent about his taking her for a ride around the countryside everyday; and Grandpa obliged her each time, even though he may not have always felt very well. I would sometimes compare them to the two characters in the motion picture, "Driving Miss Daisy." They had also become world-travelers for a period after they were first married; flying to foreign countries and enjoying the beauty of the Earth for as long as their health would allow. When it came to upholding his wedding vows, no man was ever more genuine, consistent, and self-denying in his love for his wife than Grandpa. Never once did I hear him utter a pejorative syllable about what he had to do to show Grandma that his heart belonged to her. This was part of the ongoing beauty which made him a special child of God.

The main reason why I have incorporated a description of Grandpa in this book is because his life, itself, was an essay in Christian faith. He could recite a passage from the Holy Bible in the blink of an eye without ever stuttering over a word. I will always remember that he preferred the interpretation of the Lord's Prayer to say, "...Thy Will be done *in* Earth, as it is in Heaven," as opposed to, " ...*on* Earth." I was never quite sure why he was so adamant toward this issue; but I thought if anyone was so concise about what the Son of God has to say in the New Testament, it was surely alright by me. Grandpa was a member of the Protestant faith and was a man of deep prayer and trust in God for help in every way. He once told me that the Holy Spirit grasped a hold of his conscience when he was in his middle-age years. It began to flourish one day when he suddenly realized what it felt like to set things right with the rest of the world. When he was about thirty years old, he had borrowed a garden hose from one of his neighbors that he had forgotten to return and finally took it back to the man and apologized for keeping it for so long. Grandpa was almost overwhelmed by the forgiveness which he was afforded by his neighbor; and he knew right then what the blessing of absolution felt like. If this was Christian Love, then it was for him; and he set-out for the next sixty-five years to offer his every waking moment to the Savior who had died on the Cross to wash-away his sins.

One of the most profound, and yet simple, statements that my Grandpa ever told me was after I had mowed his lawn one day and we were just sitting under his back-porch roof sipping on a glass of lemonade. We were talking about the condition of the world and about how selfish some people are. He had just gotten a bill in the mail for his annual real estate property taxes and they had gone-up a horrific amount. He later scribbled a note to the editor of our local newspaper to complain that there were thousands of new homes being built on the west side of town every year and the tax base was growing by leaps and bounds. And, yet, they chose to increase his taxes on a home that was about as old as he was and had never had any modernization or new construction done to it in decades. But, the millionaires who own the newspaper refused to print his letter. He was a Franklin Roosevelt Democrat who was woefully offended by big business trying to get every last dime out of anyone they could for their own financial gain. He did not seem to be too bitter about it as he turned to me that day, looked deeply into my eyes, and said with a sense of longing in his voice, "Son, please don't ever let hatred get into your heart." Well, Grandpa is gone now; and that moment and that day will live forever beyond my own mortal passing. If he is still able to hear my words through this humble text about faith and morals, I would like to promise him, "...I will remember, Grandpa! I will not forget what you said! I shall offer your love for me as my own gift to humankind! Hatred will never be able to conquer my heart! We shall share the Victory of Love at last!"

Many were the moments when I heard him say that he had placed his future, his life, and his soul in the Sacred Hands of his Master, Jesus Christ. Even though he was not Catholic, he still knew who the Virgin Mary is because he had known that I was authoring a book about my experiences with Her called, *Morning Star Over America*. I would get out of my car at home after going somewhere on a hot day in July and hear him and Grandma sitting quietly on their front-porch glider singing Christmas carols, just because they loved their God and Maker so much. Right before he moved away in 1996, he took me into his house after Grandma had gone to the nursing home and gave me some things from his closet; two of which were bottles of "Old Spice" after-shave and cologne. I popped the lid off of them and smelled their sweet fragrance that day, just to see if I could remember what they were like. Now, I enjoy their aroma in the privacy of my own home during my prayers which remind me of this great man; he who never knew how to say "no" to sacrifice, who always lived the dignity of hope and faith until the moment he died, who never said a discouraging word about anyone who was trying to become a better person, who never failed to forgive and forget any trespasses against him, and who lives to this day in the presence of Jesus Christ; who came to take him to dance with both legs intact amongst the Angels and Saints in the Mansions of Paradise.

An Uncanny Resemblance to Humankind at His Best

January 15, 2001

The habit of most Americans these days is to assume that daily life is somehow seeded in dismal disarray under a cloud of catastrophic despair and moves at a snail's pace toward a certain unavoidably tragic conclusion. Such malaise is not founded in the Truth because God has brought us hope within the authentic nature of His Divine presence both through the temporal characteristics of Creation and the Love which He has poured so beatifically into the dominant receptacles of our most private beings. The human heart is that key; and we realize by virtue of its generous revelations that our existence is situated not under a bank of darkness, but high above and beyond the clefs of the physical Earth. So, we now embrace a quite larger meaning for our living here; and, if we have a central theme or politick to which our consciousness always returns, it must become united with this higher purpose. Should humanity at large surrender every fiber of knowledge about life to God's husbandry and fatherhood, we would finally elevate our awareness past the wry and misdirected perception we hold against Him, His Kingdom, His Son, and our personal relationship with all three of them. Beyond the vast palatial beauty of our cathedrals and basilicas lies the greater excellence of our faith; that inner-ability we possess to perceive Love and peace in all their splendorous sovereignty. Through the power of Jesus Christ, we have come to know His Father as the Patron of our every good grace and the Fire of Truth; and yet, the smoldering Wrath who owns the desire to extinguish our inflamed opposition to His Immaculate Love for good. Even though the Almighty Father might often seem to be somewhat mysterious and unknowable at times, He is always and everywhere the Creator of unyielding Wisdom and the Master of His own transcendent vision, infallible good Judgement, and unconquerable determination.

The Most Blessed Trinity to whom we pray bears an uncanny resemblance to humankind at our best when we know how to seek-out the extraordinary virtuosity that makes us heroes in the eyes of suffering men. God is the source of our invincible power to always do better and is His own irrevocable compassion, creative fidelity, punctual submission, plentiful Mercy, and obsessive perfection. Jesus Christ is the eloquence of our speech and the propriety of our voices, the poise of our spirits, the provenance of our hearts, the sanctification of our obedience; and is forever healing, prescient, foreboding, relenting, dutiful, romantic, realistic, daunting, and exacting. His ophthalmic Love is an irreducible focus of Divine persuasion that is propulsive to the maximum grace; elusive, articulate, viscerally potent, concise, proportionately emotional, distinct, and permanent. There is an almost undefinable equity in knowing Him and in our purpose of searching for His blessing; and there is an ultimate ecstasy in our arrival in finally being found, ourselves, too. There is no other God or essence in the universe, and no other reason, consistency, or profundity. We can try to leap-frog over all of the roles which Jesus has played in our Salvation, but we will never truly know God without meeting His Crucifixion head-on. The pesky temptations of the Earth are forever trying to inhibit our progress toward this holy destiny, but we can arrive in His Arms unscathed if only we will relax the tensions which keep us so frightened and submit that we, ourselves, are not yet a perfect reflection of the Love who has made us. This does not prohibit us from becoming the likeness of His Son, however and, therefore, perfectly united with the Deity to the extent that our pristine nature can become one again in Him. The Catechism of the Catholic Church asserts that temptation, itself, is not inherently evil, but will lead us into committing error if we refuse the alliance that Christ is offering us to combat its forces. God has planned the obsolescence of sin through the power of the Cross, and we shall never grow stale if we place both our "being" and loveliness there, knowing all along that our stubborn provincialism must die in its wake.

The absolution of the human genus has already been laid-out before us in the crux of the Sacrifice of Jesus on Good Friday. It is not so much that we wake every morning and fall in love with life together, but rather we are felled by it so we can stand aright before the naked Truth of Love; to be enlightened, enhanced, and judged when everything else is done. The daybreak of this spiritual synergy comes as we are ultimately raised by the Grace of God into immortal beings to recapture the status of everlasting saints. Jesus Christ lives as *the* distinct architecture of our rehabilitated souls and our communion with the post-contemporary precision of the material world. While we will do almost anything to avoid it, we must sooner or later accept that the future beyond our mortal passing depends as much upon how we compare ourselves with the Divinity of Christ as anything good He might ever say to the Almighty Father on our behalf. That is not only the reason we must become like Him in every sense of the word, but also why we should implore His intercession in doing it right now. Rather than seeking some sort of false balance between Christianity and secularism, we would do better to open our hearts to the prospect that God sees our moderation in the spiritual virtues as being quite repugnant before His eyes. He requires far more from us than our mild intentions to replicate His Love, but also our whole certitude that we would be just as willing to suffer and die in the likeness of His Son to prove it. There is undoubtedly great trepidation hidden in this prophecy, but it bears more urging for us to be encouraged that the One who created us has already declared us all to be well prepared and worthy of entering the battle.

What propels this ensuing engagement to the climactic point of our continuing participation? It is quite simply the fact that our souls are not yet back home. We are still fighting to pierce the fog, to stagger through the forest, and to swim against the ichor channels of the so-called fabled gods who would like to boast of claiming our immortal spirits as their own. The systems, principles, and practices of our faith are wrought through the cunningness which we gain through the Holy Paraclete to fend-off His enemies by the strength of our own Love for Redemption. Even when we offer th*pater noster*, the Our Father, we are acknowledging that we are still little children who know not how to survive on our own, and never should we wish to try. It is by our voluntary admission that we repeat this holy supplication because it is one of the many on record which the Son of God has placed into legible scripture. His Spirit holds an unparalleled dominion over our technological capabilities and completely overpowers our mere human incompetence to captivate His stealthy influence. That is why we must all eventually undergo our own concession to Love, even if time has expired on the Earth before all men are borne into it from the Will of God in Paradise. Whatever He creates never really comes to an end, it only changes in form. That is how humidity becomes condensation and leaping fires incinerate flammable articles into piles of anonymous ashes. Jesus has promised to lay-waste to anything and everything that stands in the path of His righteousness. Can humankind be so naive and defiant as to deny the impending destruction of the antipathy of the globe that the Holy Gospel predicted twenty centuries ago?

We must concede that our faults and failures are no match for the gleaming streets of the City of God; for what are we lacking, instead? No sinner has ever held the capacity to know his Divine Creator without first overcoming his own corruption. Our minds may be quite proficient in an analytical sense, but we own no such logic in comprehending the suffixal right that God brandishes to bring an abrupt conclusion to anything we might initiate on our own, attempt to commission over the entirety of the universe, or even place into physical motion. We are absolutely deficient in the purpose of creating random opportunities, replenishing our spent resources, sustaining our most dire motivations, and defending our ulterior rationales. And yet, we claim that a greater sense of self-actualization is one of the more premier characteristics of a provocatively consummate man. How can we still continue to exploit our material day-dreams in the wake of what humankind is suffering as a whole? Where is the respiratory morale in the hopelessness that bashes the poor in the face everyday, while everyone else seems to prosper by the sophisms of their own blind games of chance, haphazard luck, partisan affiliations, and outright deceptive practices? On the other hand, there are those who say, "...well, I have succeeded in conquering this avenue, so where should I go from here?" This is the same devious curiosity which has already destroyed millions of marriages today, gotten upstanding young teenagers addicted hook-line and sinker to illicit drugs, caused a horrific increase in infant mortality, and depleted the collective human spirit of the energy it will require when the real battle finally comes; fighting against the devil from taking our souls away from the clutches of Christ when we are drawing our last dying breath.

Part IV - Now, It is Our Time to Respond

Roman Catholicism: Setting the Record Straight

January 16, 2001

The principal executor of our own inherited goodness is the Truth, itself, and is recognizable as being the footprints of Jesus Christ as He walks across the mortal landscape, against the seemingly invincible tides of human animosity, and through the vestiges of His Peace which live so abundantly in the Scriptures of the New Covenant. We have no viable longevity anywhere else than in His Love and in His Blood, which are one and the same Divineness from the Slash in our Almighty Father's Side. If we were to live totally by premonition and from nothing else declared in our own right, would we not continue to walk in fear that the future will belong to Him alone? God does not perceive our existence in His Kingdom in the same way that we observe certain algae or corrals beneath the seas. Have we not been told that we Christians are His chosen race, His people set apart, and a royal priesthood? The only influence that keeps us from realizing it is the feebleness of our faith. There is no pride or arrogance in claiming our portion of the Crucifixion. Heaven will not look disdainfully upon us if we struggle or fight to be the best, as long as that higher station is based upon the solid platform which is explicated through the Biblical History of the Messiah of God. The reactionary pantheism of most theologians today is more or less correct; but it is in the aspects of their implementation where some of them deviate from the Gospel Truth. Liberal interpretations of right and wrong as it has been dictated since the first century by the Holy Spirit do very little to assist the greater body of mankind to become more closely united within the Church. There is no such thing as a God who is asexual; and most all of these same heretics know it. Why they refuse to proclaim that He is a Man is beyond the grasp of most holy people.

Over the period of the past twenty years, the idea that to be so proper in defense of the Church is somehow seen as not being the true reflection of Love. If we are ever going to be perpetually faithful to Jesus, are we not remiss if we allow such distortions and myths to prolong? Are not Christians from most every walk of life getting pretty tired of hearing about so-called holy unions between homosexuals, women "priests," inclusive pronouns, and gutted sanctuaries? Would we not rather dedicate our lives to sharing the original Love of Christ as He bestowed it upon the Chair of Saint Peter from the very start of the Church? Was not Pentecost the ordination of Simon Peter as the first Pope before the lineage of many others who would follow thereafter? Now, we see priests wearing golf-shirts to ecclesiastical functions, Bermuda shorts under their vestments, and Rolex watches around their wrists. Nuns travel the streets in plain-clothes and drive fancy automobiles as if to desecrate the annunciation of their own celibacy. No apologies will be made for pointing these things out to those who are guilty of such diluvial erosions. We have spoken of maintaining the sacredness of the vocation of Holy Matrimony; but what about those who have chosen the religious life, too? Are they not especially more required to reflect the presence of God in a world which is still trying to reject Him in nearly every conceivable way?

We know that the years are passing-by quite quickly now; but do we realize the lateness of the hour? The faith we live hereby is not a notion just for a lifetime that will succeed us someday because Jesus might return any moment. His promises always eclipse and supercede the prophecies of his chosen ones because He is the God who first brought them into being. We have no right to be justified in His honor if we do not reflect this same urgency while we live. This is not to assume that we should spend our children's future or live in contempt for the weak because the fusible nature of the present and beyond is what makes Christian Love ring true. If we look at the Scriptures through such a timeless prism, we will readily see that there are truly no contradictions to be known therein, but that our own perception is flawed. Yes, we must love our wives to inevitable death, but we must also give our hearts to Salvation as though we had never been married. There is no doubt that we must remove the plank protruding from our own eyes; but this does not preclude us from admonishing our brothers about ending the hatred that has left them so bitter and spiritually blind. The Lord has come to engage the battle between the sheep and the goats, but we already know which of them has won. We, His people, are the victors who are simply waiting to receive our crowns. Those who are opposed to the Cross are the sorrowful lot who continue to fight because they cannot see past their painful losses to realize that their satanic leader has already been cast into Hell.

It is oftentimes difficult to know where the true collaborators and quislings of evil are hiding these days. Many of them are quite attractive in form, well-educated, positioned in influential places, bearing fancy titles, and revered very highly amongst pious men. Let no others be fooled by a stolen fruit which some may claim to be their own! No true child of God would ever give a hundred-thousand dollars to charity and horde another ten billion in the bank for themselves. These are quid pro quo donors, waiting with baited breath to see what accolades they might receive in return. Is it cynical for an honest Christian to ask not what was the size of the gift, but how much the giver has left in reserve? If Jesus Christ were to somehow mystically leap from the words on these pages and answer such a question, He would say,

"...absolutely not!" How do we surmise He should address those who die owning multiple millions of dollars while the rest of the world is so ingrained in poverty because of their own defense of their wealth? This most certainly speaks to the great commandment in the Bible which implores us all to sell what we have and give the proceeds to the poor. Is this the type of Spiritual Act of Mercy we should be effecting upon ourselves and our neighbors, alike? When we stand before the Throne of Almighty Justice, we should fully expect to hear that we have stored our treasures in Heaven by giving to the less-fortunate now. Most people who follow the Sacred Gospel more closely are rather confused about how anyone could make $600 payments on a new SUV every month and then drive past the food-bank to go to work everyday.

Somehow, we must strive to retrieve the solemnity and grace of the Original Catholic and Apostolic Church and turn our faces away from the bland consensus of fashioned delusion that is so popular nowadays. We have inherited a 2000-year-old legacy of decency and strict adherence to the Traditions which have made the Church under the Roman Papacy a near-perfect reflection of the Bride whom Christ is seeking to Wed at the last moment in time. There is no reason for us to stray from the upright profession of those sanctified customs that our predecessors have made before us, engraved by their own promise that no man should ever be permitted to scandalize or violate the sublime mystique which humanity has been offering God since we first came to know His Sacrificed Son as our Savior. We have no authority to amend our long-standing practice of remaining true to the Mother Church in every way; not that She is archaic by nature, but because She bears the traits and attributes of Love that Jesus still holds so affectionately inside His Most Sacred Heart to this day. However, some rogue revisionists would like to alter the face of the Church as though She is wearing a Gown that they believe to have somehow gone out-of-style. They will never once efface Her dignity, even if they should continue trying; for they shall discover at last that She has been properly attired for the Return of Jesus in Glory since the day He conceived Her into being. There are too many radicals who are refusing to maintain their Baptismal vows that are taking over too many roles of prominence in too many dioceses in America these days. And, in an attempt to avoid offending the enemies of the Catholic Church, we have chosen, instead, to placate their rancor by minimizing the sacred originality of our own true religion.

Mortal men on the Earth are risking the prospect of a melee in the middle of the streets when Heaven finally decides to come to end the world because the Saints of Old will never allow this perversion to get anywhere near the Pearly Gates, let alone within the sight of Jesus Christ. They will fight against the contemporary debasement of the principles which their exiled counterparts are now trying to revive and never be killed in the process; for they are all immortal now. We should not believe for an instant that God is impressed by our arrogant attempts to dilute the values of His Church into an ecumenical compromise because such is the lukewarmness which His Son has promised for centuries to spew-forth from His mouth in contempt. If ever there was an age in which Catholics should stand firm beside their Mother Church in the annuls of history, now is that time because we are fighting against the kings and caesars of the modernized world who are calling themselves Christians by mistake. They are trying to hide like boll-weevils under the Mantle of the Catholic Church, just waiting their chance to take another bite out of Her Sacred Crest. Heaven will defend us if we condemn their actions by invoking Christ's Holy Name; and we should never once desist in beseeching the Divine intercession of His Mother, Mary, Our Lady of Perpetual Help, in effecting our imminent victory over our foes. If we ever swear our Catholic Christianity into secrecy, humanity will never discover its best deliverance into eternal Salvation; for we are the doers and believers who effect God's bidding for the rest of the mortal world.

The Roman Catholic Church is the capitol of our state of righteous accord. Let there be no mistake about it; if we permit any forthcoming opportunists to stand in the way of the Truth or forego our responsibility to defend Her, regardless of the cost, the condition of the collective human soul will be the worse for our fears. However, we will regretfully be the harshest on ourselves once God shows us someday how we let His Son down. There is a certain swagger in the attitude of today's casual Catholic that is often bitter to the taste for those who are the true children of Mary, the disciples of the latter times who have never once left Her side. We should not be afraid of the outspoken Truth or our mandate to defend it before those who are most at risk of falling in death on their own swords while trying to run from themselves. Where are they now? They are the lay-people teaching RCIA classes who do not know enough about Catholicism to even darken the doorway in the Throne Room where the Son of God is now seated. If you asked some of them what a Scapular is, they might tell you that it is a skeletal bone in the human body near the back of the shoulder somewhere. The time has come to re-catholicize the Catholic Church and to bring our consecrated traditions back home, restoring the sacred mystery that once held Her so high above those who protest the soul-sustaining and life-giving Sacraments She provides. Jesus is no-doubt getting awfully exasperated while seeing our cafeteria-style, cut-and-paste approach to our allegiance to the Truth of His original Apostolic Church. Pentecost was not the birth of Protestantism, atheism, or agnosticism; it was the birth of the *Catholic* Church, the all-inclusive Mystical Body which follows the Son of God for eternal Salvation by its own concise definition.

So, let the world agree that the first Apostles did not live in the time of Martin Luther or John Wesley; they were the very physical human beings who walked beside Jesus Christ. And, they were Catholics by name, by virtue, by purpose, by faith, and by Redemption. When all is said and done, we will eventually discover that there is no difference between Truth, strength, and beauty as they are defined in the Saint Joseph's Bible. Most of us perceive our souls sitting in the middle of some strange void that we cannot yet define, whether it be through the parameters of spiritual health or apostasy, Wisdom and error, confidence and hopelessness, or trust and trepidation. We try our best to wrap ourselves in a tepid modesty, but those who need us the most will ultimately unravel the mystery of our being while trying to discover who we are if we do not voluntarily reveal it to them first. If we twist and turn inside ourselves in a clandestine attempt to avoid being known before men, we will only be sending our own spiritual nature into a flying tailspin in front of God and His Court. We must seek a newer cohesion right now to prepare us for the effects of Salvation. Thereafter, we will literally be capable of touching another person's soul because their spirit and their glorified body will be forever and inseparably one.

Jesus Christ Sees the World from the Inside-Out

January 17, 2001

There is no reason for us to believe that the grand years between the time we are old enough to know that we are alive and the day we become one of the faithfully departed should be a maudlin struggle against the forces of modern debauchery. No one has ever heard of a dove suffering a fatal heart attack while soaring in midflight and plunging to the ground in defeat. Thereby, the prospects for the success of peace on Earth are just as promising now as when Jesus Christ was born. How do we know this to be true? Because the Spirit of Love in our hearts bears-out the verification that the tenor of our good will shall always be pleasing to the God who gives us life. Every new day we awaken is another gift from His grace; and there is nothing to prove that such blessings will cease the charge of the Kingdom which still pours into our Covenant of Mercy from the Crucified Heart of His Son. We must remember that, even though we can be distracted from seeing Him clearly through our eyes of faith sometimes, there is nothing superfluous in Heaven. Every fond remnant we will see there is already in place beyond the limits of time and space. The basic facts of perfection, Divinity, and Glory were told by Jesus from the Cross upon which we are guaranteed a new tenancy for every age to come. There will be no need for us to take a polygraph test when we see Our Savior's Face because He already knows our confessions in the Truth of His own Judgement. If we accept the Blood of the Cross, God knows that our consciences will be clear and we will have no prior record of error to haunt us from our years on the Earth. We will be newly ordained Saints standing before Him with the Blood of His Passion cascading down our souls.

How happy we will all be to see the Glorified world as the Almighty Father has choreographed its conclusion! We will take-on the presence of little Parisian children, frolicking freely through the linear cabarets of the *Champs Elysees* on their last day of school for the rest of the summer. We must begin to prepare now for this moment of unending celebration by doing exactly what the Holy Spirit implores us to achieve in our time on the Earth. And, not only that, we should be prepared to offer the proper thanksgiving to the Most Blessed Trinity for sublimely getting us there. We would have to look pretty far and wide for people who are truly grateful for the gifts they have been given from Heaven these days. Those who are healed from crippling diseases, delivered from horrific accidents, and rescued from perilous situations should all bow in humble awe at the Love of God to keep them safe from the throes of injury or even the call of death. Rarely do we see people return thanks before a meal in a restaurant anymore; and getting a parent to even remotely consider that it is God who breathes life into their newborn children is as rare as seeing hoarfrost on the maple trees during the hottest days in July. But, through it all, we still see an entire collage of poignant visions which tell us that the Crucifixion of Jesus Christ is alive and well in the person of suffering humanity today.

The world seems to be lacking in any motivation to start praying again, so we continue through life the best we can, with the greatest know-how we can muster and in reflection of everything we have been taught by generations past. We know that there is no such thing as a game unless there is a chance we can either win or lose. This is the same way that most of us perceive the struggles which greet us as the sun rises in the East in the morning. We know that it is entirely possible for our souls to be paralyzed by the tragedies we face, which leads our hearts to being touched, but we somehow never really understand that it is happening. Many people look in the direction of God, but, by their own innate distractions, cannot really see His Love as owning any portion of their days. It is as though they are screaming so loud at the rest of the world that they cannot hear the call of His voice. The endless strain of human tears we have shed for a seeming eternity ought to teach us that we are all survivors on a remote spherical wheel called Earth, spinning in the darkness of space with nowhere else to go. The globe is a petri dish in Creation where God can see if our cultures will ever rise to the occasion of knowing His perfection or whether we can truly envision His purpose in what we have learned about why we are here.

There was a man who once lived in a small village along the Ohio River who was so unfortunate to have lost his right arm in an accident when he was about six years old. Everyone felt sorry for him because he could not accomplish the things that most of us take for granted. He could not hold an umbrella over his head and get into a car; and he once broke his ankle and could not walk on crutches while it healed. He never applauded the things that made his heart move, at least not with the clapping noise that most of us make. It was so sad to see someone else having to trim the nails on his remaining fingers and cut his meat at the dinner table. However, he knew that he was not disabled! He was as intelligent as any laboratory scientist; he could drive a semi-tractor-trailer truck with a 20-speed manual transmission, hit home runs at the ballpark with the best of them, type thirty words per minute on a computer keyboard, play a piano solo that would make a lumberjack cry, and had a pleasing demeanor which placed him high and above his more ambidextrous friends. He never once applied for public aid for his disability, and was the first to raise his only hand in school to answer a question from the teacher. Nope. This man never deviated from the normal day-to-day productivity that most responsible men contribute to societies who are so much in need of their help. The most profound trait about him of all, however, was that he prayed the Rosary with that single hand as though he was trying to lift the sorrows of the entire world onto his back. Most people pray the Rosary with two hands as the beads pass through their fingers, but he gave it all he had with the strength of his heart, knowing that God was literally holding onto the one he was missing, high upon His Throne in Paradise. He would die and retrieve it someday, using both arms to adjust his new Crown as Jesus places it on His head.

What can we say about making the most out of life when we seem to be so despondent and despaired? We often think about such people as this noble man from alongside the Ohio River. We pray in assurance with the thought of the millions of souls around the world who are agonizing in hospital beds, covered with sheets and enduring intravenous needles stuck in their arms, knowing in advance that some of their caskets are already built and are sitting in the back of a funeral parlor somewhere. Through all of this sad contemplation, God is still calling us to see His Truth in the reflection of His healing Love. That is the only way we will ever be free from seeing life as it appears to be and realizing its purpose and destiny as the Son of God already does. People in prisons have to live with this hope all the time, so why cannot those who reside along the streets rest beyond the constraints of the more immediate hours, too? We must all grow together in a more spiritual way without leaving the confines of mortality yet, knowing that our acceptance of the Love of God for humankind is our only true Light. What would happen if everyone emptied their warehouses of temporal obsession and became fully the likeness of Christ? Perhaps, then, a jury of twelve would enter a courtroom and render a verdict of, "Not guilty, because we are all sinners, too." Indeed, we could somehow go back to our youth and kneel in front of our mother's kitchen stove and watch her apple pie baking through the glass in the door in anticipation of tasting its sweetness again.

It is our spiritual vision which is still lacking, not our desire to see it corrected. If we looked at a photograph of a group of people sitting in their dress-clothes around an oak table with nameplates in front of their legal pads, we might assume that they are conducting the affairs of the day. However, we would never know whether they comprised a public commission, a board of a private business, a group of volunteers, or someone deciding the future for another segment of society. Without noticing any other signs or being able to hear what they are saying, we would not really understand the purpose of their convening. But, Jesus Christ sees the world from the inside-out. He knew that such a body of publicans was going to collect themselves to pose for this photograph back when He died on the Cross. We complain because there are so many facets about life that we may never know until we die; but we refuse to comprehend the new dimensions we inherit when we become unified in His Sacred Heart. When we suffer for the sake of His people, we are on the Cross; we have taken-on the parameters of the Divine Mercy; and we can warn the rest of the world about the condemnation they will inevitably undergo if they deny the Sacred Blood which we have already accepted. Therein lies the prospect of our clairvoyance and the vision we need to avoid taking dead-end streets in our personal and familial lives. Our first intuition is to hide from the things that make us cringe as though we are not being as giving as those societies of saints in hospice beds who are now closer to their deaths. We must comfort them, heal them, and implore them to ask Our Lord for His greater assistance if they should be so fortunate as to see Him before we hand-over our own souls to Everlasting Life.

The Ongoing Process of Christian Development

January 18, 2001

Our Almighty Father has inundated the world with billions of tiny creatures that we cannot see with the naked eye, so we secure a sample of them from the wild and place it under a microscope, hoping to discover how they affect Creation as a whole and whether our purposes might be enhanced by their presence. There are fortunes and estates spent on such research; a great deal of which furthers our capacity to discover new medical technologies and procedures. How, then, has it come to pass that we still look at the people we see with a casual glance and yet ignore what they really mean to the rest of society? Does our knack for neglecting them spring from the old maxim that nothing worthwhile is ever complete without an extended effort or a large cache of wealth? There are a great many broken hearts in the world today, not all of which are found in little children. Grown-ups are hurting, too, on the inside; mostly from the idle ignominy they receive from their peers everyday. Justice, honor, and nobility call us to take the hands of those who feel so ignored by the rest of us; we who have earned our college degrees and are now practicing workaholics who are trying to justify why we spent so much time in the classroom while learning so very little we could ever put to good use in our chosen careers. We are faced with the burden of repaying our student loans and upholding the basic decision we made to earn a higher degree; all to the diminishment of the real problems which are facing those who either went on to wage war or had no desire or opportunity to continue the process of learning in a more formalized setting.

There is hardly a person alive who has graduated with a baccalaureate degree that did not have a professor whom they did not wish to go back and slap right in the face. Oh, we have all had them! He was the one who gave us the B-minus on our term-paper in religion class because he disagreed with our basic premise of Sacramental absolution. Or, perhaps it was our female rhetoric instructor who was offended by our critique of the Equal Rights Amendment. Whomever that person was oftentimes set the platform for how we now view the people who oppose us when we are only trying to explain the essence of our beliefs from the bottom of our hearts. If only those who teach our children could be as open-minded as they require their students to be, maybe a new sense of understanding could take place in the classroom and outside the academic arena, too. We remember the story about the discussion of the Blessed Trinity in a parochial grade school one time; and the teacher asked her pupils to identify what it is and how it applied to their lives as a whole. So, a little boy in the back of the class raised his hand and promptly described the Holy Trinity as being the Nina, the Pinta, and the Santa Maria. No one else in the group knew the answer, either, so the teacher was the only one who chuckled. After deciding that the boy actually believed what he was saying, she told him that he was not quite correct, although the latter, the Santa Maria, is the Spanish name for the Mother of God. While not one in the Triune Deity, She did, in fact, have a direct relationship with the Trinity to the extent that

She gave birth to Baby Jesus and is the Spouse of the Holy Spirit. The teacher went on to explain it this way to everyone else there, and left the discussion of Christopher Columbus for some other, more appropriate day.

The things we can learn from such innocence is more valuable than we really seem to know. The impish little boy in school knew that the Trinity must have had something to do with the number three and that they were all single ships which had somehow served on a mission to discover a new world. He had inadvertently found the basis for the Most Blessed Trinity through the power of Divine Advocacy in his heart. The Father, the Son, and the Holy Spirit are those three warships that compose the Armada of Love which God has dispensed to the Earth to claim a new Kingdom for the lost. Saint Patrick would have been mighty proud of the little fellow that day for knowing that three individual aspects of one commission had flowed from a singular stem of purpose. Are we willing to take a stab at telling what we know about God before the rest of the world, even at the risk of seeming so infantile? Although our examples may not be as precise as all the doubting Thomas's may require, can we at least lunge forward into the deepest waters of good intentions to see that Jesus would never allow us to drown? There is nothing at all juvenile about the Truth, but we will certainly comprehend it better if we refrain from dissecting it through a microscope of materialism and human interpolation. It would be to the great detriment of our understanding of Love if we became entrenched in how it must be defined, rather than searching for new avenues to deploy it as it has been provided and bestowed from the Cross of Jesus Christ.

Suffice it to say that becoming a Christian is an ongoing process of spiritual development which can oftentimes take years to complete. But, the fact that we are becoming like little children again does not mean that we are regressing in faith. Of course, we must greet the future with mature goals in a quite displeasing world, but we should never once have the thought of "I" in the process or believe that our service to humanity will result in any reward which is worth the taking before God finally calls us to Heaven. If we perceive the blessings of Paradise as meeting the horizontal Earth at exactly 90-degrees, then our best prospect is to try to become the hypotenuse of an invisible right-triangle of Love that is made when we connect them both by our lives. This is to say, we mortals on the Earth may not see it, but all the Saints in Heaven will have another new polygon to shade in their coloring books. Perhaps this three-sided depiction is what that little grade-schooler saw from the depths of his infant heart. These are not the imaginary musings from someone's vivid imagination; they are premonitions to what we can all see if only we will invoke the simplicity and Wisdom of the Holy Paraclete into the dailiness of our lives.

There is no reason for us to believe that we are alone, anymore. God is within us; His faithful people on the Earth are beside us; and we, ourselves, are more than the flat-line souls who existed before we accepted the Son of God as the Savior of our souls.

Heaven Will Clothe Us All in Eternal Light!

January 22, 2001

Our newborn children deserve the privilege and birthright of being conceived into a world that is wholly free from trepidation, moral corruption, and the maddening competition which often threatens our survival amongst the corporate beasts. As we can readily see, we have been woefully unsuccessful in allowing them to live beyond the chains we have placed upon ourselves as their adult predecessors. Life must become a process of growing from the same Love in Heaven who has created us, not from some distal conspiracy that takes us through our childhood in tears, conscripts our adolescent purposes into certain factional disciplines, contaminates our adulthood with material idolatry, and burdens our senior decades with the agony of anxiety and confusion. To be given life is not a sentence of mortal punishment; nor need it be a period of sulking helplessness in our slow passage toward inevitable death. We must ask ourselves as soon as we are capable of thinking clearly and with our own sense of good judgement what posture we are really seeking. What are our motivations and plans for the future? For most of us, it is simply to survive in an environment over which we have little control, to perceive the rest of society through the most mundane prescription we can employ, to ensure that we are not the ones who are without food and shelter everyday, and to somehow muster enough courage to ask Jesus to forgive our transgressions when we finally see His Holy Face. If ever there was an unwritten charter for inadvertent isolationism, this may very well be it. We are commanded by God, instead, to wield dominion over the Earth not for the purpose of advancing ourselves or our closest of relatives and friends, but to the end of serving every nation and race in the image and likeness of Christ.

Is our every act directed toward the marketplace-collusion which makes paupers out of ordinary men? Do we aspire to achieve more in political fame than we offer to God through His Church on the Earth? Let us pray that Heaven will clothe us all in Eternal Light! There is no time to waste on drawing misconceptions which haunt shallow societies and lead them into warring over lands and wages with their peers. Dwight Eisenhower and Jimmy Carter, both from opposing political persuasions, warned us against the military-industrial complex which has become the American nation; that it might erode our desire for interpersonal cohesion, destroy our shared values of human decency and common respect, and deteriorate the fabric that keeps us from becoming a country divided by financial affairs and geographical quarter. These were leaders who knew exactly what the Savior of the World has been teaching for the past 2000 years. But, when people who have never been president choose to discuss it; when ordinary men on the street try to explain how selfish and rigid our institutions have become, they are ostracized as being radical socialists and scoffed-at as monotreme lunatics by the very people who are now conducting their lives in the way that presidents Eisenhower and Carter portended. The saddest aspect of their being castigated is that some of them often resort to behavioral disorder to make their positions known when all they are asking is for the Truth of righteousness to be given an opportunity to prevail. God sees them; and He knows the purpose of their faith. They are not left-wing extremists who are trying to destroy a freely established system of government. They are simply attempting to effect the principles of the Christian Gospel which proclaims that God has given the Earth to all His people, not just the ones who happen to succeed first or who have been so fortunate to have been bequeathed a windfall of profits by a greedy benefactor or the broker they have hired to invest the spoils of their private wealth.

The larger nations of men should stop and recognize that the drive of the human spirit was never meant to be like a rocket ship, a jet airplane, or a spiraling helicopter; but rather the likeness of a dirigible Zeitgeist, a temper of the times which stands for all Creation, through the coexistence of every man, for the purpose of uniting both the living and the dead into one era of perpetual goodness, and toward the Throne of God without the staph incongruities of poverty and surplus to preoccupy our every move. Human life, instead, is meant to be a lighter-than-air blessing from God and a process of spiritual enlightenment which cannot be derailed by such erroneous thoughts. Our souls must bloom and grow like the storied Austrian edelweiss which accompanies our way back home and sail aloft in the grace of God in a helium-like benignity that cannot be shot down by the arrows of sin or the many oppressive fallacies we have inherited from the realism of generations gone by. Some people look at the New Testament as though it was originally penned in stencil by some anonymous prophet, rather than from the Holy Spirit of God in Paradise. How wrong they are to assume that Jesus Christ did not live inside the hearts of SS. Matthew, Mark, Luke, John, and Paul as they inscribed the very words He wishes those who will be absolved in His Blood to eventually come to know. The Truth of Redemption has been laid-out by His own Hand and expressions of Love and deliverance. The mortals who recorded them were like the disciples who accept the Holy Paraclete in their hearts to this very day; sinners who are trying to do better, those who have loved and suffered by the two-edged sword of the Cross, and the smiling Martyrs who now sit at His side in the Glory of Salvation.

We can never quite port-round the facts of life by trying to distract God from knowing us in our efforts to become public men or populists from the days of classical antiquity or the years of post-renaissance. The Truth is the Truth; and we cannot hide from it or conceal our inequalities from the Light of God which can penetrate any force of darkness or impaneled shield we may implore to be our tortured defense. If we do not approach Love, accept Love, become Love, and share Love, we shall never know what it is like to see Creation the way the angels already know; we will not stand in the open fields of golden Truth that the Saints share today; and never will we be able to blossom into the fulness of our own potential-of-the-heart. We do not have to buy our way into such a blessed station in the sight of God; neither are we forced to earn it by hanging our souls out to dry. Let us remember that Jesus has told us that the poor who live among us are the salt of the Earth, and so is our struggle to help them. We have all gone into the grocery store and purchased a box of salt. It is one of the most important products we will find on the shelves because it provides the seasoning we require for our taste of life to be better defined. It is the substance we use to cure our meals and is unaffected by the frigid nature of the mortal world. And yet, it is one of the least expensive of the provisions we will ever move across the check-out counter on our way out the door. Can we envision forgiveness in our lives in much the same way? Christian Love in the image of Jesus is the most important virtue that the world will ever espouse, for it cannot be destroyed just because the cold-of-heart will not accept it; and someone can be a pauper for life and still be able to afford the full deposit of its purpose.

And yet, there are many of us who complain that we cannot see Love; that it does not hit us in the face with God's justice every time we turn around, and that we practically have to force those we hold so dear to offer their affection in return. Again, we are trying to define an infinite Divinity from the Firmament of Heaven while using comprehensible terms. There are some things that words just cannot describe, and the Love of God is one of them. This is why the Cross is such an indispensable signal that we have all been spared from the fires of Hell. Let us take into consideration the phenomenon of instantaneous combustion. We do not have an appropriate adjective in the dictionary to describe an explosion, so we try to imitate the sound it makes by saying the word, "kaboom!" Hereby, this is also true with Love. We cannot properly define its endless dimensions in the breadth of a single term, so we direct our focus toward the Life, Death, and Resurrection of Christ as our definitive explanation. This is what He asks us to do, and is no-less the priority than what God has placed before us all as we have come to know life inside the Catholic Church as She was originally intended to remain. There are some things we cannot change as easily as others, so we are forced to live alongside them in our midst as best we know how. When an incandescent bulb burns-out in our home, we do not take it apart, refit the filament, and screw it back in; we throw it away and replace it with a new one. The inner-part is far too delicate for us to repair on our own; so we have no purpose in going there. Such is a parable to what the Son of God will do if we allow our love for Him to die before He returns to redeem us. If we are not still shining as brightly as when He set us aglow 200 decades ago, He is apt to toss the world aside in favor of another one that He can truly call His own.

God knows where those filaments are glowing throughout the world today. The Light of Christ is in the hands of His humble priests as they raise His Crucified Body in Consecration at the Holy Sacrifice of the Mass before the altars in His Catholic Church on Earth. When we believe that the world is melting-down before us and that our every sense of decency is decaying before our eyes, we must feast them upon the Lamb of God who takes away the sins of the world. Our thoughts should be more stable than to doubt whether our faith will eventually save us. Every pathological and clinical disorder is the direct result of people being placed under duress by others who despise them; those who have refused to accept the ever-present perfection of the Son of God in the Communion Host. We have so oppressed other men through our desire to declare ourselves as leaders and conquerors of the material world that we have left a bloody trail of casualties in our path. Mental stress, nervous breakdowns, bi-polar disorders, depression, autism, paranoia-schizophrenia, sexual deviancy, and suicide can all be prevented if we will only reach their victims in time to heal them with our Christian Love. Our faith must become always aspirational and transcendental, not in a mere cerebral way, but in our trust in the Divine Resurrection of Jesus Christ. A tonnage of Love does not infer that dignity arrives in 2000-pound increments, but in an immeasurable lot that lifts men up, not places them under the further burden of our lack of compassion.

Our self-interest must be dissolved into a greater concern for the contemporary Mystical Body of Christ. There is no reason to read the stars anymore because they will volunteer quite vocally the Glory of their Creator to the rest of the universe and the future He has penned in our elevation of the Cross. There are no scenes of drug abuse there, no impurity, lust, thievery, or materialism in our vision of Mount Calvary because Jesus has destroyed them all. Anyone who is affected by these scourges has simply not yet sought to be healed by the power of His Sacrifice. Even those who proclaim to be free from such vices, but who are addicted to professional fame and financial fortune, are called even more urgently to kneel at the foot of the Cross for the convalescence of their ailing consciences. There is oftentimes a major difference between a politician and a public servant in that most partisans will stand by the moral Truth until it begins to impede their prospects for financial gain or securing another term; at which time they categorically deny ever having any prior knowledge of being capable of differentiating between right and wrong. These same people are also called to reconciliation with God through His Crucified Son, impaled to a Tree where every other mortal soul has been forthrightly absolved. Our lives and our love must flow into the world like a pianist performing in a chamber; from one soul into two arms, ten fingers, 88 keys, and an entire orchestration of undivided humanity; one person, one family, one society, one nation, one continent, one globe, and a singular Creation of peace. This is the true definition of unity and is the power that God wields toward the mission of making us one again in Him.

The Full Manifestation of Chivalry in Our Hearts

January 23, 2001

We enter, now, the inner-realm of the Holy Spirit by calling upon the higher senses of decency in our hearts to lionize the Son of God as the King of the Universe. No more are we slaves to the soiled past that bears the implantation of our ancestors' frames; for we are of the more eloquent age, the new listers who are preparing the ground upon which our Savior will walk again in Glory. What is it that makes this impending exultation so unattractive to those who are still ingrained in the batteries of the physical world? The answer is very simple; there are no tycoons to be hailed and no magnates to laud where we are all going. The only richness is in the Love of our Almighty Father who owns the globe and everything on it, even our souls over which we hold no dominion before Him. Here on the American continent, people are signing book deals in the millions of dollars about secular topics that Jesus Christ could not care less about. They neither enhance His Kingdom, nor detract from it, but only keep us all from knowing Him better and waste the valuable resources which we could employ to prepare our State for His Final Return. One of the first questions that will roll-off His lips is why we allowed our material resources to be illicitly concentrated in so few hands. We have forgotten that positions of power are malignant if they are not wielded for the good of humankind as a whole. Where there is wealth, there is luxury, influence, and new potential. Perhaps those who horde the greatest fortunes in America should take a time-out from their Yankee-doodles to think about what the Resurrected Son of the God who created them is going to say when it finally comes their time to be judged.

None of us is a stranger to the shock-treatment approach that capitalists use these days to lure their consumers in; from the in-your-face advertising of television, magazines, and billboards flooding our cities. Those who are responsible for such persuasive diablerie are in for the jolt of their very lives when Jesus Christ waves a red flag over their heads as they try to sneak into the procession of Saints who have gone without the barest of necessities in mortal life so the more affluent could prosper at will. Whatever we choose to call it; a cedilla, a tilde, a circumflex, or a macron; God will mark their souls for Eternity and brand them as unfit to become naturalized into His New Republic of Salvation. It is never too late to pray for them, especially now when we know that His Second Coming is so near in the offing; today, while His Divine Mercy is still overshadowing His appetite for Justice; and now, while His Blessed Virgin Mother is so profoundly beseeching His more gentle side on our behalf. The feeling of knowing in advance that we are absolved by effecting our own repentance for our sins, avoiding whatever leads us into temptation, adopting a sound platform for the amendment of our lives, and reaching-forward to evangelize the rest of the world is paralleled by none. Once we know deep inside our hearts that we can Love God and our neighbors, alike, there is no going back; no one can steal our new designation of "disciples of Christ," as long as we say our prayers.

It is like waking one morning in the spring and realizing that winter has finally gone. We hear the matin of the songbirds on the budding limbs outside the windows of our bedrooms and know that immortal life is real to us; not some prosaic, dry, or unimaginative screech from the depths of despair; never an allegation to be assessed on the merits of hearsay evidence; but a supernatural faith in the higher beliefs of our protracted souls in relation to the Love of God. We often reach-out to our comrades, chums, and buddies; but they all seem to be missing something when they have not joined us in our new quest for Salvation. They perceive us as living in some altered state; inheriting a means of survival by some mysterious deliberation that they cannot quite easily define. Now, to us, perhaps the romanticism of Robin Hood as he tackled the Sherwood Forests of Nottinghamshire can finally give our imagination a generous push. We often look at life from the obverse, face-value perspective, knowing early-on that most everything we see is available to nearly any other man; but do we ever reach-out in adoration of our infinite God to empower our own contrite confessions, appointments, and observances toward the purpose of becoming one with Him and understanding the true spiritual nature of our being alive today? That is the arena of mortality in which we will find true heroism, pageantry, fanciful mystique, sentiment, adventure, idealism, festoonery, and the ultimate renewal of the self. We hide beneath the skies of the western hemisphere like cowards crawling on our calloused bellies, never daring to tear the Gambrel roofs off our homes to allow the charismatic supernature of God to fall into Creation at its best.

Yes, we need to rest in the comforting arms of God with the full manifestation of chivalry in our hearts, to force into action our desire to be one in His Gallant Son, to impel and urge our highest regards, to search, to float, to chase, and retrieve; all in the Holy Name of Jesus Christ. By indulging His righteousness at home and abroad, and by repressing the enemies of the Fruits of His Love, we can remake our souls, God willing, into the particular pious consistency of His own stately manners; to unite and accomplish, to mend and compel, and to apply, transfer, carry, and believe. Then, we shall dare those shadowy inhibitions to try to stand in the way of our faith! "Come on! Come on!", we will shout with the courage of the Cross at the center of our being. We shall mow them down like cockleburs and burdocks because they stand no chance against the charge of our newborn Love. A reckoning is in the offing that we should anticipate like a candidate for office who has no one to oppose him anymore. It will be a future of rejoicing, glee, merriment, gaiety, and jollity for those who know their Redemption in the Blood of Jesus Christ. But, it will be a realization of wretched unhappiness for the tribes who despise Him; as their fate will be attended by unending misery, disconsolation, lamenting, hunger, thirst, contempt, and delusion. The present moment is a call-to-order for the Saints of Eternity, and also we who shall soon join them to recover from our dispersions, while rebuking the vast false-constellations who bicker amongst themselves from the Hills of Beverly, wishing that they had listened to the Holy Gospel all along, instead of bowing before the footlights which cast shadows on the drudgery of their selfish careers.

Christians are a new and distinct Creation who have cast-aside the innumerable not-so-courtly clouds of guilt that are forming in banks of accusation above the heads of those who are condemning us. There will be no Oscars or Golden Globes for those who have led their lives as hypocrites, acting as though they are nothing of the kind. There will be nary a thing so grand about the pianissimos of the hollowed-woods once the Son of God has had His final say. We know that the Love of Heaven for humanity was never poised to be a confidential grace; and there is truly no way that anyone on the Earth will ever be able to plug the leaks in the new wineskins of our overflowing jubilation to eventually tell them all off. Shyness and timidity in the Face of our very Salvation? You have got to be kidding! Never before has a society of people been so proud to succumb to the inebriation we have found in the Blood of the Cup of Redemption! No other victor in annular mortal history has ever won a campaign so overwhelming as did Jesus Christ when He killed Satan outright at midday on Good Friday; for His was not a cyclical triumph for some brassy piece of hardware. The Crucifixion of the Savior of the World is the mother of all mortal accomplishments, for now and *in perpetuum*, forever! No one in exile or already living in eternal bliss will know the satisfaction of becoming the greatest Champion the universe has ever seen. However, the miracle does not stop there! That feeling of irrevocable joy has been passed-along to us! We, too, are teammates of this Grand Warrior because He has invited us to become united with Him on the same Beatific Cross. Now, the superlatives which might attempt to describe our own sense of perfect being are much too inadequate to ever suffice.

We have an opportunity to succeed today; one which those who reject Our Lord will never own so that our souls are lifted to the status of princes and knights who can finally stand upright before the Throne of our Almighty Father and proclaim with surety, "*Ich Dien*, I serve!" The pale helplessness we have known for years is now completely destroyed, minced, mangled, and blown into smithereens. Our trite snafues have been mysteriously transformed into acute senses of better judgement, acts of overwhelming succession, and profound statements of prophetic Truth. The spiritual architecture of our new awareness has been redesigned from the stick-built porticos of human despair into an Ionic and Corinthian series of heretofore unknown achievements; for we now are piloting the Concorde Cheyennes of our souls into the Sacred Heart of Christ. The "will" is our own to finally accept Him; for we are free to choose our destiny in absolution; and not a soul who is ordered by evil forces to be our enemy or dispatched to coerce us into quitting can do anything about it. We stand before Jesus as people of good faith; and no bribery can take us away from knowing His Omnipotent Father in Heaven again.

No Crypt Can Hold Us Now; No Burden Do We Bear!

January 24, 2001

Our Lord and Mighty Savior, in whose favor our souls shall ever rest, is the Heraldry of the ages and the comfort of the blessed! How awesome and wonderful is the honor You bestow upon us to cadge our Resurrection without a mere pittance in return. Your Cadmean Victory is the Glory of the Cross; You, who have been the politeness of an angry God, who instills the beauty of the ages into the fabric of our hearts; You, who alone have suffered so prettily in the place of we who were so guilty of scandalizing the piety of the perfection we once owned! How we pray to You to be our true Imperialist; that Your Love will conquer the surface of the Earth; that Your Truth will saturate every land; that Your Justice will consume us inside the fires of Everlasting Life! We wait for Thee with spirits and honey locusts in our thoughts and the royal poinciana of a much greater Kingdom resting at our feet. The crests of crimson clovers cannot haunt us anymore, but raise us to the crystalline affection which sails across Your tears. No crypt can hold us now, no burden do we bear, no phantoms to wreck our dreams; for we are now and forever handfast in Your Grace, citadels in a world of small accomplishments, and wanderers over the higher plains of destiny which is Your Sacred Heart. Will You not calibrate us with the warranty of Your Passion to bind us in moral excellence? Shall not Your inheritors and those who pray the moniliform Mysteries of the Most Holy Rosary experience the Stations of the Cross while never parting their gates or cowering in the parlors of their homes? Under vows of chastity and obedience, do we not all come calling upon the surplus of Your Love with our spirits laid wide open?

You are the sole libation for the parched renditions of which we sing; suffering our state of feverish envy because the Saints can see Your Face right now, while our vision is yet dimmed by the fazing trespasses that keep blinding us in disgrace. Our souls know no other lover than Thee! Our prerogatives are ostentatious if we do not deposit them over the levees of Your Truth, casting them to the winds and into the wilderness in which You live in such harmony with the Creation You have made. We shall only flabbergast our own fledgling helplessness should we ever decline Your penchant to be the Truth! For now, all the past is gone and our horrors have been done; there is nothing more we can do, it seems, to make You Love us more. It is only in You that we are one again, that we dress the Crispen cruppers which adorn the tails of the steeds upon which Your Mercy has finally found its peace! Now, all Love is united once and for all in Your Suffering, dominion, diplomacy, opulence, oceans, streams, briskets, brine, and Sacraments! We offer You our very selves, broiled and broken, penniless and aching, sparse and foolhardy, eager and intoned. Now, You touch and Love us affectionately when nothing more do we deserve. You dote over our impotence when all we wish to know is where the Truth began! Yes, we are too routine, mechanical, fixed, habitual, and coarse of memory!

But, all in all, we have come to know Your Wisdom again, to realize that we shall never end religious wars through political fashions in the expanse of our lifeless times! We are the silkworms who have vested the lot of our years in harboring the sweetness of Your Fruits for ourselves, too stingy to pass them along to the rest of the brood and too dilatory to admit that our aggression is at fault and our transgressions are to blame! How sorrowful we are to have offended Your Salutatory Peace when we only wish to hold a little share of it for ourselves, our friends, and those we hope to marry someday. How hollow are our midnight wares when we leave You out in the cold and darkness for far too long, evacuated from our hearts like a virus on the loose, too doleful on our own to make the oceans quiver on our journey or quaff the waves of Your Passionate Blood along the way! We might declare that it does not matter anymore if it is all the same to You! How extraordinary is Your kindness to not take us to the docks in retribution for our sinfulness, never holding back from willing Your Crucifixion to the dead who are laying in the streets, more than generous to the touch when we are cringing in such pain. Your bludgeoned Wounds will always forbid us to ignore the Love You hold for humankind, the isosceles parity in which Your Virgin Birth made You One of us; save Your everlasting sinlessness. How much farther will You go to take away our loathing and sensations of the flesh? Do we not grow numb waiting for Your Paraclete to light upon our sordid souls and warble a tone to cradle our cares into a more fathomed sleep?

If we shaved our heads and donned a wig, would You not concede that our reclusive follicles are trying to deceive You into believing that they are like our inner-selves, holding-out in terror so they will not be harvested like the goats who live in segregation from the sheep? When life hurts, the pain is real; but somehow deep inside we know that You are, likewise, weeping too. The leafstalks which hold our shivering palms within Your grasp are growing crisper by the age; but we shall never stop dipping them into the waters of our Baptism to keep them growing upward to Your Throne. When our hearts are filled with sediment, will You not turn the world upside-down again and make Your Blood come rushing to *our* heads? Then, our intuitive discourses can be filled with the Psalms of Your embrace and our funeral dirges will resound with new meaning once again. We remember the Great Deluge which was Your premonition of the foundering of our sorrows in the containment of the Cross, and a mutual pair of every kind which You had specified should prosper before its passing wake. But, now the True Species have become Your Sacred Body and Your Blood, whole and uniformly, individually and collectively the Most Holy Presence of Your Sacramental Divinity from the Altars of Your Catholic Church. Let not Your detractors take away the beauty of Your fineness before the world or lead anyone to believe that these Elements are not Your Crucified Soul which has been Resurrected from the Grave! We will fight with diligence to the severance of our heads to witness that You are truly the Manna of Life from the Kingdom of Paradise, come to Earth to be our spiritual nourishment and Salvation once again.

The spattered hesitance of the protestors who march against Your Streets of Gold are only yellow-bellied pond lilies who stand in stagnant waters, just waiting for the chance to grab-hold of someone with a weaker faith, take them hostage before the world, and attempt to prove that Your Holy Eucharist was never really You. The fact remains, however, that no one in the annals of recorded or uncharted history has ever proved that You are not the Bread of Absolution whom You proclaim to be! You are the Sacrament of the annihilation of their mutiny and the reason they will be so ashamed that they have been too wicked for so long. Perhaps their blindness is not because they are turning their faces away from the blessings of Your Priestly Office; but because, in vengeance, they have plucked their own eyes out by mistake! The essence of Your Truth is its own prophetic Will; and many years of wonderment have taken their toll against the people You have sent to tell the world in advance of Your march to send Your enemies into the pitfalls which churn so deeply beneath the seas. Do those who utter "nay" dare to raise their heads against the ripples of Your gentile Love before Your Sacred Heart swells into the whitecaps that will bore like knives into their stubborn breasts? Is there any man alive who will spend the rest of time in completeness at Your side who has never come to grips with the expediency of Your discipline before he shall die? Are there any ghosts who bear the likeness of Your Saints who have come to haunt us in their place?

Sometimes we think that our sugar-shacks do not hold their sweetness anymore because we have somehow lost our taste for them. Is this not like the semblance of our consciences which we have cordoned-off from landing point-blank against the Truth for which You Died so profoundly 2000 years ago? Is Your humanity not attempting to conceal the hardening of our hearts while we have already heard Your Sacred Voice today? The lessons from the Scriptures are the promulgation of Your Laws which have rendered Your Creation a wholly justified armament in the battles of human romance. Will we comply with them or concede at last that we are too frail and weary to face the trumpets of self-sacrifice at the break of dawn when tomorrow finally comes? We are Your scarlet warriors who shall never leave Your side, Your signature paratroops who have fallen intrinsically in Love with Your Kingdom which stands within the reach of our fingers now. So, we beg Your pardon and ask that You will bless us with the engagement and fullness of Your bountiful Heart, ringing-in the final years of mortal Earth without an instant to spare on those who would be damned as they spate into Your Holy Face while choosing to plummet down the shaft of Hell that Your Mystical Body leaves behind. The scent of our Redemption is pleasing to the touch; and our huddled icebergs that lurch with such clandestine treachery beneath our feet are melting through the hearth of the Divine Love in which You have warmed the Earth. We can sail to greet You without worrying anymore if only You will chart our course and be a Lighthouse in our dark and dreary times.

Responsibility is a Characteristic We Must Learn to Wield

January 25, 2001

Will we not ultimately be required by God someday to revise the floor plans of our mortal residency to prepare a broader room for His Crucified Son; the same Savior who already owns the right-of-way for our passage into greater things, where our conscience and reality, the Truth and absolution, and peace and civility all finally intersect? Walking through life is quite a waiting game; but they who stand aside while expecting the skies to clear before they take a step might be mistaken as being "rigor mortis" when someone comes to call on them! Indeed, there are media moguls who would take a dive to get their hands on the date of the Second Return of Jesus Christ so as to cash-in on the profits of achieving their prediction. But, in the interim, they seem not to care the slightest about the conditions of the world before He finally arrives. The Associated Press correspondent Skip Wollenberg reported from New York that the CBS Television Network was raking-in 2.3 million dollars each for the 60 half-minute advertisements in the Super Bowl XXXV football game of January 28, 2001; a whopping $76,667 per second of air-time. We cannot wait until Judgement Day to see what excuses these merchants and networks try to peddle to the Son of God when He shows them a picture of the rest of the world on the day this game took place. Is there any more that needs to be said about the distribution of wealth which is now ongoing in the new economy of the American nation? What about the argument that large corporations put forth which states that their companies employ tens-of-thousands of people who all benefit from such advertising? Do these same laborers, like the corporate executives, make millions of dollars in annual salaries; or are they the ones who must settle for the bare minimum wage that the federal government forces their bosses to pay?

Our focus has shifted from whence we once shared our candy bars in the park with our friends to whether we can purchase the entire confectionery company before our competitors have a chance to gobble it up first. If we could anticipate the intonation of the Will of God today, we would hear Him command that we go back to those earlier years and try to find-out how we lost our innocence since then. Every young boy can remember folding the tongue of his red "Radio Flyer" wagon back over its bed and sitting with one knee inside, while using his other leg to paddle his way down the sidewalk. We felt as though we were really in control back then because we allowed cooler-heads to mind our ways; our parents, teachers, and private guardians. This is exactly the same kind of trust that we should place in God and His Court of Angels right now. However, most of us reject this kind of benign demeanor until we finally get caught with our greedy clutches in the till, at which time we undergo some strange metamorphosis of denial and ask someone almost rhetorically, "What are you picking on me for?" When we look at our own profile, we can see the distinctions by which we are known to other men; our casual mannerisms, senses of humor and compassion, our capacity to prevail over the forces which try to diminish us, and our perspectives of human life as we perceive them to be in general.

Responsibility is a characteristic we must learn to wield through the lessons of our peers, the repercussions of our own adventures, and the messages and teachings of Jesus Christ through our allegiance to His Holy Catholic Church. If we decide that it is easier to scoot our burdens across the floor of human life than to pick them up and carry them, we will be generating a lot of senseless noise and disrupting the peace in our lands; we will do an immense amount of damage to our own spiritual presence; and we will mar the Earth with the evidence of our own shoddy ambitions. Living as a good Christian is much the same way. There is a demarcation we cannot see anywhere else except in Jesus' Holy Cross that guides our steps and defends us against the temptations which almost inevitably lead to the committing of some type of mortal sin. When we say that we must never cross the line into impropriety, we should know in advance that the Holy Cross *is* the line between living and dying, condemnation and Salvation, war and peace, and Love and hatred. The Crucifixion is our shield against the baron forces of evil who, in their spiritual incongruity, are trying to pilfer our Salvation for themselves like wolves clad in the linens of sheep, when they know full-well that they will deny the Blood of Jesus Christ over and again at the end of time. Their poor station before God and against His righteousness is a fitting sentence for the crimes they are committing against humanity. When all is said and done, what we have accomplished for Our Lord during the passage of our years figures to be the main criterion which He will employ to determine whether we are worthy of entering His Kingdom at last.

This is the reason why we should wrap ourselves in the cloak of servitude and personal discretion, knowing that our greatest work is yet to be done. The sky is the limit, but most of us are quite content while leaving the birds of a feather to inherit the profits of the superior winds. When some people reach the top rung of a ladder and discover that they can go no further up, they either stand there in amusement of the greater world which seems much too enormous to ever conquer, or retreat to their bungalows in defeat, hoping that someone more creative than themselves will evolve from the crowd and finish the work they first began. They seem to be unaware that, in Christ, there are much longer ladders to be had; a thought which has not yet entered the minds of most everyday men. We squelch our higher potential and squander our opportunities because we are still afraid to discover the tools which will help us build a better modern-day world. If there is anything that the greatest heroes who ever lived had in common, it was that they, too, were once afraid. They were fearful of failing, anxious about the final outcome, and sometimes too weak to travel. But, they all succeeded because they mustered the courage that only the human spirit can provide, the invincible creativity which comes from the power of God in our hearts. If we bequeath a legacy for our children to discern, let it be that we succeeded in effecting change for the better, in rolling-up our sleeves and soiling our hands, and watching the beads of impassioned sweat drop to our feet while we labored to make their future more in tune with the glories of the Heavens.

It seems like wise men are always saying things that most of us stop to write-down, but we often fail to employ the reasoning for the Wisdom which led us to pause in the first place. Does not the experience of our precedent mortals allow us to see the ramifications of human life with a sharper edge? There is no doubt that no one except the Son of God is all-knowing, all-seeing, and Omnipotent, but such does not preclude us from communing with the Truth through the fruits of our prayers, the Divine perception that is garnered through the Sacraments of His Church, and the Sacred Mysteries which are proffered from the Hand of God through our engagement with the Angels and Saints. We are told that His Peace keeps flowing like a river into the bays of human existence; but most of our progress is dammed by people who continue to hate the rest of society, by introverts who seem not very interested in what the rest of the world is like, and through the prissy imperfections which make ordinary people seem prudish to their potential neighbors and friends. If Jesus Christ had ever issued a blanket Commandment in the Holy Scriptures saying that humankind was meant to be isolationist in their approach to interpersonal communication, would those who are so offended by our healthy casual speech try to kick the rest of us off the edge of the globe? The answer is probably "yes," but it does little to address the fact that He did *not* issue such a mandate and that He, instead, requires us to this day to join hands in the common cause of being one humanity. So, why are we not searching every meadow and valley for our brothers and sisters in Love? Because we are still too reluctant to put-forth the effort; and this is also the reason why we are not complying with the rest of the Statutes of His Holy Word.

We enjoy the freedom which comes with walking down the public byways and never even looking those whom we encounter in the face, let alone inquiring as to how they are feeling, whether they have the basic commodities to make it through the night, or which supplications we may offer to God on their behalf to bring-forth His consolation to whatever might be disconcerting them these days. It is as though we see the body of humanity as being a nondescript sandstone wall around which we must walk to get to where we really wish to go. If we perceived our brethren in Christ like a giant mirror flashing the Truth of our own disregard in our faces, would we be as apt to try to walk away? Do we not truly wish to know what evidentiary facts that our enemies hold in their clutches which might serve to indict us someday? It is all based upon a senseless social fear that has been festered by our misunderstanding of other people just because they are different from us; other colors and customs, foreign cultures, varying interests, and wholly opposite perspectives of right and wrong. This is the basis of why Jesus Christ asks us to unite in His Sacred Heart. He has created us all, He knows our souls, and He is confident that He can serve as the Mediator who will finally make us all one.

The Infamous "Rule of Law"

January 26, 2001

When we finally die, go to Heaven, and see Our Savior's Face, we will discover that there is really no such thing as a converse side to Creation and that we have been living blindly in the presence of God all along. However, this will not be the case for those who give their souls to Satan; for he and they will never be allowed to step-foot in the greater parameters of the phenomenon of human immortality. Back in the early days of Christianity, the Love of God for His people and the interpersonal affection between them was called their *agape*. This same Grecian term is employed today by many religious societies and prayerful organizations. Why? Because the Love of our Creator has never changed from the very first moment He placed our spirits into being. Whether someone lives in Athens, Jerusalem, the Congo, Antarctica, Tokyo, Bangladesh, Santiago, or Ashland, Illinois, the favor of our Almighty Father rests deeply upon those whom He has given life; in the womb, to the cradle, through the broadness of middle ages, and beyond their death. Jesus has often spoken of mortal life as being not unlike a flat plane in an otherwise spherical universe; and we walk with the Light of His Crucifixion through the perils which try to keep our hopes face-down on the mat. God is trying to teach us through His Son that human life serves a greater purpose than this. It is meant to be a support for the endless ages which have come before us; and our service to them is to resonate what God has had to say long before we were ever born. He sees us in the likeness of the Saints who have become the baluster spindles under the handrails of mortality to which we all cling during our ascension back to Heaven.

One of the strangest ironies in modern times is that our greatest strength to survive does not reside in our capacity to destroy our neighbors by either brute force or technological superiority. What good is there in conquering an enemy if we simultaneously go to our own graves in the process? No; the real strength and vigor of a race of people is in their ability to invoke the spiritual assistance of the God who gave them life. The sinews of a great nation rest not in its eminent potential to be a superpower amongst the lot of weaker states, but in its desire to avoid conflict through the invocation of God's common sense. Of course, this requires constraint, not only in the area of the field of armaments, but also the generation of a greater tolerance for those nations who are still developing inside and amongst themselves. What good is our prominence if we isolate our wares from the rest of the globe by taking control of the world's wealth to procure what we want for ourselves and leave the rest of them with nothing in their pockets to enter our shoreline borders and banks as patrons and friends? Our intentions are wholly false-hearted if we struggle to grab every good thing from the Earth and, then, hail our sovereign nation as a great benefactor while we slowly and methodically piece-meal our enemies' resources back to them like fishes to a seal.

Sometimes we look at our brothers and sisters like we do the cicadas that screech in our backyard trees in the summertime. We are not sure what they are buzzing about and we do not know how to mute them. They seem to be the most repulsive thing that God ever created short of a slug; and only the arrival of winter seems to make them go away. Is this how we perceive different peoples from other nations whom we do not really understand? We cannot speak their language; they often seem to invade the privacy of our own national consciousness; and they never seem to be as physically attractive as ourselves. So, just like the winter, we exterminate them by the coldness of our hearts and the isolationism we employ in turning our backs on them and closing the door. While our lives of western society seem to be mottled with the diversity of talent, fiscal solvency, social order, and timeless customs, the rest of the world often seems almost alien to us. Are we not forsaking the Christian Doctrine that our reverend ministers and priests have been celebrating for over 225 years in America today? There are too many influences that are manifested in our boasting of the famous "rule of law" which has kept our republic in line for so many generations. This "rule" has not always been applied equally since our nation was founded. Is it not true that the Emancipation Proclamation which President Lincoln signed into law was missing from the conventions in the late 18th century? Was it not exactly100 years later when the law was changed again so our African-American citizens could inherit their just and due civil rights?

The Law of God has never, and shall never, undergo such an evolution because He has included the Redemption of every nation and race from the moment Jesus Christ was conceived in the Womb of the Blessed Virgin Mary. Sadly, however, humanity has done practically everything in our puny power to reject His Divine presence in the same way we would still like to exterminate the songs of those cicadas from ever piercing our ears again. The Son of God appeared into the world as a baby Child whose Blazonry was the sinless perfection in which He was begotten by the Will of His Father in Heaven. Ever since He first set-out to change the tone of human behavior, to teach us about the evil nature of hatred and sin, and to welcome us into the embrace of Paradise by becoming one in Him, we have been battering Him with lies and distortions about His reconciling purpose and holding Him off from succeeding by surrounding ourselves with material possessions and the distractions of perverse sexual excursions and an outright rancorous arrogance. Humankind has attempted to stultify the Divinity of our Lord Savior ever since He reprimanded us for being the transgressors who first offended Our Maker and plunged us to the Earth in exile. As if this is not enough, our predecessors decided that they would take their secular law into their hands and killed the Messenger by nailing Him to a Cross. But, what they could not have known back then is still ongoing; both He *and* His Message are still very much alive! He has undergone no change of Heart; His tenets are still the same; and His intentions are just as Salvific.

Let it be understood by readers and listeners, alike, that the men who have authored the very book in which these words are inscribed are Caucasian males who can see that our peers have tried to dominate the American democracy from the very first moment it was chartered. This is not a levy or judgement about how certain races always behave; it is more a function of how reluctant any society of people is to create a more inclusive ordinance in their communal approach. We have claimed to be a single nation under God, founded within the auspices of His good Graces. How, then, can we know our Creator so well if we must be forced by the blood of wars and revolutions to conform to the Beatitudes of the Holy Gospel? Why does the Pope of the Holy Roman Catholic Church have to keep reprimanding us about our ulterior motivations of greed, isolationism, the culture of death, and immorality in the streets? How can the greatest democratic nation on the face of the Earth be so afraid of people on other continents who only wish to share their due portion of the blessings which continue to flow from the generous cornucopia of the Sacred Heart of Christ? Reprimand, indeed! Has not the Holy Father told the peoples of every corner of the globe that the culmination of our mortal existence will be filled with as great a Justice as it will the Merciful Blood of

Jesus Crucified? The question remains to be answered as to whether we will be judged as a collective republic by the echo of the Cross as well as each of our individual deeds. Does God see a conspiracy in our American nation which has held our states hostage to materiel and fashion at the expense of the development of the rest of the world?

The prognosis for our recovery from our sickness of imperialism does not look very appealing as we enter the 21st century. Perhaps there is a bit of hypocrisy in the Preamble to the Constitution of the United States if we do not heed the words which have been uttered so profoundly from the lips of the likes of Sir Winston Churchill, Bobby Kennedy, and Martin Luther King. Their generous hearts and prescient spirits told them many years ago that independent countries which enjoy political freedom do not always comply with the Commandments as they have been set forth through the Holy Bible. If we wait for greater leaders to come along to teach us more about public righteousness and moral equity, will someone not kill them too, in the same way that Jesus Christ was murdered on the Cross? Where is the guilt in trying to make the whole world a better place? What does any group of citizens stand to gain if their rulers are selected by the majority of the electorate? Does it necessarily imply that the broad population of a given country is incorrupt if they do nothing to prevent their representative icons from being executed at random by some in their midst who see themselves as superior to the rest? The vision which the Holy Gospel provides is much more revealing than that; and Heaven is more inclusive than any democracy has ever attempted to emulate. This is why God is the King of Creation and we are His humble servants. He is the Truth and we are His subjects who are still trying to discover what it means to comply with His empyreal Domain.

Parceling-Away the Miracles of the Universe

January 27, 2001

Did not our sweet Lord make preparations for all souls to be returned to the sunshine of Paradise because it is what would make *Him* the most happy, too? Would He not have been blue and forlorn to know that His children would never gather around His temples again, that we could not play in the corolla fields outside His parlours anymore, or that our cries for consolation could never again be heard by the Love who is so profoundly polite? He did not desire to endure the mourning which accompanies the survivors of the lost, they who remain holding the memories of their helpless departed ones; these anguished hearts who can do nothing more than smile through their tears, rise to their feet, look back just one last time, and go into the future aggrieved. We must thank our Creator that He wished not to know this kind of sorrow for the endless ages; the same agony which pierces our hearts when the bodies of our young sons are placed like baggage onto jet airliners and brought back home from war or those who die in the middle of an intersection after having been struck by a police car chasing someone else they thought was so criminal that catching them was worth the risk of losing another innocent life. How must we feel thereafter when we discover that the party being pursued had only changed driving lanes without using the proper turn signal? Is this not how God felt when we lost our souls to Satan; the evil who felled us from Grace by chasing us around the Garden because we wished only to flee from his malevolent temptations? We know that the Kingdom of God is a most beautiful sight for the soul to behold! But, we must move to the flourishing Love of Christ if we expect to take-in the pleasing aroma of the flowering plants and Fruits which He has borne for our eternal remaking.

There are some people who have wondered what the finality of Creation would have been like if God had chosen, instead, not to make-way for our return to Heaven through the begetting of His Only Son. They are parceling-away some of the greatest miracles that the Universe ever revealed; for there is a Sacred Mystery inside the Most Blessed Trinity in the mandate of Our Redeemer. We are quite aware of the Father, the Son, and the Holy Spirit as being the Triune Deity which gives us new life and our blessed opportunity to be delivered from death. This concentric Mystery lives equally inside the Second Person of the Most Holy Trinity because it consists of the Life, Crucifixion, and Resurrection of Jesus Christ. He is truly the Father, Son, and Holy Spirit in Himself, as much as the other Separate Ones share His Divinity and perfect presence. What about the prospect that might have been, should our Almighty Father not have chosen the "III" sumptuous manifestations of His charitable Love to absolve humanity from our sinfulness, laying-waste to our ensuing mortality, and conquering it at last through His Son's Victory over the Sepulcher? We can imagine the scene just subsequent to when we were pronounced dead for having followed Satan's hatred in the march against the Omnipotent Supremacy of God. The air would have taken-on the solemnity of the processional ceremony which is afforded to highly regarded heads of state when they pass-away, are eulogized, and are carried so sorrowfully by cortege to their final resting place.

In the case of fallen humankind, Angel after Archangel would have stepped to the podium to mourn the loss of such a pretty race. The final obsequies would include their wailing cries of why a massive people with such Divine potential could have violated the oath of Truth under which they were created. We were at the break of dawn in immortality, it seems, when Adam and Eve laid down their swords of dignity and were lanced, themselves, by the perils of temptation and pride. As with any other tragic passing upon the Earth, they rued what might have been if only they could have had those precious few immortal moments back again to change their minds, to amend their wills, and to entrench their deeper impressions into the loveliness of God. They would have wondered why they chose to squander their most pure intentions upon the feline curiosity that was so offensive to the Paradise which had been their sartorial Crest. Next in the process of this Requiem would have been the Salutations as given by the Orders of the other Angels, each of them pouring their tears upon the floor of the sod-moistened Garden of Eden. There would be no need to embalm God's people yet because He had planned our deaths upon a much more dreadful globe, away from the pearly Lights of Heaven's best Providence, and beyond the Gate that would have never been ajar if not for the fault of humankind. The Kingdom of the Father would have remained united with His children; we who would have otherwise had no bowels to chase and no reason to hide. Our admission was not in our failure to be His rightful lot, but inside our wanton decision to violate the perpetuity which made us so unwitting as to what our newfound corruption would bring.

Down to the ground like a waterfall splashing against the bedrocks, we were thrown to the dogs to teach us a lesson about the deployment of the human will. We have permission to take a road that leads away from God, but our new destiny never holds the sweetness of His Love; our quarters are absent of His protection, and our sleep is filled to the hilt with nightmares and hordes of images from the dismal abyss which is our permanent grave. How sad for God to know that there were no longer any Saints in Heaven when Adam and Eve took their Fall because they kidnaped every one of us with them when they left. The Almighty Father gave our immortality a proper burial, though, as He dressed us in the cosmic architecture of the temporal Earth, with Her stately grandeur of rolling meadows and towering trees, with rising mountains and teeming seas! Our dais would become His footstool while He held His mighty Hands to His chin, wondering what to do with such an empty Palace. Let us be more than grateful that the Fruit of His contemplation would be to send His Prince of Peace to bring us all back home again! Now, the hollow chambers where we once played would echo anew with our laughter of restoration! At the precise moment in His prefigured Plan, He knew that the Cherubim and Seraphim would have reasons replete to chant the Final Triumph of His Sacred Heart! There was no doubt that, in our stubborn and adamant lack of self-control, we would defy again the presence of His Truth; that we would detain and interrogate His Prince, and finally kill Him in reply; just as we had committed the self-inflicted wounds of sin which cast us from His Side on the day we were buried with the lost.

Regaining our souls into the bounty of new Life would take the power of His Paraclete, a Holy Spirit to reside inside our hearts! It would require a Roman Catholic Church of Apostolic Saints who would, themselves, be killed in the likeness of their Teacher; save one, whom Jesus spared to reciprocate for another who defiantly kissed Him on the cheek and proudly ran away. This Highest Priest was sent to the Earth as the Anointed One, the Christ, whose Name would become "Jesus" as soon as Mary Immaculate bore Him from Her Womb. Now, new wars would begin, battles against the races would ensue, torrents of grievous hatred would continue to resound; but, through it all, His Church would always prevail. There would be numerous Popes, Martyrs, Doctors, Deacons, Seven Sacraments, Eucharistic Vestments, Litanies, and Mysteries; all Sacred in the sight of the God who justified the reason why His Creation would be born again; because He Loved us then, He Loves us now, and He shall Love us evermore! Every spirit in His Divine orchestration would point to the yonder skies and proclaim with the strength of their holy beings that we are all supposed to return there soon! There would be mouths and vestibules of rivers to pursue, groves and vaults to conquer, and many ages of sorrow to somehow overcome. The passageways would be lined with civic processions and entourages of more eloquent men; those whose hearts could travel beyond the ordinary grace of the finer things to see the Greatest One; the vision of the intercourse between Heaven and Earth that would make all the difference in the world.

Amongst the wonderment of the mourning which must have taken place that fateful day in Paradise when God would inter His precious humanity past the Narrow Gate through which we must all eventually return, there stood Six White Horses so stately present, preparing to pull the Caisson that would take us to the Earth. How grand they must have looked with their manes and forelocks braided with the silken embroideries of such a grieving Court, their breath puffing from their nostrils into the coldness of our hearts, their heads randomly nodding in their trademark equestrian fashion like the motion of a pump-handle flying in the breeze. The sun must have glistened from their silvery polls and reflected from the garnish so carefully applied to the pastern over their hooves. The strength of their poise would portend something greater than our deaths; for God meant for these steeds to take us gently into the night, being careful not to fracture us, harboring more Merciful plans for us to come. Their girths were decorated with the ribbons of His forgiveness that the Savior whom He would send to redeem us shall wear around His Mystical Body like a cummerbund as He finally brings mortality to a close. So, the clopping sounds we hear in our sleep sometimes are not the thunderous clouds billowing overhead, but the preeminent return of the Knight Rider of these Six White

Horses who is coming back for us; not bearing a Caisson this time, but pulling the Chariot of our Divine Salvation in which we shall all be delivered back to God in Paradise, our souls in His embrace as the Gate of Heaven is finally encased behind bricks and mortar like the Holy Pontiff in Saint Peter's Basilica sealing-off the Great Jubilee Door.

Locating the Ulcers of Tyranny Stinging the Earth

January 29, 2001

Sometimes we wonder what the Earth must feel like as humanity continues to fill its hollow voids with our bloody fields of ultra delirium, corruption, violence, and unmitigated cerebral deception. If it would ever be possible for the globe to suffer a bout with ataxia, now must be the time when its limbs and mosses seem the most helpless of all. Our relationships with other people are certainly a discovery deposition as to why there are wars still being perpetuated by people who have never even met. It is oftentimes quite easy to fall in line against our neighbors because we may not understand their styles of life or ancient customs. It seems, sometimes, as though our external relationships turn toward the elimination of ongoing disputes only when we are attacked by a common foe, when we are called together *not* as friends, but to conquer another "...enemy of my enemies." Is this not why the globe sheds Her tears inwardly, flooding the crooked valleys with the horrors of our shame? Can we not take a lesson from nature, knowing that the flowers in the meadows and the birds of the air share the same lands, sunshine, and breezes? What in the Name of God do we have to lose by trying? The answer is more simple than we would truly wish to know; the majority of souls who inhabit the several continents seem to have enough to worry about within their own families and native states to be concerned with the welfare of other people half-way around the globe. And, yet, according to the Gospel of Jesus Christ, this is no excuse, nor is there a credible one to be poised.

What we often fail to recognize is that our own sloth makes slaves out of other people. When we turn our backs on the large effort required to make peace around the world, men will continue to go to war. We have defiled nearly every conceivable opportunity to stop the bloodshed which is still raging at this late hour in human history; but, short of a few good souls, most of us read about it in the newspapers and go about our business as though it is some kind of tragic novel we have read. Those of us who refuse to reach-out to the greater hemispheres which are still battling the squalls that lay-waste to their personal lives are like the drones in a colony of bees; never making any honey, and impotent to take a jab at lancing the opposing forces which serve to bring societies down. Other people who are quite capable of supporting themselves and their families often run to the government for financial assistance because they would rather watch football games on television; thereby reducing the amount of funding that could be feeding the children of the "legitimate" poor, if ever there is such a thing. Are these not among the continuing reasons why the Earth on which we live is still groaning from the burden of supporting so many factions who it realizes are only molesting it for their own devious survival? Jesus Christ said that He is going to set the world aflame someday. Is He speaking of the globe as being the sadly-neighing thoroughbred whose spirit we have broken, so burdened by the hatred of humanity that She has collapsed under the weight of our transgressions? There is no doubt that the fires of which Jesus spoke refers to the cremation rites He has accorded to a world that we have practically annihilated in our reckless path.

The onus has been spread over the conscience of humanity to do a better job in locating the ulcers of tyranny which are still stinging the Earth with jealous malice and subterfuge, and root-out the thugs who are responsible for it. We are commanded by the Son of God to make way for the rising of His righteousness in the spiritual sense, starting with our own inner-beings. We can set the record straight only after we understand the facts that He wishes to be known, those which are explicated quite explicitly in the New Covenant and the Catechism of the Roman Catholic Church. Let us not be deceived by a so-called Methodist *Book of Discipline* which tries to strip the faith of every prayerful soul who clings to the Seven Sacraments for their spiritual strength and the intercession of the Angels and Saints who have stood more for Christ in the last millisecond than the descendants of John Wesley have espoused during the past four-hundred years. The repugnance which they are describing about the Romish Traditions is the very essence of their own lack of faith, not of the ancient Rites of the Holy Roman Catholic Church. When they say that the Holy Sacrifice of the Mass is "repugnant" in their eyes, they are also affirming that they are taking a position which is counter to the Sacred Cross that has saved them, and that they are "anti-Cross" and, therefore, "anti-Christ." And yet, if we were to approach 90% of those who profess to be Methodist, we would discover that their flock would never be able to say what the *Book of Discipline* is about, let alone that the United Methodist Church maintains such an anti-Catholic stance in their approach to Christianity at large.

When somebody proudly states that they are in complete union with the faith of the First Apostles, and yet continues to efface the Original Catholic Church in the process, they are making a statement which is about as ridiculous as having us believe that they look less like themselves in person than they do in their favorite photograph. This same twisted logic is what they are trying to get Jesus Christ to believe to this day! They may certainly arrive at the end of time to be judged worthy of entrance into Paradise, but there is no doubt that there will be many others who profess to own no religion at all who will walk-in ahead of them. The Catholic-bashing which has been ongoing in such places as Bob Jones University and others is a pungent affront to the Crucifixion of the Savior of the World; and Jesus will remind them of that someday. He has given them a brush which is filled with the blessings of unity and good will to paint the world in peace, but they have chosen to dip it in their own discriminatory Protestantism and mar the Earth with their divisive graffiti instead. Pope John Paul II has more righteousness beneath the nail of his little pinky-finger than in the entire collective body of human beings who have represented the Protestant Church since they turned-tail and ran away in the shadows of Judas Iscariot over four centuries ago. What many people fail to realize is that we are all meant to be children of the Holy Eucharist as God brings it to the Altar of Sacrifice in the hands of His priests. Every one of us is meant to be a living and breathing "pix" who leaves the Mass with the Crucified Son of God in our souls, prepared to prudently evangelize the Truth of the Most Blessed Sacrament to everyone we meet.

The pseudo-argument that Jesus Christ would never deposit His Sacred Body into a mortal human being is wholly without merit. How, then, could He ever instill His Holy Spirit in Protestant people who are proclaiming to be His witnesses before the rest of humanity while they stand so firmly against the presence of His Sacrificed Flesh, Soul, and Divinity inside the communicants who are departing the Eucharistic Table with such thanksgiving grace? The fact is, anyone who denies that the Most Blessed Sacrament is the Son of God in all ways conceivable is an outright enemy of the Holy Paraclete Who founded Christianity on the Feast of Pentecost, only ten days after Jesus Ascended into Heaven. There is no doubt that He is the Living Fruit of the Holy Mass and that He is the Manna from Heaven about which all human absolution ultimately revolves. Yes, those who receive His Eucharist are sinners; and that is why we proclaim just prior to Communion, " *O' Lord, I am worthy not to receive Thee; but only speaketh Thou the Word and my soul shall be Refined* !" There are facts which are subject to discussion, and others which are beyond reproach. The Eucharist is the Body, Blood, Soul, and Divinity of Jesus Christ, the Son of God, The Savior of the World, The Prince of Peace, Mighty God, Wonderful Counselor, The Holy One, Land of God, Prince of Life, Lord God Almighty, Lion of the Tribe of Judah, Root of David, The Word of Life, Author and Finisher of our Faith, Advocate, The Way, Dayspring, Lord of All, Shepherd and Bishop of all Souls, The Messiah, The Truth, Almighty Savior, Chief Cornerstone, King of Kings, Righteous Judge, Light of the World, Head of the Church, Morning Star, Sun of Righteousness, Chief Shepherd, The Resurrection and The Life, The Horn of Salvation, Governor, The Alpha and The Omega, I AM; and there is nothing any Protesting mortal man can do to stop it! That is the last word about this irrefutable discussion; and it is the Truth.

Once a soul has accepted the Most Blessed Sacrament as being He Who Is; that the Sacrament of the Holy Eucharist is both the Physical and Spiritual Divinity of Jesus Christ still living among us; life thereafter is never quite the same. The skies become more clear, no matter what the weather patterns on the horizon may portend. There is something more magical about the midnight blue that is wholly awesome to behold! The grotesque illusions of self-defeat and materialism all disappear like the turning of a switch; not just the passing fad of a nova in which we see a sudden burst of fate that eventually pales in time, but the perpetual apex of celestial joy that makes the imaginary Zodiac look like a frisbee in the mouth of a newborn Chihuahua. In the Most Blessed Sacrament, we are free to dream again and to impale the darkness which leads our hopes into despondence with the Saber of Resurrected Love. We can sail atop the seas of Anointment without a shipboard beneath our feet! We can hope now in communion *with* Hope, instead of against it all the time. The world is made aright with us, through us, and because of us! Our spirits seem almost able to take the sun from the skies with our most impressionable poetry and bounce it like a ball off the backboard-vacuum of outer-space. Jesus *is* this invincible Life inside our hearts! He is freedom, vision, splendor, reality, transference, time, Eternity, forgiveness, pardon, and peace! The Tiara that sits atop our Pontiff's head is a prophecy and likeness of the Crown which we shall all enjoy in the Light of Paradise; so we should run to receive his Papal blessing wherever he shall travel in his dispensation of the indulgences of his High Office in the sacred likeness of Jesus Christ, Himself. So, let those who Protest against this Holy Vicar and his Catholic Church wallow in their secular amphitheaters and phantom-carpeted board rooms; for we shall follow the dignity of Saint Peter and the throngs of men who still believe, those who continue to hope for the restoration of the Church under Jesus Christ as She was originally intended to be, where the Altar of Sacrifice yet remains in time for God's children to partake of Him in Eternal Bliss, where the statuary monuments of our living faith still stand as prayers to His early dignitaries, and where confessionals are appropriately placed so that God-fearing men can go and have their Baptismal Gowns washed clean in a Penitential Rite before they greet their Salvation at last!

Indeed! We Are a Good Humanity!

January 31, 2001

We must discern at last that we are a human race which is prone to accident and error, who are more infantile than malicious, and much too spiritually inadequate to ever overcome the forces of our exile without the Almighty Love of Jesus Christ at the center of our hearts. For page after page, I have been recording the description of why we are failing Him and how we embrace such lame excuses not to do any better. I am not a pessimist when it comes to realizing that God can make saints of us all in the matter of a mere instant. Just as He previously allowed in the Garden of Eden so long ago, He still wants the decision to be ours. If we pore over our mistakes long enough, we will ultimately discover that most of them are only a function of our lack of knowledge, rather than a vast conspiracy to undercut our brethren in the process of conducting the affairs of life. There is no reason to believe that we are predisposed to commit wanton hatred against each other because too many people from frail places have made a glorious difference in improving the greater world. For all it is worth, we are more afraid of one another than we would like to be; and this unintentional shyness often manifests itself as smugness and isolationism. What frightens us about the human species in its entirety is what causes the numbness in our hearts as we try to discover what motivates us as a whole; and that is the confusion which greets us when we fall asleep at night and awaken in the morning. It would not be fair to judge the children of God without using the same criteria that Jesus Christ will employ at the end of time. Anything which violates His Love is the nature of sin; and we are responsible to always avoid it.

The Son of God defines corruption as any aspect of the human constitution which is not in alignment with the Will of His Father. Does He expect us to critique ourselves in the process of accepting that Will? Yes, of course; and He is the standard by which we should evaluate our progress toward that end. It is also why His Sacred Heart is the course by which we walk and the destiny we shall all reach. Christ told us at Pentecost that He would never leave us orphaned and that He has implanted His Spirit in our hearts to prove it. He is, in effect, leading us back to Heaven by placing the essential Love of God inside our mortal shells. What our souls have to say about this is in accordance with how we dress our will. Do we accept the profession of faith which takes us away from the things of Earth and leads us to the Glory of Paradise? Are we more interested in what the Holy Spirit has to offer, rather than the summoning of the flesh? How we answer these basic questions is the barometer as to whether we are accepting the discipline required to become like Jesus and, therefore, worthy of being granted Salvation through His Blood into the Kingdom of the Saints. Our task is not an easy one because there are so many influences in the mortal world that defy and reject the spiritual aspects of Christian conversion. We are tempted everyday to become immersed in material possessions and distracted by entertainment. We are certainly not required to become monks in order to be saved, but there is no doubt that our lives must include many hours of prayer each week if we ever expect to shed the burdens of life which keep us from knowing God better.

Yes, humanity is basically a good body of people when everything we have accomplished has finally been taken into account. We support one another when there are tragic losses to face; we rush to the side of victims of natural disasters; most of us voluntarily pay our proper share of taxes without having to be forced into compliance; we attend our particular churches with great fidelity; we hold the same prayerful anticipation at the center of our beings which says that life will eventually improve for everyone in time; and we really mean it when we stop to think long enough. There would not be sufficient room in the world to hold the books where our transgressions and misgivings might be recorded; but it would also suffice to say that we have been equally as benevolent in our own right, too. There has been a huge difference in how we have approached each other through the past generations because we have only become more developed and self-sustaining in the past seventy-five to 100 years. Before that, property owners would help their neighbors farm the fields, mend ways between disputing families, haul well-water to one another during periods of drought, travel in wagons together to procure provisions for their personal use, and join under the stars at night to sponsor square-dances and community picnics. Now, in the 21 st century, we work away from our residences, travel by ourselves to get there, eat in the farthest corner of a cafeteria during lunch hour, and arrive back home exhausted and ready for bed about 9:00 p.m. Of course, there are some who might watch the news and a couple of dramas on television, but again, always to the diminishment of our relationships with our neighbors and friends.

Once upon a time, the home was the hub of the wheel around which all other activities short of attending church on Sunday revolved. Wives were homemakers who were interested in raising their children instead of struggling to establish a career in some professional field. I will leave it up to America's sociologists to decide whether this has had any formal bearing on the composition of families in the contemporary world. The point I am making is that the status of our culture, population, and desires continues to be an evolving process, not unlike the phenomenon of democracy, itself. Those who were previously marginalized by whatever outside forces bound them to repression are now becoming contributing members of societies. This sort of progress is good for everyone involved, especially toward the elevation of the dignity of those who had it so bad for too long; while those who have effected these developments are to be commended well. How, then, do we transform this bottled energy into creating the greatest of all human cohesion, that of collecting ourselves under the Cross? The government has already said that it is disinterested, that it would even be illegal for them to ever become involved. There is a move now underway to bring faith-based organizations into the public limelight by allowing them to share in collected taxes for the purpose of assisting the poor and disadvantaged. But, how far does the majority of our citizens really wish to travel down that road?

Indeed! We are a good humanity! If not, perhaps, for the forsaking of our own potential as much as we deny God, nature, the universe, and our neighbors; the world would become a far better place should we embrace them all! We are short of being wholly Divine because we keep cutting ourselves down and off-of the vine of Love upon which we can grow to any dimension we desire. If we conclude that there is far more to life than the practice of possession and control, then we should also be forced to acknowledge that there is little of this world which is worth pursuing or crafting for our personal use. If not for our good sense of humor and our stubbornness to succeed, many of us would have given-up on ever being happy in life at all. We remember the story about the young man who weighed about 350 pounds who once told his friends that his mother had named him Jason for a very good reason. His premise was that he weighed so much when he was born that it took him from July through November to completely emerge from his mother's womb; hence, his name was given for the acronym of those months, JASON. Such self-deprecating humor is, quite obviously, the signature of a humble soul. This does not imply that we should tear ourselves down in order to lift each other up; but there is truly no room for pride or arrogance in the process of reuniting humanity or in the cause of extinguishing our biases and characteristic differences. There seems to be an underworld afoot that we cannot yet see where God breathes life into newly-conceived offspring of every species, where grassy-fields bloom so slowly that no one even notices the process, and as our prayers rise expeditiously to the Throne of the Almighty Father aboard a spiritual procession which is often unbeknownst to us.

Let us go looking for that subliminal world in which graces fall from Paradise like rain! What is to inhibit us from knowing our Creator better by at least trying to live in the image of His Son? We have manifested a world which is filled with so many contradictions; marketplaces amidst fields of corn, slums surrounding the White House in Washington, taverns next to churches, hospital maternity wards across the street from cemeteries, hermits leaving millions of dollars from their estates to the impoverished who could have used it long before they died, doctors who have taken their Hippocratic oath to preserve human life at all costs who are still aborting tiny babies from their mothers' wombs, policemen who arrest prostitutes and set them free again for the exchange of sexual favors, judges who sentence convicts to prisons that are in far worse condition than their dog-houses at home; and on, and on, seemingly without end. However, our potential to do better and to become more genuine people is as great as any other force in the universe. If not for our outright laziness and the lack of anyone to push us in the proper direction, we would have attained it long ago. We claim to believe in God, but we relinquish almost every opportunity within our grasp to prove it. It seems as though we are slaves to some inherent desire to cling to materials and fashions, while refusing to wrap our fingers around the more spiritual aspects of mortal possibility that will help us make the most of human existence. In the final analysis, do we fight for the things which matter the most? Do we assume that God has come to us and, therefore, we need not ever move any closer to Him? Is there a whit of shame in our hearts for having let Him down?

We are sometimes asked to bring to mind the first thing we can remember as little children. Some of us can recall an incident or two that may have occurred before we ever turned five-years-old, but most of those moments are somewhat poignant in nature. Others can remember having attended kindergarten classes somewhere, and how they played together with their friends. Almost everyone can recall learning how to read and how difficult our phonics was to understand. We are grateful for having graduated from the study of inflections, irregular verbs, genitives, additive adjuncts, relative clauses, finite post-modifiers, and dangling participles. No one really cares whether their contemporary English grammar is that concise anymore. Quite so, it is probably not very important, anyway. But, the reflections we should harbor are the things which made us little children, not in a delinquent way, but only innocent so as not to wish for the materials in our neighbors' hands or crave a prospect that might tend to lead us away from our harmless demeanor. Whether we have now grown-up to become president of a corporation, a famed movie star, a chemist, a congressman, or an international peacemaker; that little child has remained within us through our maturation into adulthood. Remembering such simplicity is the essence of an open heart; and it is also the nostalgia of Love for which Jesus Christ pines to know us best. His Divine Will first placed our innocuousness into motion; and our internal guidance and conscience should always lead us back to Him.

The Theology of Absolutionism

February 1, 2001

Perhaps we tend to perceive our inner-goodness in a lesser light than we should, hoping that somebody else will take-up the slack when we grow weary or burdened from the battles of disrespect. There are no improper actions in our efforts to thwart the wicked and bring peace where there is no rest amidst the terrors of war. When we utilize our military prowess to preempt an evil attack somewhere, we are displaying the acronical colorfulness of the sunset of a good day. There are very few people who do not become sentimental, emotional, patriotic, loyal, and generous at least during some moments in their lives. We give alms during the proper seasons, say our prayers before meals, pick-up someone's articles that they drop in front of them on the street, send greeting cards for various anniversaries, offer Masses for the deceased, visit the sickly and dying, and anonymously offer our money to different charities when the opportunities arise. There has never been a question as to whether we are a decent people, but whether we are willing to treat our enemies in the same mannerisms that we offer to our friends. This is the true test of our allegiance to Christianity. When we bid hello to someone we like as we see them passing by, Jesus says that sinners do as much. The question remains; are we as equally prompt to greet those whom we regard as our opponents in every sense of the word? Perhaps we should look more at life through the eyes of spiritual faith in the Son of God than we do the logical rationalism which tries to push His miracles out of our way. There are a lot of people who have their heels stuck in the burrows of the mortal world who believe that human reason, unaided by Divine revelation, is the sole guide to all attainable religious Truth. This, unfortunately, is the part of humanity which is not so good.

There can be no true productivity toward the growth of the inner-self without attaching our philosophies to the Holy Gospel of Christ. The term "secular" need not be profane in the eyes of God; but humanity has simply defined it that way. The everyday lives of many people are characterized by irreverence toward His sacred purposes; including unholy, heathen, and pagan rites that sound like a clamoring gong in the middle of an empty auditorium. Whatever terms one might choose to employ, those who refuse to know God are blasphemous, sacrilegious, impious, and unduly temporal. And, yet, there is hope for these endangered souls to convert to the Truth of Christianity. When Jesus said "..it is finished," from the Cross, He meant that there would still be ample time to every purpose under Heaven, and that all souls who will eventually rise with Him on the last day of Earth still have time to discover it. Why else would He have allowed 2000 years to expire if He did not expect our conversion in His Blood to take so long? He was telling us about everything that would occur since then; that it has been completed, and is yet unfolding as we live today. Perhaps He was waiting for the people of the 21st century to finally conquer the pro-Darwinian forces who have tried for so long to lead His humanity away from the Truth of His Creative genius.

The genial climate of Christian goodness skewers the doctrine of those who say that reparation was never necessary for the reconciliation between God and man. When Jesus Christ was put to Death on the Cross, God was sufficiently pleased that such reparation had been made for the sinful nature of Adam and Eve and all peoples everywhere who would live in exile on the Earth below. Hereafter, there is no reason for us to hide anymore or to claim before the shores of Paradise that we are too naked to depart our rafts in the sea of disgrace. In Christ, we have been clothed in grace and absolution so that all which is of God can be restored in us again. Since we are such a good people, there is no reason why we should ever cower in fear from accepting our new "being" in the Blood of the Cross. It is not only more logical than anything any empiricist could procure; it is the only factor which is available to finally link us to Heaven after so many generations have gone by. Let us never forget that mortal experience and observation alone have nothing to do with the convalescent nature of the Holy Paraclete as He lives so comfortably inside the human heart. Even the field of medicine threw-out the philosophy of relying solely upon experimentation as the source of knowledge while calling it "quackery" long before most of us who are alive today were ever born. Some doctors are even hailing the power of religion and prayer as having a measurable and sustainable benefit for those patients and their families who choose to espouse it in the process of their physical healing.

If we are meticulous about keeping track of where God seems to go in life, we will discover that He calls equally upon the rich and poor to prove their sense of loyalty to the Beatitudes which have been set-forth by Christ. There has never been a millionaire who did not eventually die; and there has never been a pauper who did not arrive in the foyer of the everlasting riches of Paradise as soon as his spirit left his flesh. Whether they all elected to accept the Divine Mercy of Jesus is a matter we will have to discover when we, ourselves, get to the Pearly Gates. It has long been said that Christianity is no democracy and death is common to every man. We can all take to our knees and thank Almighty God that His Kingly Reign is one of a more generous Spirit and not a mandate of endless slavery. And, what about the mortality which serves as the great equalizer for all who have been born? We can fully escape its effects if we offer our souls to the Resurrection of Jesus from the Grave. However, we are not excluded from also sharing in His Passion and Crucifixion along the way.

Somewhere, there is a frankly outspoken Saint who might say that it is just the cost of doing business in the process of being redeemed. And, before Creation comes to its final conclusion, we will all assuredly discover the real reason for hope; that there has never been a source of suffering that was not a portion of the Cross to which Our Savior was nailed. In the words of our modern-day youth in regards to the crises we face in our lives, Jesus Christ has already, "...been there, and done that!" Now, it is our turn to make reparation for the still ongoing sins of those who choose to reject His Holy Sacrifice.

A familiar poet named Ralph Waldo Emerson once said, "Why not realize your world?" His thesis about faith was basically correct, but like many of his era and those thereafter, he forgot to include the theology of absolutionism which is the main principle of the Christian Doctrine. If only such writers would have spent more time offering their inspirational phrases about the exculpatory nature of the Mercy of Jesus Christ, perhaps the collegiate professors who are still teaching us about their works would have gone into the religious vocations, themselves. Where does our future rest and our destination lie? Not in the theatrical or oratorical works of moderate men; not in the exit fulcrums, climaxes, and epilogues of literary works; and not in the passive philosophies of romantic critics; but in the Promise which has been made through the New Testament of the Saint Joseph's Bible. The Messiah from Heaven, the Savior Anointed, the Christ for all the ages is the present-day Living Word of God Who shall never grow antiquated or be torn asunder by any man or woman, alive or dead, or by any conceivable facet of the human curiosity or imagination. No matter how many arsenals that the dictators of the world can boast of owning, none is the equivalent of the power of the Son of God to bring peace or wage war, to destroy and remake, to punish and reprove, or to cast-way and retrieve; all in the Name of the God Who has created us. This is truly raw power! It is not dependent upon a cycle of the select or the side-effects of transferable goods. The strength of Heaven comes from within the soul, where no thief can lay-in-wait for the owner to come home.

Therefore, we are left in time to accumulate a legacy of goodness in the image and likeness of the invincible power that will take us all back home. We must never allow our guard to be dropped, even for a moment, because the world is filled to the crust with forces which are trying to keep us from succeeding. Our perpetuity in the fields of greatness must begin now; as it is often described, 24/7/365; every hour, everyday, and all year long. It would not be imprudent for us to remember that the Son of God was forced to traverse through the same perils of time, even though the Eternity of Heaven lived inside Him all the while. This, too, is what He wishes us to know about ourselves as we are given to the Love in His Sacred Heart. His critique of humankind stops short of a full endorsement of everything we do, but it is laced with such sincerity and Love that we cannot keep from taking it most seriously. There is a whole gamut of distractions which detain us from acknowledging this sometimes, but most of them are much ado about nothing. Rather than seeking-out the arts of other men who, perhaps, do not know as much about God as they think they do, we should make the most of Him inside our own consciousness so we will not be shocked at the end of mortal life when we see how far away we might have been from total righteousness. There is much more we can do in simple ways to effectuate our professions of faith. Our Father has given us broad smiles to offer to the rest of His children, but we fail miserably to employ them for the good of their purposes. We grant assurance and peace to others when we smile upon them affectionately. Indeed, we should all pray that we will see such a beaming expression on the Holy Face of Christ when we finally die.

The key to understanding our spiritual health is whether we allow ourselves to become elevated by the same Love which God has dispensed through His Almighty Son. This does not imply that we must temporarily accept His Eternal Being and, then, go searching for something else. Just because someone is falling through the air does not mean that they are flying of their own accord. The Love and Peace of Jesus Christ are our two wings which hold us upward in His Grace so that our souls will never come crashing back to the ground in faithlessness and despair. There is no substitution for knowing ourselves well; and that is the tone of how Jesus will assess our ability to live our outward compliance with Him, too. If we effect His Love in all ways known to man, then we will recognize Him when we die as He reciprocally welcomes us into His warm embrace. Indeed, finding out who we are from the inside is not that difficult a task. Contrary to popular belief, it is rather easy to walk through a house of mirrors without colliding with any of them; we must simply move in any direction in which we do not see our own reflection. This is the same self-denial that can make us saints as we travel through human life; looking always beyond our needs to the greater suffering of men while deferring our presence to the Dignity of God; and He will thereafter lead us to the door of His unparalleled consolation. The Holy Spirit is in us as our guide and Shepherd because He knows that we are flying blind through the dangers of the material world. His Grace is the supernatural art which imitates life when we accept His Love to the perfection of our own potential. We must remember that singers cannot fake their own voices like players acting on a stage. Two people who might play the roles of Romeo and Juliet can certainly appear to be someone they are not; but, a soloist before a crowded room in contemporary clothes is who he is; and this is the same candidness which Jesus Christ seeks from us.

Wielding the Divine Sense of Inevitability

February 2, 2001

Once our conversion to the Gospel of Christianity has been made, there is no longer any reason for us to wonder how the world will ultimately end and what the Son of God will have to say to those who have spate upon His Face. Should we feel sorrowful for the few who will remain defiant against the very Cross which has saved them from the perils of death? According to the Blessed Virgin Mary, they wilfully choose to do evil instead of good and, therefore, are not worthy of our compassion as they cast themselves into the fires of Hell. If a person is an unrepentant follower of Satanic works, he is certainly no comrade of ours. Indeed, if many of them had it their way, they would choose to take our souls into condemnation with them. Of the many ways that Christians can be described, one of the most profound is that, through the Wisdom of the Holy Spirit, we are intelligent enough not to be snagged by the traps which Satan's sorcerers and fiends have set before us. People who have taken a stance against Jesus Christ are all losers; they will never taste the sweetness of Eternal Life; their souls will agonize in the pit of darkness below the Earth longer than any imagining; and they will rue the day when their pride first forced them into surrendering to the forces that led them from grace. It is their decision, their choice, their making, and their eventual fate; made by the witting employment of their human will to the lasting damnation of their pitiful souls.

Contrast this, now, to the Victory which is ours in Christ. Christians see human life like the end of a football game when the winner has already been declared before the clock has ever run out and we are all walking across the field of mortal life with Triumph in our grasp while the remaining seconds slowly tick away. Even though we have yet to die as the wage for our sins, we know that our passing is not forever and life is not ended; it is just changed as we are pulled into the realm of the Spirit World of God in Heaven, where we will be granted a glorified body which is lacking in any of the corruption that we know now. This is why staying affixed to the things of the Earth is such a decadent consumption of time. If we do not accept the Spirit of Christ in our hearts while we live, our entire composition is already rotting atop the surface of the ground. The blessings which are reserved for righteous men are beyond the reach of those who would choose to be any other way. By remaining in the grist of faithlessness, they are like automobiles in a demolition derby whose drivers are never allowed to make contact with the competing cars. How can they ever succeed in defending themselves if they cannot move out of the way? What would be the use of having the ability to impact the rest of society if they are never allowed to wield it? Such is the fate of those who deny the existence of God to the depths of their own hollow agnosticism.

What Christians wield that everyone else cannot sustain is the Divine sense of inevitability. Prayer to the Holy Trinity is like speaking to God, Himself, on a cellular telephone; but those who reject His Holy intercession are bound to beating rocks on the sides of the stone walls in which they have imprisoned themselves to see if there is anyone else still alive to hear them. It would be an awfully gruesome prospect to know that everything you will ever become has already happened to you, that the light of the noonday sun is brighter than anything else you will ever see, and that the saline oceans contain the freshest water you will ever drink between the continents of despair which you have only wrought upon yourself. But, this is exactly the destiny of choice for thousands of people who still profess to be reprobates, atheists, and other enemies of God. The same can be said about those who wholeheartedly embrace mortal sin as being a "natural" part of life. We cannot profess to be the children of God and simultaneously walk in the footsteps of the Prodigal son who ran away from home seeking the glitzy fashions of the temporal world. Our Father in Heaven will not allow us to deny Him forever, especially while He knows that He has given us ample time to repent of our transgressions and return unpunished into the fold. The wasteful, reckless, extravagant, lavish, and impure lifestyles of many people around the globe today is most repulsive in the tear-filled eyes of the Almighty God who has created them in the Divine Providence of His Love.

There are parents who would destroy their entire empires to have their children back at their side again; but they never once took one of them aside to explain what life is truly like in the alleys of sorrow behind the facades of the glamorous streets of fortune and fame. When it is too late, they ask, "What did I do wrong?", as they wring their hands in sorrow. The answer is quite obvious; they declined to give their children the Love of Jesus in their hearts, while trying to purchase their honor with material profits. Our Creator is a genius without peer; and He is a prophet whose premonitions are now coming home to roost in the conscience of men. We have been told time and again in the Sacred Scriptures to fend-off the temptations which always roll in-tandem with personal wealth and public fame; that we should seek only the things of the Spirit, instead. Put more plainly, Jesus has been telling us for centuries that we shall reap what we sow and, therefore, our children are addicted to drugs and pornography because we did not fill-up their senses with the Holy Gospel while the bidding was at its best. We pay the price through our own grief, the agony of knowing the pain in the lives of our families, and in the incessant phrase which keeps piercing our thoughts every day of "...what might have been." The point in all of this is; do we grovel in the terror of what our past has brought, or do we give every ounce of our beings to Jesus Christ and begin anew? Maybe we can never take away some of the decisions we have made in the past for which innocent people might have suffered, but we can assuredly hand them over to the Son of God for reconciliation before the stateliness of His Grace. This is a prayer that He will always hear because He is the prime source of our health and posterity, not only for the past and today, but for all the future to come.

Jesus Christ will set things right between parents and children in the same way He brings peace between the nations. We often feel violated at the same time we are offending those who live so closely to us. The Holy Gospel nullifies all of this error because, by accepting its tenets as our guide to life, we become new citizens of a higher Kingdom that knows only the preservation of peace and good will. This is the purpose of Love and the direction in which the New Covenant will lead us. Jesus has told us time and again that wherever two or more are gathered in His Name, He will reside also in their midst. If father and son join hands and hearts inside the repose of Jesus' Sacrifice on the Cross, no enemy of peace can ever divide them again. Satan might come snooping around to see what he can corrupt, but he will only be burning his nose in the flames of regret if he tries to sniff his way in. It does not take a fortune of materials to either gain or lose in the process of engaging the lovingness between the souls of two people; it only requires that they open their hearts and allow the Holy Spirit to enjoy His rest in them. Indeed, if this can be done between a father and his child, there is no stopping the seed of cohesion from spreading throughout an entire race and across the continents of the rest of the Earth. Perhaps the first kiss of justice and peace are the proverbial mustard-seed of faith which has welcomed humanity into the family of a greater community.

Let us cast-away the esoteric assumption that Salvation in Jesus Christ is only for a select few who own some sort of first-wage or seat at the inner-circle of pious accord. After all, He came not for the conversion of the righteous, but for the purpose of saving sinners through the power of His Blood. How do they know this to be true? Because His Holy Paraclete convinces anyone who is kind enough to lend an ear during appropriate moments of the day. When someone asks Jesus why they are poor, His response is that He wishes them to become more like Him. There are rarely any people who ask God why they are rich because most of them have already cast Him aside as a fad for another day. Yes, there have been such millionaires in America and around the globe who have stated that religion is only an illusion in the minds of the poor or those who have a weak self-disposition. Now, there is some Satanic babbling for you! There are hundreds-of-millions of good Christians just waiting in the offing, rubbing the palms of their hands together, waiting for the Son of God to drop the atomic bomb of Truth on such wealthy souls and blast their arrogant materialism into tiny pieces flying through the swirling breezes of His Divine Justice. It is kind-of like waiting for the battle between good and evil in a motion picture that you have already seen. But, the ending which depicts the good guys' victory is so profound and touching to the heart that you cannot stop watching it time and again; while the tears of thanksgiving to God keep rolling down your cheeks.

Our faith in Jesus Christ is consistently compared with the differences between Light and darkness, genuineness and deceit, and punishment versus eternal reward. The reason for this series of dichotomies is not too difficult to understand. Love, in the way that Our Lord has explained it, is quite definitively greater than anything which is *not* His Love. The human spirit knows the difference as soon as we are exposed to it because the inherent nature of goodness was instilled inside us when we were first given the breath of Life. Christians never get out of bed in the morning and act surprised by the works of evil that keep pelting us in the face everyday; we have come to expect it as a natural result of defying the forces of the world which keep tempting us into abandoning our faith. What feels so good about it is that we know that Satan and his followers are only wasting their time because we are given to Jesus Christ for protection, dominion, strength, guidance, and deliverance. Hereafter, those who oppose us might as well close the book on ever expecting us to reverse our course. The Redemption of our souls has become complete by the oath we have taken in our Profession of Faith in the Savior of the World. Evil rogues can carry placards outside the doorway of our hearts all they might; but we shall never back down, our allegiance to Christ is non-negotiable, our blood is filled with the Sacraments of the Cross, and our final drive is for the Gateway of Heaven, come what may. This is not to say that we are yet perfect in the way that Jesus wants us to be; but there is absolutely nothing that is less than saintly about our determination to become one with Him in the Light of Paradise, much to the regret of those who oppose our relocation under the Throne of His Holy Father.

We may not yet be able to promise God that we completely understand Him or that we can see the plat which He has laid-out before us as clearly as He wants. But, we are always moving in the direction of discernment because, like the first Apostles, we have nowhere else to go; there is no other Savior than His Son who surrendered His Life on the Cross so we would know perfection again. Indeed, we may not yet be able to profess full knowledge of the Will of Heaven for everyone who is still alive on the Earth, but we can certainly pray for our concessions to be most pleasing in His sight until we gain the full parameters of our own unobstructed vision. This does not imply that the vicious world must tear us limb-from-limb to get us to understand how excruciating was the pain which Jesus suffered during His Passion and Crucifixion on the Earth. For the most part, our grief is shared with His Agony in the Garden on the inside where we feel betrayed by those who scoff at us for beholding our faithful charge in the Name of God before the rest of humanity. Of course, those who suffer physical ailments are the direct descendants of Our Lord on the Cross and, they too, are assisting in the mitigation of the error which has overcome the world with such apathy and greed. When we realize that we are the Light of the world like the Savior in whom we choose to believe, we will have come full-circle in taking-up our crosses and sharing the sacrificial nature of His Divine Love.

"With Cross in Hand, I Sign My Name!"

February 3, 2001

We can allay our apprehensions about stepping toward Jesus in faith by simply doing it anyway because the worse that can happen is that we will discover the Truth on God's terms rather than by our own misguided assumptions. We have a somewhat migrant sense of good judgement at times, not knowing what to rule-in as an aspect of our behavior and what to leave-out. Most of us have only a variable capacity to toe the line of never wavering from the lessons of goodness we have been taught since the days of our youth. Forget the metaphors about summer heat-indexes and winter chill factors; we are still trying to discover the real temperature of our ability to perceive the world as it truly exists without the confusion of someone else's hyperbolic rhetoric. Someday, God will come before us as we stand in His presence and ask at last, "What did you do?", and we will wonder how to respond because two different avenues will leap into our mainstream of ponderance; does He mean what did we do wrong, or what did we do right? At first blush, it will appear as though He will be looking for signs of our compliance with everything we have known about Jesus Christ, and whether we accepted our role in His Kingdom, or cast our crosses aside and walked around them. Did we watch for His signs and pray to understand them? Did we carry our burdens gladly, or were we part of the greater suffering which was heaped upon our friends? Did we humble ourselves before humankind, nurture the weak, and pardon the wicked? Even though our actions may have been tempered by a bitterly-fought struggle for swifter justice, there is no reason to believe that Jesus will deny us His absolution if our aggression is toward the forcing of the conversion of our faithless peers and the diminishment of every distraction which keeps them from knowing Him in the way we have come to enjoy.

We often walk through life as though we are stuck behind the curve of attaining the true rightfulness that keeps eluding the grasp of benevolent men. It is a curious proposition to know whether those who surround us are really as in Love with Heaven as they would have us believe. They point us in the direction of different theological works they may have read, but they rarely portray the gentler spirit of the authors who placed them into writing. We have absolutely got to stop looking at Christianity as though it is some sort of novel code of conduct in which we are spectators looking-on from the sidelines somewhere. There is no greater hypocrisy in Creation than to state that we are Christians and then live as though we have never heard of the Holy Gospel. There are Cadillacs driving around the United States with bumper stickers which say, "More Lord," and "WWJD, What Would Jesus Do?" Those who see such phrases are quick to inquire whether these people are really asking for an opportunity to purchase another new limousine on which to display more vitriol that the owners, themselves, are still violating. The response Our Lord would surely give to the query of "...what would Jesus do?" is that He would sell the very Cadillacs on which these bumper stickers appear, admonish their drivers for their hypocrisy, and give the proceeds to the poor.

There should be no vagueness in how the world sees our faith in the Gospel of Christianity. We have seen images of a pen and notepad laying on a table somewhere in an office or home into which we have been invited; and we know that there are words penned in handwriting that are not sufficiently close for us to read. This is how many people see those who do not wear their Christian faith outwardly so the entire world can see the Love inside their hearts. They know that we are capable of witnessing to the Truth because they have seen the distant images of our intentions inscribed into the surface of the globe; but our purposes are just aloof enough that we will not allow the greater family of man to discover the darkest secrets in our souls. If only we would move closer to the Cross, we would definitely better understand the Word of God who has been Crucified there. Our attention would be drawn to a clear focus upon Jesus' Wounds, the meditations of His Sacred Heart, the bequeathing of His Eternal Will to man, and the final petitions which He raised to His Almighty Father in Heaven on our behalf. If we perceive the Earth as being that pad of paper and the Cross as the instrument in God's Hands, we would be able to read the story of our lives written plainly within eyesight; "I Love you, I have Died for you, and I will Save you into the Heights of Glory!" This is when we will finally discover the invincible jurisprudence that belongs only to God in Three Divine Persons and His Judgement which proves that we are the intrigue of His curious intellect.

It seems as though many of us would rather play in the rain than in the open fields of sunny bliss at times. We do not often know why; but it certainly says a great deal about who we are; that we often feel more free about facing the elements than we do the ordinary tick of time; that our souls are still searching for the dynamics which are unavailable to us through the normal constraints of daily life; and that even our own deaths cannot destroy our desire to see Creation from the other side before God featly calls us to our death of His own consent. We often tempt the fate which makes us less than invincible before the facets of the globe and wave a flippant hand toward the danger that warns us of troubling times ahead. Why? Are we dissatisfied in knowing that the Angels will protect us only if we live in a prayerful Light? Does our tension, envy, and lust for independence become so great that we would defy the ordinances of metaphysics in the hope that we will somehow discover a new way to become more free? This may be alright for now; but we tend to look at other men who disagree with us to the moderation of their own good judgement and confess that our attitude toward them places them amongst the most despised people of everyone we know. There is a rather curious process now ongoing whereby we have been issuing personal indictments against our admonishers and concurrently dispensing pardons for those who like to wallow in the plush of our similar sinfulness like tossing candy canes into a crowd of mischievous little children.

Perhaps a brief review of the moral Virtues and Vices which are delineated in the ecclesiastical works would not be unwelcomed by those whose spirits are only now being moved toward the greater Light of Wisdom. There are three basic theological Virtues which relate immediately to God; Faith, Hope, and Charity. It has long been known that these are stitched together by the common thread of Love which comes through the power of the Throne of God, present in the Blessed Trinity; Father, Son, and Holy Spirit. We become virtuous in them because we must see them from the center of our hearts without the enhancement of the physical sight of our eyes. We know that God is the Truth, and there can be no other verity because Christ, Himself, has told us this from the first moment when He sent the Angel Gabriel to seek His Mother to bear Him into the world as a Child at Bethlehem. The Holy Trinity is also the Unity of our unseeable God in the Presence of the Divine Three. Most of the Popes in history have taught that the Almighty Father resides in Eternity as a Spirit without a discernable Body, seeable only when He chooses to become Incarnate before the rest of Creation. This is what He did when Jesus Christ was born. He became Flesh in the Person of His Own Son for the

Redemption of all humankind. Moreover, we are aware of the Cardinal Virtues which are Prudence, Justice, Fortitude, and Moderation. These co-Beatitudes are clearly mandated in the Book of Wisdom 8:7, and lay-out the simple aspects of the human spirit which bring the absolved soul into alignment with the Holiness of the Divine Messiah.

If ever mankind starved his appetite for the good of the physical world and hungered for the Fruits of the Holy Spirit, God will fill him to the brim of his soul with Love, Joy, Peace, Patience, Kindness, Generosity, Faithfulness, Gentleness, Continence, and Chastity in accordance with the Book of Galatians 5:22,23. Thereafter, no longer will we cringe in sorrow from the pangs of being lesser than what God has intended us to be; upright and just, holy and servile, penitent and benign. What great graces does He give to the followers of His Sacrificed Son! The Holy Paraclete dispenses His Gifts to the world in the form of Wisdom, Understanding, Counsel, Fortitude, Knowledge, Piety, and Fear of the Lord; all in accordance with the Book of Isaiah 11:2,3. There is no greater goodness than to pledge our allegiance to these benisons from our Divine Creator! He is our health and Salvation from every Vice that could ever tempt us into failing to keep His Holy Commandments. Through our conversion, we defeat pride with humility, covetousness with liberality, lust with purity, anger with meekness, gluttony with temperance, envy with brotherly Love, and sloth with diligence. These are the Virtues through which every Capital Vice will eventually be destroyed. But, there is yet more for us to defend! We should never yield to the sins against the Holy Spirit, which are presumption, despair, violation of the Gospel Truth, jealousy against another's spiritual goodness, obstinance in the face of grave sin, and final impenitence before the Deity of God.

We have been told in no uncertain terms that vengeance belongs to the Lord and to no mortal man. The Holy Scriptures delineate Four Sins which are crying-out to Heaven for Vengeance; willful murder (Genesis 4:8-16), the sin of Sodom (Genesis 18:20; 19:12,13,24,25), oppression of the poor (Proverbs 14:31), and defrauding laborers of their due wages (James 5:4). If any human being is willingly harboring any of these grave sins, he should move swiftly to confessing before the Lord in the Rite of Reconciliation, amend his life, and avoid all occasions that would lead him back into such transgressions against the Divinity of God. And, not only that, we can be held equally as accountable by aiding in the sins of others. How do we do this? By giving *false counsel* to them, *commanding* them to commit a wrongdoing with our superior station, *consenting* to agree with their error, by *provoking* them into the committing of wrongdoing, by showering them with *undue praise* when we know they are entertaining the presence of sin, by becoming an *active partner* in the sins of other people, by *remaining silent* in the face of sin, by *defending the wrong* that has been done by others, and through our *concealment* of sins which have been committed by turning our faces another way. This does not imply that we should run around the world poking our fingers at the poor souls who fall to such temptation; but we should gently guide them to the Truth by directing them to the proper Sacraments that will assist them to heal their lives and their souls before God.

So, we have a great many works by which to become better children of Love, not only through the eminent good works of prayer, fasting, and almsgiving, but through our direct interaction with our brothers and sisters in Christ. Many of us have even accepted such humble evangelical counsels as voluntary poverty, perpetual chastity, and entire obedience as our way of living-out our faith in the Savior of the World. It is not necessary for us to become priests and nuns to be as holy as these dear ones who have entered such vocations with great fidelity; but we should take their example as our own for the service of the same God in whom we believe. There are four things we should remember if ever our thoughts should become so lame as none others could possibly survive; Death, Judgement, Heaven, and Hell. When we acknowledge both the existence and effect of each of these manifestations, we have transcended the mortal world in which we live toward the greater spirituality of our own perpetual existence. We are living the New Springtime of our lives on the Earth already and our beginning has flourished from the Sacred Soil of the Holy Scriptures. There is no altering the Truth which God has displayed therein through the obedient hands of His chosen Apostles who have been so faithful to His Kingdom. If only every mortal man could understand what it really means to accept these things in our weary hearts, no longer would there be any vagueness to our faith, no more would our partisan propensities exist, and long would live the power of the prophesies we have sustained in Jesus Christ.

Conciliatory Enlightenment and Omnipotent Power

February 5, 2001

We savor the strengths which help us live through the suppressions that often try to make us feel as though life is not worth living because they are like the sentinels guarding us during our darkest hours. If we were to sum-up the worthiness of our waking moments, what do we really find ourselves accomplishing these days? Many people are lost in the satisfaction which is wrought through food, sex, music, politics, sports, wage-earning labors, or drug and alcohol abuse. Not much time is devoted to religiosity and spirituality anymore. When life becomes too difficult, we are prone to compare our days to the contrast of smoothness versus roughness. If we perceive life through such an analogy, we probably should consider what it looks like from the other side of mortality. Perhaps God is saying that if our pathways are always smooth to the touch, we might be more apt to slip and fall on them when the monsoons of strife pummel against our hearts; whereas, if our time is filled with the suffering and self-sacrifice that Jesus has endured, we are less likely to fall prey to the desperation which often consumes our thoughts. Just as there are flaws and fallacies in statistical thinking based upon the anomalies of substandard logic, we can also entertain an errant perspective of the spiritual aspects of human existence if we believe that Christianity always means that we maintain a perpetual cordiality with everyday life as though we are walking-out of Church, shaking our Pastor's hand, and smiling every time we get out of bed in the morning. Reality is oftentimes more caustic than that; and our own demeanor is always effected by how we react to it. It would be interesting to see what humanity would do if God decided to hasten the rotation of the Earth on its axis, almost to the point where centrifugal force would toss humanity completely into the higher atmosphere. Would we cling to the world just the same, or would we let go and see what God allows to happen to us. This is an extreme example of our allegiance to His Omnipotent power; but it is also a quite applicable parable to ponder.

On the other hand, if we did not have a natural instinct to become one with life hereafter, we would not entertain such a penchant for seeking-out its beauty; men and women would not be climbing mountains, exploring the wilderness, writing poetry and musical lyrics which bring tears to our eyes, painting awesome pictures, sitting by the seashore, watching the sun setting on the western horizon, or blasting-off into outer-space ever so often. These are the things we can seemingly accomplish on our own terms. But, there is no doubt that the Son of God asks us every day to meet Him on His Court to see how our talents fare against the unknowns of the supernatural realm. This can be done only by our invocation of the Holy Spirit because we have never been able to calculate a means of seeing past the material world any other way. We cannot lay-down to sleep at night and willingly choose what we will dream about; which proves that the intellect is not the source of our greatest control of power. Only the Truth of Love in our hearts has the authority to prevail over every other aspect of our subconsciousness and the way we present ourselves through the day. If we walk through a plant nursery and try to single-out the aroma of the *mabel grey*, do we suppose that our instincts are clear enough to recognize it from amongst the rest of the flowers? Indeed, most of us could not; and therefore, would be detained by another fragrance which is just as pleasing to our olfactory senses. We should seek the entire dimensions of the Love of God in this same way; walking through life with a clear mind and welcoming disposition to whatever gifts He chooses to dispense, bar none. Our isagogic studies of the Holy Scriptures, the history of the Church, and the modern pathways to perfect holiness should be no less inclusive as well.

There are many more ways to throw Satan off our path than he has in return to misguide us. We might ponder the story about the President of the United States who was scheduled to appear across the border in Mexico one time, but there had been many threats to his life in the recent past. So, in order to protect him while he flew aboard Air Force One, the U.S. Defense Department surrounded the aircraft with a contingent of fighter jets completely guarding his circumference during the entire flight to the southern Nation. They were loaded to the gills with guided missiles and other sophisticated technology that would allow them to deter anyone or anything from invading the airspace bearing their Commander-in-Chief. After landing in Mexico City, the pilot taxied the President's jumbo-jet down the runway and onto the tarmac where he was to deplane. Then, to the great surprise of all the reporters and awaiting public at the terminal, the leader of the free world poked his head *not* out the doorway of Air Force One, but from the balcony of a private office building located near a flight-control tower where he was brought after having been taken to Mexico by automobile some forty-eight hours prior. We can throw Satan off our path in the same clandestine way if we decline the fanfare that often accompanies becoming a healer of nations and continue to do our work of humility amongst the rest of God's children on the ground. This is not a means of distracting ourselves from the diversity which often surrounds our Christian conviction, but ensures that the simplicity of our actions will be rewarded by the surprise of many people who did not know such servants of Christ were living in their midst.

When we look at the overall record of time, we will discover that Christians are not the slightest bit intimidated by the forces of the world because we redefine them in accordance with the Gospel in which we believe. Why should mankind be overly concerned about the perils of physical life that we know have already been defeated by the conciliatory enlightenment and omnipotent power of God's Mystical Grace? There are some people whose approach to life is so adverse that the only way they can put a smile on their face is by forcing a frown onto someone else's. Not so with those who adhere to the civil-heartedness of Jesus Christ; not so at all! The spiritually pious nature of His faithful flock is quite a stark contrast to the cavalier approach to daily existence that contemporary hedonists often make to human life in America these days. Whatever pleasures we discover while we live on the Earth should be toward the satisfaction of our responsibilities in the Holy Gospel, much to the dismay of the modern-day pagans who still believe that Creation is somehow a strange quirk of nature or chance, and nothing to do with God. These are the irreligious heathens who will clutch the ground like leeches should the Almighty Father ever crank-up the spinning of the globe in outer-space to see who surrenders their "being" to whatever counter-physical manifestations He might choose to deploy. The daily fortitude in our relationship to mortal life as we know it depends upon our faith in realizing His power without having to see it with our eyes. The most delicate aspects of the Earth are all girded through the invincible Nature of the God who has created it. We have all seen the exquisite beauty of porcelain sinks in the mansions of many-a-fragile royalist; but we often fail to remember that their pearl-like appearance is sustained by some of the most durable cast-iron ever known to man. We can polish the surface of everyday life all we want; but there is no denying that the hard-core reality behind it is the perpetual architecture of the Wisdom of God.

There are new dimensions aplenty when we accept the Divinity of Heaven as it has so profoundly consumed the Earth. It is like the aura which is so often referred to as being two worlds that have finally collided. In the instance of the Kingdom of God, however, there was not a humongous explosion when Jesus Christ was born; peaks did not plummet to the foothills of the mountains; and the stars did not fall from the skies overhead. A little Child in a Manger, surrounded by His Mother Mary, step-father Joseph, and a few domesticated animals, slipped quietly into Bethlehem and changed Creation forever. Not to worry, though! There were plenty of thunderclouds booming overhead on the day He was killed on the Mountain of Calvary; and there will assuredly be an eruption of Justice when He comes back again in Glory to rival the occurrence of all the earthquakes and volcanoes that have stricken the globe with tremors and ashes combined. This is the type of forced righteousness that those who believe in our Resurrection in Christ Jesus have come to anticipate. There was once a still-photograph which appeared in a newspaper of a Blue Jay sitting on the handle of a car-jack that was holding-up an old sedan alongside a country road while the driver was apparently away from the scene having his punctured tire repaired. There was obviously no way that the bird could know what he was perched upon; and the prospects of his ever understanding enough about the situation to the point of assisting the driver when he returned were quite slim, indeed. But, the photographer knew of the keen contrast which existed at the intersection where humankind and nature met that afternoon; so he chose to share it with the rest of the world.

Such is the common citizenry that most people who look beyond mortal life have come to expect through the implementation of their faith. It is like experiencing all the possibilities which could somehow combine what nature has to say in tune with our actions, and how we answer back. Our inner-selves are often like the focus of that picture of the Blue Jay on the jack-handle. We take pride in the fact that our identity is separate and individual from everyone else, while going out of our way to become one with the phenomenon of Nature. Do we suppose this is the case because we can control the elements of the tangible Earth more easily than we can change our fellow man? After all, chipmunks and squirrels do not require much from us when we sit in the shade where they live. Turtles and butterflies never ask us to proffer them an advance on their paycheck or the loan of our tools for a couple of days. Who can blame anyone for taking a walk deep in the woods and getting away from it all? But, wouldn't you know it? The mosquitoes, flies, and snakes keep driving us back into our dwellings to deal with the problems we are required to face that never left us while we were gone. Are they admonishing us to remain as a part of the whole, connected with the great society of humanity to whom we owe the debt of our service before the Cross of Our Lord? Even though we try to blend into anonymity with the lilies of the fields, we are required by God to never quit the fight for remaking the Earth into the likeness of His Kingdom. There will be plentiful Eternities for us to walk alongside trickling streams once our work here has come to fruition.

We often strive to attain our own personal distinction, creativity, inner-peace, and acknowledgment; and yet, we travel in vast numbers to public events, becoming one of the body in a congregation of realists, and latching-on to certain fads like they are going out of style. How can we be so impressionable when we simultaneously fight to be our own distinguished "person?" Perhaps it is not so unnatural for us to remain at peace within ourselves and still become a fruit of one humanity than it is for a Blue Jay to light upon the handle of a raised car-jack sitting in the country. We can only hope that Jesus sees our effort to maintain our individual discretion in His Most Sacred Heart at the same time we are fighting for the common goodness of the rest of His people. If we ever see streaks of lightning coming down to the Earth in the middle of a cloudless sky someday, maybe it will be Him taking our photograph for presentation to the saintly Societies who now live above the Firmament in Heaven. We can only hope that He sees us this way; that we are trying our best to blend into one species of greatness under the Cross; that Heaven and Earth are filled with His Glory because of the Love inside our hearts; and that He will return to the site of our helpless agony, just like that driver bringing back his tire which has just been repaired, to get us back on the road toward the destiny of Everlasting Salvation where our every act will be blessed.

The Rise and Fall of the Western-American Culture

February 6, 2001

To evince and manifest the best of all possible worlds on the only Earth we have at our disposal, it is high-time we stopped to think about how purposeful is our custodial nature and how we utilize what little passage we are given to walk the paths of the ethical sureties under our control. How great a society America would become if we never again heard of a shooting in the middle of the night like a pack of wolves pouncing on a doe drinking at the center of a brook. We grow-up believing that survival means dominating everything within reach and controlling whatever gravity we can get our sticky fingers on. Do we actually believe that we hold the inalienable right to force the change of the globe in accordance with the standards which were engraved in us by such a secular approach to our human development? Animals in the wild do as much. Whichever of them is the more powerful is the king of the jungle and at the top of the food chain; inherited by their genetic composition and physical stature. Let us not fool ourselves anymore; there is little difference in how we treat one another in our variant strata of socioeconomic dispositions. In the first decade of the 21st century, we ought to be intelligent enough to have learned from the past. The fashion of ignoring the plight of nations which are foreign to our own has been quite a miserable failure. Nearly every conceivable weakness that has befallen Europe, Asia, Africa, and the Far East has eventually made its way to our domestic shores. We have inherited their civil unrest, lack of cordiality, unstable customs, and even a certain number of their crippling and fatal diseases. If only we would have spread the healing that we once enjoyed so prolifically in the 1950s with the rest of the world, chances are good that we might have avoided most of the frailties which have now entered our continental borders.

God is an absolute genius. There is no doubt that He was looking toward us back then with the intention of urging us to pursue the agony of the rest of the world with our high markets and sleeker lifestyles. When He discovered that we were almost totally isolationist in our approach to many social and medical problems overseas, He brought them to us, instead. There is no doubt that America is the reason why freedom prevailed in World War II; but would we have gotten involved in such a vast global conflict if our own national security was not at stake? Such a rhetorical question leads us to better understand the true reasons why we reach-out to other people, even inside the circumferences of our independent states. If only we would be more proactive and preemptive at times, many of the tragedies which continue to eat-away at the fabric of our societies would be nipped in the budding-stage before they ever sprouted into anything more harmful than they are. The time is ripe for action now because we live in such a global age of communicative, technological, and medical advancement. The gratuitous liberty we wield in forcing our way into most other countries makes us look like hypocrites when we stand only to grow our trade relations for capitalistic gain and ignore the internal affairs which keep them from becoming more self-sufficient of their own accord. If anyone would look at the Random House Dictionary these days, he would see that there are about 135 given definitions for the word "run;" more than most any other term in the English language. But, it is quite an applicable verb to describe what America does when we see poor people in other nations suffering anything but a war in which we have some kind of vested interest in the outcome; either economic, strategic, or militaristic. We have been described as among the most selfish nations on the Earth, although we are the wealthiest, when it comes to granting aid to other countries whose people are starving to death, but not under fire for the survival of their political sovereignty. For every dollar that some of the Scandinavian peoples give internationally for aid-to-the-poor, the U.S. gives about three cents. This seems somewhat disproportionate to most of our allies.

For whatever unknown reason, we do not appear to hold any squabbles against spending billions of dollars filling outer-space with satellites and spy equipment, holding-stations, telescopes, and undisclosed military apparatuses. We have explored the ionosphere, mesosphere, exosphere, stratosphere, and thermosphere; and we seem to be just as curious and paranoiac as we ever were before. Our creativity seems to be somewhat out of balance, and we care to do nothing about it. Is it our national pride that makes us spend ourselves into oblivion while trying to see what we can do next with our overly-developed industrial strength and coldly-calculating minds? Do we actually believe that we are impressing the rest of the nations on the globe by continuing our advancements into realms which have little to do with human sustenance in the face of such world-wide poverty and crime? We are only depriving the other hemispheres of their due prosperity, encouragement, and enthusiasm if we ignore their calls to lend them a hand as long as their objectives are truly genuine in maintaining peace in every precinct and taking care of the disadvantaged who reside within the configuration of their own dominions. The disposition of America's approach to the family of humankind could use a little pep-talk from the God who has placed the breath of life into our lungs. But, too many people do not care what He has to say because they have prepared Him no room to coexist in our democracy any more than some of the least advanced aristocracies on the face of the Earth.

How can we really assume that assisting other countries to establish meaningful democracies within themselves is such a repulsive prospect when this is exactly what we are doing to reform our own welfare system right here in the United States? We complain that the disintegration of our families is to blame for most of the poverty in America, but we refuse to believe that the same problem exists anywhere else. As for them, we speak as though they are just ignorant of the facts about the new world order, that they are all too primitive in their approach to creating a public system of economic progress, and they are far less educated than they should be in this day and age. Well? What are we going to do about it? We complain that we should not just throw money at problems which will not seem to go away, but we never see any massive teams of experts leaving America for far-off shores to actually assist those who are most in need to draw-up civic constitutions not unlike our own. If we are such a great example of democracy at its best, why do we send only an emissary or two to remote places that are in such need, or our Secretary of State where there exists the imminent possibility of war, or an ambassador to take-up residence with them so we can say that we are keeping in contact with their local government heads? What we really need to do is take their plight and apathy by storm and increase the roles of leadership that we share within our own democratic state. The Red Cross, Catholic Relief Services, Food for the Poor, the Peace Corps, and other such international relief agencies are all well and good; but they are only slowing the leak of dignity which keeps seeping from the lifeblood of our foreign neighbors. Why is this an issue in faith and morals? Because we are sinning if we do not respond to the depravity of poorer nations any more than to give them three-cents out of our deep pockets of trillions of dollars and tell them to have a nice day.

America is a fat country of out-of-shape zealots who often concern ourselves only with how we can collect the debts that are owed to us by other countries and how we can inject our ulterior motives of making consumers out of the rest of the world in order to keep our capitalistic machine running here at home. We waste energy and resources like wild carnivores devouring their prey, deplete the qualities of our global environment, and make landfills and potholes out of the previous acres of wilderness in which the most vicious animals can no longer survive. Many species are becoming extinct because we have hunted them all down for game and the marketing of their pelts; and there is no way we will ever get them back again. Wealthy Americans have traveled south and shaved the rain forest down to its nubs in so many places that the available oxygen of the entire Earth is being depleted. Our internal-combustion engines are spewing-out poisonous gases that can be seen for miles, and factories are filling the skies with acid rains which fall on our neighbors like pandemic plagues. We spend billions of dollars per year generating hydroelectric power, refining fossil fuels, trafficking narcotics, brokering stocks on the open market, and developing advanced computer technologies. And, yet, if we ever took a tiny microchip the size of a pea out of a $40,000 automobile, we might as well sell it for junk because it would never be able to be driven again. Insurance companies are taking us to the cleaners, healthcare and pharmaceutical providers are robbing us blind, our waste-sites are bursting at the seams, the prison population is growing by thousands of beds every year, and corruption and ineptitude are the order of the day in our own civilian, national, state, and local governments.

This is not even the tip of the iceberg when it comes to how far we have fallen toward the bottom of the dismal abyss of shame in America today. We are allowing our children to poison their minds and ruin their lives with the filthy productions that are coming from Hollywood; lust, crime, and perversion are the norm these days on many college campuses and neighborhood streets; gambling casinos are running amok beside legalized brothels; women are getting abortions on demand; and our adolescents are using contraceptives like someone is forcing them into promiscuity. Bold atheists are taking-over the public lecterns; the American Civil Liberties Union is fighting like Green Berets to keep Christianity away from our government; students are shooting one another in our schools like scenes from the Civil War; millions of Americans are worshiping at the "altars" of materialism and political power; and the breakdown of the sacred institution of marriage is a source of national disgrace. Not only that; we spend more money in the United States on veterinarian care for our dogs and cats than most other nations expend to keep their entire populations from dying in their beds. Boom-box noise that is somehow mistakenly called "music" and violent video-games are pulverizing our children's sense of decency; magazines and motion pictures glorify sex for pleasure; our teenagers wear clothes that hang on their bodies like rags when the extra material could be used for dressing their counterparts in the poorer regions of the world; there is a general fantasia in the air of "do unto your brother *before* he does unto you;" and the havoc and madness in the public marketplace has left us anything but a civilized society of respectable people.

All of this is part of the decaying fiber of our moral being that will eventually leave us standing naked before the rest of the world with nothing else to wear but the embarrassment which we have heaped upon ourselves. When we try to stop it, a kind-of national anxiety sets-in and our citizens complain that we are infringing upon their constitutional rights of freedom of expression and the power of their creative prowess. It seems like Americans are free to do anything but become part of the entire body of humanity which is seeking its decency in the Holy Gospel of Christian goodness these days. We often advance ourselves by bribery, pandering, stolen opportunities, and elitist partisanship. We can be seen in all this confusion milling around between the pillars of hatred and horror, wondering if the insanity will ever come to an amicable end. Instead of behaving like eagles in flight in the way of our previous generations, we are acting like ostriches with our heads stuck in the sands of outright indifference and unmitigated mortal treachery. Rather than warehousing our possessions against an uncertain future, we should be hunkering-down for the battles of Truth which lie in our nation's path when a great reckoning will befall the error we have allowed to spin completely out of control over the past thirty years. Instead of "waste not, want not," we have mortgaged our children's hope by our aggressive gluttony and left them a world that has been pillaged by our lack of respect for each other, for the society in which we all live, and for the value of life, itself. The Judgement of God will come swiftly and appropriately; and we will have no venue through which to complain if we do not reverse this terrible course before very long.

Making the Case for the Impeccable Nature of Man

February 7, 2001

The time has come for God's Creation to realize that we must choose to either be rendered Divine again in the likeness of Paradise or risk the long, permanent fall into obliquity when He finally returns to bring the mortal Earth to a close. Jesus Christ has impearled His Crown with our rehabilitated souls and is now walking around Heaven with a proud beam in His Eyes because the rest of us will be coming Home soon. With all due diligence to everything He has taught us, there is no way that we can fail if we will only adhere to the civility and advocacy we have inherited by foundering in the Golden Cup of His Blood. There will come a time when humankind will be taken in chains into a Higher Court before the Almighty Father, and Jesus Christ is the only Savior who is capable of setting us free. His Testament, alone, is proof that we are worth the Mercy which God will dispense to those who accept it. Of course, the Saints who are already there will be able to witness to the number of times we called on their intercession toward the greater piety of our souls; but our true acquittal is found in the Cross on which Our Savior was Crucified. Even the consultative intercession of the Blessed Virgin Mary is as important as our own prayers for Salvation; but the decision to bow-down before Her Son ultimately rests upon us. Let there be no mistake; if we have the capacity to choose to be errant, we can certainly employ this same human will to select the more irreproachable Light of propriety as our last act of intelligence. We are not yet completely faultless or sinless; but there is no way that our Creator will see a blemish anywhere on our "being" if we ask Jesus to cleanse us in the power of His Blood. We are capable of becoming like Him while we still live on the

Earth because He said so; and that is all there is to it. How? By becoming the Love He has espoused during the Eternity in which He is living, both at our side, and in the Kingdom of Paradise.

The Holy Bible speaks about a wedding between the Son of God and His Mystical Body on the Earth, composed of all the souls whom He will deliver to the Throne of His Father when He Returns again in Glory. There are two things we always remember with great distinction in our life and times; and they are marriages and funerals. We have already held the Last Rites for Jesus when He was buried in the Sepulcher before dusk on Good Friday. Much to our advancement, however, those eulogies were never meant to be etched in stone because the God-Man whom we laid to rest got up again and walked-out of His Grave. So, we have discovered at last that we are not very good at interring God for very long, either in a hole in the ground or under any transgressions we might still be trying to conceal from Him. We turn our attention, then, to the Nuptials that will take us back to Paradise where we, too, will be raised from our tombs. This is a ceremony which cannot be reversed; and neither would we ever wish it to end. We will not be singing "Here comes the bride," on that day, but rather, "When the Saints go marching in." If only we would look at our destiny in the Arms of Jesus in the same way that a bride and groom anticipate their wedding day here on the Earth, most every problem which exists between us would suddenly go away. We would realize that our souls are individual, but somehow mysteriously inseparable in the Sacred Heart of Christ. This is what it means to be one faith, one Church, and one humanity.

Let's get the facts straight; we are not an inherently evil people. It is not natural for our souls to be condemned because God has prepared our way back to paradisial impeccability. There is no tint of error, wrong, or miscalculation that can survive in the Holy Cross upon which Jesus of Nazareth was slain. For anyone who is looking for a bellwether, a benchmark, a line in the sand, or a clarion call, the Cross is every bit the formal announcement they should require that God has forgiven us of everything we have ever done to offend Him and all His Creation. The case against us has been dismissed; we are off-the-hook, free to go, relieved from charge, released from bondage, and given the keys to the front door! The same Divine Father who threw us down from the Garden of Eden has made-way for our entrance again in the Passion, Death, and Resurrection of His Only Son. Our Redemption cannot get any more concise than that. The war is finally over and the race is won! We need not be concerned that our actions will never be perfect in His sight because He has changed our *own* vision so as to show us what behavior He would rather condone. We are not players who are involved in an event which has already been decided against us; we are on the winning-team of righteous Christians who are wearing the uniforms of our Baptism back to the clubhouse of Paradise where our champagne celebration is waiting to ensue. Once a person knows that he is victorious, he will never look back at a mistake and say, "...if only I would have...." Our errors have been dissolved in the Crucifixion of Jesus Christ; and we must take a stand to believe that they are gone! There is nothing left before us to bind our spirits to such doubt anymore.

Now, we can be insistent before the rest of the world which assumes that we will likely never amount to anything. Those types of false accusations have already been condemned by the Messiah who has delivered us from transgression. We can climb-up our television towers and scream-out for joy to anyone who can hear that we *belong* to someone, that our souls matter now, and our future has been charted. The pattern of everyday life makes sense to us now because we are able to form them into steps on our march toward Everlasting Life like connecting the dots on the calendar-page. We can behave like our existence is meaningful again because we have discovered the presence of its purpose. Why is it so possible that we can be perfected in the power of the Holy Spirit? Again, because Jesus Christ said so. How much more plainly can He make it? We see all the signs of this Truth in Nature, in our friends, in the solace which comes in prayer, and through the miracles that splash against our faces everyday like a garden hose spraying water out-of-control through the air. If we are not happy with human life as it is today, we have the power to change it by simply imploring God to eradicate every wicked force from the environment of our newfound holiness. The spiritual aspect of our inner-being is more powerful than any physical form, more preeminent than all the prophesies that ever came true, and more imperial than any mortal king could ever hope to become. No weapons, provisions, materials, numerations, distractions, or nullifications can steal, alter, or destroy the perfection we have gained in the power of Our Crucified Lord. One of the main problems with people who call themselves Christians is that most of them errantly believe that their Salvation is supposed to be kept secret from the rest of the world.

This is our age in contemporary time to devote to the evangelization of the rest of the globe in the dignity we have gained through the Love of our Triune God. When we pump our fists into the air in jubilation and say, "three cheers for Jesus!", we are offering one-each for the Father, the Son, and the Holy Spirit. He answers us by taking a bow before our souls when we toss our every care into His Grace like confetti into a crowd. Through all of the cheering that the Angels do, we can see His Right Hand beckoning us to join Him on the stage, waving rapidly as we walk somewhat timidly to the front of the platform where our spirits will be fitted with the luxury of His Mansions.

We should feel special in knowing that this is true! We should walk with the assurance of the Heights of Glory in our hearts because God has never once let us down. We seem to crawl around on our bellies like we are worthless wretches in His sight; but He is telling us to get-up onto our feet and stride with the rest of the dignitaries whom He has set aright through the power of His Sacredness. Why would we reject this? How could we possibly deceive ourselves into believing that none of this is true? There is hope for our refined dominion because of the Paraclete we cannot see which has inhabited the hearts of His people whom we can see. Let us look to one another now with a blessing of gratitude because we shall all someday perceive ourselves again in a greater Light, where there are only blue skies and cool breezes, where there is no more pain to suffer, when every pathway will have been made smooth and every valley raised to the plateau of His Love.

Humanity is the most important part in this process because we are the ones for whom Jesus Died on the Cross. Why else would He have suffered to the degree of Expiration if He did not believe that we would return to the Father someday through His plentiful Grace? God can only tell the Truth; and we must choose now to accept it. Creation has nothing to lose and everything to gain if we will simply raise our eyes to the New Horizon of Life beyond the portals of our death here below, throwing our doubts aside and standing firm in the faith that the future and everything beyond it has been claimed for us in our likeness of Christ. When He said, "Be perfect, as I am perfect," He was not implying that we should polish our fingernails or comb our hair in some way which implicates our physical stature in Him. He was talking about our very souls, our inner-beings, our capacity to be like Him in every way, especially in full reparation for any hint of human sin. Of course, there are temptations which keep battering our consciences everyday; but these same taunting gestures buffeted Jesus as well. He could not have sinned if He wanted to; and that is the newness we will inherit if we remake our image in His Divine Love and know that the Kingdom we are all seeking is not of this world. Call it miraculous if you must; but this is the Living Gospel Truth for which He Died and is the same conviction that He seeks in us today. There is no pride or audacity in standing before humankind and saying that Jesus Christ has made us perfect again. This is what He is expecting us to say; it is the same reason why His Apostles and countless Martyrs who followed Him were killed outright, stoned and bludgeoned to death, burned at the stake, fed to the lions, and decapitated in the middle of the downtown square. They were simply telling the rest of the world that they had given their souls to perfect Love and, therefore, became perfected in Christ because of it. They were accused of blasphemy and executed for describing the world to be exactly the way their Savior told them it would remain, if not for the presence of His Grace.

The Prophecy of our Salvation was first heralded by the Archangel Gabriel who was sent to ask the Virgin Mary to give birth to the Messiah whose imminent arrival was predicted in the Mosaic Law that God handed-down before Him. He has come and done His part to preserve our Grand Pardoning in the wake of such an awesome Revelation which has been disclosed through the New Covenant Gospel. We are not orphans anymore; our souls are no longer dead; our spirits can fly again; our existence has been transformed into a perpetual state of blessing; and the intentions of the God who has manifested it all will prevail at the end of time. We should now have the courage to sprout, grow, and bloom high into the air without fearing that anyone else will be able to cut our future off at the knees. We can reach for the stars and really touch them, clicking our heels together in the process, allowing the entire universe to acknowledge our acceptance of the ongoing supernatural transformation in which our souls are being evolved. This is the genuine heartiness of our commencement from faithlessness into our full conversion in the magnanimous blessings from on High. Why would we desire to reclaim any passing material world when we know that our true treasures are already waiting for us at the doorway of Paradise? Who could reject such an enamoring benison or turn their back to this most elegant Feast of Restoration that our souls have gained in the favor of the Most Blessed Trinity?

The Truth is, we all have our individual aspirations, no matter how modest they may be; and we must eventually choose which of them are the most appropriate to pursue. Our hearts yearn to be deep in Love with someone or something, but we often do not know if it is actually with another mortal person or whether we are chasing the shadows of who we really wish to become; or even the intangible essence of superior life which comes only after we let ourselves go and become united with the Higher Spirit of God. We have often heard the saying that He makes no junk, and that there is hope for everyone on Earth to convene in Heaven someday. Our sadness is usually manifested during the interim while we watch everything we have ever held-closely or fondly admired slip slowly into the voided acreage of the past. What we can never lose, however, is the greater perception of ourselves, the more explicit definition of who our souls will become when this journey of life is through. If we permit our nightmares and darker imaginings to overcome our joy, we will be bound to the fate of permanent unhappiness and detained by our self-induced prophecy that we may never know true greatness again. We often read books, open our eyes to the tenor of outdoor Nature when we wander down unkept country lanes, and whisper prayers to the angels who are closest to our hearts;

but the Truth always remains intact that we should keep striving to become the Saints whom our Divine Creator wants us to be. He has set our mortal lives into motion in the inexplicable universe, counting every last pulse of our being, and soothing the agonies of our temperament when we seem to be finished for the day.

If all the Earth is truly a stage, then Paradise must be our reality; and we should never cease-the-chase for the holy righteousness that will deliver us there someday. Even as bad as life may seem at times, our mortality bears a sacredness which only the enlivened of heart will ever know; those who are given to the Fruits of Love, to the Divinity of power that is compassion within us and the Wisdom to see beyond the present-age into the open fields of immortal beauty. We see light and dark amidst the swelters of our meandering days; but we are mostly blind as to how God is leading us by the hand. No rhymes, melodies, panoramas, or succinct memories can quite compete with the cascade of perfection and jubilation which is our Salvation; but we are caught-up in it now and most of us do not yet realize it. The Earth is a portion of the endless horn of plentiful Grace that falls like snowflakes from the summits of the mountain ranges overlooking the Celestial City which every living Saint among us will call their new homeland someday. So, let us all hope together in peace and mutual confession, walking gently upon the tightrope of this tangential life, holding hands, embracing hearts, sharing every blessing we can summon from the Love inside our better selves. God can see and hear us; He can feel the inside of our consciences and even knows the temperature of our sincerity. Let us give our "all" back to Him, palm-to-palm in Love with the Genius of His Plan to take us to His majestic Kingdom of happiness very soon.

Should we decide to genuflect upon our knees and bless ourselves with Holy Water, He will respond in-kind to our hope by raising us back to our feet again and showering us in Divine Mercy which is waiting like an ocean behind a dyke to force His Triumph that is ours to share. As soon as we remove the plank of indiscretion from the center of our eyes, Jesus will take His finger away from the hole in that fateful Dam and set us all free in the highest-tide of His generous Love. Our souls are His, and His alone; not the world's, not given to fear or hesitation, and never to evil or desecration; but to royal dignity and Light, to joy and peace, and to rest and Holy Communion. Let no man stop us from getting there; let nothing impede the progress of our infant steps; let not a single sliver of disinclination ever bring a solitary wrinkle to the bridge across our brows. All in all, we live a good life in salutatory gentleness; the Hosts of Heaven are not stalking us for our resignations quite yet; and we are thankfully filled by the sustaining piousness that the Holy Spirit has implanted at the core of our inner-being. If our thoughts require the nourishment of initiative in order to survive, our souls also need the food of greater holiness; a wholesome goodness which can only come through Love. We must all become the ever-present witnesses of sound commitment to each other again, valuing what we know in-fact to be worthy of discernment in our most hallowed of times, deepening our desire to understand the surety of absolution after all the babbling is done by those who would tempt us into going some other way.

Yes, we are a humanity of decent accord, worthy of being called the children of the Lamb, and destined for truer greatness before the Earth has had its final say. Perhaps we have not been the most worthy of visitors who have ever lived upon the globe, but our earthen friend has been quite a gracious host after all, sustaining the exiled people from another place until we have only now achieved our opportunity to defy the forces of gravity by escaping through the auxiliary door of death and being Resurrected through our Christianity. Is this not the same hope which sustains those who are incarcerated against their will in public penitentiaries and dungeons below the surface of the ground? Is not the desire for the sweet taste of liberty just the same? We are free because we have already been excused from the throes of imperfection by the Sacrifice of Jesus on the Cross. He is our hope and inextinguishable Light; and we are His, too; perfected by His Bloodshed, Redeemed in His consent, and poised to touch His Sacred Heart for good when He finally comes again. How do we lift Him-up before mankind? How can we reach-out and touch the hem of His Garment from here? By becoming the little children whom He wants us to be; by coloring the world with the hues that distinguish us *not* as men of the tillable soil, but of the solid foundation of Truth, peace, justice, hope, and faith. Christianity is not a revolving door because once you are in, you are in forever. When other men come to quiz us about our newly-acquired conviction, we will be able to see by the nature of their first question whether they are followers of the Holy Gospel, too.

We sometimes wonder what life would have been like if only we had been converted to the Blood of Jesus Christ sooner than we were; what goodness could have been wrought; what dreams might have come, and the gruesome battles which could possibly have been averted. We do not call the Holy Gospel the "Good News" for no good reason! God's Love is timeless; our misgivings and omissions have been mitigated; our reconciliation with our Maker has arrived; and we can all start living over again. Fathers can now say "I Love you" to their sons with their own sense of urgency; and really mean it, too, without fearing the loss of their midday composure or giving-in to some gyrating maudlin sentimentalism. Indeed, we have all perceived a spiritually-tired mother sitting in her fabric rocking chair, straightening a doily over its arm with tears rolling down her cheeks, wishing that the world and her children, and everything else about mortal existence, was less harmful to the human spirit; that she could have kept all of her little children under her care forever; that her babies would never have grown-up to become bitter or indifferent, or much too distant to even be recognizable as they were once before. The vast entirety of all Creation has seen the inside of these beautiful people, perhaps trying the best they know how to *be* true Love. They have all already succeeded in Jesus because He has remade them into the likeness of Himself; and there is no greater Love than that. The roof under which we have lived as individual families is common to everyone, for we are, indeed, one humanity by the Virtue of God; and we are all going back home to Heaven to see Him someday very soon. Let this be the reason why we leave the world smiling as we exit the door. Are we perfect? Perhaps not yet; but we are well on our way. Impeccable? Probably not by most standards; but we shall get there quite quickly through the Love, Compassion, Mercy, and the Infallible Judgement of Jesus Christ.

The Supernatural Presence of the Blessed Virgin Mary

February 8, 2001

We know that the common American citizen has never been viewed as being the soothsayer, prophet, or marabous of the physical world, but we do own the right to shape the future by the choices we make. Indeed, most people do not really wish to discover what their latter years will behold, short of perhaps having advanced knowledge of things like lottery numbers and vital dates of uncertain survival. Those to whom we are strangers cannot read a great deal into our actions because we are mostly bland in them and work well off-the-cuff most of the time. Such is the nature of the ordinary populist, never quite rising to the surface of any transcendental plane and usually content while watching life go by a day at a time. Does this necessarily make us a deficient species? There are certainly plentiful reasons for us to be concerned, given the thesis of some of the more critical essays in this truthful transcription. A huge number of people claim that they have never really been summoned to make a difference anywhere, except perhaps to line the pocketbooks of the endless string of telephone solicitors who keep bothering us during suppertime everyday. If we are not attending our jobs somewhere or talking with our friends, we are usually nursing our gardens along or cultivating the soil around our peonies and marigolds. There is certainly no malevolence in this because so many of us have been told by highly regarded theologians that "...they also serve who only stand and wait." Far be it from anyone else to place our neighbors' arms in stocks for not going door-to-door with instructions on how to pray the Holy Rosary when we have plenty of others trying to knock them down with crowbars in the middle of the night. The first is a shame, and the second is a reckless crime.

How, then, do we move toward making societies more holy again? How do we help them to recognize that the Life of Christ is the presence of God in the world, and *only* through Jesus will our souls ever be redeemed? It certainly does not help matters much when we have so many emotional speakers taking to the public airwaves and saying that God will accept anything for the expiation of our sinful nature. It has been quite clear for the past 2000 years that only the Crucifixion of Jesus is the full and unparalleled reparation for every offense we have committed against His Will. Newspaper editors and other publicists can claim that we must accept all religions as one under the sun, but most of them are only trying to keep the battle from entering their own front doors and lobbies. They can even become somewhat testy when you confront them about it, as though you are requiring them to lay down their lives for the cause of human conversion and let their surviving associates print it in the paper. The entire concept about accusing Christians of being less-than tolerant when they are only trying to speak the Truth is hatched from their adversaries' defiance against complying with what God has to say. Their position is that they should not have to respond to Him if they decline to accept His Reign altogether. This may be alright for the immediate future, but what would happen if their life ever came to an abrupt conclusion and they had to explain their denial right to His Face? Such a prospect should bring the essence of "terror" raining down upon their souls.

Humanity is faced with quite a dilemma these days because most people of differing faiths are willing to fight to the death to defend them. Although such allegiance is quite noble in nature, what happens when they, likewise, arrive at their deaths and discover that they have allowed themselves to be killed for reasons which were never in alignment with God? So, let's just cast the idea of intolerance aside for awhile and acknowledge that the miraculous presence of Jesus Christ is simply too profound to ignore. His Immaculate Mother has been factually appearing throughout the world for many centuries now, and most of the apparitions have been scientifically proved as being authentic, and some are already confirmed to be true by the Roman Catholic Church. When the sun descended from the skies following a rainstorm in Fatima, Portugal on October 13, 1917, as was witnessed by 70,000 people, hardly anyone could cast such a supernatural event aside. Through three small shepherd children, Lucia dos Santos, and Jacinta and Francisco Marto, Our Lady said to humankind, "**Do not offend the Lord our God anymore, because He is already so much offended**." She asked for personal conversion, recitation of the Holy Rosary, for world peace, prayers, and sacrifices for sinners who have no one to pray for them. She further requested of everyone who would hear Her that we all go to confession, receive Holy Communion, and pray five decades of the Rosarian Mysteries every day. Pope John XXIII said that the Shrine of Fatima is the center of all Christian hopes. Pope John Paul II echoed his earlier predecessor by saying that "Mary's message at Fatima can be synthesized in these clear, initial words of Christ," he said, "The Kingdom of God is at hand! Repent, and believe in the Holy Gospel!"

There is hardly a soul on the Earth who has not heard of Pope John Paul II; they know who he his, the power of his papacy, and the intentions of his words. And yet, like those many ordinary Americans who sit on their porches in the evening and watch the cars go by, we smile at his remarks and shrug them off as something for only those living religious vocations to do. Over eight decades ago, the Mother of God lowered Herself above the skies of Fatima to speak to all of us, not just those three children or the 70,000 people who had to shade their eyes from the sun spinning in their faces, or even those who are cloistered in prayer in the dark rooms of convents. Mary is talking to every living and breathing soul on the surface of the globe; Catholic, non-Catholic, agnostic, atheist, and anyone else who will respond to Her Voice. The idea that the mission of Christianity must somehow be retained inside the circle of those who call themselves such is quite an errant philosophy. There are a billion things we could be doing to assist the spiritual healing of the population around the world, but most of us prefer to never leave the security of the fences around our lawns. Let's put the fancy-face aside; God is going to make us all pay for this someday because we are the ones to whom He has been talking for so long. We might understand how He could excuse the first thousand years or so after the Ascension of His Son into Heaven for the message of the Gospel to catch-on. But, we have been exposed to the Truth of His Love for over twenty centuries and counting! It is not like we have never been offered the chance to accept Him, after all. It is our own outright obstinate rejection of His Mystical purpose that is growing our problems these days.

Secular facts are always relative to the conditions in which they are presented and are subject to the variables and coefficients that surround their procurement. Religious Truth is more dependable than this because its very foundation is seeded in the God who has created it. While we are certainly welcome to live-out our faith in Him, we are not allowed to skew the precepts of His Love and Commandments to suit our own personal lives. Our Creator has not granted legitimacy to our error, but our own existence must be ultimately absorbed in His power by our obedience on the Earth. We will all eventually arrive at a moment when our sense of spiritual duty will overcome our shameful lack of effort; and that is the time when we will cup our hands above our eyes, look-up into the sky, and stare directly into the sun. The arrival of the inner-marvels of our most recessive insights should come to the fore and we shall stand and pronounce our names before the Truth which will ultimately judge us; while a deep-bodied and openly brilliant *responsory* must sound from our lips in acclamation with our union in the intrinsic perfection of Love. We cannot become our own men unless we place our entire beings in Christ, for He allows us to remain in union with every goodness we possess, as long as its definition is befitting to the excellence of God. Without His intervention, we are nothing, not even the remotest glitch on the matrix of Creation, and we shall never be heard from again. If we have*not* Love in our hearts, our identity is defiled, bridled, suppressed, and constrained. This is why we must subject our souls to the Truth of God's indivisibility, because Truth and Love are reciprocally One.

We recall the Charles Schulz "Peanuts" cartoon-depiction of the little beagle, "Snoopy," lying flat on his back on top of his doghouse. This image is the likeness of where humankind will remain if we continue to decline God's invitation to unite soundly in His affection forever and beyond. If we refuse His overtures in time, the scene of Snoopy reclining on his roof will look like a rocket in-flight to the souls who will be incarcerated below the pit of lasting perdition. No matter how far we try to run in an opposing direction, we cannot escape the presence of Jesus Christ or the power that has been vested in Him to set the world aright. He already regulates the course of human events by declaring His Will before any of our other actions; and He watches in pity as many of us struggle to run away. He must assuredly smile upon our helplessness sometimes as though we are little mice trying to scale our way out of the bottom of a claw-footed bathtub. We need to come to the understanding that God has not only placed a moratory suspension on our movement toward defeat, He has ended it without condition altogether, ripping our souls completely out of the jaws of Satan like a page from an open book. To the blessing of all the ages, He has also framed us inside the Glory of Paradise and thrown the rest of the chapters away because that is where the story of human mortality ends. Now, we can take-hold of our self-esteem once again, but we are simultaneously forewarned to stay away from the damning impulses of pride and selfishness.

Vanity is a scourge which will only hold us back from coming-of-age in the finer things of life, like spiritual perfection and choosing to pursue the sanctity of chaste behavior. When we rise above such oppressions, the years that have passed behind us look like stars twinkling in the night, some brighter than others, as our memories come and go. There are many months that we would just as soon not remember at all, so we pray for rain and hope that the clouds will seal them away from ever entering our thoughts again. If we are to become the royal people whom Jesus has called us to be, we must stand upright and proclaim it to the world, with only a modest concession before the Angels, and then walk down the center aisle amidst the crowd of naysayers whose less-than sedentary doubts can never prevent us from succeeding. If there is anything practical about our sentiments, let it be that we have gained a priestly form to our consistency, that our conscience is proper in certitude, and that we are forever willing to take-up the slack for our unrefined brothers-in-arms. If we fully employ the authority of our Divine persuasion and the holy inducement of our better judgement to convince the rest of humanity that Jesus Christ is the Savior of the world, they will come along; the truly wise will follow; and the rest will bring-up the rear behind them, just to be able to say that they were not the first to succumb to the Dominion of God. Such is the nature of human hesitation. Sometimes, it seems as though Jesus really takes a pause for reflection over these last hold-outs, and He has a special reward for them as we are told in the Holy Scriptures. After all, "...many will lose what little they have, while others will gain more atop their good fortune."

There is going to be quite an interesting culmination to the fate of the world someday. The suffering-poor will be declared to be the best-of-a-kind; God will tell the rest of us whether we were the comfort of His more helpless lot who served them due compassion when their chips were down and they were felled as victims of sorrow and depression. He will know whether we responded with Love in their most dire of times or if we thought to remind them of His healing Mercy during every opportunity that landed in our hands. We will always place our souls in harm's way if we willfully rescind the protection of Saint Michael at our side or stand with our faces in the corner when there are only two walls before us to converge. We often choose to place our lives in chains and circumscribe the outcome of our future in a counter-productive direction, producing no more than additional shame toward the goodness for which we would otherwise be known. The list is long that would recount the number of disquisitions in which we have debated the proper approach to Christian conversion, but it is always better to simply surrender to Christ with our hands in the air and leave the conclusions to Him. When the enemies of Salvation put us to the test, we should always proclaim that we have sworn an oath of Love to spend the rest of Eternity in Heaven, and they will all drop their weapons in defeat and leave our presence with their heads hanging to their knees. Our stature has been raised beyond most temptations now; and we can conquer the rest of them by offering our humble prayers. Let us move forward with this assuredness close to our breasts and to the singing of the Cherubs resounding through the air.

All of this is why the Mother of God has never given-up on our own success in being Redeemed in the Cross of Her Son. It is also the reason why there are still so many ongoing supernatural manifestations occurring at Her Marian Shrines all around the world these days. That famous Holy Site of Fatima has been the source of scores of miraculous healings of the sick and infirm, the conversion and enlightenment of millions more, and the awakening of the Christian conscience for the pilgrims who are called there by God to pray. Thousands of other people have been cured of their disabilities and diseases in such locations as Lourdes, France and Guadalupe, Mexico in the Holy Waters which have sprung from the places over which the Mother of God has appeared to seek the best from humanity toward our deliverance from evil by collecting us in the Sacred Heart of Her Son. Our lives have now become distilled from all the impurities which have previously held us down and have been transformed from the stagnant plane of confusion to the aerodynamic Wisdom of our higher righteousness. It does not matter that we have not forcefully engaged the Heavens or sought a reason for such marvels; our role is only to accept them as being even greater evidence that God loves us more than we realize before we see His Precious Face. Indeed, Jesus Christ was placed on trial under Pontius Pilate for Loving His people on the Earth too much. There was a sufficient case that everything He said was true, and humanity sentenced Him to die by Crucifixion at the stroke of noon on Good Friday.

It is a normal function of the human expanse to awaken in the morning and say to ourselves, "what next?" While it seems to be an appropriate question, we can now look back upon the Earth from which our souls have hereby extended and proclaim with certainty that we have already gone; moved-on to the finer things in Creation, to the values of Truth, Grace, and Peace, beyond the arc of the horizon in the skies, past our own sad wakes, and into the Providence of God. There is no fear before us now; nothing in time can force our hearts into amnesia, for we shall long remember the Sacrifice which has taken us back into dignity; Jesus Christ, sparing no grief or pain of His own, looked death straight in the eye and pronounced it to be deceased, itself. The term "jubilation" is an insufficient one to describe the feelings of those who have come to realize the broadening of their faith in Him; and "victory" seems too shallow a word for the comprehensive celebration which is about to begin in every single galaxy in Creation as God turns His Kingdom loose on those whom He has made, remade, adjudicated, and absolved. It is our own arrogance that made us fall from Grace; and it is our humble submission to the Resurrection of Christ that will take us back again. There is an aromatic, labiate herb with blue flowers called "hyssop" whose twigs were once used in the ceremonial sprinkling of God's anointing graces onto those who knelt before Him. This same minty freshness is growing in the lavender backgrounds of our mutual forgiveness now, just beyond the scope of our mortal eyes. If we are to be like Jesus, we must learn to accept each other again without any remembrance of the transgressions that have kept us all apart. We have become pastoral shepherds of one another's soul; and such is the commission for which we shall all be reunited someday. Let us never submit to squabbling or hopeless despair, but rather lift our collective hopes and charity to the shores of the picturesque Divineness which Our Savior has placed before His Father's Throne in all Eternity.

Refusing to Extol Our Lady's Highland Grace

February 10, 2001

After all the exegesis is rendered, do we ever ask ourselves what effect, if any, that our critical observations and syntactical scrupulousness has had on our endearing transformation into the image of the Most Sacred Heart the world will ever be blessed to have encountered? Do we force the heavenly Fathers and Doctors of our faithful past to take a second look, and perhaps an exacerbated sigh from on-High, as we hammer their spiritually-crafted pruning hooks into spears and their penance-drenched ploughshares into swords, all the while really hoping to craft a measuring stick to size-up our opponents and cane the backs of the stubborn wretches who cannot seem to grasp the scholastics which our elevated prowess has so arrogantly mastered? Of all the things that the inferior human intellect does with such pseudo-nobility is capture the beautiful and the bold, the majestic and the breathtaking, the miraculous and undefinable and incarcerate them within the darkened parameters of a wounded Adam, hoping to make all that is Infinite subservient to our feeble will and at the command of so fearful a dominion who have yet to collectively embrace an omnipotent Lamb who is, Himself, the Shepherd in the soul of every good man. Where in the analytical Christian continuum does the siege of conscience end which is inflicted upon the audience that is selfishly cultivated by moral academics who, in their crass ingenuity, have created a maze from which no one has the mental-juggling capacity to extricate themselves? When do the imperial gates of the Kingdom open, allowing the subjects to advance with the fertile blessings of ecclesiastical trust and the seeds and saplings of a new and extended empire of Catholic grace?

The mortal intellect has set us into a spinning contortion as we run through life, following a tail that we have yet to realize as being attached to our own making. How else can we explain a group of minds who profess that God speaks to His people and guides us with His Holy Spirit, then when He does, the unfortunate soul who is witness to such magnanimous greatness is practically pureed in the theological winepress of certified doubters and eventually spit-out as a bad seed when he could not contort his witness into a shape acceptable to his faithless interrogators? By what spirit is this done? Are we saying that God does not speak to each human heart, but only interacts with the souls of those who are hierarchically anointed? Are lay-children so far down the ecclesiastical chain of life that, if God does send them into the world with a message, no one is really required to believe anything that may come from their lips anyway? What does this do for the integrity of Christian Evangelization? Is not everyone called to humble submission before the sublime prodigies of our Almighty Father and the merciful admonishments that come from them? Is it not the same Heavenly Creator talking? If God cannot deny Himself, then how can those who are administering the hierarchical Church deny the miraculous manifestations of the Holy Spirit through outright indifference and refuse to accept them as being worthy of belief?

The human mind is not very multi-dimensional at all. How many thoughts can a person ponder in a given moment; or how long a string of numbers can someone repeat that is not in sequential order? The grand question this invokes is who is influencing the containment of our limited-scope of thoughts during each given instant of our lives? Is it the Holy Spirit of Jesus, or academicians, instead, who are trying to define for everyone just how large God really is? In the view of many theologians, whether they wish to admit it or not, the measure of living in union with Christ is directly related to the cornucopia of historical facts about the Catholic Church through the ages, reams of scholastic theological objections, and a memorized arsenal of apologetics that can be immediately recalled from within the human mind at any given moment in time. One's intellect must be an ocean that is bursting at the seams with answers and views about every nuance of Christian fact or fiction before our inquisitors will humble their egos to accept as credible anyone claiming to have any simple input regarding the wisdom of the Holy Spirit through the course of time. Then, in God's great plan of Redemption, He miraculously sends His Mother to innocent little people in order to capture the attention of Her children for Salvation's sake, hoping all the while that the thoughts we will entertain in the small dimensions of our world will be the ones being delivered by His Immaculate Queen. But instead, these private recesses within the soul of every person are stormed by the mortal voices of theologians who are ultimately seen by the Heavenly Hosts as being presumptuously interruptive by pompously usurping the Mother of God. Indeed, when is the last time we have ever heard any moral authority courageously share one of Our

Lady's messages with anybody else? Do they actually believe that their own words provide greater light and wisdom to the world than do the strains which proceed from the lips of the Queen of the Universe? How can we condone the snuffing-out of the flicker of Light and hope that is ignited by a "private revelation" of the Blessed Virgin as young souls naively approach a learned Religious and are overwhelmed by an intellectual deluge of pious refutation and complex abstract theoretics which culminates in the statement "You don't have to believe in anything like that," or "It's not part of the Deposit of Faith." Does not the Deposit of Faith teach us to have faith; to walk by faith and not by sight? It is this very Deposit, in itself, which gives us the beatific capacity to believe in miracles. Indeed, it is the height of imprudence to deny the fruits which come from the very faith we possess. In practice, we are being taught to chuck our enlightening experiences into a trash receptacle and to only proceed into the world in fear and trepidation of every word that comes to our hearts which has not already been pored-over for centuries by Saint Aquinas and his successors. This is the truth. When will you ever receive support from your fathers for repeating anything other than a direct quote from the Catechism or the earliest Church Patriarchs? God bless their souls! What has happened to the Light of Love in our hearts and the confidence and peace that proceeds from their sacrificial witness?

I recently heard an orthodox moral theologian defending this kind of position. He validly contended that God is in complete control of the hierarchical process of discernment and, therefore; it is really a secondary matter whether anyone responds to the intercession of the Most Blessed Virgin at all. What this man callously failed to recognize is the suffering which humanity endures within the perfecting process, depending upon whether we collectively invoke our faith in order to avoid impending moral tragedies. God will purify us either way; but if we listen and respond to Heaven's direction, we are saying "yes" to our opportunity to participate in a mercifully peaceful culmination to Creation. But, it is apparent that many of them would rather us all endure a purifying bath of bloodshed instead. Wasn't the Second World War a sufficient admonishment for us to summon greater obedience to the revelations of our Blessed Lady? If these same moral theologians cared one iota greater than a pea about suffering humanity, they would be pleading just like Our Lady for every child of God to listen and obey everything She is telling us through all of Her miraculous manifestations. Instead, they are stressing that we are not required to believe them at all. I humbly ask; who do they think they are? They are required by the Almighty Father to be the pinnacle examples of the living faith that they preach as being necessary for Salvation. Are they too close to the picture to realize what is happening right before the eyes of their hearts?

It seems as though they are standing with a white-knuckled grip on the railing of a ship which they refuse to allow to grow large enough to safely navigate the treacherous earthly swells with a more peaceful and stately grace. How can anyone claim to be a faithful follower of the Most Blessed Trinity after this very Union manifests the fruit of God's infinite blessedness and still refuse to respond in humble obedience? No man can say that he loves apple trees and the fruits they bear, then purse his sour face when confronted with their succulent abundance just because they are yellow, instead of the red he was expecting. What a great test from God to reveal whether we really trust Him at all. Is it a display of any degree of faith and abandonment to the Holy Spirit to stand-by in mocking indifference before the face of such supernatural manifestations of grace from on-high? After all of the excuses are stripped away, what does your heart tell you?

Epilogue

February 14, 2001

There must be about a million, or perhaps even a billion, poems, books, songs, articles, and elegies that have yet to be written; those endless miles of highways which stretch across the breadth of our hearts and spell-out what we really want to say about living in a world of such dread and fear; an existence knowing only what it means to look-out and wonder what next will befall a humanity whom God has blessed so well with dignity, restoration, and forgiveness. Why will we not see that those volumes of pain, or perhaps joy, are real nonetheless; and that Creation will ultimately know how much we have suffered inside on our own, and altogether, in shame and sorrow; and how the world might have changed if only the many opportunities for our self-expression would have come sooner? We look back on the years with pride, and often with thankfulness, but mostly through some strange sense of nostalgia that the pain and remorse of the seemingly everlasting dailiness of life has led us to a present-time in which only the aching in our hearts seems to matter. We may never know the effect of our errors and misgivings upon other men until we die; but we can assuredly respond to the call of the greater human spirit which reveals far in advance what God already thinks of us. If we do, then our consciences are alive and there is still hope for a better future for the universe of which we are only a passing and diminutive part. Whether we choose to accept it or not, humanity en masse is an integrally-connected body of mortal beings who already have somewhere to go because we cannot remain stagnant forever. Our personal addresses often change and we might migrate from shore-to-shore sometimes; but we are ultimately one people on the Earth under the Almighty Father of Love who has created us all.

There is a huge cloud of suspicion looming above us as to how we will be remembered, what the cumulative effects of our actions will be, why we could not quite span the breach which keeps us from knowing one another better, and why we allowed benevolence to die in the face of our slothful indifference and the turning of our backs upon Love; when Love is the only fact that ever mattered in the history of the world. We have finally discovered that reality is not composed of concrete, wood, rubber, metal, plastic, cloth, and glass; but only of the human spirit as we walk the ground in fatal flesh, taking-in everything we possibly can through our senses, and often casually fending-away any impulses which might serve to lead us into a closer relationship with Heaven. What we see, hear, and touch are superceded by the intangible aspects of mortal life; and no one on Earth has either the power or evidence to refute them. If only we would set-out to seek God, He *can* be found; for I am convinced that He is placing enough miracles before us that, if ever we connected them all together like dots on a page, we would finally recognize the image of His Truth and the purpose of our faith clearly etched upon the surface of the globe. There seems to be a fine line separating the agony of the pooled existence in which we live and the ecstasy that flows from His Sacred Heart beyond the distant horizon of our everyday paths. We oftentimes play the world like a pinball machine while watching our opportunities to become better people carom off the parameters of time as we shake-down everyone who steps into our traps and steal the best they have to offer from their hands, throwing the rest away. Thereafter, we behave as though we are taken by surprise when God has finally had enough of our selfishness and chooses to emblazon the word "tilt" like a gigantic explosion of dynamite in the darkness of the skies.

If only we could become more kind and proficient in admonishing other men in view of their transgressions, we might be able to take a more concise look at our own conduct as well. Most of us, however, do not subscribe to the theory that sinners hold the proper authority to reprimand other sinners because it looks to be like one great pretense of hypocrisy. However, when we step to the podium to deliver their eulogies upon their deaths, we enlarge their legacies to be far greater than we ever thought of them before; perhaps because we wish to be known to have been associated with such fortunate people who are now staring God right in the Face. How much longer can we continue to live like recluses in the midst of the greater world and then tell anyone who will listen how great were the strangers who have died that we never really took the time to know very well from the start? The Truth is, most of us reach for almost anything we can gather to ensure our own peace-of-mind, place it inside the chambers of our hearts, and climb-in beside it to escape the perils, strangeness, and uncertainty of the physical world. Perhaps we forget that such a system is finite, not unlike the collection of words uttered by a 100-year-old man. His syllables may number in the hundreds-of-millions before he draws his final breath, but there is a definitive quantity to the very last one. His passing, itself, is proof-enough of that. Everything about us is equally as limited if we refuse to embrace the Divine Love of Jesus Christ. In Him, we know no such boundaries because our souls are one with the endless expanse of Creation.

The Nativity, Crucifixion, and Resurrection of Jesus has rocketed humanity like a spacecraft off the launchpad of the material world; and the Holy Gospel is God's instructions for our conversion, our "roll-program" per se, to set us onto the proper trajectory to reach the heights of Glory where His High Throne is seated. Why so many people have inexplicably turned a deaf-ear to His Wisdom is a source of great curiosity to those who know Him well. We hold our greatest vows and oratories in our hands right now, but we approach humanity as though we have opened the door of our linen closets and poked our heads inside. We refuse to address or facilitate the needs of the greater Earth by cowering in our little shells like chickens that are yet to be hatched, cringing in fear that we are going to offend somebody else by speaking the Truth about human Salvation. Many other people have difficulty recognizing the miracles of the Holy Spirit because they forget that their own service to humanity is supposed to be part of the equation. They might have been given a clue that their soul needs to be reborn by seeing the Pope on television or reading about the installation of Roman Catholic Cardinals in the newspaper somewhere, but they often stand-back in a lackluster state of disinterest, waiting for their hearts to rebound into the maturity of a larger faith. This does not imply that they are supposed to jump onto the platform of Creation and foster a movement of hysteria about some unknowable God. We are required to be mature about our childlike beliefs in listening to what the Bible has to say to every soul on the Earth. We must remember that the forbidden fruit was placed on a tree which was located at the exact center of the Garden of Eden. Was God telling us that He does not want us to proudly walk onto the center-stage of Creation and take a bow, just because of who we are supposed to become? His purpose is that our own humility and integral cohesion inside the body of mankind and our service to, within, and among all peoples is the most important to Him.

If only we could be confident in knowing that every intention of other men was generated from a charitable spirit, perhaps we would not be so apprehensive about approaching them first. We dream about a magic wand being waved over the heads of everyone alive to make them never desire to be greedy or famous; but why would we wish to be so hypnotized in order to overcome our own inequities when God is already calling upon our human will to set our courses straight? If not for material gain, would there even be as much as a whisper between complete strangers anymore? I finally realized that capitalist marketing was a farce when the father of a very close friend of mine passed-away, and he received a letter in the mail certifying that the vault in which his father's casket was interred carried a "Full Lifetime Warranty." Who's life? The man for whom the product was purchased was already dead in the grave! This is the type of deception that makes hermits out of ordinary people because they wish to get away from solicitors knocking on their doors, calling on the telephone, and sending junk-mail to get to the hard-earned money they hold in their pockets. We also turn to our lending-institutions to borrow enough resources to purchase a modest home to call our own, and the financiers who lend it at usury never blink an eye in asking double the amount they advanced to satisfy the interest on the loan. There is something seriously wrong with a system in which a $50,000 home mortgage costs $90,000 to retire just because the borrower's salary is too small to allow him to pay it off any sooner. Are these people being punished for being poorer than those who can repay the same loan within a year and be charged only $5,000 in carrying fees? This is an injustice that keeps the wealthy always rich, while those who are not as fortunate are forced to pay for the lavishness of the well-to-do.

It is no wonder that most of us have become cynical about material things; but God is calling us to a higher grace of immortal life now. He knows what it means to be poor because His Son was born into absolute poverty. I would not even venture a guess as to how He will judge those who see it as a crisis every time one of their children hiccoughs and they have to take him to the emergency room; while countless other children lay dying under railroad-passes from pneumonia because they have no provisions for their healthcare in place. There is no doubt that Jesus sees all of His people as living upon the same "level" of mortality on the Earth; but He must also recognize the social strata we have allowed to fester and divide His brothers by economic scale, social status, and personal self-identification. It seems as though the acquisition of money makes some people's eyes grow shut as to what is actually occurring around them. Indeed, the mountains have met their match if they believe that they can ever compete with the stubbornness of humankind with regard to our slow movement toward sharing the provisions of the physical world. Some people have no grain to grind into their meal and no water to quench their thirst. They can be seen emaciating to skin and bones, while other citizens of the Western world spread their faces across television screens and accept trophies for their "outstanding artistic achievements;" just prior to climbing into their glistening Porsches and driving back to their mountainside mansions in Beverly Hills. Many others are so obese that they spend fortunes buying pills to help themselves eradicate excess body-fat and cellulite while they continue to stuff their gourds at the dinner-table every night.

We must become a more globular people with an accent on the disadvantaged-multitudes by calling upon the Kingdom of Paradise not only until we die, but to the very end of the mortal world; even if it means our having to work as Saints in Heaven to intercede for our exiled counterparts who are crawling-around on the Earth before Jesus comes again in Glory. The disproportionate distribution of our resources is not acceptable to the Son of God; and tens-of-thousands of greedy people are going to have their feet placed into the Fires of His Wrath someday because of it. It is true that our sins have been expunged from Creation by the Crucifixion of Jesus on the Cross; and even our honest mistakes have been edited from human existence like film out-takes on the bottom of a cutting-room floor. But, if we decline to recognize the unmitigated selfishness that is flying in the face of God's Holy Justice, those who are responsible for it are ultimately going to regret the day their laboring mothers ever gave them birth. This is not some idle warning just to induce rich people to share what they hold in the bank; it is the plain Truth that is recorded in the Sacred Scriptures. Christians are not making a judgement about how worthy their brothers' souls might be prior to the influential Mercy of the Blood of Jesus Christ; we are just repeating what He is asking us to say. Through the power of the Holy Paraclete in our hearts, we are admonishing those who are the most greedy to give-up the fight to conquer the material world and thereupon surrender their souls to God. There is nothing either implicitly or explicitly judgmental about their having learned it first-hand from their brethren in Christ before being scolded by His Father when He takes them before His Celestial Court to assess the uncharitable nature of their extravagant lives.

Of all the criteria by which our souls will be judged someday in accordance with God's Sacred Commandments, the Beatitudes given through the teachings of Christ, the Blessed Virtues, and the Fruits of the Holy Spirit; surely our compliance with how we share our basic resources is amongst the most important. We will be seen through the eyes of our charity, or lack of it; and whether our self-denial became the epicenter around which every other aspect of our behavior has revolved. There is a fundamental decency about human life that we must embrace and certain lines we must never dare to cross. There are rules which should never be broken and standards that must always be upheld. And, on the reciprocal side, there are goals which must be accomplished at all costs, if they serve to promote the mission of Jesus Christ. There are certain actions which must be averted and engagements that must never be allowed to unfold. We should always learn to recognize these things and make our decisions wisely by the lessons we take-away from our mortal experiences within the body of the Church and remembering the lives of the great men and women who have preceded us in death. There is a concept that was introduced in my first book, *Morning Star Over America*, called the "placid temperament" of the human spirit; and it means precisely what it says. How we effect the gifts of sharing, caring, beholding, serving, praying, consoling, and loving says a great deal about who we are as a domesticated people before the Cross of our Salvation. Each new day we live is like tacking another shingle upon the row of roofing we are laying toward the highest peaks of our inner-holiness; it serves to seal and protect its predecessor for all posterity to come. This is likewise how we should enforce our moral code of conduct, ensuring that our legacy is equally as suited in history and eternity, alike.

The squalls at the appendix of life will eventually retire, and we already know it. Whether we are prepared to face them is quite another matter. Now is the time for us to censor everything about our souls which is profane and obscene before the eyes of God so that our personal conduct is always acceptable in His sight. This collection of spiritual *Essays* will never become the final word in the discussion about the faith and morals of humankind; but, perhaps, they will instill the courage in some of us to step-forward and try with greater compassion to succeed in making the nations an identical replica of God's Kingdom again. Any anonymous third-party should be able to look upon the Earth and not really know whether he is perceiving Heaven, too. It all boils down to our decision to become the little children of Jesus; whom we have been called to emulate since that cold wintry night when He was born in Bethlehem. Before our parents had the availability of "velcro" to hold our diapers on our bodies, they were forced to use large safety-pins to keep them from falling off. Sometimes they would work their way loose and skewer us in the hip like a huge hypodermic needle; and we would scream at the top of our lungs until our mother found-out what was bothering us. Now, we have grown to be adults, and we still have a Mother who always knows our pain, who is aware of the pangs of the world which impale our capacity to live in peace, who anticipates the most serious difficulties we will ever face in life, and answers our call to even the least significant of our concerns. God has given us the Blessed Virgin Mary, the Immaculate Queen of Paradise, as our own Matriarch of Eternal Salvation on our journey back to His side.

There is no way that the role of Our Lady in human Redemption could ever be overstated. She is the same Woman who first asked Jesus to perform miracles when He walked the Earth in sinless Flesh; and She has never relinquished the majesty that She holds in His Sacred Heart to intercede for us now. The purpose of Our Lord in transforming water into wine at the wedding feast of Cana was not just to satisfy those who were celebrating their Nuptials that day; it was God's premonition that we could all summon the help of His Mother toward accomplishing every good thing we do now in His Holy Name. Indeed, when we petition Jesus Christ to save our souls and set the world aright by invoking the advocacy of His Immaculate Mother, we can rest assured that it shall be done. It is not necessary for our souls to be lanced by the scourges of the world in order for us to call upon Her aid; for our aching hearts are pain enough for Her to respond. She wields the power of the Holy Spirit in ways that are given to no other Saint; and humanity would do quite well to remember why Jesus made us Her children when He was dying on the Cross. Most Protestant faiths reject the role of the Virgin Mary as the Mediatrix of all Graces toward the final destiny of human Salvation; and their piety is much the poorer for it. How can we become the little children whom Jesus has asked us to be if we deny knowing the very Mother He has placed before us to teach us the difference between right and wrong? Mary and Saint Joseph are the parents of the Man-God who has saved our souls from rotting in the flaming cauldron of Hell. If He tells us to call upon their intercession in the process, we had better listen to Him profoundly, like there is no tomorrow.

Maybe it would not hurt the male population to be a little more gentle on the women of the world, too; especially those who embrace the blessings of motherhood rather than striving to become the stuff-shirt "businessmen" of corporate America and fist-waving leaders of atheistic cults. Let's face it, the institution of the family took its most severe turn for the worse when strong-headed women decided to disavow their role as mothers and started killing their unborn babies in their wombs and using contraceptives so they could enjoy the pleasures of the flesh and still hold-down their $75,000 job everyday. Now, we are told that breast and cervical cancers are being blamed on birth-control pills and other substances that are used to preserve their cosmetic beauty. Their God-fearing great-grandmothers would come back from the grave and kick their tails with a cast-iron skillet if Jesus Christ ever allowed them to. But, we must still be gentle in the way of His Holy Spirit until they finally learn that the role of "mother" is far more important than whether they can maintain their homes in the western suburbs. After all, God did not cause "man" to suffer any lasting pain or leave any permanent scars on him when He opened his chest, removed a rib, and created the first female to be his partner. This is sufficient evidence to prove that God is truly a Man, creating mankind in His own image, and fashioning "woman" from under the crest of the male. And, in His creative genius, He decided that our children would be conceived inside and borne from the female womb, as well. Women are a special people; and it is our life's duty to treat them with dignity, support them in every way we can, and nurture their self-image in communion with the holiness of the Blessed Virgin Mary so they will become the little girls whom Jesus will greet with golden barrettes and pretty bouquets at the Gate of Paradise someday.

God always speaks to us through the specific facts of the everyday world; man, woman, child, father, mother, sibling, and earthen nature, alike. We can know what He is saying by how well we listen with our hearts and respond to His overtures in-kind. There is no means through which we can out-do Him in generosity; but we will never know the fullness of His charity if we refuse to listen. He is apt to say, "...spare Me the crocodile tears, little ones," when we tell Him that life is too tough for us to bear sometimes. He already knows it; and He is also fully-aware that He is our help and our Shield whom we are doing our worst to betray in almost every conceivable way. We can know Him best by approaching His Sacred Heart ever-more sincerely as the hours continue to pass. And, *that*, in itself, is the purpose of human life and is the essence of Truth which lies beyond our future.

ALPHABETIC INDEX OF ESSAYS

www.ingramcontent.com/pod-product-compliance
Lightning Source LLC
Chambersburg PA
CBHW060252100426
42742CB00011B/1722

* 9 7 8 0 9 6 7 1 5 8 7 1 6 *